THE
DEATH
OF ELVIS:
WHAT
REALLY
HAPPENED

THE DEATH OF ELVIS:

WHAT REALLY HAPPENED

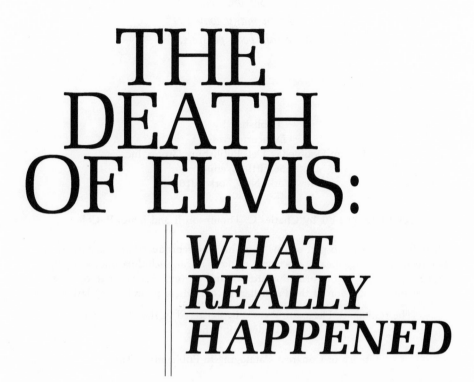

Charles C. Thompson II
and James P. Cole

Delacorte Press

To the memory of
Harold Sexton, M.D.,
who in many ways
made this book possible.

Published by
Delacorte Press
Bantam Doubleday Dell Publishing Group, Inc.
666 Fifth Avenue
New York, New York 10103

Library of Congress Cataloging in Publication Data

Thompson, Charles C.
    The death of Elvis : what really happened / Charles C. Thompson II and
James P. Cole.
        p.   cm.
    Includes bibliographical references and index.
    ISBN 0-385-30228-2
    1. Presley, Elvis, 1935–1977—Death and burial. 2. Rock musicians—United
States—Biography. I. Cole, James P. II. Title.
√ML420.P96T5   1991
782.42166'092—dc20
    [B]   90-38915
                                                                              CIP
                                                                              MN

Manufactured in the United States of America
Published simultaneously in Canada

January 1991

10 9 8 7 6 5 4 3 2 1

100796

CONTENTS

Foreword   vii

I. EP/DOA   1

II. The Last Book   12

III. Inside the Autopsy   30

IV. The Cover-Up Begins   43

V. Hometown Boy   61

VI. Two Investigators   69

VII. The Shit Files   87

VIII. Irresponsible People   98

IX. Dr. Feelgood   116

X. The Entourage Revisited   130

XI. The Cancer Question   144

XII. Suspicious Minds   157

XIII. Preserving Presleymania   173

XIV. The Pharmacy   192

XV. Drug Watchers   204

XVI. In the Can   226

XVII. Reactions and Undercurrents   241

XVIII. Uncovering the Cover-Up   253

XIX. COD from Scandinavia   269

XX. The Hearing   287

XXI. Unspeakable Chores   312

XXII. The Western Swing   328

XXIII. Pallbearers and Phantom Friends   343

XXIV. The Trial   365

XXV. The Story That Won't Go Away   378

Bibliography   399

Index   403

FOREWORD

THIS BOOK represents more than ten years of interviewing, researching, reporting, regrouping, writing, and—above all—persisting.
Why all this effort for a medical-legal book about Elvis Presley? In
the beginning there was a mere hunch that something wasn't right
about how Elvis's death was investigated. However, as we began
reviewing old evidence and turning up new, we discovered more
than a disagreement among pathologists, more than a question of
heart problems versus drugs. We found an injustice, both to legitimate medical inquiry and to diligent law enforcement.

So we've kept after it, regrouping after each setback and
going forward with each dribble of new information. In hundreds
of interviews from Memphis night spots to West Coast laboratories
to the office of a dentist who owned no equipment and made house
calls, our questions have been the same. What was the real state of
Elvis's health before his death in 1977? What were the circumstances surrounding that death? And what really killed him?

In 1979 we produced an hour-long program for ABC's
20/20 entitled "The Elvis Cover-Up." To a considerable degree this
program answered the first two questions. Going beyond the whispers of kiss-and-tell memoirs, it established that Elvis was a pre-
scription-drug addict. It reconstructed Elvis's last hours, the discovery of his body, and the futile efforts to revive him. But a solid
answer to the last question—what really killed him?—has been
more elusive.

"The Elvis Cover-Up" is remembered today as the story
that put Dr. Nick—Dr. George C. Nichopoulos, Elvis's physician—
in so much hot water. But the drama didn't tie up the loose ends.
Why, for example, did the last drug prescribed for Elvis fail to
show up in the toxicology reports?

Holes like this bothered us, but what nagged us more was

the official criticism. Dr. Jerry T. Francisco, the medical examiner who ruled Elvis died of heart trouble, contends that our broadcast was good entertainment but crummy journalism. We weren't privy to full details of the Presley postmortem, the medical examiner insisted—details, we must add, that Dr. Francisco conveniently chose to exclude from his official files.

Hence, while we stand behind the results of our initial investigation in 1979, we have persisted—an interview here, a follow-up there—until we tracked down three new troves of information.

First, there are tape-recorded interviews with notable and otherwise inaccessible figures in Elvis's life, including Colonel Tom Parker, Elvis's manager with the Midas touch; the mystery girlfriend who came on the scene late enough to give a vivid account of Elvis's depressed state of mind; and assorted aides and flunkies who worked to preserve a phony image and cash in on it after Elvis's death.

Second, there are the autopsy records shedding fresh and conclusive light on how Elvis died.*

And third, there is a detailed account of how the autopsy was conducted in 1977 and how it has become a sore subject not only with Elvis fans but also among many pathologists and toxicologists who regard this as a case that needs daylight.

Inextricably, the autopsy details are part of the story that Dr. Francisco claims we missed. We include these details not out of ghoulish curiosity but as an essential element in the full account of how Elvis died, how those who regarded themselves as Elvis's friends anticipated it well ahead of time and tried to bury what really happened.

CHARLES C. THOMPSON II   Memphis, Tennessee
JAMES P. COLE   January 8, 1991

---

* These revelations should lay to rest a host of unfounded theories such as the preposterous claim that Elvis committed suicide.

I

EP/DOA

THE MODULAR REV AMBULANCE was built for speed and durability. Mounted on a General Motors chassis with a heap of horsepower, the boxlike body was threading an orange and white trail through midafternoon traffic northbound on Interstate 240. At the Union Avenue overpass the throttle eased into a sweeping left turn. Then the engine roared out for three more anxious blocks west. It lurched to a stop just beyond a large cross painted on a concrete helipad and beside a set of double doors leading into the Baptist Memorial Hospital emergency room. A swarm of men emerged from the rear of the ambulance. Stealing glances at unsuspecting onlookers, they surrounded a stretcher as the paramedics wheeled it inside.

A receptionist hurriedly filled out an admission form. It identified the patient as Mr. John Doe; home address, 3764 Elvis Presley Boulevard; age, 42; occupation, self-employed entertainer; home telephone number, unlisted. The form further stated that he was suffering from cardiac arrest. The line for diagnosis would remain blank for another forty-five minutes. Across the top of the page the receptionist scrawled "No publicity."

The patient was wearing pajama bottoms and had a gold

necklace and drop hanging around his neck. As the stretcher and entourage scuttled past, an emergency room technician stripped away the necklace and for safekeeping handed it to Mrs. Marian Cocke, a hospital nurse who knew the patient well.

Also in the emergency room was Maurice Elliott, Baptist Hospital's wiry administrative vice president. He eyed the security guards, who were mindful that news reporters soon would be trying to claw their way in. On the publicity front, Elliott was a veteran handler of newshounds, but the rush of events was leaving him with a numb, unprepared feeling.

Further inside the emergency room a Harvey team was assembling in trauma room No. 2. A Harvey team is a bring-'em-back-from-the-dead component that includes doctors, nurses, respiratory therapists, and EKG technicians. When a Harvey team is summoned, it's akin to the sounding of general quarters on a U.S. Navy ship under enemy fire. The one at Baptist Hospital was well regarded in medical circles, but here it needed to work a miracle.

The shock/trauma team, headed by Dr. Otis Warr III, worked on the body, but the lack of vital signs was discouraging. "Most people are warm," one doctor said. "He was cold and looked like he'd been that way for some time. He was blue. His lips were blue. His chest was hard to pump."

The doctors administered three shots of Epinephrine and two shots of Isuprel. In cardiac arrest cases, these drugs often are used to stimulate the heart. Epinephrine also has another use—to relieve the symptoms of anaphylaxis or the sort of shock caused by an acute internal reaction to a substance. The team also injected sodium bicarbonate to stimulate the heart and administered a 5 percent dextrose solution diluted with water.

The doctors made a surgical incision, called a thoracotomy, on the left side of the chest, between the fourth and fifth ribs. A surgeon poked into the incision with a tube and tried to reinflate a lung that had collapsed during resuscitation attempts. The incision also permitted an open-heart massage. The massage produced no results, however, and later the incision was sewn up.

To slip tubes down the patient's throat and open an airway, the team members had to smash out the front teeth. A residue of vomit blocked the airway. It was suctioned out. Then the

2

stomach was pumped. In the flurry of activity, the throat and stomach contents were dumped down a sink, a dumb move that would go unnoticed for six hours and have lasting consequences. One nurse later said she had "better things to do than save samples for an autopsy."

These futile efforts puzzled Kim Davis, a young Harvey team nurse. "Why are we working on this corpse?" she asked. "He's dead."

Her teammates exchanged smug looks. "Because he's Elvis Presley," one of them said.

"Oh," was all Kim Davis could think of to say.

———

Meanwhile, Dan Warlick was finding August 16, 1977, a bona fide dog day—a lifeless, windless 94 degrees that even by Memphis standards was oppressive. Warlick, twenty-eight, was the only investigator for the Shelby County Medical Examiner's Office, but even as a one-man show he had run out of official business by noon. With lots of red-headed energy, he agreed just for grins to help two friends in the sheriff's department serve a warrant. Usually Warlick was investigating wrongful or sudden and unexplained deaths for the medical examiner. But this warrant was something different—an indecent exposure offense, a "wig-wagger" who had gone public with his private parts in front of a young woman right out on a sidewalk of midtown Memphis. It had happened a couple of nights earlier just around the corner from George's, the barroom site of the annual Miss Gay Tennessee Pageant and God knows what else. The victim worked for the Medical Group, a clinic of internal medicine where coincidentally Elvis Presley's doctor practiced medicine. She was a good friend of the two detectives. The wagger ought to be locked up, the detectives said. He had a prior. Their suspect worked a production job at the Firestone plant in North Memphis and his shift would be punching out about three o'clock.

Warlick met his deputy friends at a downtown restaurant for a late lunch and a little arrest action. But they dreaded the thought of climbing into their assigned tan police cruiser, knowing that as usual the air conditioner wouldn't work. Sure enough, the air inside the car hit them like a blast furnace. As a deputy gunned the engine, they cranked the windows down and tried to cool off using what officers call "four-forty air conditioning"—four windows down and forty miles an hour. Three shirts were drenched in sweat by the time they got to the tire plant. The trio and warrant were waiting for the flasher when he walked out of the factory. He surrendered meekly. The deputies handcuffed him, threw him in the back of the cruiser, and headed for the county jail—just another routine arrest and another quick-draw artist off the streets for a while.

Warlick, feverish from the sun yet in good spirits from a change of pace, dropped back in at his office just before 3:30 P.M. He had just enough time to grab his lab coat and see if anything unusual had come over from the city's charity hospital next door, known to medical students as "the knife and gun club." If nothing was happening in the office's control center on the fifth floor, he planned on checking out at 4:30 P.M. for the air conditioning of his own apartment and maybe a cold beer.

Warlick was one of the few investigators for a medical examiner anywhere in the country. There was little precedent for the occupation. His job description was worded vaguely enough so that in effect he did what his boss, Dr. Jerry T. Francisco, told him to do. It might mean an assignment to chase down a medical record at a private hospital when the health department flagged a suspicious death certificate. Or making the scene of a homicide investigation. Or down in the morgue seeing that the correct identification tag was slipped over the correct toe. On occasion a corpse would wind up over in the nearby University of Tennessee medical school cadaver pool by mistake. But that was the sort of foul-up that Warlick usually managed to stop.

Warlick's efficiency so pleased Dr. Francisco that he gave him the title of chief medical investigator for the State of Tennessee. Since Dr. Francisco was also the Tennessee medical examiner as well as Shelby County medical examiner, which really meant Memphis, he had the authority to bestow such grand titles. And after all, Warlick was taking graduate courses at the University of Tennessee Medical School, the same ones as aspiring M.D.'s.

As the hour approached 3:30 P.M., Warlick took the elevator up. In the corridor the atmosphere was abuzz. Secretaries and technicians were bustling. The push buttons on the telephones were lit up and blinking. Dr. James S. Bell, the portly majordomo of the office, was adither with a bottleneck of calls.

Bell was grossly overweight—about 260 pounds packed in rolls of pale fat on a six-foot frame. Having dissected more than his share of charred lung tissue, Bell nonetheless chain-smoked a couple of packs of Kools a day. At this moment, as Warlick was to recall it, Bell was "excited, out of breath, and in a state of turmoil."

A crisis, particularly one involving press and public, wasn't Bell's squeeze. Outsiders unnerved him. He preferred routine. He rarely ate breakfast or lunch but was seen frequently in the morgue munching on a couple of Twinkies as he eyed the corpse of a crime victim about to be autopsied. Even among homicide cops, who had seen most that life's underside had to offer, Bell was regarded as a ghoul. "He liked to tell them graphically," Warlick recalled, "all the details about a particularly bloody accident or his favorite techniques of dissection."

Circumstances on this afternoon clearly were beyond Bell's control. He grabbed Warlick by the lapels and thrust a small piece of white notepaper into his hands. "It just had the initials 'EP, OD? DOA BMH'," Warlick said.

"I asked Dr. Bell what it meant." Bell drew him closer and enunciated, "EP, OD, DOA, BMH. The big EP."

The message registered in Warlick's mind. Elvis Presley. Maybe an overdose, don't know. Dead on arrival. At Baptist Memorial Hospital, the huge hospital a half block away across Madison Avenue. That was Elvis's hospital. He had been a patient there five times in the past seven years. Warlick had been working in the medical examiner's office for four years and now, unexpectedly, here was the big case.

"But what are we going to do?" Bell gasped, breaking Warlick's concentration.

"Do? Why, hell, we've got to find Jerry." Warlick meant Dr. Jerry T. Francisco, their boss.

But Bell was flustered. "Jerry's in a meeting with the head of the medical school and can't be disturbed."

"He damned sure can for this," Warlick said. But before alerting his boss, an inner voice nagged Warlick to stop. What if Jim Bell with his Gomer Pyle gullibility was the victim of a hoax?

Warlick picked up the phone and called Baptist Hospital. Patched into the hospital's administrative offices, the investigator was assured that Bell's information was not a prank and that Elvis Presley, admitted under the name of John Doe, was indeed dead in the emergency room, even though there was still a futile attempt going on to revive him. Next Warlick called the dean's office at the medical school. He persuaded a secretary that Francisco must be interrupted and should call the medical examiner's office back as soon as possible.

Minutes later, Francisco returned the call. Warlick relayed the sketchy information he had and said he was leaving for the emergency room. "If there was a question of a drug overdose, I wanted to seize that body, so no one could alter, do, or have anything done to the evidence before Francisco arrived," Warlick explained later.

Before leaving, Warlick told Bell to contact the homicide bureau and set up a rendezvous with their detectives in the Baptist Hospital emergency room. Bell was relieved to be assuming a subordinate role in the case. As he was to explain later, he already had "a morgue full of bodies."

Memphis police were already on the case. As Warlick reached the street he spotted Lieutenant Sam McCachren, a burly, ham-handed police veteran dressed in a nondescript suit and narrow tie. Joining up and heading toward the emergency room, Warlick and McCachren found a hubbub. A stunned crowd of several hundred people milled around the helipad and grassy plaza sprawling out to Union Avenue. The word was out that Elvis had been brought there by ambulance. Reports on transistor radios sprinkled among the crowd blared out that Elvis was "in respiratory distress," which was true as far as it went. He wasn't breathing.

Picking their way through the crowd to a side door, Warlick and the homicide detective flashed their identification and were admitted inside the emergency room. They saw an assortment of white coats mixed with the grays and blues of security guards and uniformed policemen. Warlick thought McCachren seemed unsure of himself and decided the lieutenant might be more at ease taking in the aftermath of a double-ax murder than remaining in this madhouse.

McCachren was assistant homicide commander and was scheduled to retire to rural Mississippi the next year after twenty-five years of service. He was winding up an eight-hour shift when his bureau picked up the ambulance broadcast about Elvis. Warlick and McCachren had worked together before but always in trauma cases. The Presley death presented something new. Neither had worked a celebrity case, and Elvis was certainly some kind of celebrity.

The Harvey team was still working on Elvis's corpse when Warlick and McCachren entered trauma room No. 2. Warlick noted that livor mortis had set in—a condition characterized by a purple coloration that doesn't blanch when pressed. Livor mortis indicates that the victim has been dead for more than two hours. Coupled with the corpse's stiffness, Warlick told himself that Elvis had been dead a lot longer than that.

Standing to one side of the Harvey team, Warlick recognized Dr. George C. Nichopoulos, Elvis's physician. Nichopoulos, known as and called by friends and patients "Dr. Nick," admitted the futility of the team's efforts. "It's no good; he's gone," he said. The time was 3:40 P.M.

As the Harvey team was disbanding, Warlick gave instructions to emergency room personnel not to move the body without permission of the medical examiner's office. The body was placed in a cooler in the hospital's pathology department, and an armed policeman was stationed in front of it. Warlick said he issued his order after reviewing the verbiage of Tennessee's postmortem statute almost unconsciously. "Sudden death while in apparent good health . . . Death unattended by a physician . . . Death under violent, suspicious, or unusual circumstances . . ."

The word "unusual" stuck in his head. So did the knowledge of how medical examiners sometimes lost jurisdiction in high-powered cases. Dr. Earl Rose, medical examiner in Dallas, for example, asserted his authority in President John F. Kennedy's assassination only to be rebuffed at gunpoint, Rose said, by the Secret Service. Kennedy's body had been trundled off to an airplane. The resulting autopsy involved a host of doctors, at least three legal jurisdictions, medical evidence scattered from Dallas to Bethesda, and had become forever enshrined in the "how-not-to" lore of forensic pathology.

But at 4:00 P.M. on August 16, 1977, Dan Warlick was convinced that there would be no such criticism of Francisco and the Shelby County Medical Examiner's Office for the handling of the Elvis Presley case. Warlick was determined that this case would be conducted by the book.

At that point, Nichopoulos said he wanted to go back to Elvis's home and personally tell Vernon Presley, Elvis's father, that resuscitation efforts had failed. He told Maurice Elliott not to release news of Elvis's death until he called back confirming that Vernon knew. Nichopoulos took an autopsy consent form with him and said he would urge Vernon Presley to sign it.

Through a mousetrack of corridors, McCachren knew his way from the emergency room to the administrative offices all the way over to the east wing of the hospital. Warlick trooped after the detective. Only then did Warlick notice a third member of the party. He was Jerry Stauffer, a cherubic assistant district attorney built close to the floor. Stauffer, a prosecutor with but one year's experience, had been begging Sam McCachren to take him on a big case. As luck would have it, Stauffer was hanging around the homicide bureau hobnobbing with the detectives when McCachren got the call.

Apart from riding in police prowl cars at night, Stauffer distinguished himself by carrying around a plastic vial for his chewing tobacco spittle. Wiping his portable spittoon clean and tucking it away, he had tagged along with McCachren today. For two years Stauffer's boss, the Shelby County district attorney, would be ignorant that he had a man involved in the investigation of Elvis Presley's death. And for two years Stauffer's role would be the only link between the death and the prosecutor's office.

The investigators found a din of jangling telephones in Elliott's office. A full complement of secretaries was there to fight the phones and placate impatient reporters with coffee and doughnuts in an adjoining room. For now the hospital was sticking to the "respiratory distress" ruse. Joining Warlick, McCachren, and Stauffer was another veteran homicide detective, Sergeant John C. Peel, a short, barrel-chested officer who practiced a no-nonsense style of investigative work.

Elliott greeted the four investigators hurriedly because it was plain enough that he was in the throes of a public relations man's nightmare. What was the hospital to do? What was it to say? Would the body be moved? Would there be an autopsy? Would the medical examiner perform it? What about security? The crowd was growing outside. Elliott needed information quickly, but not just for the press. Some of Elvis's close friends were secluded in a back room. He needed to keep them posted. Press relations were not Warlick's strong suit. He balked at advising Elliott what kind of statement the hospital should issue about the body once the death was made known.

Warlick was conducting an investigation, and he and the detectives wanted to talk to Elvis's friends to see what they knew or could tell them about his death. Elliott said that Joe Esposito, Elvis's road manager, could best describe what happened down at Graceland, the Presley mansion.

One might have guessed from Esposito's appearance that somehow he was connected to the entertainment industry. He was wearing a jogging suit, zipped down to display a crop of chest hair. He had a piece of heavy gold jewelry suspended from his neck on a 14-karat chain. It was a lightning bolt with the initials T.C.B., standing for "taking care of business" in a flash. This was Elvis's motto for how he wanted tasks accomplished. Elvis had distributed T.C.B. charms to Esposito and other important members of the Presley entourage.

Esposito was one of the few Northern-born members of this Southern-bred fraternity. Under normal circumstances Esposito was a take-charge guy, a skilled juggler of concert schedules, baggage, and accommodations for as many as 200 Presley followers. An old army buddy of Elvis's from 1958, Esposito might have been managing a parts warehouse if it had not been for the singer. And now, unexpectedly, Elvis was gone.

9

The Death of Elvis

From the hospital Esposito had called Portland, Maine, where Elvis was to have launched an upcoming tour, and relayed news of the death to Colonel Tom Parker, Elvis's longtime manager. There at the hospital Esposito intended to make an announcement of the death to the press himself if he could get his emotions under control. But he was having trouble. Bouts of tears interrupted his recapitulation of that afternoon as he gave a statement to Warlick, McCachren, Peel, and Deputy Prosecutor Stauffer.

Charlie Hodge, another member of the Presley entourage, was there and also was having a hard time keeping his emotions and tears in check. Hodge, forty-two, a diminutive back-up singer and musician on many of Elvis's records, was best known at concerts as the follower who threw his Elvis scarves to women in the audience. With Esposito, Nichopoulos, and two more members of the Presley inner circle, Hodge had ridden in the ambulance carrying Elvis's body to the hospital. He was bawling when the four investigators met him.

Esposito, as road manager, had come from California to Memphis a day earlier to manage the upcoming concert tour. He had been staying at a Howard Johnson's motel near Graceland with his girlfriend. He said there had been no foreshadowing of Elvis's death.

Elvis had been batting a racquetball around the courts at Graceland until about 6:00 A.M., Esposito said. Elvis's current girlfriend, Ginger Alden, was there. Everybody was excited about the upcoming tour. Esposito had scheduled departure for 1:00 A.M. on August 17.

Sunrise was Elvis's cue for some sack time, and this day was no different. At the first streaks of daylight, he and Ginger went upstairs to the bedroom suite. Warlick wondered what went on upstairs, as if Esposito should have drawn him a picture, but listened quietly, taking no notes. Sergeant Peel was writing it all down. Esposito said he heard nothing more out of Elvis or Ginger until about 2:00 P.M. At that point Ginger called downstairs on a house intercom to tell a maid that Elvis was out cold on the bathroom floor. The maid contacted Al Strada, a bodyguard who doubled as a valet. Strada went upstairs to Presley's bathroom and found that Elvis had fallen off the toilet and was slumped over on the floor. Strada called downstairs for help to pick Elvis up, thinking that he had passed out or fallen and injured himself.

Esposito said he had just walked in the door at Graceland when Strada called for help. When Esposito reached the bathroom, he said he found Elvis lying in a flexed position on the shag carpeting in front of the toilet with his head next to the wall. Esposito said that when he rolled Elvis over, he noticed that his tongue was out and that he had bitten it. Elvis's jaw was stiff and wouldn't move. He was unable to push the tongue back into the singer's mouth. The road manager noted that when he turned Elvis over, his arms and legs stayed in the original position.

"He realized that this was a very significant, serious situation, and possibly Elvis was dead," Warlick said later. "At that time, he told me that they called the ambulance. And it seems like he said he tried mouth-to-mouth resuscitation." Esposito said he also telephoned Dr. Nick, who at the time was making hospital rounds.

In addition to Presley's general stiffness, Esposito said he noticed the cold blue complexion of Elvis's face and neck. Despite all these danger signs, Esposito told Warlick that Elvis's body was moved to the bedroom. Later that night Esposito would tell the press that Elvis was found dead while peacefully lying in his bed. But that's not where the Memphis Fire Department paramedics found Elvis's body when they answered the call to Graceland.

II

THE LAST BOOK

AT ELEVEN O'CLOCK on the night before Elvis Presley died, Sam Thompson was sitting in the kitchen of Graceland, drinking a cup of coffee, talking to the maids and playing cards with Dick Grob, the mansion's chief of security. Thompson and Grob had primary responsibility for security at the twenty-three-room home and the thirteen acres surrounding it.

Elvis had bought Graceland, which was named for the original owner's wife, back in 1957 for a little over $100,000. He intended it to be a gift to his parents. But his mother, Gladys Presley, died in 1958 of cirrhosis of the liver. It was publicized as a heart attack. Vernon Presley remarried. And ultimately Elvis settled at Graceland himself.

Thompson, twenty-nine, had come to know the house and grounds quite well in a year's time. He had grown up in Memphis. Tall and trim, articulate and well educated, Thompson seemed out of place in his job as a bodyguard and errand boy for a rock-and-roll superstar.

"I never looked at it as a career move," said Thompson, who later would earn a law degree and sit on the juvenile court bench in Memphis. Thompson was working as a sheriff's deputy when his younger sister, Linda, started dating Elvis Presley in 1972. That was the year Elvis's wife, Priscilla, left him for karate instructor Mike Stone. Priscilla's divorce became final in 1973. And long-haired, lovely, and good-humored Linda became Elvis's live-in girlfriend and traveling companion for the next four and a half years.

In July 1976 after a number of fist fights and brawls resulted in more lawsuits than were tolerable, Elvis had Red West, Sonny West, and Dave Hebler fired as bodyguards. But the kidnap and death threats weren't going away and had to be regarded seriously. Elvis believed he needed more level-headed people, preferably with a law-enforcement background. After three job offers, Elvis persuaded Thompson to sign on.

Looking over his cards there in the kitchen, though, Thompson was planning on jumping ship and returning to his old job as a deputy. He had found out firsthand that the stories his sister had told him about Presley's taking pills by the handful were all too true. "I felt Elvis was developing a very strong dependence on some type of medication," Thompson told state investigators later. "I just felt like Elvis's health was not going to continue for a great number of years and that there wouldn't be a future in that business for me." Elvis's worsening drug habit was unknown to the general public. Nevertheless, Thompson worried that one day it might jeopardize his own reputation in law-enforcement circles.

From Sam Thompson's perspective, there was another problem that wasn't going away, either. Elvis's new live-in girlfriend, Ginger Alden, was openly hostile toward him from time to time. "There was some friction there, you know. I mean, Elvis and my sister had broken up, and she was the new girl on the scene. And I think maybe I felt some friction there, certainly on her part and on mine, too, candidly, because of the relationship between my sister and myself, and Linda and Elvis, and Ginger and Elvis—a little love triangle thing.

"I know that all the members of the group that I was aware of resented Ginger Alden being in that situation. Nobody felt like she was really taking care of Elvis. When I say that, I mean in terms of his medication and watching him and taking care of him.

Like we all knew that the personal aides and whoever was with Elvis, in terms of a girl, they would have to do that."

Thompson hoped to be out of Elvis's service and back in his deputy's uniform by September 1. But before he could leave his current job or the kitchen or his card game, for that matter, Thompson had to finish a task his boss kept putting off. Elvis's nine-year-old daughter, Lisa Marie, had been visiting at Graceland for about two weeks, and Priscilla was becoming angry out on the West Coast. Elvis kept delaying his promise to send his daughter back. Thompson knew Elvis was leaving on tour within twenty-four hours, and he was marking time waiting for his boss's high sign to gather up Lisa Marie, her gifts, and baggage and take her back to her mother.

Thompson looked up from his card game and saw Elvis coming down the kitchen stairs. Elvis was followed by Ginger Alden, Billy Smith, one of his cousins, and Charlie Hodge, the rhythm guitar player, who often seemed like Elvis's miniature shadow. Elvis said he was going to see a dentist, Dr. Lester Hofman, to have a filling attended to. He led the group out the back door to the oversized carport where a low-slung, customized, black Stutz-Blackhawk was waiting.

An odd-hour venture, such as a dental appointment at 11:00 P.M., was typical both of Elvis's upside-down routine and his city's willingness to accommodate it. In a day before home videos, Elvis would rent entire movie theaters after hours for himself and his friends and shell out extra for a projectionist to replay a particular film segment that appealed to him.

As he left for the dentist, Elvis said nothing about what to do about Lisa Marie, so Thompson waited until his boss returned. It was 2:00 A.M. Elvis went straight upstairs to his living quarters, but soon he called Thompson on the kitchen extension of the house's internal phone system. Elvis instructed him to fly to California on American Airlines late that afternoon with Lisa Marie.

Thompson knew he had a long day ahead of him. After dropping Lisa Marie off in Los Angeles, he had to take another commercial flight back to Portland, Maine, to rejoin Elvis and the entourage on the first leg of the concert tour. This meant a transcontinental flight and in less than twenty-four hours a transcontinental return. The prospect was wearying. Thompson immediately went home and climbed in bed around 5:00 A.M.

Thompson was awake and packing his bags for the trip at 2:30 P.M. that afternoon. At that moment an emergency went out to 2147 Elvis Presley Boulevard—fire station No. 29, located a mile and a half north of Graceland. By 3:00 P.M. Thompson was nearing the front gates.

"As I drove through the gates, David Stanley [one of Elvis's stepbrothers] was driving down," Thompson said. "He had a Datsun 240Z, a little sports car, and he was driving really fast. And he came down, and he stopped, and he just said, 'Have you heard the news?' And I rolled the window down, and he said, 'Elvis is dead.' And he just roared off." David Stanley was in a hurry because he was trying to smuggle out a friend who shouldn't have been at Graceland.

Outside the gates, and typical for any hour of the day or night, there were plenty of gawkers hoping for a glimpse of the most famous citizen of Memphis. They hardly expected to see a fire department ambulance making a sharp left turn and roaring through the gates at 2:33 P.M. Martin Davis of Chattanooga, a construction projects engineer with a discount store chain, told *The Memphis Commercial Appeal,* "The ambulance damn near ran over me. It hit the gate as it was going in. Shortly after the ambulance got there, a gold-green Mercedes also hit the gate going in. Someone said it was Elvis's father, Vernon Presley. [Actually it was Dr. Nichopoulos.] When they took the stretcher in, the gear in, I knew something was happening. They went in the front door."

Ulysses S. Jones, Jr., twenty-six, a Memphis firefighter and emergency medical technician, was riding shotgun in ambulance unit No. 6 as it made its high-speed run to Graceland with its siren blaring. Jones eyed the crowd as his partner, Charlie Crosby, negotiated the turn and headed up the winding driveway to the white-columned mansion.

Both Jones and Crosby had completed an eighty-eight hour course in emergency medical aid and had several years of experience in their jobs. Instantly they had recognized 3764 Elvis Presley Boulevard as Graceland, but nobody told them the identity of their patient. "We were told a party passed out or a party was having difficulty breathing," Jones said. "It isn't unusual anyway for us to get a call to Graceland," Crosby added. "Ambulances are often summoned there to the front gate because of fans fainting and traffic accidents."

Unloading some of their gear, the two paramedics were ushered through the front door and directed upstairs by a uniformed guard. Crosby said they still didn't know who their patient was. Vernon Presley, he suspected, "because I've transported him before when he had a heart attack."

Jones and Crosby entered Elvis's huge bedroom and noticed an oversized bed. It was about nine feet square, Jones estimated. It was unmade, and the room was in disarray. The two technicians were led to an adjoining bathroom where seven or eight people, both men and women, were hovering over something. Jones saw a man and a woman giving mouth-to-mouth resuscitation to a fat man, who was naked except for a pair of gold-colored pajama bottoms pulled down around midcalf. The man was lying face up on thick, deep red carpeting. When he first entered the bathroom, Jones said the blue coloration fooled him into thinking the prostrate form was that of a black man, about six feet tall and weighing over 250 pounds. Jones was shocked to learn that this was Elvis Presley.

The oversized bathroom was in even worse disarray than the bedroom. Papers were strewn about, and the people were in a state of emotional chaos. "People were crying and saying, 'Do something' or 'Do that!' They wanted to know if he was dead right then," Jones said.

Charlie Hodge pleaded, "Don't die! Please don't die!" Vernon Presley entered the bathroom, saw the body, and cried, "Oh, no! My son is dead!" Vernon clutched his chest, and the medics feared that he was going to have a heart attack.

Amid the wailing, Ulysses Jones turned to a dark-headed young man in gold-rimmed designer sunglasses and a football jersey lettered Hawaii '75. He looked Polynesian or Hispanic. Jones asked what had happened.

"We think he OD'd," replied the man, later identified as Al Strada, one of Elvis's bodyguard/valets.

Strada's reference to a possible drug overdose caused "a

16

kind of funny stir in the room," Jones said. Jones asked Strada to find the medicine that might have caused the overdose. Strada promised that he would. Elvis's doctor, Dr. Nichopoulos, was on the way and would know more about the medication, Strada added. But neither Al Strada, whose normal job was looking after Elvis's wardrobe, nor Nichopoulos ever produced any medicine or ever told Ulysses Jones what Elvis took the day he died.

Jones and Crosby fitted a life support mask over Elvis's face and continued efforts to save him using CPR (cardiopulmonary resuscitation). Jones said it was hopeless. The two technicians were unable to find any vital signs of life. Elvis's pupils were pinpoints. He had no pulse or blood pressure. His body was cool and was beginning to stiffen. Still the technicians continued their efforts for several minutes, then wheeled the body downstairs to their ambulance.

Just before the paramedics drove away, a short, white-haired man ran up, introduced himself as Elvis's physician, and asked to ride along. Nichopoulos said he was at Doctors Hospital several miles away when he received a call telling him to get to Graceland as fast as he could. Four members of the Elvis entourage —Joe Esposito, Charlie Hodge, Dick Grob, and Al Strada—climbed into the back of the ambulance with the doctor as it left. Nichopoulos helped Jones administer oxygen to Elvis, but he couldn't get a tube down Elvis's trachea and had to settle for a mouthpiece instead. The doctor administered a chest massage. It had no effect.

Over the ambulance's siren, Jones heard Nichopoulos hollering, "Breathe, Presley, breathe!" Jones regarded this as more of a prayer than a realistic plea. Beside the stretcher Esposito told Nichopoulos that he had heard Elvis breathe in the bathroom when he turned him over and felt him expel some air from his lungs.

As the ambulance raced toward the hospital, the signs of rigor mortis were spreading. Rigor mortis is a rigidity of the muscles that occurs usually four hours or more after death and normally first affects the muscles of the face. The eyelids, then the muscles of the jaw, become stiff. The process spreads gradually from the muscles of the head and neck to those of the thorax, abdomen, legs, and feet in that order. Pathologists can plot this stiffening process and usually give a fairly accurate estimate of the time of death.

Nichopoulos ordered Crosby not to head for the nearest hospital, Methodist Hospital South, but to go to Baptist Hospital about seven miles away in the city's medical center. Nichopoulos typically admitted his patients at Baptist Hospital and when it came to admitting Elvis, the hospital administration always had cooperated in supplying cover stories hiding Elvis's real health problems.

Nichopoulos's order contradicted Memphis Fire Department emergency procedures, which say that in a life-or-death situation the ambulance must stop at the nearest full-service hospital. Jones said he thought Nichopoulos's order was strange, but he decided that since the doctor was Presley's personal physician, he was entitled to take Elvis to any hospital he wanted. The ambulance pulled up to Baptist Hospital's emergency room at 2:56 P.M.

Jones and Crosby waited around the emergency room for about an hour until Nichopoulos called off the Harvey team. Jones told the team what Al Strada had said about a drug overdose and added that Nichopoulos had yet to fill in any details. After pronouncing Elvis dead, Nichopoulos asked the firemen to drive him back to Graceland in their ambulance. He had the unpleasant job of telling Vernon Presley that his son was dead. No telling how he would react.

Vernon Presley, sixty-three, had a serious heart condition. This was reason enough for the doctor to worry, but there was something else. For a time Vernon had been a Nichopoulos patient himself, but he had grown to mistrust the doctor. Vernon Presley, who was to die two years after his son, told several associates he blamed Nichopoulos for Elvis's death. "I mean Vernon was really upset. He mentioned things about maybe who killed his son," Sam Thompson said. "I think he resented Dr. Nick. I think maybe he might have resented him all along, but I do believe that after the death he resented Dr. Nick as far as his relationship with Elvis and drugs and that type of thing. Maybe even blamed him."

Vernon knew about his son's drug usage and the doctors who were the suppliers. Several years earlier Vernon had quietly hired two private detectives in California—John O'Grady and Jack

18

Kelly—to investigate Elvis's drug habits in detail. The results of that investigation were far less than comforting.

If Nichopoulos was mindful of Vernon's private fears about Elvis and drugs, he didn't mention it to the paramedics when he asked for a ride back to Graceland. He expressed only the fear that news of Elvis's death might trigger another heart attack. Jones and Crosby called their office and received permission to escort the doctor to Graceland. When they arrived, they wound around the drive to the back of the mansion. Nichopoulos entered through the rear door. He met with Vernon and a group consisting of Minnie Mae Presley, Elvis's eighty-eight-year-old grandmother; Delta Mae Biggs, Elvis's aunt; Sandy Miller, Vernon's girlfriend; and Tish Henley, one of Nichopoulos's nurses, who was stationed permanently at Graceland.

Sam Thompson witnessed the tearful scene. Nichopoulos broke the news to Vernon and the others and persuaded Vernon to sign an autopsy consent form. Moments later Thompson was called to the telephone. It was Dick Grob, the mansion's rough-hewn chief of security. Calling from the hospital, Grob said, "It finally happened." Thompson took that to mean that Elvis's unbridled use of drugs finally caught up with him. "We didn't get into a lot of detail," Thompson said.

Thompson and Grob had already done a lot of detail work. They had drawn up contingency plans, assisted by Esposito, for sneaking Elvis's body back to Memphis in the event he had a fatal overdose in another city or died in flight on his private plane. As Thompson later described the plan, they would "cloister his body and wrap him in a sheet and take him out, you know, à la Howard Hughes or something and get him back to Memphis before anybody knew what was going on."

A year earlier, reclusive billionaire Howard Hughes died of neglect and drug addiction in Mexico, but his aides smuggled his body back into the United States and claimed he died in this country of other less sensational causes. In time the aides were caught and their plot uncovered. But they had set an ample precedent for the type of cover-up of a celebrity death that Elvis's staff seriously discussed and planned.

"I guess we were primarily concerned with the fact that we

19

did not want him, if he was going to expire, to expire from any type of drug overdose and for it to reflect on him as an individual," Thompson later said. The "Memphis Mafia" members thought that Elvis's hometown was an easier place to cover up a drug death than any other city in America.

But now the contingency plan was moot. Grob told Thompson to take charge of security at Graceland. That wouldn't be easy, Thompson thought, but at least he didn't have to fly to California to take Lisa Marie home. That trip had been canceled. The little girl was to remain in Memphis until her mother decided what to do with her.

As Thompson was hanging up the telephone, he observed Ulysses Jones and Charlie Crosby entering the mansion. The emergency medical technicians were returning to Elvis's bedroom and bathroom upstairs to retrieve the equipment they had left in their rush for the hospital.

But when they entered Elvis's suite, they got a surprise. "Everything had been cleaned up," Jones said. "The bed had been made, the restroom and everything had been cleaned up. The papers were all gone."

The cleanup, however, had failed to remove all suspicious evidence as Dan Warlick, the medical examiner's investigator, was to discover moments later.

———

After leaving Baptist Hospital, Warlick raced to his office across the street, shucked off his lab coat, and grabbed a Polaroid camera. Nothing beat having a few photos of a scene when his memory or powers of description failed him. Warlick planned to ride to the Presley mansion with McCachren and Jerry Stauffer, his DA sidekick. Meanwhile, McCachren had time to reach Jerry Francisco on the telephone. The lieutenant was satisfied by the conversation that Francisco had taken command of the investigation. An autopsy would be performed. But there was still some uncertainty about where it would be performed—at Baptist Hospital or in the county morgue. Stauffer used these few minutes to call his wife.

Without mentioning Elvis, he told her, "I might be a little late getting home tonight. I'm on a big case."

Warlick caught up with McCachren and Stauffer at the homicide cruiser parked outside the emergency room. A fast jaunt down Interstate 240 to Elvis Presley Boulevard put the cruiser at the Graceland gates in fifteen minutes. Uniformed policemen, who were told belatedly to secure the death scene, let the four-door, worn-down homicide car enter. Sergeant Peel was already there with his regular partner, Detective Roy Millican. Peel and Millican had driven Joe Esposito and Charlie Hodge back to the mansion in their squad car.

Warlick told himself to freeze the scene. He had never been to Graceland before. His memory needed to be at its sharpest. Maintain any evidence that Francisco might need. Willy-nilly, though, the winding driveway, lush grounds, and tall timber combined to work their magic. As Warlick was entering Elvis's entrance hall, he took in the gaudy, three-inch-thick carpets and some garish Spanish drawings on the wall to his right. There he caught a glimpse of a little girl with a face that looked remarkably like a younger Elvis Presley. She was being comforted by a middle-aged woman in a white dress, a nurse or servant, who was to remain anonymous to him.

Warlick identified the girl as Lisa Marie Presley, Elvis's only child. She would be in line to inherit all her father's wealth one day. She was crying. "I got sad," Warlick recalled later. "I thought, 'She just lost her daddy.' I thought, 'Do your job right. These are people. They have feelings.'"

Down the hall Warlick recognized a beefy, red-faced man with white hair. It was Vernon Presley. He seemed composed. "My baby is dead," Warlick heard Vernon say into the telephone. "They've taken him. He's gone. My baby has died." Then Vernon burst out crying and was overcome by uncontrolled spasms of grief that nearly buckled him in two. Whom did he mean by "they"? The angels, perhaps, Warlick thought. When it wasn't being ignored, religion was country fundamental at Graceland. "I've seen some really bad things working for the medical examiner, and they usually don't get to me, but this did," Warlick said. "This is Elvis Presley. To the rest of the world he is a god or a demigod. And here

21

The Death of Elvis

I come to do an investigation, and the first two people I meet are a little girl who has just lost her daddy and a daddy who has just lost his son. It really made me somber. It really got to me."

Sam Thompson led Warlick, McCachren, Peel, Millican, and Stauffer up the staircase to a second-floor hallway. Thompson stopped twice to unlock a couple of doors sealing off Elvis's bedroom suite. The second door led into a combination den and office. Scattered on couches forming a complete perimeter of the room was an assortment of teddy bears. They were everywhere, facing obediently toward an oversized desk with a placard reading ELVIS PRESLEY, THE BOSS. The walls were covered with leather or Naugahyde, probably leather. The decor might look cheap—Warlick called it "your basic tacky"—but you could bet it was costly. All put together, the room blended a childish air with hard reality beginning with the largest stuffed animal and ending with the syringe Warlick noticed in front of the placard. The syringe was empty. It contained no needle. It reminded Warlick that he was not intruding on Elvis's turf as a curiosity-seeker.

Warlick walked past the desk and out of the office-den into the bedroom. On the far wall he spotted two or three television sets perched on a deep bookcase and staring at an angle toward the biggest king-size bed that Warlick and the cops had ever seen. On top of the case he found a second syringe, just like the first. "I'll tell you, those two injectable syringes really made me wonder what in the world was going on here," Warlick said.

Over on a chest of drawers he noted a pistol. Stauffer said he saw a number of guns in the bedroom. Elvis was a known gun nut and owned an extensive firearms collection that included an M16 fully automatic assault rifle, a Thompson submachine gun, and a breakdown, high-powered assassin's rifle that came equipped with a detachable telescopic sight.

The bedroom was sealed off from the outside world. Long ago the windows in the room had been blocked out, creating a false sense of timelessness. Warlick looked around the room and then was struck by something all wrong. "The bed's been made up," he exclaimed. "It shouldn't have been made. Somebody has cleaned up the place." Stauffer watched Warlick's anger boil as the investigator asked Sam Thompson if the bathroom had also been cleaned.

Thompson told him the maid had also been in the bathroom and had cleaned it.

At this point, Esposito came upstairs and accompanied the investigative team during the remainder of their Graceland inspection. Before joining the group, Esposito had attempted to console Elvis's dad, who was still downstairs, and placed another call to Colonel Parker. Esposito nervously ushered the group through the bedroom door to the bathroom. It was more than a bathroom, though, having been expanded into a dressing area and wardrobe room. The carpet was deep red. This room was Elvis's inner sanctum, and nobody, absolutely nobody, entered without knocking. A yellowish throw rug lay in front of a black toilet, located to the left of the doorway. The commode was slung close to the floor, inclined slightly toward the tank, and had a padded seat—a veritable Cadillac among crappers, a true throne for "the King." From seatside another television was in clear view. Two telephones and what looked like an intercom were mounted next to the toilet-paper dispenser. Comfortable arm chairs were stationed around the bathroom.

Dominating the room was a circular shower about seven feet in diameter. The shower walls were done in a combination of brown, black, and white tiles. A cushy vinyl chair rested in the middle of the shower, fighting a losing battle to mildew. To the right of the doorway from the bedroom was a twelve-foot-long light marble counter with a built-in purple sink. A mirror rimmed with oversized light bulbs ran along the wall at counter length.

Stepping to the counter, Warlick inspected a black bag. It was like a doctor's bag with a big flap folding down to a latch in front. Inside was a complement of tiny black plastic drawers. All of them were empty. The bag could have been a disguised jewelry case, but more than likely it had contained drugs. And that was the strange thing about the Presley suite. Warlick had looked through countless bedrooms and bathrooms in his four years as an investigator, but this was the first one where there was a total absence of drugs. Where were they? This latest discovery triggered his natural suspicions as much as the two empty syringes had.

Neither Warlick nor McCachren nor Stauffer, who could have offered a pretty good legal opinion if asked, discussed the question of a search. An overview would suffice. No warrants. No rummaging through drawers. No questions on the whereabouts of what had been removed. No interview with the maid who had cleaned up. Don't pry too much. Don't offend. For God's sake, don't confiscate anything. This is Elvis Presley. Leave everything to Francisco. All that really matters is what the body contains, not how it got there.

Then Esposito volunteered, "He was found here," and pointed to the floor beyond the toilet. The body was found on its left side, knees drawn, and gold pajama bottoms down past the knees. Blood was in his nostrils, Esposito said. "Are you sure about the position?" Warlick asked, mindful that this was a far cry from the version that Esposito had given at the hospital.

Esposito called Al Strada to the bathroom for backup. Strada was the first bodyguard to arrive in the bathroom after Ginger Alden called for help. He verified what Esposito had told Warlick and added another detail. Strada said Elvis was reading a book when he was stricken. It was lying open and facedown on the counter among tumbled-over cologne and after-shave lotion bottles. Warlick examined the book's location, took in the knocked-down positions of the bottles on the counter, and theorized that Elvis had tossed the book when whatever killed him first struck. This observation would loom large in the official account of how Elvis died. Esposito added that Elvis was clutching the book in his hand when Esposito first saw him on the bathroom floor. Warlick considered how quick Esposito was to shade his facts and rejected this assertion.

Warlick took time to examine the book. It was a large volume with glossy illustrations, lots of them. It wasn't the King James Version of the Bible, as some Presley entourage members would later claim. It wasn't a book about the Shroud of Turin, or religion or psychology or mysticism or light bedtime reading either, as other Presley intimates would variously claim.

"It was raunchy pornography," Warlick said. "Hard core by 1977 standards. It was definitely not the type of book you would read to put yourself to sleep. It was a combination of sex and astrology. Like if her Pisces is in this position, then your Capricorn should be in this position when fornicating. It had drawings

—pretty graphic stuff—just to make sure you didn't miss the point about where your respective astrological signs should be when copulating. I don't know how this nonsense about him reading a book about mysticism or religion ever got started," Warlick said.

Warlick turned to Esposito and Strada and asked, "Had he vomited? Are there any specimens? Is this exactly how it was when you found him?"

"No," Esposito replied. "The maid's been in here and cleaned up."

"What?" Warlick exclaimed, unable to check his anger for a second time. Maybe the room had been cleaned with the best of intentions, the investigator rationalized. He didn't think so, but he didn't pursue the subject further.

Then Warlick looked down on the carpeting and discovered a moist discoloration in the three-inch-deep shag. It was located at the point where Strada said Elvis's head came to rest. Warlick knelt down and sniffed. He detected the odor of vomit and gastric fluid. He laid himself on the carpeting and stretched his six-foot-long frame out from the moist spot back to the toilet. He came several feet short of reaching the toilet bowl. Warlick was about the same height as Elvis. The investigator now believed he had his second significant clue. He was certain then that Elvis had not just fallen off the pot in a stupor, but rather had stumbled or crawled several feet before he died.

Warlick paused long enough in the bathroom to click off a few photos. As they spewed out of the Polaroid SX-70 camera, he checked their quality, stuck them in his pocket, and returned to the office. Ginger Alden was waiting. The twenty-three-year-old girlfriend was as much of a knockout as Warlick would have predicted —a life-size ornament of a woman with dark hair, flawless features, a willowy body made to order for a movie magazine. As she began answering his questions one level above a shy whisper, it was apparent she spent more time on her preening than on her intellect. For the first time that afternoon, Warlick began jotting down notes. Ginger was dressed in street clothes, and her hair was neatly coiffed in place. It was obvious that she had been crying, but she was not crying when she talked to Warlick.

There had been this trip to the dentist, Ginger said. That

seemed, you know, the best starting place. It was about 11:00 P.M., a routine beginning for Elvis's turnaround days. Elvis had taken a carload of the gang along. The dentist worked on a few fillings and cleaned Elvis's teeth. He cleaned hers, too. Nothing unusual. Ginger failed to mention—and Warlick failed to ask—whether the dentist had given Elvis any medicine. Afterward they all returned to Graceland, and they played racquetball until about 6:00 A.M. Elvis went upstairs to his bedroom accompanied by his cousin, Billy Smith. Elvis and Billy went into the bathroom to dry off from the heated game. Billy, who lived with his wife, Jo, in a trailer behind the main house at Graceland, left shortly after that, Ginger said. But at this point, the former Miss Mid-South neglected to tell Warlick that Elvis then called downstairs and told his twenty-three-year-old stepbrother, Ricky Stanley, to bring up his packet of sleeping pills. She failed to tell Warlick and the detectives that Ricky Stanley would bring up other packets of medication to Elvis later that morning. And she didn't say anything about how she was in pain from menstrual cramps. Elvis called Graceland's resident nurse, Tish Henley, and ordered her to bring up a sedative to help Ginger sleep. Even though Ginger withheld this information for two years and had great difficulty keeping her timing of events straight, Warlick regarded her as "basically truthful and honest."

Warlick scribbled notes as Ginger continued. About 8:00 A.M., she estimated, Elvis was having trouble sleeping and went to the bathroom to read. It was a book about "psychic energy," she said. Warlick smiled at the description. Years later Ginger identified the book as one entitled *Sex and Psychic Energy*. She told her family that "they," meaning those in charge at Graceland, ordered her to keep quiet about the book. She never identified who "they" were.

Ginger told Warlick that a few hours after finding herself in bed alone, she called out, "Elvis?" There was no answer. Between 1:00 and 1:30 P.M. she said she woke up again. Still no Elvis. This time she went to the bathroom, found the body, and called downstairs. Thus Ginger's estimate of when she found Elvis's body was thirty minutes to an hour earlier than the 2:00 P.M. distress call that Al Strada mentioned.

As Ginger was finishing, George Nichopoulos slipped into

26

the room. Warlick recognized the wavy, stark-white hair and a face that looked like tanned putty. Dr. Nick was soft-spoken and accustomed to pursing his lips and pausing before answering the simplest question. He could have passed for Harpo Marx.

✱ Warlick asked what conditions Elvis suffered from and what drugs were being prescribed to treat them. A chronic colon problem, Nichopoulos answered. He was prescribing medication for that. There was this "U.R.I." Warlick knew the jargon. That meant upper respiratory infection. Medication was being given for that. Always the term "medication." The EKGs—they had shown some fluctuation in Elvis's heart rhythm and a bit of hypertension, but nothing significant. And there was the dentist, Dr. Hofman, whom Elvis had visited the night before. The dentist had given Elvis two painkillers, one while he was in the dental chair and one when he left. Sergeant Peel asked if Elvis drank. Nichopoulos said Elvis didn't drink at all.

During the interview Warlick thought the doctor was "distraught but not frantic." Actually Nichopoulos must have been a frightened man. In the preceding twenty months he had prescribed almost 10,000 potent pills to Elvis. These consisted of uppers, downers, tranquilizers, and narcotics. Most recently he had written eight different prescriptions of this type for Elvis on August 15— the day before Presley's death. Two of these prescriptions were for Dilaudid, a powerful narcotic normally given to terminal cancer patients to relieve excruciating pain. In addition, in the early morning hours of August 16—the day of the death—Dr. Nick telephoned the all-night pharmacy at Baptist Hospital and authorized the dispensing of six more four-milligram-strength Dilaudid tablets to Elvis. This was the strongest version of that narcotic. This Dilaudid prescription was the last one written for Elvis. If taken together, the Dilaudid tablets were enough to put most anybody under for good. Nichopoulos had good reason to be jumpy.

"I asked Dr. Nichopoulos if he felt like there was any chance that this was a drug-related death or that Mr. Presley had overdosed," Warlick said, "and he said he did not believe so." Nichopoulos said the only medications he prescribed for Elvis were kept by a nurse, Tish Henley, who lived on the estate. Warlick summoned Mrs. Henley, who told Peel that in addition to the medication the doctor had mentioned, Elvis had also taken two five-milligram-strength Valiums and had perhaps taken one other unnamed type of pill "during late evening or early morning."

Following this recitation by his nurse, Nichopoulos concluded that he could volunteer no hypothesis for Elvis's death. According to Warlick, "Nichopoulos really didn't have a whole lot to say."

Having spoken to Nichopoulos, Warlick was satisfied by what he had asked and what he had learned. He had gathered enough information to report to Francisco. He had taken the initiative in putting a hold on the body. Plus he had interviewed the individuals who first found the body, the man who had taken charge of it, and the decedent's private physician. He had the photographs. McCachren agreed they had covered the essentials.

At 5:55 P.M., McCachren called the homicide command post at the downtown police station and gave a summary of what he and Warlick had found out at Graceland. McCachren also said that he had talked with Francisco. The medical examiner had agreed to conduct Elvis's autopsy at Baptist Hospital "under his direction" rather than at the county morgue. McCachren said he was bringing Warlick and Stauffer back to the hospital.

While the lieutenant was on the phone, he noticed a nattily dressed man with a ready smile and a handshake enter the mansion and go over to Vernon Presley to console him. McCachren recognized the visitor as the county's elected sheriff, Eugene Barksdale. As McCachren and Peel walked out of the mansion, they looked at Barksdale unctuously talking with Vernon and shook their heads. They knew that Barksdale, who was up to speed on the vices of the city's rich and famous citizens, wasn't here to do an investigation. But there's only so much a flatfoot can say. They just shrugged and left.

Warlick's thoughts were elsewhere. He was suspicious of the sparkling bathroom, the generally sanitized smell of it, and the absence of drugs. And Warlick still had found clues there, despite the efforts to hide them.

McCachren gunned the engine and headed the cruiser

north onto Elvis Presley Boulevard. Those at Graceland were happy to see it go, for they knew the death of Elvis was neither unexpected nor untimely nor really all that shocking. It had been coming for a long time.

III

INSIDE THE AUTOPSY

THE ELVIS PRESLEY AUTOPSY marked a rare event in the specialty of pathology. Converging on the second-floor suite as the corpse was being removed from the cooler were two distinct breeds of specialists.

Medical examiners, as the position evolved from the old coroner's system of medieval Britain, hold a public position. Frequently they are at work in county morgues without rubber gloves or surgical masks. Their patients are all dead, examined on referral from a dice game shootout, a head-on collision, or maybe an apartment fire. Forensic or legal pathology is the grim business of medical examiners and revolves around life's underside. Its purpose is to assign an official cause and manner of death—not only for filling in the blanks on a public death certificate but also for prosecuting crime.

In contrast, hospital pathologists are the clinicians. Typically they are tracking the disease process of a living patient and are helping other physicians find a remedy. If the patient dies, then they may perform an autopsy to determine if the death resulted from that disease being tracked or something collateral, like heart failure associated with emphysema. Unlike medical examiners,

30

hospital pathologists serve no direct public function. They don't sign death certificates. And given the nature of their clinical role, the deaths they encounter usually aren't sudden or unexplained.

On the night of Elvis Presley's autopsy, Dan Warlick questioned Francisco's wisdom in agreeing to conduct the autopsy at Baptist Hospital. He knew Francisco's penchant for making snap decisions and then locking them in concrete. "An experienced medical examiner learns you do an autopsy in your own morgue and then throw away your specimens after you test them," Warlick said, "because that way nobody can ever second-guess you. Jerry lost control then, and he never got it back."

As Warlick walked into the autopsy suite from his fact-finding trip to Graceland, he saw Francisco harmoniously chatting with some of the nine Baptist Hospital pathologists present in the room. There also were three uniformed Memphis policemen as well as two uniformed hospital security officers standing just inside the door. Warlick pulled his notebook and Polaroid pictures out and began to give his boss a briefing. Francisco had on his white lab coat but was not wearing latex surgical gloves as the other doctors were. Most of them also had on surgical scrub uniforms and plastic aprons.

Warlick guessed that Francisco wouldn't participate in any of the actual dissection work. The medical examiner was smoking a cigarette. During their brief conversation, Warlick and Francisco stood apart from the hospital pathologists. Warlick began to pour out his findings and then noticed that Francisco hardly seemed interested in what he was telling him. Warlick continued anyway. He told Francisco about Elvis's sitting on the huge black toilet, about finding the two syringes, and about the empty doctor's bag. He summarized what he had gleaned from Ginger Alden, Joe Esposito, Al Strada, and Nichopoulos. Warlick said he found no pills but was suspicious that drugs were somehow involved in this death. Then as Warlick tried to explain the importance of the clues he had found at the death scene, the medical examiner cut him off. Francisco thanked him politely for his information, invited him to witness the autopsy and then rejoined the other doctors hovering around the famous corpse like birds of prey.

It was about 7:00 P.M. The crowds outside the hospital were

growing, hoping to hear more about Elvis as the sun began setting on this feverish day. Inside the autopsy suite, the scene was positively sepulchral. Elvis's corpse was stretched out on a porcelain surgical table rising about three feet from the floor. At the foot of this table was a stainless steel drain pipe to catch any blood or body fluids that might be spilled during the procedure. A bank of bright lights, complete with reflectors, was already turned on, illuminating the body and the center of the room. Another table, covered with thick corkboard, was located close to the main surgical bier. Water ran across the surface of this table and into a warren of steel drains. During the autopsy, organs removed from Elvis's body would be placed on the corkboard for precise dissection.

Warlick had equipped himself with a white lab coat and a pair of latex gloves. Given half a chance, he intended to participate in the autopsy, even if his boss didn't. He was standing behind Francisco.

Dr. E. Eric Muirhead, the patrician chief of pathology at Baptist Hospital for the past twelve years, stood next to Francisco. Tall, slender, and white-haired, Muirhead looked every bit "the chief," as his understudies called him. He was a graduate of Baylor University Medical School and had taught at Southwestern Medical School in Dallas. While in Texas, Muirhead helped establish the medical examiner's system and certainly was no stranger to forensic pathology. Later he had been on the faculty at Wayne State University Medical School in Detroit before coming to Memphis.

In addition to his position at Baptist Hospital, Muirhead also was a full professor in the pathology department at the University of Tennessee Medical School and later would serve as department chairman. Eric Muirhead, who had been practicing medicine for thirty-eight years, was considered senior to Jerry Francisco, both by position and stature. In truth, Muirhead didn't want to handle this autopsy, but he had his back up. Periodically his department would notify Francisco of a suspicious case and request that a corpse be transferred to the county morgue for further investigation. Consistently Francisco waved off such referrals, preferring instead to piggyback on Baptist Hospital's findings. And now here was the big case, and Jerry Francisco was all too quick to take over and remove the body. There was no doubt in Eric Muirhead's mind that this was a medical examiner's case all the way, but perhaps there was a way to establish some sort of joint working arrangement that would keep the corpse where it was.

Through Nichopoulos, Baptist Hospital officials got word to Vernon Presley that there was a mob scene growing outside the hospital. Maybe the wiser course of action would be to avoid transferring the body across Madison Avenue to the morgue. Vernon Presley approved of the idea of performing the autopsy at Baptist Hospital with the medical examiner's participation. The stage was set for what was to become a bitter disagreement over how Elvis died.

Standing next to the frosty, reserved Muirhead was one of his top assistants, Dr. Harold Sexton. A quiet, slightly built man, Sexton would be in charge of collecting specimens and later would oversee the work of outside consultants in this bizarre case. After graduating from the University of Tennessee Medical School and beginning his residency as an internist, Sexton was drafted into the army in 1967. He spent two years in Vietnam as commanding officer and surgeon at a medical clearing unit hospital. His unit handled more than its share of shot-up and war-blasted casualties.

Those two stressful years took their physical as well as their emotional toll on Harold Sexton. When he returned from the war, he finished his residency in cardiology but found that branch of medicine just too draining, especially as he began to experience serious heart problems at an early age. He switched to pathology in 1973 and became a protégé of Muirhead.

Before entering the autopsy suite, Sexton ducked by the chemistry department and gathered a stock of acid wash glassware, sterile vacuum tubes, and sterile syringes and needles to take those samples he judged appropriate for testing. Harold Sexton was wearing gloves, an apron, and a scrub suit. Apparently wary of Jerry Francisco's reputation, Sexton brought in more containers than a Tupperware salesman. He wanted to be sure that at least two samples of every specimen taken from Elvis's body were preserved—one for the medical examiner and one for the hospital. Francisco would be unaware of this split-sample arrangement until later, when many of the hospital's samples had been dispatched to nationally recognized experts for independent analysis.

Dr. George Bale, another slightly built pathologist sporting a salt-and-pepper beard, was standing near Sexton. Bale was a health nut in terrific condition. He kept himself in shape by daily running up and down the hospital's twenty flights of stairs. Also suited up for surgery was Dr. Thomas Chesney, another pathologist with a cardiac subspecialty. After this phase of the autopsy, he would spend three months with a microscope examining and analyzing tissue slides taken this night.

Another pathologist, Dr. Noel Florendo, was adjusting an electron microscope at a work station in another part of the room. Florendo had been born in the Philippines. Dark-complected, big-shouldered, and stocky, he seemed more like a pulling guard in football than an expert in microscopy at a celebrity autopsy. Two years later, Florendo unwittingly would become an important source of information about the autopsy on national television.

There were four other Baptist Hospital pathologists on hand in the autopsy suite—Drs. Raul Lamin, James Holbert, J. A. Pitcock, and Roger Haggit. They would take part in the procedure as their specialties were required. Why so many doctors and why were so many subspecialties of pathology, like chemistry and cardiology, represented here?

"Because he was Elvis," said Harold Sexton. "And I think that was obvious. Everybody was concerned, and everybody was eager, in a hurry, and so forth. I think you could probably compare this to the [President John F.] Kennedy autopsy. And because he was Elvis Presley, you know, most of the people on the staff were called in to help so that nothing was missed."

In addition to Warlick, Francisco, eight hospital doctors, two hospital security officers, and three uniformed policemen, there were two others in the autopsy room.

One was Nichopoulos, who had just returned from Graceland. He handed over the autopsy permission form that Vernon Presley had tearfully signed. The form, which listed Elvis as "single and divorced," had been witnessed by Nichopoulos and Elvis's security chief, Dick Grob. It stated that after the autopsy, Elvis's body should be sent to Memphis Funeral Home for burial preparations. After delivering the form, Nichopoulos played virtually no role in the autopsy, even though he stayed in the room through most of the dissection. Looking haggard and dejected, Nichopoulos gave Muirhead and Sexton some limited background information about Elvis's medical history. Nichopoulos also attempted to brief Francisco, but the medical examiner seemed uninterested.

Medical charts from Elvis's previous stays in Baptist Hospital had been pulled and were in the room for the doctors to consult. Most of the records were not listed in Elvis's name. For example, an electrocardiogram from October 15, 1973, bore the alias Aaron Sivle, an anagrammatic cover using Elvis's first and middle names. A pulmonary physiology report from another hospital visit on August 29, 1975, again listed Elvis as Aaron Sivle. The use of phony names was not an unusual practice for Elvis, who for years used the pseudonym John Burroughs when he made hotel or plane reservations. He also frequently used other people's names when he had drug prescriptions filled. Muirhead had gone through the records and found two admissions for drug detoxification and methadone treatments. Off the bat, the chief had an idea of what might be involved here.

The other man present in the autopsy suite was Isaac Henderson, a black technician employed by Baptist Hospital. Henderson played a critical role in the autopsy. He was a diener. That's a fancy term meaning he was a pathologist's assistant. The requirements for becoming a diener are usually a high school diploma, a background as a butcher, or at least some rudimentary knowledge of human anatomy. In an autopsy the diener makes the initial incisions on the cadaver's chest, saws the ribs, cuts open the stomach cavity and head, and removes the vital organs, so that the pathologists can make the fine cuts required in a proper post-mortem examination. Being a diener is a messy, bloody way to make a living and requires a strong stomach.

Before Isaac Henderson went to work, Dan Warlick had time to make a careful examination of Elvis's body. The investigator said he had to overcome his "sense of awe" before beginning the inspection. First Warlick looked for needle marks on the body. He checked the arms and found no intravenous needle tracks. This wasn't surprising since Elvis was known by his valets to take the liquid form of drugs through intramuscular injections.

Warlick tried to be thorough, even checking for needle marks between the toes, but found nothing. Warlick didn't check Elvis's buttocks, though, and later said it never occurred to him that Elvis might have himself injected there.

Warlick checked Elvis's nose, observed a trickle of blood seeping from the nostrils, and prepared swabs from the nose to test for cocaine use. For reasons never explained, however, the medical examiner's office never bothered to run a chemical analysis on the swabs. Warlick said he took these samples even though he observed no deterioration of the singer's nasal septum that would have indicated heavy and prolonged usage of cocaine. Former associates of Elvis said he used cocaine from time to time but that it wasn't one of his favorites.

As Warlick continued his inspection, he made notations on a Shelby County medical examiner's investigation report. He noted that Elvis wasn't circumcised. He also noted a "pale pressure mark" parallel to the left eye and a "sutured thoracotomy" on the left side of Presley's chest—the thoracotomy that had been made in the emergency room by doctors attempting open-heart massage. The form had a blank space for "profession." It stumped Warlick. "I thought, 'singer' and thought, 'No.' I thought, 'recording artist' and thought, 'No.'" Then a mental light came on and Warlick wrote down "entertainer."

Warlick turned the form in to his office that night and several days later saw to his chagrin that Jerry Francisco had copied it verbatim in his own handwriting and signed it. Francisco had been an expert witness in court proceedings for a lot of years. It wasn't unusual for a lawyer to ask, "Is that your handwriting, Doctor?" And the medical examiner wanted to be able to say, "Yes." Of this bit of stolen authorship, Warlick would say later, "I mean he didn't even correct my errors, spelling, or grammar. He just copied it over and signed it!"

Warlick observed that Elvis didn't seem as tall in death as he thought he had been in life. "Of course, how big is a guy supposed to be that you've seen standing twenty-five feet tall on a movie screen, if you get my drift. But he seemed small in death."

Elvis's associates described him variously as being between six feet and six feet two inches tall. Red West, who had known Elvis since their days together at Humes High School in Memphis, explained the height discrepancies in his book, *Elvis: What Happened?* West said Elvis wore lifts in his shoes—even his house slippers—to enhance his height. Elvis's height was five feet eleven inches. Warlick didn't note a height on the official report. He examined Elvis's hair, though, and thought it looked dyed. It probably was, if you believe Elvis's hairdresser, Larry Geller. Geller claimed in his book that he had been dyeing Elvis's natural light brown hair jet-black for years. Geller added that near the end of his life, Elvis's hair had turned a stark white color just like Vernon Presley's. The hairdresser said he asked Elvis to leave his locks naturally white, but Elvis regarded that change as too radical for his image and insisted on raven-black hair. Warlick wrote that Elvis's hair was black. He described Elvis's eyes as blue and noted that Elvis had no mustache or beard.

The investigator also thought that Elvis weighed much less than the 255 pounds that the fire department paramedics estimated when they carried the body from Graceland earlier that day. Warlick decided Elvis was overweight, maybe weighing 220 or 230 pounds, but not the lardgut that others were saying he had become. During many of his last concerts, Elvis wore a girdle to appear slim. He also was known to gird his midrift with Saran Wrap before going on stage. The purpose of the Saran Wrap was twofold —to hold his gut in and to help sweat fat off at the same time.

As the autopsy would reveal, though, Elvis had a physical problem that girdles, plastic wrap, and even dieting couldn't overcome. It made him look much heavier than really he was. And it probably made Warlick's estimate of his weight more accurate than one made by the emergency medical technicians. Nonetheless, Warlick failed to write down a weight on his form. He did note that the body had "congestion to the face and upper torso." Other than the pale pressure mark and thoracotomy that he had already recorded, Warlick found no other bruises, abrasions, or scrape marks on the body. He said Elvis's face was pale and lacked expression. "I mean, he looked bad," Warlick said.

Moving to other blank spaces on the form, Warlick wrote

that livor mortis had set in and was fixed and that rigor mortis was also present. Warlick checked the body for edema, an excessive accumulation of fluid in the tissues that causes swelling. Ankle edema, or dropsy, is seen in certain cases of poor heart function. He checked the ankles and discovered no signs of this type of edema. He pressed his thumb against the body in several places to test for pitting edema. If the tissue didn't spring back when he removed his thumb, this was evidence of edema and could mean resultant heart failure. He found no problem there. But he failed to look for traces of edema around the eyes. Puffiness there is a good clue of drug abuse. Putting these indicators together, the doctors estimated that Elvis might have died as early as 9:00 A.M.

Warlick looked into Elvis's mouth. He saw the teeth that had been smashed in the attempts to put a tube down Elvis's throat, but he saw no evidence of vomit or choking. He didn't attach much significance to this, as he correctly figured that Elvis had been aspirated in the emergency room. At this time, he did not yet know that the mouth, throat, and stomach contents had been flushed by the Harvey team. However, he did remember finding traces of vomit and bile on the deep red shag carpet in Elvis's bathroom.

Warlick had his Polaroid camera with him in the operating room. Although it was standard procedure in the Shelby County Medical Examiner's Office to take face shots of the subject before an autopsy, he took no photographs. "The reason you took photographs," he explained, "was to tell who this was, so there wouldn't be any doubt later about who this was." Francisco ordered Warlick not to take any photos in this case and he didn't argue with his boss.

It was about 7:30 P.M. when Warlick had finished his inspection of Elvis's body. At that time, Lieutenant Sam McCachren entered the autopsy room, singled out Francisco, and asked, "How's it going?" Francisco only shrugged his shoulders. McCachren said he came in "to see if I could enlighten or be enlightened any further in the investigation, possibly for a quick determination of the death or the cause of death." Seeing that any quick answers were unlikely, McCachren made arrangements for Warlick to call the homicide bureau after the autopsy was finished and tell

Sergeant Peel the results. McCachren left the room, called his office and went home for the night. He was fated never to be involved in this investigation again.

Isaac Henderson, the diener, now began his work. Taking a scalpel, called a Bard Parker No. 22, Henderson began cutting on the left shoulder. The scalpel looked much like the blades that children use to sculpt model airplanes. The diener had started a procedure known among pathologists as "cracking the chest." Henderson applied pressure to his blade, cutting to the bone, and drew it down at an angle to the xiphoid, the lowest point of the breastbone. Then he drew his blade back up from the xiphoid in an opposite angle to the right shoulder. This formed a V-shaped wedge. Then he used the scalpel to shave the muscles away from the rib cage. The chest muscles in that wedge or flap were pulled back over the face, exposing the rib cage.

From the very bottom of the V-cut at the xiphoid, Henderson pulled the scalpel deeply straight down, circled the navel, and then returned to a straight-line abdominal incision all the way to the pubis bone. The V now looked more like a Y. In fact, pathologists call these initial autopsy incisions "making a Y-cut." The muscles covering the abdominal cavity were shaved back laterally on each side, exposing that area.

The diener then picked up a Stryker bone saw, which is named for its manufacturer, and plugged it into a power outlet. All the doctors and Warlick were standing around the autopsy table intently watching Henderson work. The electric bone saw hummed as it cut through the clavicle, better known as the collarbone, extending from the sternum or breastbone to the shoulder tips. The saw's blade is serrated and shaped like a half-moon. It is attached just below a grapefruit-size electric motor. Henderson gripped the saw by a goosenecked handle attached above the rounded motor. The Stryker saw is also used to cut off plaster casts. It isn't supposed to cut flesh if it slips from bone.

While cutting through the ribs, Henderson's saw occasionally hit small veins and sent up tiny splatters of blood. Having cut through the ribs and sternum, Henderson set the saw aside and tried to lift up the breastplate. But some of the organs underneath were stuck. He had to shave away more muscle with his scalpel blade.

Now the breastplate was lifted freely, and the heart, lungs, thymus gland, esophagus, trachea, and larynx were exposed. The doctors peered into the chest cavity to make sure the lungs were in their proper position. They were. They weren't "smoker's lungs." Warlick, who had attended hundreds of other autopsies, thought they looked like regular lungs and saw nothing significant about them at this point. The doctors also examined the chest area to see if Elvis had suffered hemorrhage here. They were looking for the rupture of an aneurysm. An aneurysm is an abnormal condition characterized by the stretching or distending of a portion of the wall of an artery. The aorta is particularly susceptible to an aneurysm formation. Nothing like this was found in the chest cavity, and a later check of the abdominal cavity showed nothing amiss.

Isaac Henderson used his scalpel to cut down from the diaphragm to the pubis through the abdominal layer of fat, called the panniculus. He pulled this layer back, exposing the abdominal organs—the large and small intestines, liver, spleen, stomach, gall bladder, and pancreas. Henderson used his blade to expose the neck organs. He cut through the floor of the mouth below the tongue and continued slicing through the neck column. He pulled the pharynx, larynx, esophagus, trachea, lungs, and heart down to the abdominal area and then out of the body. Those organs were laid out on the corkboard-covered table with water running over its surface. The physicians took over the dissection process on this table.

Bale and Chesney did most of this work with Muirhead, Francisco, and Warlick looking over their shoulders. The two doctors first began making probes of the lungs. They were looking for one of the main causes of sudden death—a pulmonary embolism. An embolism is the obstruction of an artery by an embolus, usually a piece of clotted blood that breaks away from one part of the circulatory system and travels to another. Physicians also refer to this clotted blood as a "thrombus." The autopsy pathologists carefully cut the pulmonary artery that came off the left side of the lung to the right side of the heart. Using surgical scissors that had one blunt edge and one sharp edge, they meticulously dissected the left pulmonary artery. They found no embolus. They repeated the procedure on the right pulmonary artery with the same results. These arteries, which carried blood to the lungs from the heart, were clear. The doctors now carefully dissected the rest of the lungs, the three lobes on the right and two lobes on the left. They found no embolus or thrombus. The airways were clear, and they found no evidence of lung disease. Samples of lung tissue were taken for microscopic analysis. Pulmonary embolism was now eliminated as Elvis's killer.

While Bale and Chesney were making their dissections, Sexton had his hands full taking samples. He collected cerebral spinal fluid, blood, urine, and tissue from all of the major organs for testing. Soon Sexton had a portion of the blood spun down and had the serum separated. Many of the samples were quick-frozen and placed at minus 70 degrees centigrade. Sexton carefully split the samples—one set for Baptist Hospital and another for Jerry Francisco.

Dr. Noel Florendo stayed busy on his microscope examining frozen samples that Sexton handed him. Other samples were fixed in formalin preservative and had colored dye added to them. These would be available for microscopic analysis in twenty-four hours. Dr. James Holbert took a sample of bone marrow for testing. At this point in the autopsy, one of the doctors informed Muirhead that no stomach contents were found for testing. Sexton called the emergency room and learned that the mouth, throat, and stomach contents had been flushed away. This was a blow to the autopsy team. The suspicion was growing stronger that this was a drug-related death. If there had been any undigested drugs in Elvis's stomach, that evidence was now lost forever.

From time to time as Muirhead saw something that interested him, he turned to Jerry Francisco and said, "What do you think about that, Dr. Francisco?" The medical examiner answered him, but took no active part in the work and gave only one special instruction about a sample to be taken. He asked Sexton to make sure to obtain a sample of the contents of the gall bladder. Bile taken from the gall bladder is often a good place to look for evidence in drug-related deaths.

Chesney now began to examine Elvis's heart. He trimmed

it away from the lungs. Everyone in the room was watching as he worked. Chesney held the heart up from the table. It was extremely large. Instead of looking like red muscle, this heart looked like brown flab. A normal human heart weighs about 375 grams. Warlick guessed this one weighed at least 80 grams more than normal, maybe as much as 480 grams. Actually, Warlick was short 40 grams, even with his highest estimate. Elvis's heart weighed 520 grams. Its size was a sign of hypertension, no doubt, and in this case, perhaps, congestive heart failure.

Symptoms of congestive heart failure are retention of salt and water due to impaired heart function, shortness of breath, swelling of the legs and feet, and poor circulation of the blood. Warlick already had checked for edema—the swelling and fluid retention associated with congestive heart failure—and found no evidence of it. Death from congestive heart failure is usually a slow, fairly predictable process. It wasn't how Elvis died. His fat, flabby heart may have failed him, but it didn't fade out slowly and predictably. A heart attack was a more likely candidate, and there was only one way to find out if that killed him. Elvis's heart would have to be dissected bit by bit and checked out. That's just what Chesney planned on doing as he picked up his Bard Parker No. 22 scalpel and prepared to cut.

IV

THE COVER-UP BEGINS

THE PATHOLOGISTS had been dissecting the body of Elvis Presley for more than an hour on the night of August 16, 1977, and clearly understood they were not operating in a vacuum. Even though the doctors had taken their time and had already methodically eliminated two possible causes of death, they knew they were fighting the clock. It was now about 8:00 P.M. and they were running out of time. This was no ordinary corpse they were dissecting. They didn't have two weeks or two days or even two hours. They needed an answer now. The whole world wanted to know what killed Elvis Presley.

Two of three U.S. commercial networks had led their evening news broadcasts with Elvis's obituary that night and said the cause of death was still unknown. That fed the frenzy for more information. Switchboards at the local newspapers were flooded with calls. The wire services were besieged from newspapers everywhere with requests for information. Memphis, a second-tier city with a population of about 750,000, was being flooded with Presley's fans descending from all points of the compass. They were streaming into the city to find out what happened to their hero and to pay a final tribute. The networks were comparing this mass phenomenon to the fan reaction to actor Rudolph Valentino's death a generation earlier. On this night many Elvis Presley fans were flocking to Baptist Hospital, clogging the streets around it, and causing traffic jams. A horde of newshounds, armed with cameras, microphones, and notebooks, were among them and contributed more to confusion than enlightenment. Rumors, some of them wild, some of them unbelievable, were rampant. Sergeant J. N. Willis of the Memphis Police Department's homicide squad told reporters that Elvis died either from heart failure or an accidental drug overdose. The police brass later retracted both of Sergeant Willis's death theories.

Reporters nosing around Baptist Hospital's emergency room heard Elvis had "aspirated." They checked with medical sources and found out that if Elvis had indeed aspirated, it meant he vomited, then inhaled the stomach material into his lungs, and choked to death. These same sources told the reporters that this condition is commonly found among people who are under the influence of alcohol or drugs. These sources had no pipeline to the autopsy suite, the only place where this rumor could be verified or denied. But it spread like kudzu nonetheless. They also heard that Elvis died from an uncommon disease known as lupus erythematosus, an acute skin disease evident mainly on the face and hands. Only three to six cases of lupus occur in a population of 100,000. Sometimes the disease attacks the internal organs and causes death. This systemic form of lupus killed southern novelist Flannery O'Connor in 1964. And when it came to exotic diseases among journalists covering Elvis's death, lupus was tops. Despite its wide and intermittent circulation, the lupus rumor was incorrect.

Another rumor that would take on the proportions of a hoax held that Elvis died of bone cancer. It took on a life of its own that night and is still circulated from time to time in books by Elvis entourage members.

A hospital source, obviously one trained on the nonscientific side of health care, told an out-of-town reporter, "His body was just worn out. His arteries and veins were terribly corroded." That baffling gibberish eventually made its way into *Rolling Stone* magazine.

Other wild speculations made it into print and onto the commercial airwaves that night and the next day and are still floating around. Among them is the notion that a mysterious intruder caught Elvis unawares in the bathroom and murdered him with a karate chop. If it's plausible that a team of seasoned pathologists in desperate search of a cause of death could overlook such blunt trauma to the neck, then maybe Mona Lisa was a man. And of course the most outlandish rumor of them all maintained that Elvis was really alive. Elvis zealots clinging to this notion contended that the corpse being dissected on the hospital's second floor belonged to somebody else. Somebody else had volunteered to die for Elvis or had been killed by Elvis so Elvis could disappear. Elvis was unhappy and wanted to get away. Hence, an ever-resourceful Elvis faked his own death to make good his escape. Whacked out, crazy, weird, whatever—that crackpot story is still very much alive, years after Elvis's burial. A best seller has even been written on the subject and has its believers.

Reporters and fans that night could hear any and every story they wanted to hear. Gossip was as good as truth because as the minutes became hours outside Baptist Hospital there was as yet no official story to hear and believe. The autopsy was continuing.

Although there was no communication between the news-hungry mob outside the hospital and the doctors inside the autopsy room, the pathologists seemed to know by osmosis that the crowd was there. They sensed the pressure on them for determining the cause of Elvis's death. And soon.

———

Thus every eye in the operating theater was glued on Dr. James Chesney as he used his scalpel to dissect the left anterior descending coronary artery of Elvis's heart. This artery, which is located on the outside of the heart, is about the same size as a rawhide lace on a boating moccasin. Or as Dan Warlick described it, about the same size as regular spaghetti, not vermicelli.

Pathologists consider this artery a good place to start look-

45

ing for evidence of a killer heart attack. Chesney made repeated cuts about every millimeter along the artery. As he cut, he pulled his scalpel back and looked into the middle of the artery. He was searching for an obstruction of any kind—for a thrombus or an embolus or a fresh clot. He also was looking for severe arteriosclerosis, a hardening of the arteries often caused by a buildup of cholesterol, or for a complete closure of an artery or for a closure of more than 90 percent. As he finished dissecting the left anterior descending coronary artery, Chesney found none of these signs of a heart attack. He noted only mild atherosclerosis, or hardening of the inner lining of the artery. Chesney estimated that the artery was about 40 to 50 percent narrowed. A narrowing of 70 percent, however, would have thrown up a red flag as a symptom of heart attack. But Chesney regarded what he found here as insignificant.

Chesney repeated the dissection process on the circumflex coronary artery. Again, he found no significant anatomical evidence of a heart attack. He repeated the process a final time on the right coronary artery and obtained the same results.

Now he began a process known to pathologists as "running the heart." He cut open Elvis's heart in the direction of the blood flow starting on the right side at the atrium, the upper chamber of the heart, which receives blood from the veins. He laid the heart open like a book and again began looking for obstructions and closures. He found nothing to indicate a heart attack. His dissection of the aorta, the large artery originating from the left ventricle or chamber of the heart, showed only minimal hardening of the inner lining. Chesney later wrote that Elvis's heart "has an overall configuration of mild left ventricular hypertrophy without dilation." That meant Elvis had some increase of the size of his left ventricle or heart chamber that caused mild hypertension (high blood pressure). "Without dilation" simply meant that Elvis's heart hadn't failed. In other words, he didn't die of a heart attack.

Dr. Noel Florendo had taken time from his microscope to watch most of the dissection of the heart. "I did not think there was any evidence of a heart attack," Florendo said. And although Dan Warlick was no doctor, he knew clogged coronary arteries when he saw them. And he didn't see any that night.

Hence a third major cause of sudden death had now been

eliminated. Pulmonary embolism was gone. A ruptured aneurysm was gone. The atmosphere in the autopsy room was now nearing the panic stage. The doctors were running out of obvious causes of what killed Elvis. They now looked to the brain to provide them with an answer. Maybe Elvis died of a cerebrovascular accident or apoplexy? That is, maybe he had a stroke caused by a hemorrhage or clot within a blood vessel in the brain.

Diener Isaac Henderson picked up another scalpel with a big X-Acto handle and began cutting into the head. He made his first incision behind the right ear and circled the cut to the back of the head and then upward to the top of the crown. Then, starting again at the right ear, Henderson reversed the direction of the cut up to the crown, joining the back incision. He repeated this entire process on the left side. He pulled the front scalp flaps over the face and the back scalp flaps down behind the neck. The skull cap was now revealed.

Henderson picked up his Stryker bone saw and made a circular cut around the skull. He made two notches—front and back—to take the guesswork out of fitting the cap back on the skull after the autopsy. He now lifted up the cap.

The exposed brain was picked up gently and severed just above the spinal cord. The brain was placed on the corkboard table. Some pathologists believe that before a proper dissection of a brain can take place, it should be soaked in formalin preservative for two weeks. This hardens the brain tissue, causing it to take on the consistency of rubber and permitting easier dissection. Normally, forensic pathologists don't have two weeks. And tonight, neither did members of the Elvis Presley autopsy team. They began cutting on the brain as soon as it was placed on the dissection table, first removing the cerebellum or the part of the brain responsible for muscle coordination. They started probing the circle of Willis, a group of arteries surrounding the base of the brain. These arteries feed blood to the brain. The doctors dissected them and found all of them to be open. There were no leaks, no holes, no clots, no hardening. Now, as if they were slicing two loaves of bread, the pathologists made front-to-back cuts of the two brain hemispheres. They were looking for hemorrhages or large bloody areas. They found no evidence that Elvis had suffered a fatal stroke. A cerebrovascular accident had not killed him. The fourth and last major obvious cause of sudden death was now eliminated.

By now Francisco and Muirhead were out of time. Earlier they had agreed to hold a press conference at 8:00 P.M. It was almost that time now. With nothing positive to report, the two pathologists nonetheless proposed to leave the autopsy room and face the press. Dan Warlick thought this was idiotic, since all that could be said with a straight face was, "We don't know, fellas." Warlick thought the physicians should at least finish the gross phase of the autopsy before they opened their mouths. And even then, he thought, the doctors would be able to say only that they must await chemical tests before making any pronouncements about what killed Elvis.

Muirhead assumed they would report that the autopsy was inconclusive pending further tests. Inasmuch as Francisco was the medical examiner who had charge of the case, it was a foregone conclusion that he would be the point man at the conference. At that Francisco, Muirhead, Sexton, Bale, Nichopoulos, Holbert, Haggit, and Pitcock left for the press conference.

Isaac Henderson, the diener, as well as the three uniformed policemen and two hospital security guards, also left the room. The guards were now stationed outside the autopsy room. Only Drs. Tom Chesney, Raul Lamin, and Noel Florendo plus Dan Warlick remained inside the room to complete the autopsy. Another hour's work lay ahead of them.

———

Francisco was still wearing his white lab coat when he walked into the hospital's press conference room and seated himself before a bank of microphones. He was flanked on his left by Nichopoulos, Muirhead, and Bale. They were also wearing white lab coats. Standing out among this group of drab, staid-looking doctors was Nichopoulos with his white, flyaway hair, his diamond-studded rings and gold jewelry. His open-necked black silk shirt clashed garishly with his white medical smock.

Francisco opened the press conference, saying with a

straight face, "The results of the autopsy are that the cause of death is cardiac arrhythmia due to undetermined heartbeat." Put another way, Elvis's heart stopped beating. Muirhead was aghast. What a silly diagnosis, he thought. The heart must stop beating before a person dies. And for the heart to stop, it goes into some kind of arrhythmia or irregularity of beat.

But the reporters gobbled up this glib nonsense, not pausing to digest it. Francisco continued: "There are several cardiovascular diseases that are known to be present. One is a mild degree of hypertension that had been under treatment for some time, and that there was hardening of the arteries, the coronary arteries of the heart, known as coronary atherosclerosis."

That was true enough, but Francisco didn't say that Chesney, the autopsy team's heart expert, had rated the coronary atherosclerosis as mild and the atherosclerosis of the aorta as minimal. Nor did he say that the autopsy team found no clear sign of heart attack as a cause of death. And yet he was clearly pointing to atherosclerosis as a likely cause. He backed off just a bit, saying the hardening of the arteries didn't do enough damage to cause the arrhythmia.

As Francisco's words were broadcast from Memphis to Missoula, millions of Elvis fans breathed a sigh of relief. Their idol had died of natural causes—a heart attack. Or, anyway, that's what they understood Francisco to say. As a cautionary note, the medical examiner added about cause of death: "It may take several days. It may take several weeks. It may never be discovered." He told the reporters that although Elvis was taking drugs for hypertension and a chronic colon problem, there was no evidence of any drug use contributing to his death. "He was using medication to control his blood pressure and for a colon problem, but there is no evidence of any chronic abuse of drugs whatsoever," Francisco insisted, glossing over Warlick's evidence to the contrary—the syringes, the black bag, the hasty cleanup job in the bathroom. Furthermore, not a single chemical test had been completed, and the absence of any noticeable cause had been a giveaway that the toxicology reports would have a lot to say about how Elvis died.

Muirhead was noticeably embarrassed. He winced as Jerry Francisco ran roughshod over the physical evidence with a lot of cardiological double-talk. But he didn't contradict the medical examiner. "I wish I had spoken up," Muirhead told his colleagues later. "But I didn't know about the toxicology."

Before turning the microphone over to Nichopoulos, Francisco disposed of the Elvis lupus rumor, at least for the night. He told the reporters there were hospital test records in Elvis's files that clearly eliminated lupus. Nichopoulos, the man who had ordered a powerful narcotic prescription for Elvis just hours before his death, seemed positively jubilant by what he had heard from the medical examiner. He told reporters that Elvis had been taking "appetite depressants" to curb a weight problem, but he added that those medications were not amphetamines. As Elvis's private doctor for ten years, Nichopoulos dismissed rumors that Elvis had been taking hard drugs. "If he was taking cocaine, I would have known about it," he asserted. He added that he had given Elvis an extensive physical five days before and found him in fit condition. "He was getting over an eye infection and a sore throat, but overall he was a healthy man," Nichopoulos said.

———

News of the press conference filtered back into the autopsy room. Francisco's words, which, given the tense circumstances, had come off as a pronouncement, surprised the three remaining pathologists and Dan Warlick. Warlick thought that if his boss wanted to call it straight from the shoulder, he should have said Elvis died of "idiopathy." That simply means of unknown causes. But as it happened, Warlick termed Francisco's statements "total, complete, unmitigated bullshit." Florendo was more muted but also disapproved of what the medical examiner had said. Florendo defined cardiac arrhythmia "as an irregularity in the heartbeat sufficiently irregular enough to cause death." He had seen no evidence in the autopsy to warrant this diagnosis. Over their specimens, the three pathologists shook their heads at this tour de force of medical mumbo jumbo and got back to work.

Dan Warlick examined Elvis's larynx, the voice box, situated between the base of the tongue and the windpipe or trachea.

The larynx contains two bands of tissue called vocal cords, which make speech and singing possible. The sounds are created by the expansion and contraction of the vocal cords as air passes between them. Warlick was checking for edema. He was looking for a swelling in the larynx—an indicator that Elvis had suffered an allergic reaction to drugs. He found nothing unusual, no signs of bruising or choking.

While holding the voice box in his hand, Warlick became sad and introspective. "As I looked at Elvis Presley's vocal cords, I thought about all the millions and millions of lives that he had affected with the songs he had sung and the music he made. And I thought what a pity it was that he would never be able to sing again."

Next the team began checking the abdominal organs, all of which proved to be large. Warlick said all of Elvis's abdominal organs were oversized. "It's not a disease," Warlick explained. "It's just a condition where your organs are bigger than other people's, and he had big abdominal organs." His spleen weighed 340 grams. A normal spleen might weigh about 75 grams. But his spleen was neither swollen nor distended, nor did it show any evidence of an inflammatory disease nor any kind of acute bacterial infection.

His kidneys were large and in fairly good shape. Chesney made the following notation about the kidneys: "Renal papillary necrosis, confined to single papilla." That means one of the kidneys contained a small nipple-shaped protrusion of dead tissue. This was not a serious problem and did not contribute to Elvis's death.

His liver weighed 3,500 grams. Chesney noted the liver enlargement, describing it scientifically as "hepatomegaly." He wrote the liver had "mild fatty metamorphosis," suggesting that the fat caused by alcohol or drug abuse had transformed the appearance of the liver. Elvis's liver problems first were noted by doctors at Baptist Hospital in January 1975, when he was detoxified for drugs. A biopsy had been done on his liver then, and it revealed damage to the organ brought about by severe drug abuse. Chesney observed that the liver wasn't in terrific shape, but he eliminated it as a cause of death.

Noel Florendo and Raul Lamin were now at work doing a

messy job over a stainless steel sink where a constant stream of water was flowing. They were standing about ten feet away from Chesney and Warlick. Florendo held an odd-looking pair of surgical scissors in one hand. The scissors looked like the ones that nurses use to remove bandages, only they were three times larger than bandage scissors. One blade of these scissors ended with a flat bill that had a hook attached to it. Florendo was using this instrument to perform an autopsy dissection known as "running the gut."

"Hey, look at this!" Florendo shouted, startling both Chesney and Warlick. They rushed to the sink. Florendo was cutting the colon or the large intestine with Lamin assisting. The colon is approximately five to seven feet in length in a person Elvis's size and should have been about two inches in diameter. By Warlick's estimate, however, Elvis's colon was at least three and a half inches in diameter in some places and as large as four and a half to five inches in diameter in others. As Florendo cut, he found that this megacolon was jam-packed from the base of the descending colon all the way up and halfway across the transverse colon. It was filled with white, chalklike fecal material. The impaction had the consistency of clay and seemed to defy Florendo's efforts with the scissors to cut it out.

Everyone paused. It was obvious to all four men that Elvis had a severe bowel problem. They believed he must have suffered pain and discomfort from the fecal impaction and could only speculate about the number of days Elvis had gone without a bowel movement. They all understood that this bowel problem was a clear symptom of prolonged drug abuse. As Warlick described it, "When you take downer-type drugs, depressants, narcotics, a lot of them, most of them, have the concomitant effect of slowing down the digestive system. In other words, the locomotive action of the bowel quits working, so it gets packed with food, and then it gets packed with more food. And it sits there distended and full of food, and that causes the colon to stretch."

This colon problem caused considerable concern among doctors who had treated Elvis during his hospitalization and drug detoxification in 1973. Dr. Lawrence D. Wruble, a noted Memphis gastroenterologist who treated Elvis then, later testified that Elvis was addicted to drugs. Wruble said the drugs caused most of Elvis's intestinal problems. His wild eating habits and fondness for high-cholesterol food—greasy cheeseburgers and French fries by the bagful, burnt bacon and peanut butter and banana sandwiches fried in butter, ice cream by the half gallon—also contributed to his intestinal problems. Warlick believed the distended colon explained why some people thought Elvis was a lot heavier than he actually was. And it also explained why Ginger Alden said Elvis spent so much time in the bathroom that morning. "The poor guy must have been in misery. He must have suffered some real discomfort," Warlick said to himself that night.

But as bad as the colon problem seemed, it didn't kill Elvis. Or did it? Maybe it did indirectly? Warlick mulled a cause of death theory that began coming together in his mind after he discovered several clues in Elvis's bedroom suite at Graceland that afternoon. Drugs played a role in his hypothesis. He considered running it by the others in the room but kept it to himself.

Warlick helped the three pathologists finish collecting and preparing the specimens. They were to be sent to laboratories around the country for chemical testing. And he made sure that specimens taken from the kidney, liver, and blood had been sent to the University of Tennessee toxicology lab across the street from the hospital. Francisco, unlike the Baptist Hospital pathologists, relied on this lab for his chemical analyses.

The diener, Isaac Henderson, had just come back in the room and helped stitch up the body. None of the organs were sewn back into the body. They were preserved for testing. Arrangements had been made to transport the body just three blocks down Union Avenue to Memphis Funeral Home for burial preparation.

———

Security was tight at the hospital as the body was moved, and it was about to get tighter. Uniformed hospital guards came back into the autopsy room and took possession of all the notes and forms that the doctors had used. These papers, slides, and preserved specimens were all locked in the hospital's vault for the night. Rumors of ghoulish plots to steal documents, pictures, and even Elvis's body were circulating in Memphis. The hospital administration was taking these rumors seriously. Police detectives had informed them that a burglary might be attempted on the pathology department's filing cabinets. The police were being tipped that several sleazy tabloids were offering huge amounts of money for the autopsy information. And as this week wore on, attempts to steal or purchase the autopsy information became blatant.

For example, according to Maurice Elliott, the hospital's executive vice president, a private detective called a hospital employee in the laboratory's business office and offered $10,000 for the Presley documents. "This fellow [the detective] asked him [the employee] did he know of a way to get the record," Elliott said. And a Memphis man connected with the weekly *National Enquirer* approached an undercover police agent with a plot to burglarize the medical examiner's office to get the autopsy report—which had not yet been written—and photos of the body—which had never been taken. Police said the plot was never carried out and no arrests were made.

That night Dan Warlick's car was burglarized, and the small spiral pad he used to take notes at Graceland and in the autopsy room was stolen. Apparently the culprit was unaware of the notebook's potential value because Warlick's notes were never exploited.

Another man believed to have been associated with the *National Enquirer* approached a secretary at Baptist Hospital and a secretary in Francisco's office with offers of $2,000 for photos and the autopsy report. Warlick's photographs of the Graceland death scene somehow disappeared from the files. The medical examiner denied that they were stolen, and produced them two years later in complying with a subpoena.

Several days after the autopsy, undercover police officers met with a *National Enquirer* reporter staying in room 411 of the Holiday Inn Rivermont and came very close to arresting him. The police apparently cooled the man's desire to obtain the Presley documents illegally. But the Memphis cops didn't stop the *National Enquirer* from playing tawdry journalistic fun and games right up to and including Elvis's funeral. The *Enquirer* equipped one of Elvis's third cousins with a miniature, spy-type Minox camera and paid him to take a picture of Elvis lying in his coffin. This tasteless photograph was published as a cover shot in the newspaper.

Warlick walked back to his office across the street, passing some Elvis fans still lingering outside the hospital on Madison Avenue. It was about 8:50 P.M. now. The air was still humid and stifling, but at least the thermometer had dropped several degrees since sundown. Back in his office, Warlick stored the nasal swabs in the refrigerator—the ones never tested. Sitting at his desk, he remembered promising McCachren that he would call the homicide division after the autopsy was completed. He picked up the phone and dialed the bureau. He reached the duty officer, Lieutenant G. E. Jordan, and reported that Francisco had preliminarily ruled that Elvis's death was a result of "cardiac arrhythmia, causes unknown." The lieutenant asked if that meant Elvis had died of natural causes. Warlick told him that that was his understanding of what his boss had said. At that point, the lieutenant jotted down "natural causes" and closed Memphis Police Department case No. 2793, the death of Elvis Aaron Presley.

After Warlick completed his call, he pulled out his notebook and the investigative form he had partially filled out in the autopsy room. He looked over the form again and assigned it Medical Examiner case No. 77-1944. He left it for Francisco.

As Warlick walked out of the office, he glanced at his watch. He just had time to drive home, open a beer, and watch the late television news. He was curious about how Elvis's death and autopsy were being covered. Climbing into his car, Warlick dropped his notebook on the seat—it was the last time he would see it—and started the car, heading south to his apartment. It wasn't far from Graceland. It had been a hell of a day, one he would remember for a lifetime.

Once home, Warlick turned on his television to discover how a tentative pronouncement with little substance can be transformed into an unqualified declaration. He heard a local news announcer say that Elvis died of a heart attack. "That's a goddamn lie," Warlick swore, then caught himself. He almost threw a perfectly good beer at the screen and gained a better understanding of why Elvis shot out television sets.

That night, two of the major television networks ran special half-hour-long Elvis tribute programs following the local news. Geraldo Rivera, a hip, long-haired, controversial reporter, anchored the ABC-TV broadcast. Rivera was receptive to preliminary indications that Elvis had died of heart problems. He told his viewers that although Elvis's death was sad, "at least 'the King' had not followed in the melancholy rock 'n' roll tradition of Janis Joplin, Jim Morrison, Jimi Hendrix, and all the others" who died of drug abuse. Regarding Elvis as the first antiestablishment rock star, Rivera was a longtime Elvis fan.

The other network special that night ran on NBC-TV. David Brinkley, a brooding southerner who was very much aware of the Presley phenomenon, anchored the special. While more professional than Rivera's broadcast, Brinkley's show stirred up a heap of flak from Elvis fans. Brinkley introduced a panel that was supposed to talk about Elvis and his music. It included Steve Dunleavy, who had written the book *Elvis: What Happened?* with Red and Sonny West and Dave Hebler. Dunleavy, a bearded Australian, described Elvis's weird life-style, his weight problems, and his fondness for drugs. Then, as he waved a cigar, Dunleavy made a dreadful mistake for which NBC later apologized. He called Elvis "white trash." Those are fighting words to many poor rural whites who were local Elvis fans. Dunleavy's words probably caused a few more television sets to be shot out that night in memory of Elvis.

———

At Baptist Hospital, Dick Grob, the former California police sergeant who headed security at the mansion, had asked to be present in the autopsy room but had been turned down. Grob managed to stay busy in the hallway, however. He ran off two reporters, Craig Schwed and Susan White of United Press International, who were trying to get a glimpse of the body at the hospital after the autopsy. Schwed and White were both wearing white hospital laboratory coats and were attempting to blend in with several of the pathologists discussing the autopsy as they walked out of the operating room. Hospital employees, wearing green coats with the words "refrigeration technician" stitched on their breast pockets, were then entering the autopsy suite with a cart. Grob confronted the two gawking reporters, told them they had no business where they were and ordered them to leave.

That was not Dick Grob's last experience that night with a prying newsperson. He had a later run-in with a photographer at Memphis Funeral Home after Elvis's body arrived there from the hospital. Grob finally persuaded the police commander at the funeral home that problems with the press would become worse. The commander doubled the guard detail and placed the funeral home off-limits to working journalists.

Confident the situation was now under control, Grob headed back to Graceland to do some investigating on his own. He couldn't understand why Elvis had lain on the bathroom carpeting for so long without anybody noticing and calling for help. Grob suspected that Ginger Alden knew more than she had told so far that day.

The security chief also wanted to talk to the maids at Graceland. They were alert to little things, such as buttons on the kitchen telephone console, which lit up when calls were made from Elvis's bedroom suite.

He also wanted to talk to Elvis's stepbrothers, David and Ricky Stanley, who were supposed to be on duty all the time Elvis was laid out on the bathroom floor. Grob already had heard from Sam Thompson that David Stanley was hightailing it out of Graceland shortly after the ambulance arrived.

———

While Dick Grob was puzzling over the elements of an in-house investigation, Vernon Presley was trying to control his anger. And that anger was directed toward Nichopoulos. He couldn't help blaming Dr. Nick for his son's death. He even harbored the suspicion that perhaps Elvis had been poisoned. Those autopsy papers he signed ought to lead to some answers, and Vernon hoped soon. Meanwhile, he was going to have a showdown with Nichopoulos—and have it before the funeral—to get a few financial matters straightened out.

In 1975 Nichopoulos borrowed $200,000 from Elvis in exchange for a promissory note. On March 3, 1977, an additional loan of $55,000 was made by Elvis to Nichopoulos at 7 percent interest. At the time of the second loan, the first was modified to call for 7 percent interest and both were consolidated. The consolidation agreement called for monthly payments of $1,082.85 beginning April 1, 1977, through February 1, 2002. The loans went for construction of Dr. Nick's outlandishly gabled, custom-built house in fashionable East Memphis—a potential nightmare for a real estate agent if it ever had to be put on the market. However, Elvis never signed the consolidation agreement.

On the Thursday after Elvis's death, Vernon met with Nichopoulos and had his showdown. As executor of Elvis's estate, Vernon signed the consolidation agreement. Then he fired Nichopoulos as his personal physician and warned the doctor never to be late making any monthly repayments of the loan. Later, Vernon would order Baptist Hospital officials never to show Nichopoulos a copy of the autopsy. Under different circumstances he wouldn't mind exposing doctors who handed out pills by the sackful, but this time it would expose his own son. Above all, Vernon wanted to preserve the public myth of Elvis, the clean-living entertainer who opposed drug abuse. Also in the interest of appearances, Vernon allowed Nichopoulos to participate in Elvis's funeral as a pallbearer.

Over the next several days, Nichopoulos attempted to mollify Vernon and get back in his good graces by spinning a fanciful tale. As investigators were to ferret out later, Nichopoulos told Vernon that it was a good thing that death came when it did because Elvis was suffering from incurable, terminal bone cancer and was in terrible pain. There was no medical evidence, then or later, to support this assertion, and apparently Vernon sensed that the doctor was dissembling. The ploy did not work.

On the same day of his confrontation with Vernon, Nichopoulos was also attempting to protect himself on another front.

This second move would have headed off whatever role drugs played either as a cause or a contributing factor in Elvis's death. With the autopsy far from complete, Nichopoulos signed and attempted to file an official death certificate for Elvis, listing "cardiac arrhythmia, coronary artery disease, hypertension, and diabetes mellitus" as the causes of death. He also listed "fatty liver" as a contributing factor. Apparently it was a botched attempt at a cover-up, and it was intercepted.

According to Tennessee law, Nichopoulos had no legal right to sign the death certificate. Moreover, with the autopsy test not even completed, Nichopoulos's death certificate would have been quite embarrassing had it then surfaced in the press. The Tennessee Department of Public Health, recognizing that Elvis's death was currently under investigation by the Shelby County Medical Examiner's Office, rejected the death certificate and sent it to the medical examiner. In effect, Jerry Francisco voided it by keeping it secret in his files and replacing it with a death certificate of his own.

Vernon's anger at Nichopoulos apparently did not end with their showdown before Elvis's funeral. A month after Elvis's death, Nichopoulos had a scary experience that kept him looking over his shoulder and pondering Vernon's irate state of mind.

The scare happened while the doctor was watching a Memphis State University–Utah State University football game in Memphis's Liberty Bowl Memorial Stadium. A friend, Dr. Charles Thomas Langford, a kidney specialist at Baptist Hospital, was sitting directly behind Nichopoulos. Langford was Nichopoulos's guest at the football game. Near the end of the game, a bullet struck Langford in the right shoulder. At first, police feared that Langford had been wounded in an attempt on Nichopoulos's life, and they assigned Nichopoulos round-the-clock bodyguards. The police never learned who shot the doctor, but they later concluded that the bullet was probably a stray that either had been fired outside the stadium or from much higher inside the stadium and had not been aimed at Nichopoulos. They withdrew the bodyguards.

Shortly after this bizarre shooting, Mrs. Jo LaVern Alden, Ginger Alden's mother, and Vernon Presley were discussing Elvis's relationship with Nichopoulos. Jo Alden said the strange wounding of Langford came up in their conversation. "I asked him what did he think really happened," she said. "Vernon looked at me coldly and said, 'They shot the wrong damned doctor.'"

V

HOMETOWN BOY

YELLOWING WITH AGE in a picture frame among other notable editions in Memphis history, page one of *The Memphis Commercial Appeal* for August 17, 1977, is instructive
not so much for what it reported but for what it didn't fathom. The
lead story across the top of the page reads:

> Elvis Presley died Tuesday, apparently of a heart
> attack, at Graceland mansion.
> The 42-year-old "king of rock and roll" was found
> unconscious in his night clothes at 2:30 P.M.
> Presley was found by his road manager, Joe Espo-
> sito, and was taken by ambulance to Baptist Hospi-
> tal's emergency room where he was pronounced dead
> at 3:30 P.M., police said. Hospital officials announced
> the death at 4 P.M.
> Esposito told authorities he could find no sign that
> Presley was breathing and could not detect a heart-
> beat. He began emergency resuscitation efforts and
> called a Memphis Fire Department ambulance.
> Shelby County Medical Examiner Jerry Francisco,
> who performed an autopsy, said the death was due to

The Death of Elvis

**"an erratic heartbeat" but added that the exact cause
of death may never be determined.**

The newspaper article then went on to quote the medical
examiner uncritically—there was "severe cardiovascular disease
present," which in combination with mild hypertension probably
caused "cardiac arrhythmia"; there was "no indication of any drug
abuse of any kind" because there weren't any needle tracks; and
without any qualification, "basically it was a natural death."

Elsewhere the story quoted the police as saying that Joe
Esposito discovered the body, and several paragraphs later it identified Ginger Alden as the last person to see Elvis alive.

Twenty years earlier, back when the Memphis newspapers
were geared up for daily war, there would have been a confrontation at the press conference, an attempt to talk to another doctor,
another source to verify this cardiac arrhythmia foolishness.
"Whatdya mean, his heart stopped? That got announced this afternoon. Who were the cops on the scene? You got any pictures?"

But the Memphis press was tame and deferential in 1977,
not fighting to get the story so much as to win over a public relations specialist and get the handout first.

Hence it's not surprising that the lead story in *The Commercial Appeal* shifted quickly to easier aspects of the story to report—
the events outside Graceland. There were the phone calls pouring
into Memphis, the run on Elvis records at local shops, and requests
engulfing hotels and motels for room reservations. Here there was
a crunch. A Shriners' convention had most rooms booked up.

As the lead story reflects, the Presley entourage in tacit
alliance with Memphis officialdom was glossing over embarrassing
details if not lying about them outright. To enumerate:

- Esposito hadn't found the body, as *The Commercial Appeal*
  would straighten out later in the week.
- "There was evidence of severe cardiovascular disease."
  This remark from Francisco was well off the mark. The
  final autopsy report would conclude that while Elvis's
  heart was oversized at 520 grams, the 60 percent narrow-

ing of the coronary arteries was not unusual for a man his age.

- "No indication of any drug abuse of any kind" didn't square with Elvis's impacted colon, discovered in the autopsy room, or with the syringes that Dan Warlick found in the bedroom suite, or with the suspicious-looking black bag he saw in the bathroom.
- The needle track comment, with its underlying assumption that drug abuse necessarily would involve street drugs, was a handy diversion that in the short run satisfied reporters looking for a hot angle or aiming to beat a deadline.

And what about Ginger? Was Elvis alone when he died? If with Ginger, was there a sexual angle, like the reported coitus interruptus death in 1979 of former Governor Nelson Rockefeller in New York?

After Elvis's funeral *The Commercial Appeal* published an exclusive interview with Ginger. She reminisced about how two months earlier Elvis had proposed to her on his knees in "the lounge area" of the very bathroom where she would find his body, about the eleven-and-a-half carat diamond ring in a green velvet box, and about how she regarded Elvis as "a part of me."

But she had Elvis falling out of a lounge chair, not off a toilet seat. She said his face was buried in thick carpeting in the bathroom and that "it was like he breathed once when I turned his head." The police report quoted her as saying Elvis's body was slumped to one side with his head against the wall.

If Ginger had any comments about Elvis's drug-taking, they weren't to be found in *The Commercial Appeal*'s exclusive. The story did contain, however, a remark from Ginger's mother that she never worried about her daughter staying over at Graceland.

Of overriding significance, as suggested in this and other early news stories, was how firmly Dr. Jerry Francisco assumed control of the investigation.

Unlike the Martin Luther King case nine years earlier, there was no suspect to be identified and captured, no apparent crime committed, no real leads to follow, unless you were a toxicologist with a sample and a microscope.

The fire department paramedics played a fleeting role in the day's events, but their superiors told them not to comment about details, certainly not to repeat Al Strada's remark, "We think he OD'd."

Already the homicide detectives were off the case. At Francisco's instruction, Dan Warlick had called the bureau and told them to close out the case as a natural death. The detectives' written report would be concealed from the press for another two years.

Already Francisco had served notice on reporters that many weeks would be needed to complete the autopsy. And already he had cautioned that there might never be any firm conclusion about just how Elvis died.

Shut off from much prospect of hard news follow-ups, the press fell back to cover a sociological spectacle—mass mourning outside the gates of Graceland, where tragically two young women were killed by a drunken driver. There were countless interviews with the hodgepodge of fans about why they had come. There were the memories of friends, beneficiaries of free Cadillacs, and easiest of all, old reporters who remembered back when Elvis drove a truck for Crown Electric Company.

Beneath all the fluff reporting, though, *The Commercial Appeal* was the news organization that stood the best chance of ferreting out the truth of how Elvis Presley really died. To an outside journalist, the newspaper had everything going for it. It was located on the scene. It had sources sprinkled in key spots through the police department and medical examiner's office. And it even had an old-line reporter who was considered to be a part-time member of Elvis's entourage, a good friend to Elvis's family named Jim Kingsley.

Nonetheless, *The Commercial Appeal* blew the story. Despite the hometown advantage and a tenacious reporting job by its medical writer, the newspaper knuckled under to the myth of a hometown hero, to fears of taking on the medical establishment, and to an impulse to put the big story in the past and get back to light features and spot-news reporting.

Rather than pulling out the stops for a full-dress news investigation, *The Commercial Appeal* employed a cute scandal-sheet tactic and sneaked a reporter disguised as one of many undertakers into Elvis's funeral without a notebook. There wouldn't be any prizes awarded for local coverage in the Elvis case. As William Sorrels, managing editor of *The Commercial Appeal,* was to admit later, "We knew there was a problem, but we couldn't prove it. We didn't do a good job."

The Commercial Appeal and its afternoon competition, *The Memphis Press-Scimitar,* had a common owner and, from a business standpoint, joint managers for circulation and advertising. The two newspapers operated out of a five-story, solid brick building once occupied by the Ford Motor Company at 495 Union. The fourth-floor production operation separated the two editorial staffs—*The Commercial Appeal* on the third floor and the *Press-Scimitar* on the fifth. The two newspapers also shared a garish green-and-yellow interior decor that looked like leftover paint from a Holiday Inn. But at bottom the two staffs were none too chummy. *The Commercial Appeal* employees looked down their noses at the *Press-Scimitar* staff as bush leaguers manufacturing superficial stories and embellishing the headlines. The folks at the *Press-Scimitar* regarded *The Commercial Appeal* as a conglomerate of stuffed shirts who took themselves far too seriously and who daily waged war on the adventure and flair of reporting the news.

The animosities were historic. Part of the *The Commercial Appeal*'s self-proclaimed reliability was its consistent support of E. H. "Boss" Crump, who controlled Memphis politics as a benevolent dictator from the dawn of the Progressive Era after the turn of the century until his death in 1954. Crump left a legacy—if not of hero worship, at least of hero deference.

Elvis benefited from that legacy. If a cop dared to write up a speeding ticket for Elvis, it never got to court. And if that *Commercial Appeal* reporter covering Elvis's local concert thought he could get away with calling the local boy "a pudgy reminder of the 1950s who ought to accept middle age"—well, the editor's No. 1 pencil was quick to knock that out of the review.

Not surprisingly, when the police squawkbox on the metro desk blared out that an ambulance was on the way to Graceland mansion, *The Commercial Appeal* was off balance, inexperienced in key positions, and under pressure to tackle a tough assignment. And Jim Kingsley wasn't about to cover "the big story," either, even with his inside connections.

Kingsley had known the Presley family—Vernon, Gladys, and Elvis—since the hardscrabble days in Tupelo, Mississippi, where Elvis was born. Kingsley was starting out in the newspaper business in the early post-war years as a reporter in *The Commercial Appeal*'s Tupelo bureau, located about midway between Birmingham and Memphis. And his migration from Tupelo paralleled that of the Presley family, which moved into a poor white section of North Memphis in 1948.

While most reporters coming into *The Commercial Appeal* newsroom were looking for a way up the editorial ladder, Kingsley was content to be a reporter—handling general assignment duty, filling in for the regular night police reporter on Sundays and Mondays, writing a weekly entertainment column, and picking up a regular weekly paycheck.

In addition to his assignments on the metro desk schedule, however, Kingsley handled the Elvis beat, whether in the newsroom, at the police station, or at home, which happened to be Whitehaven, Elvis's part of town. When a tip came in that Elvis had bought a new Cadillac for a total stranger or had flown to Dallas on the spur of the moment just for a special sackful of cheeseburgers, then Kingsley would get the call.

In turn, Kingsley would call Vernon, who would check out the tip. Vernon might or might not know, might not want to know. The story might or might not get written. It was Kingsley's call. The newspaper trusted him implicitly to handle the Elvis beat and washed its hands of any delicate stories on the subject. The editorial brass was well aware, for example, that after Elvis's army hitch, his teenage girlfriend was living without benefit of clergy at Graceland. You didn't see that story in *The Commercial Appeal*. So long as Kingsley scooped the rest of the nation with an exclusive on Elvis's latest tour schedule, which he did with regularity, then who was to complain?

Yet over a period of time it became apparent that Kingsley was turning a blind eye to any hard news about Elvis personally.

Once on tour with Elvis in Las Vegas in the early 1970s, Kingsley checked in by telephone with the metro desk. Almost as an afterthought, he mentioned that there had been a threat on Elvis's life—no big deal, really. The night metro editor thought otherwise. Pumping Kingsley for information with question after question and demanding answers, *The Commercial Appeal* produced an unbylined story about intensified security at the Hilton where Elvis was playing. The story rippled to the far reaches of the globe and appeared on page one of the Vegas papers with a Memphis dateline.

"Kingsley was very protective of Elvis. He would frankly lie to us," said William Sorrels, *The Commercial Appeal*'s managing editor in 1977. During the last year of Elvis's life, Sorrels said he and another editor hotboxed Kingsley with questions about Elvis's frequent hospitalizations and mounting medical problems. But Kingsley dodged the questions and left the impression that Elvis's difficulties were minor.

"All you had to do was look at the pictures of that last concert. It wouldn't take a genius to figure out that he was a very sick man," Sorrels said. As for assigning another reporter to write about Elvis, Sorrels said, "Nobody wanted to, nobody pushed. We gave Elvis a free ride."

Two weeks and a day before the death at Graceland, three of Elvis's former bodyguards—Delbert "Red" West, Sonny West, and Dave Hebler—had published a paperback book entitled *Elvis: What Happened?* It opened with an account of the near-fatal overdose of a young woman picked up in a hotel for Elvis. The so-called "bodyguard book" took the first public glimpse into Elvis's private world of pills to wake up, pills to sleep, and pills to relax.

In its coverage of the death, *The Commercial Appeal* published a story without a byline about the bodyguard book. Rather than accept *Elvis: What Happened?* as a challenge to dig out the Elvis story independently, the newspaper merely climbed out on a short editorial limb. "The picture that is drawn," *The Commercial Appeal* said of the bodyguard book, "is very much at odds with the clean-living image Presley and his manager, Colonel Tom Parker, wanted the world to see."

In other stories, the newspaper interviewed Joe Esposito,

the road manager, and quoted him as saying Elvis didn't use drugs, "none whatsoever." Esposito added that Red West and the other authors must have been "very bitter" to have written the book.

At the *Press-Scimitar,* the primary Elvis writer was Bill E. Burk, a gossip columnist who stretched fluff journalism to new limits in Memphis. After the death, Burk wrote about his first meeting with Elvis at a barbecue stand in 1955, about a psychic who had warned him that Elvis would die on tour, and about the letter he had received from Graceland complaining about a column. "The full contents of that letter and my answer to it," Burk confided to his readers, "shall remain personal."

Burk did have his contacts, however. And two days later, August 19, he managed a telephone interview with Linda Thompson, Elvis's girlfriend after the divorce. In order of priority, Burk had Linda telling the readers about: (1) how Elvis constantly read books on religion, including that last tome in the bathroom "about Jesus' skeleton being found"; (2) how Elvis sent a check every week to a youth he had seen in a wheelchair at the Graceland gates; (3) how Elvis spent a roll of cash having Linda's dog, Getlow, treated unsuccessfully at a special clinic in Boston; (4) and finally, how she didn't believe reports of Elvis's rampant use of drugs.

"Elvis had taken sleeping pills," Burk quoted Linda as saying. "He was in a high-pressure business. A lot of people in this business take sleeping pills, but he was not really on drugs. He has taken Demerol for pain, but it was always prescribed. He said, 'That's what medicine is for if you don't abuse it.' Elvis did not like pain. Everything he took he had a prescription for."

Little did Burk know that Linda Thompson's private observations about her four-year live-in relationship with Elvis would provide a big clue years later to the medical mystery surrounding the death.

VI

TWO INVESTIGATORS

LOOKING BACK at how Memphis reacted to Elvis's death, a story written by Beth J. Tamke foreshadowed the medical-legal controversy that would follow. Tamke, then age thirty-two, covered the medical beat for *The Commercial Appeal.* A tough-minded, tart-tongued reporter from Senatobia, Mississippi, she had paid her dues covering the police station and the religion beat, or, as she called it, the "God squad." In both positions she had exposed swindlers and charlatans because Beth Tamke was as nosy as a church auxiliary. Now as medical reporter she had inherited a beat that had been handled with kid gloves as disease-of-the-week and profiles assignments.

Tamke and her notepad were two blocks away from the mounting hubbub around Baptist Hospital when Elvis was brought in. Oblivious to what was happening and bored, she was covering a drawn-out meeting of the Memphis-Shelby County Hospital Authority. "The main topic on the agenda was whether cigarettes ought to be sold in a public hospital," said Tamke, who in those days could run through a pack of Salems in an afternoon.

"I didn't have any idea what was going on until I got back to the office and got on the elevator. The whole building was electric. Riding up the elevator, somebody told me what was happening and I said to myself, 'Fuck cigarettes, I'm doing a story on Elvis.'"

Finding the old Presley clippings in a shambles, Tamke managed to pick out short, spoon-fed, one-column stories about Elvis's hospitalizations—going back to 1960 when he broke the little finger on his right hand. "It was impossible to get through by telephone to Baptist Hospital. So I went down there and badgered the administration to release a rundown on when he was admitted and what for."

After obtaining accounts of Elvis's previous hospitalizations since 1960, Tamke found it a simple matter to check them against the news clippings back in the newspaper morgue.

"It didn't add up. From that night and for the next two months my assignment was to get the autopsy," Tamke said. "During that time I saw that in getting the autopsy, a by-product might be getting the medical examiner. But the editors didn't see it that way."

Writing her story on the night of the death, Tamke reported, "The diagnosis of Presley's ailments released Tuesday night do not correspond with those given out at the time of his hospitalization." What had been reported as pneumonia and pleurisy in October 1973 was now hypertension. What was identified as a liver problem in January 1975 was now hypertension and an impacted colon.

Tamke had been in the business long enough to know she was on to something. Two months later she would write the first story with hard evidence to suggest that Elvis, the hometown boy, was a chronic drug abuser. A month after that, Tamke would be transferred to one of the newspaper's Siberian gulags—handling consumer complaints for the "Action, Please" column.

———

By 8:30 P.M. on the night of the death, Dr. Harold Sexton had prepared a urine sample in the pathology lab at Baptist Hospital. He was looking for a quick qualitative test identifying what drugs were in Elvis's system. Sexton labeled the sample as that of "Ethel Moore," a fictitious name he would use later on.

While Baptist Hospital was the largest hospital in Memphis and touted itself as being "the largest private hospital in the world," it had no toxicology lab. Earlier in the evening, Sexton had turned over samples of whole blood, urine, cerebral spinal fluid, and gall bladder tissue to Francisco.

But Sexton didn't expect much help from Jerry Francisco's toxicology lab. He held it in low esteem. Hence, unbeknownst to the medical examiner, Sexton sent the urine sample down Union Avenue a few blocks away to the Duckworth Laboratory at Methodist Hospital for a drug screen.

"This was a personage of some note," Sexton said with wry understatement later on, "and we didn't want to neglect anything that might be of any significance in the autopsy. And so we did just a routine screening work-up, as you might do in any number of cases."

The tests over at the Duckworth lab were preliminary—aimed at giving Drs. Muirhead, Sexton, their colleagues at Baptist Hospital, and presumably Francisco a clue about what killed Elvis or a direction for focusing further medical investigation. The Duckworth screen was qualitative, identifying the presence of particular types of drugs, not quantitative, saying in what strengths these drugs were present. In addition, the Duckworth screen tested only urine, not blood or cerebral spinal fluid.

Overnight the results came back to Baptist Hospital. The tests were positive for four types of depressants—barbiturates, meprobamate, benzodiazepines, and ethchlorvynol. They were negative for a host of other types, including amphetamines, cocaine, and notably morphine and codeine.

In contrast, Francisco's toxicology lab at the University of Tennessee issued a report a few days later randomly combining tests results for both blood and urine. The UT work-up identified ethinamate, methaqualone, codeine, meperidine, chlorpheniramine and unspecified barbiturates as being present in either blood or urine. It reported all of those drugs as being in concentrations "less than the toxic or lethal levels," but otherwise failed to enumerate just what those levels were. In the world of a toxicologist, therapeutic, toxic, and lethal ranges were in a perpetual state of redefinition.

The results of the UT urine screen, which represented a direct comparison with the Duckworth lab, was of particular interest to Sexton and later would loom large in Francisco's official ruling. The UT test showed no presence of ethchlorvynol, more commonly known under the trade name of Placidyl.

"This was a very important element in the overall toxicology analysis," Sexton would say later. "The Duckworth lab knocked it off that very night while Francisco's lab didn't find it at all. Ethchlorvynol smells just like dirty socks—really noticeable. But if you start your temperatures too high in testing for it, then you'll burn it off. It was plain enough to me early on that this is what Jerry's technicians did. They burned it off."

Within a week's time after Elvis's death, therefore, Sexton and "the chief," as he called Muirhead, knew they were up against not only a medical examiner who shot from the hip but also a public laboratory that some doctors believed to be staffed with underskilled, fumble-fingered technicians.

"We wanted to pick the best independent toxicology lab we could find to help determine how Elvis Presley died," Sexton explained in 1979. "We asked around discreetly all over the country and the name that kept cropping up was Bio-Science Laboratories in Van Nuys, California."

On August 19, 1977, Sexton looked over his checklist of samples—3.5 milliliters of cerebral spinal fluid, 9 milliliters of blood, 2 milliliters of urine, 124 grams of liver tissue, and 139 grams of kidney tissue. Placing the samples in sterile containers packed in dry ice and then Styrofoam, Sexton sealed them up in a box and shipped them Airborne Express to Drs. Ronald Orynich and Norman Weissman at Bio-Science. The autopsy number was A77-160, the patient's name was listed as Ethel Moore.

Beth Tamke was making it her business to meet every working pathologist in Memphis to establish a network of information for what was looking like a long assignment. But in the newsroom she was catching flak.

Angus McEachran, metro editor at *The Commercial Appeal* was gruff, arbitrary, and ambitious to rise within the news executive ranks of Scripps-Howard. McEachran wanted that autopsy and wanted it fast. Secretly he knew the chain soon would be sending him down to *The Birmingham Post-Herald* as editor. In retrospect, Tamke believes the Elvis assignment would have turned out differently if McEachran had stuck around longer. Beyond his ingenuous personality, McEachran understood hard news. His replacement, in contrast, was far more comfortable with a feature story to warm, not dissect, the heart.

"McEachran was on my ass the entire time," Tamke said. "He kept telling me I wasn't doing enough." Whether correct or not, McEachran's criticism kept Tamke's gray cells on overtime as she dreamed up ways to get another story in the paper and to find some leverage to use on Francisco.

"I went to Muirhead and told him I was writing a story, not on Elvis but on pathology. Muirhead said, 'Fine, but you'll need to read this.' It was a book on the history of pathology, but he couldn't find it at his office. So he sent his secretary to his house—right then—to get that book. She got a speeding ticket on the way back. I offered to pay for it, but Muirhead wouldn't let me. But I want you to know, I read every goddamn word in that book. It was interesting but told me a whole lot more about pathology than I wanted to know. Anyhow that's how I got to know Muirhead."

Tamke also got to know Dr. George C. Nichopoulos, but in a more confrontational fashion. "Dr. Nick wasn't returning my telephone calls. So finally I just went down to his clinic one morning—made sure I was there when they opened the doors."

Along with her purse, notebook, and tape recorder, Tamke was carrying a copy of *Elvis: What Happened?*, the bodyguard book now gaining so much attention since Elvis's death. "Dr. Nick's receptionist asked me if I had an appointment. I told her no, that I had been trying to get one and would be happy to wait until he could see me. The receptionist said I couldn't see him without an appointment, but I wasn't planning on leaving."

The Death of Elvis

Tamke found herself a seat, rechecked the list of questions she planned on asking Dr. Nick, then opened the bodyguard book and began reading. As the clientele for the Medical Group, Dr. Nick's clinic, was processed through the waiting room, Tamke noticed a pattern. Young women, mostly on the seedy side in appearance, were coming in and asking to see Dr. Nick. They, too, didn't have appointments. And Tamke was making it a point to make eye contact over the top of her book with the receptionist who was so quick to cite an office policy obviously so rarely enforced.

"It was plain enough to me as the morning wore on," Tamke said, "that these patients were in the habit of dropping in for a refill without notice. But all the receptionist could tell them was the same thing she told me—you can't see him without an appointment. They finally let me in right before noon. Dr. Nick told me I had ten minutes."

Extracting information from the bodyguard book, Tamke added a question about Elvis's shooting out television sets, particularly when Robert Goulet appeared on the screen. Elvis hated Robert Goulet. Otherwise Tamke's questions, which she fired off rapidly to make the best use of her limited time, gave her the basis of an exclusive story that appeared across the top of page one on August 25, 1977.

"What sticks in my mind about that story—other than the fact that most of what I was told wasn't true—was when I got back to the office there wasn't anybody there who would transcribe the goddamn tape. That was a helluva note. I spent the rest of the afternoon transcribing it myself and barely had time to get the story finished for the first edition."

In the lead paragraph, Tamke quoted Dr. Nick as saying Elvis didn't have a drug problem, "at least not in the last three years of his life."

Staring at a cold cup of coffee on his desk, Dr. Nick said he was trying to put his life back together. He didn't mention his worries about what Elvis's toxicology reports would show or his tense relationship with Vernon Presley.

But he told Tamke that Elvis had been unhappy in recent months over problems with Ginger Alden, that "medication" was kept from Elvis because he might wake up in the night and take too many sleeping tablets, and that Elvis probably had been dead for several hours before his body was found.

Dr. Nick told Tamke he didn't believe Elvis was an overdose victim. "No, I don't think he had anything there to OD on. He had taken a couple of sleeping pills or he was given a couple of sleeping pills. Whether he had taken them or not, I don't know. And the only other medicine he had on hand was some medication he used for his colon and medication that he used for his sinus."

As for heart problems, Dr. Nick described Elvis's hypertension as "mild," a condition for which there was no need for drugs. "At a time when he was getting ready for a tour or he was having emotional problems, he had very labile [unstable] hypertension. There were times [when there were] certain stresses would run his [blood] pressure up to 170 to 200 systolic and diastolic anywhere from 90 to 110. And there were times when he was at home resting or just convalescing from a tour or whatever, he may have had a normal pressure of 130 over 80."

Dutifully, Tamke reported that normal blood pressure ranges from 100 to 150 systolic and 60 to 100 diastolic. She had been hitting the medical books.

So what killed Elvis? Dr. Nick, who had been present during some of the autopsy's gross phase, rambled like Casey Stengel about the medical examiner's preliminary ruling. "I think that this is a presumptive ruling, a backdoor diagnosis, which everyone has to have a cause of death. And taking a given individual who has heart-risk factors like diabetes, hypertension, and plus obesity, plus some degree of hardening of the arteries, vessels to the heart, and you don't find other causes of death like blood clots to the lung or stroke or heart attack where the muscle itself is damaged, then you are left with this presumption that playing the percentages and odds, that this [cardiac arrhythmia] was the cause of death."

A week later, *The Memphis Press-Scimitar*, the city's afternoon paper, managed a weak follow story on Dr. Nick, who disputed rumors that Elvis had lupus. "Those were the worst two months of my life," said Peggy Burch, the *Press-Scimitar* reporter who was assigned to knock heads with Tamke. "It seemed like every morning Beth would have the story I'd been trying to get."

"What hurt Peggy the most was her appearance," Tamke said. "These were pretty straitlaced people we were dealing with." Burch, a Pennsylvanian fresh out of college, was a product of the 1960s with flyaway hair, plain-Jane paisley dresses, and an earth-mother look about her.

Tamke, having beaten the opposition to Dr. Nick, continued to keep in touch with her contacts within the pathology community and to persist in her calls, either in person or by telephone, to the medical examiner's office. She got through to Francisco on August 26.

The medical examiner was sticking to his guns. Very likely, Francisco told Tamke in an interview, the cause of death would be heart attack. Why? Well, Elvis's heart was enlarged. His liver contained fatty globules. His coronary arteries were abnormally narrowed. And apparently from either talking to Dr. Nick or reading Tamke's exclusive interview, Francisco said he had been told of Elvis's wide swings in blood pressure.

On two key points, Francisco either deliberately misled Tamke or hadn't bothered to find out.

First, he said Elvis's stomach hadn't been pumped during resuscitation efforts and that the stomach contents revealed "nothing identifiable."

Second, Francisco told Tamke that Elvis didn't have an impacted colon. He said it looked normal at the autopsy. Of course, the medical examiner was at the news conference when Baptist Hospital pathologists, along with Dan Warlick, were running the gut back in the autopsy suite and gaping at Elvis's jam-packed megacolon.

At the bottom of Tamke's story, however, was an ominous paragraph. "[Francisco] said the autopsy report will remain private unless the case becomes a medical examiner's matter or unless Presley's family decides to release it." At the time, she didn't attach much significance to it.

Two Investigators

Harold Sexton was in close contact with Bio-Science Laboratories by telephone. His primary contact was Dr. Norman Weissman, director of toxicology. Weissman, a slender, distinguished-looking man in his early sixties, had built up a reputation as a meticulous and scrupulous researcher. And never before had he seen a more alarming case than this Ethel Moore test sent in from Memphis. Weissman got on the phone to Baptist Hospital and tracked down Sexton. Ms. Moore, whoever she was, must have been gobbling up prescription drugs like a kid in a candy store, Weissman reported, because the first tests at Bio-Science were showing 10 types of drugs in significant concentrations.

At that, Sexton decided to let the hepcat out of the bag. They were talking Elvis, he confided, and Baptist Hospital wanted nothing less than an exhaustive investigation.

———

In 1977 Bio-Science Laboratory was a pacesetter in the field of toxicology for its mastery of the Gas Chromatography-Mass Spectrometer, or GC-MS. Chromatography is a process capable of separating complex mixtures so that each chemical component can be analyzed independently. This step produces a spectrum of chemical components or a chromatogram. As the chemical components are separated, they enter an "ionization chamber" where they are bombarded with electrons and fragmented into segments that have a characteristic pattern, component by component, molecule by molecule. A mass spectrometer, which determines the relative masses of atoms, has a computer that reads these patterns and codes them with bar graphs like those found on grocery products. Over a period of time, toxicologists have built entire libraries with thousands of these bar graphs, distinguishing not only chemical compounds but also the same compound in a variety of concentrations. Once new drugs come on the market, they are run through the GC-MS process and new bar graphs are catalogued.

GC-MS technology was state of the art when Elvis died. A toxicologist without GC-MS was like a stenographer equipped with a manual typewriter. You might be able to get the job done, but it would take time and there might be some typographical errors you didn't catch. Francisco's laboratory at the University of Tennessee didn't have GC-MS technology when Elvis died.

Out in Van Nuys, what stunned Weissman and his colleagues in the "Ethel Moore" case was not only the sheer number of drugs their computer library identified but also the high concentrations. Toxicology has a basic scheme. Once a particular drug is identified, its blood and tissue concentrations fall into one of three classifications—therapeutic, indicating the concentration is in line with a legitimate medical purpose; toxic, indicating that a harmful amount of the drug has been taken; and lethal, producing death.

Haziest are toxic ranges. Drug manufacturers define therapeutic dosages and, once on the market, drugs and how they behave at different blood concentrations are monitored closely in clinical settings. On the other end, accumulations of drug overdose cases in the last generation have established generally documented lethal levels for both street drugs and prescription medicines. Toxic ranges, however, are under constant revision as researchers learn more about side effects, tolerances, and results of drugs working in combination. In this last area, Weissman knew he was looking at what one day would be a textbook case. But Bio-Science wasn't satisfied with going it alone with this conclusion, and the fellow who was writing the books on forensic toxicology was down the road in Orange County.

Picking up the telephone, Weissman called Robert H. Cravey, chief toxicologist for the Orange County Sheriff's and Coroner's Department. Weissman was then president and Cravey vice president of the California Association of Toxicologists, and they were close personal friends.

A bald, clean-shaven man with slight paunch and friendly presence, Cravey has a gift for taking complicated scientific information and distilling it into straightforward testimony understandable to the average juror. Cravey's peers consider him fearlessly honest and independent. Dr. Thomas Noguchi, the controversial coroner of Los Angeles, often called on Cravey to run toxicological tests to double-check his own lab or if he had instrument problems. Cravey and two other toxicologists later would compile and annually update a reference book entitled *Courtroom Toxicology,* today the bible on the subject for trial lawyers and forensic specialists.

When Weissman called Cravey, he didn't mention Elvis Presley. Instead he said he had a sensitive case and would like to hand-deliver a series of specimens for independent testing. Given the high sign, Weissman drove fifty miles from his laboratory in the San Fernando Valley just north of downtown Los Angeles to Cravey's facility in Santa Ana. With him was a carton packed in dry ice and containing samples of Elvis's blood and tissue.

"Even though I hadn't been told it was Elvis's case, I suspected it was," Cravey said. "I knew that he was the only important person who had died about that time period."

Withholding the Bio-Science results and asking for a second opinion as a favor, Weissman looked over Cravey's shoulder for the four hours needed to run the samples through Orange County's testing procedures. Assisting was a young understudy named Dwight Reed, whom Cravey described as "one of the brightest people I ever had." Later, Reed would run the actual tests for Noguchi, dubbed "Coroner of the Stars," in the drug overdose death of John Belushi. Reed regarded Cravey as "Toxicologist of the Stars."

Weissman watched as Cravey and Reed finished their tests. Cravey jotted numbers down on a notepad. They matched up with Bio-Science's.

The pharmacopoeia shocked Cravey, but he also was puzzled. Why hadn't Weissman brought him any stomach specimens? He recalled how critical stomach contents were in the Marilyn Monroe case. Noguchi's lab hadn't tested them. "I thought that was a major screwup in the Monroe case," Cravey said. "I didn't ask Norm Weissman about it in Elvis's case because I was not supposed to know it was Elvis Presley I was testing, but I thought it odd that there were no stomach contents."

Cravey's conclusion was straightforward. "In view of the lack of significant pathology [disease process] to explain death, and considering the vast number of sedative-hypnotic and analgesic drugs found in concentrations ranging primarily from therapeutic to toxic, the combined effects of these drugs in combination must be considered. These findings would be consistent with coma and certainly would be fatal."

Weissman thanked his friends, packed up his specimens, and drove back to Van Nuys. Then he contacted Harold Sexton in Memphis and arranged for him to pay Bio-Science a visit and see their testing procedures firsthand.

═══════

Sexton arrived in mid-October 1977. He reviewed the laboratory data that Bio-Science had prepared in support of its report in the Presley case. In exchange, Sexton showed the toxicologists Baptist Hospital's autopsy protocol detailing the condition of Elvis's vital organs at death. There was no cardiac or other pathology to explain death. Sure enough, Weissman and Sexton agreed, this was an overdose case.

After receiving a full briefing in southern California, Sexton packed up his reports, returned to Memphis, and huddled with Muirhead and his other colleagues at Baptist Hospital. All were convinced that the cause of death was clear and that their investigation was nearing an end. It was October 17, 1977, two months and a day after Elvis's death.

Muirhead assembled a group on October 18 to visit Vernon Presley at Graceland mansion to explain the autopsy report. Francisco was there. So were Maurice Elliott, administrative vice president at Baptist Hospital; Sexton, who was prepared to go into minute detail about the report; Ms. Marian Cocke, the Baptist Hospital nurse who attended Elvis during his hospitalizations and frequently at Graceland; and Ms. Sandy Miller, Vernon Presley's fiancée. Absent and uninvited was Nichopoulos.

Before delving into the toxicology report, Muirhead noted that Elvis's body displayed four conditions—a minor edema, or swelling of the lungs from a small buildup of fluid; conjunctivitis, a swollen and inflamed condition around the eyes; cyanosis, or blue coloration of the lower abdomen with a distinctive line of demarcation showing how Elvis was curled in a semiflexed position; and from that abdominal line upward, hundreds of small hemorrhages or petechiae. These petechiae, Muirhead noted, indicated that Elvis had lived for a short time, allowing the blood vessels to burst, after falling to the floor. All of these conditions, he added, were consistent with death by drug overdose, which as the toxicology report showed was what killed Elvis.

Francisco chimed in that he was 90 percent in agreement but would need to review the autopsy report further.

As Maurice Elliott recalled the meeting two years later in a sworn deposition:

"Dr. Muirhead reviewed in some detail with Mr. Presley, Vernon Presley, how the autopsy was performed, what sort of tests were done, and basically the results of those tests and our staff's conclusions as to the cause of death."

"And did Dr. Francisco make any report to Mr. Presley at that time?" an attorney asked Elliott.

"No. Dr. Francisco at that time stated that he was in general agreement with our conclusions but that he wanted to take the complete report and review it with his staff before coming to an official conclusion. And he indicated at that time, after he had done that, that he felt obligated to make some statement to the press."

———

Tamke was aware of the Graceland meeting although she knew too little about what was said to write a story. She also was aware that the assignment she had lived with for two months was coming to a head. As Tamke sized it up, the worst case scenario would be to find out what the autopsy concluded while sitting in a morning news conference with the news break going to *The Press-Scimitar*.

Tamke's homework paid off. Francisco was reviewing the case with his associates in the medical examiner's office and was keeping a lid on the story—except that the medical examiner had to sign a death certificate. According to normal procedure, it would be sent to the Memphis and Shelby County Health Department and from there to the Tennessee Department of Public Health in Nashville. Under state law, death certificates are confidential documents sealed from public view for fifty years. Nonetheless, as Tamke knew, there were many pairs of eyes between Francisco's office and Nashville.

By that time McEachran, Tamke's boss, had moved to Birmingham. His replacement as metro editor was E. B. Blackburn, longtime editor of the newspaper's Sunday magazine, *Mid-South.* Blackburn, known around the newsroom as "Blackie," was a jovial but opinionated editor who had measured most of his news career in column inches on the copy desk. *The Commercial Appeal's* news side made him uneasy. Hard news made him nervous. And hard news pertaining to Elvis Presley made him paranoid.

On October 19, the day after the Graceland meeting, Tamke patched together a story derived from the pathologist sources she had developed during the past two months. "Pathologists are like anybody else. They want to know what's going on, particularly in their field. They all had been talking about the Elvis case."

Tamke's story, which quickly hit the A wire on both Associated Press and United Press International, said multiple drugs might be ruled as the cause of Elvis's death. Burrowing in on what had taken place at Graceland, Tamke reported that Vernon Presley had learned of ten drugs that had been found in Elvis's system. While all the drugs were within prescribed levels, Tamke's story speculated, together they could have triggered an interaction affecting the singer's enlarged heart. Her story correctly listed Elvis's heart weight, aorta and all, at 520 grams.

Francisco wasn't commenting on the story, but inside the medical examiner's office he was sounding off to his staff that Baptist Hospital was trying to dictate the final ruling in an unseemly alliance with the press.

Jim Bell, the medical examiner's pudgy understudy, remembered Francisco calling an in-house powwow over it. "Our conference concluded that the report from Baptist Hospital, and [in] my opinion, was wrong and that the conclusions were wrong and that the newspaper article was in error," Bell said in a deposition two years later.

Just what was going on between the Shelby County Medical Examiner's Office and Graceland during this critical three-day period is murky. But Dan Warlick remembers Francisco talking frequently over the telephone to Vernon Presley, who had been shaken by the autopsy's findings as detailed by Muirhead. Now Vernon Presley apparently was being given a second, and contrary, opinion that somehow made Elvis's death seem more palatable.

Francisco told Tamke to hold up on writing any more stories until his news conference scheduled on Friday, two days away. But Tamke wasn't waiting. She pulled all stops to nail down what Francisco was putting on the death certificate.

"The story about the death certificate was the key to everything else I did," Tamke said. "I had a source—I'm not telling who or where—who saw the death certificate. There was no mention of drugs. Up until that point I had been able to verify unattributed information from two separate sources. My source who saw the death certificate was absolutely reliable, but I knew I wouldn't find a second one.

"Blackburn wouldn't have run the death certificate story," Tamke said flatly more than ten years later. "Fortunately, I got my information at home over the telephone at night. John Weed [an assistant managing editor] was in charge. I explained what I had, and also what I didn't have. Weed told me to come back into the office and write it."

Appearing on the morning of October 21, Tamke's story reported that the cause of death listed on the certificate was a heart ailment. Drugs weren't mentioned, her report stated, even though tests commissioned by Baptist Hospital showed the presence of at least ten drugs in Presley's system. Francisco had signed the certificate the day before and had it hand-delivered to the local health department.

The repercussions from the death certificate story were threefold. One, the Baptist Hospital team had a clear indication that Francisco had double-crossed them. Two, those with access to the autopsy were mindful that Beth Tamke had the wherewithal to get the hard evidence into the newspaper. And three, Jerry Francisco was persuaded forevermore that these hospital pathologists had stepped over the line into the forensic realm and were trying to tell him his business. Not surprisingly, Francisco scheduled his

83

news conference for Friday morning, October 21, 1977, at an hour that would give Tamke's afternoon opposition the newsbreak.

As foreshadowed in Tamke's reports, Francisco handed out a press release ruling that the cause of Elvis Presley's death was hypertensive heart disease with coronary artery disease as a contributing factor. Drugs, Francisco ruled, played no part in the death.

In an effort to add clout to his ruling, Francisco said the entire staff of his office—two other forensic pathologists and a toxicologist—supported the conclusions. These were Francisco's employees—Drs. Bell and Harlan and David Stafford, a chemist with no experience in forensic toxicology until Francisco hired him.

In addition, Francisco said, "two other toxicologists in the United States," who were to remain unidentified for two years, had been consulted in the case. All put together, two toxicologists (Stafford and an unidentified outsider) believed the drugs made no significant contribution to death. The third toxicologist, another mystery expert, said that "all medications were in the therapeutic range and individualy [sic] did not represent an overdose." Or at least that's what Jerry Francisco's press release said.

Then, aiming a zinger at Muirhead and the others across the street, Francisco added to his press release, "All the toxicologists agreed that the decision whether these medications played any role in death causation should be left to the forensic pathologist."

As for the hard evidence that might cast doubt on the medical examiner's opinion, he continued, "The autopsy was not ordered by the district attorney general and thus is not a part of the file of the medical examiner."

Francisco was having it both ways. As a medical examiner's case, he could issue a ruling and talk freely about Elvis's death. But the naysayers, all within the private sector, were stymied.

Muirhead, an internationally recognized expert in hypertensive heart disease, was livid but held his tongue. "Vernon Presley has my report. Our dealings have been entirely with the family. He is the only one who can release it, if he wishes. That's all I am going to say."

But Tamke had her sources, ones she had worked hard to establish and the newspaper brass failed to appreciate. Those sources, which remain unidentified today, slipped her a key portion of Bio-Science's toxicology report. Tamke's story covering and expanding on Francisco's news conference revealed drug concentrations in Elvis's bloodstream for the first time. The results were:

- Codeine at ten times greater than a therapeutic dose with morphine, what becomes of codeine when the body metabolizes it, at a near-toxic concentration
- Methaqualone (Quaalude) at a toxic level
- Diazepam (Valium) at a low therapeutic level but its metabolite on the borderline of toxic
- Ethinimate (Valmid) high in the therapeutic range and possibly toxic. Research hadn't established a firm toxic level for this drug
- Ethchlorvynol (Placidyl) on the toxic borderline
- Pentobarbital high in the therapeutic range
- Butabarbital within the therapeutic range
- Phenobarbital in a low therapeutic range

In street terms, all these drugs are "downers." Acting together, Tamke reported her sources as saying, they would result in death by polypharmacy. Tamke's editors refused to allow her unidentified experts to go any further than that. Otherwise, she would have reported that the codeine alone in lower concentrations than Elvis's had put people in their graves.

In response to Tamke's questions about the Bio-Science findings, Francisco said the tests from his own lab as a forensic shop were more reliable—a remark that brought titters from forensic specialists familiar with the caliber of Bio-Science. Francisco went further to state that Placidyl, identified in three other labs, wasn't really present in Elvis's system.

How could Francisco's tests—the ones performed in a public lab, commissioned by the medical examiner and made a part of the full autopsy record—be kept out of the public domain? Indeed, couldn't it be argued that Francisco's contribution to the autopsy, as slipshod as Muirhead and Sexton believed it to be, had in fact transformed the entire autopsy into a public record?

In the aftermath of Francisco's devastating news conference, Tamke was asking herself these questions as she thumbed through the newspaper's copy of *The Tennessee Code Annotated* in search of answers.

"I remember what happened as plain as yesterday," Tamke said. "I was looking through the lawbooks when Blackburn walked by my desk. 'You're not a goddamn barrister,' he told me. 'Get your nose out of those lawbooks and write me a story.'

"So I wrote stories about Legionnaires' disease, about cricks in the neck, about water on the knee."

With that, Tamke knew she was off the story. Her hardearned documentation of Elvis Presley the drug abuser went to an unobtrusive cabinet in the newspaper morgue containing what was called "the shit files." The press in Memphis lost the initiative that Tamke had established singlehandedly.

"Beth called me up after it was all over," Peggy Burch of *The Press-Scimitar* recalled. "We went out to a bar to talk it over and got stinking drunk."

VII

THE SHIT FILES

IN THE SUMMER of 1979, two years after Elvis Presley's death and most likely because of her stories about it, Beth Tamke was running the "Action, Please" desk. That meant checking out consumer complaints about crummy air conditioner repairs, bum land deals in phantom resort developments, and bogus coupon offerings. To her mind the Elvis story was dead. *The Commercial Appeal*'s management, led by editor Mike Grehl, took the view that reporting the presence of drugs in Elvis's system marked the end of the newspaper's assignment. Journalists, so their argument went, weren't doctors or lawyers. Let the medical professionals sort out the significance of the drugs and resolve their own squabbles about cause of death.

Besides, there were heaps of other Elvis stories to write. Lawsuits about who had the right to market Elvis's name and image. Tax claims about the value of Graceland and how much the Presley estate owed the Tennessee treasury and the Internal Revenue Service. The solvency of the estate itself, which was valued at about $7 million right after Elvis died, was being threatened by mounting costs to maintain the mansion. And there were always the fans and visitors. Worldwide, they kept coming to Graceland, which the Memphis city government was considering buying and turning into a museum.

Then there was Vernon Presley's health. Country-shrewd and stingy, Vernon as executor of the estate had managed to hold the embattled Elvis fortune together. But on June 26, 1979, he died at Baptist Hospital of that bad heart.

Paying little attention to any of this news in 1979 was Charles C. Thompson II, a network television producer and one of the coauthors of this book. Thompson grew up in Memphis and was back in town for a couple of reasons, official and unofficial. Officially, he was poking around to do a story on Elvis with Geraldo Rivera, the rambunctious wild-card correspondent of ABC's *20/20* news magazine. Unofficially, Thompson was laying out some money-saving logistics that would allow him for a good part of the summer to bring in his wife and three sons to visit his parents, who lived in retirement 100 miles east of Memphis on the Tennessee River.

Charlie Thompson, thirty-seven, used to work at *The Commercial Appeal,* and he knew where the newspaper kept stories that the editors regarded as too hot to handle. In 1962 Thompson spent a summer as an intern in *The Commercial Appeal*'s library, or morgue, where he worked under a gnome-sized man named Glen Allen. Few characters on the staff went back further than Glen Allen. During the great Mississippi River floods of the 1920s, Allen provided the only communications link between the newsroom in Memphis and its bureau correspondents in Arkansas, Mississippi, and rural West Tennessee. On the roof of the newspaper building Allen maintained a roost of carrier pigeons that flew dispatches back and forth from isolated bureau correspondents. Long after the flood waters receded, Allen kept the roost going just in case the waters ever rose again. But by the 1950s the pigeons became another victim to mass communications and Glen Allen kept to the morgue.

As with all interns, Allen schooled Charlie Thompson in the morgue's peculiar logic. Korea might be under *K,* but if you didn't have any luck there, try Manchukuo. Files for proper names, or people files, ordinarily were alphabetical. Subject files, such as

88

Homicides or Maid of Cotton Pageant, would have an assigned number, and you needed to look that up in the card catalogue.

That wasn't the only bifurcated filing system in *The Commercial Appeal* morgue, and Glen Allen taught Thompson about that, too. Except for short, inconsequential items, all local stories were to be catalogued and filed. "Then there's this set of files," Allen confided. "We call them the shit files." More than once, Allen said, the top editors had summoned prominent Memphis citizens to the newspaper to view their own shit files or ones reporting the misdeeds of their children. "It really makes an impression on them," Allen said. After four years in the navy as a commissioned officer, including two combat tours in Vietnam, Thompson returned to journalism in 1968 and found his way from the print to the broadcast side. As an investigative reporter and producer for a television station in Jacksonville, he came up with a documentary series on pollution that identified his own station as a major contributor to that problem. Hence he returned to *The Commercial Appeal* for four months in 1970 and quickly received a tough reminder about the shit files.

Thompson was assigned to investigate a brutal policeman, one so vicious that cops in the same precinct were calling the newspaper anonymously and pleading for an exposé. The cop in question avoided picking on blacks. The police department was becoming too sensitive about civil rights complaints. Instead he got his thrills from working over white derelicts, boozers and dopers alike. They weren't your most credible witnesses.

Thompson assembled his story by putting together interviews of victims, bystanders, and police sources. He also cited medical, court, and arrest records. Given the large number of victims injured by the cop, the story made compelling reading. He turned it in, and an editor told him that although it was good, the paper didn't intend to run it because it "might inflame the police department." The editor said he would call the police chief, arrange for him to look at the story, and then suggest that the cop should be taken off the beat and assigned someplace "safe."

Thompson believed there wasn't a safe place anywhere on the police force for this sadist. But as he found out in arguing with the editor, the boss isn't always right, but the boss is always the boss. The brutal cop was moved to the city jail where his duties could be supervised more closely, and Thompson's story went into the shit file.

Thompson had moved on to work at CBS News when the cop died in a freak traffic accident about two years later. The paper resurrected Thompson's story from the morgue, put another reporter's byline on it and ran it. The story inflamed some policemen, who thought it had appeared about two years too late to do any good.

In 1978 Thompson joined ABC News where *20/20,* a news magazine, was being established to compete with CBS's well-established *60 Minutes.* Challenging his old network sounded inviting, but after a year of breaking his back trying to keep *20/20* on the air, Thompson was dubious that either he or *20/20* would be around to see 1980. The ratings were lackluster. During its first year, *20/20* was seen weekly in the summertime and in prime time only once a month during the other nine months of the year. ABC's executives planned on making the show a weekly prime-time feature in September 1979. But Thompson and the show's other reporters and producers believed the weekly schedule would be short-lived without more viewers.

The famous face that Charlie Thompson was working with in the summer of 1979 was Geraldo Rivera, as unlikely a pairing as a muffaletta and moonshine. Both were in their mid-thirties—Thompson, thirty-seven, and Rivera, thirty-six—but from there the similarities were scarce. Rivera sported long hair and a bushy mustache. Thompson's thick hair was prematurely gray and cut short to round out his clean-shaven look. Rivera was into a third marriage and had a son. Thompson had been married only once, was still married to the same lady, and had three sons by her. Rivera spoke in the hip jargon of New York City. Thompson, when he wasn't riled up, spoke in a soft southern drawl. Yet Thompson and Rivera had a common approach to getting after the news. Both came out charging.

Thompson's friends at CBS News warned him that Geraldo Rivera was a hot dog and an embarrassment to serious broadcast journalism. While Thompson understood that Rivera was controversial, he also believed Rivera was the victim of too many bum raps.

By ancestry, Rivera was both Jewish and Puerto Rican. By training he was a lawyer practicing criminal defense law in 1970 when a group of Puerto Rican militants in New York City asked him to become their spokesman. Geraldo was so effective as the militants' mouthpiece that ABC executives hired him to work at the network's flagship station, WABC-TV, that same year.

Never content with conventional beat reporting, Rivera scored big at WABC and built up a personal following. Perhaps his most memorable story called for breaking into Willowbrook, a state-run institution for the mentally retarded. With that sort of daring, Rivera exposed conditions so deplorable that viewers and public officials alike overlooked lawbreaking as a method of news-gathering. The Willowbrook broadcast resulted in government reform and lent credibility to Rivera's shrill, unorthodox style.

By 1974 Rivera was working for the network as a host of a late night show, *Good Night, America.* From 1976–78 he worked for ABC's *Evening News* as a feature reporter. For traditional network correspondents Rivera's brand of "personal journalism," at times to the point of crying on camera, was too much. By his own admission Rivera was a womanizer, and he seemed to take peculiar glee in seeing his name in the tabloid headlines. Rumors emerged that his real name was Jerry Rivers and that he had used the Hispanic version of his name in order to qualify for a racial minority hiring quota at ABC. And after a Middle East assignment, there were whispers around the studio that Geraldo doctored the sound tracks with canned gunfire suggesting that his life was in peril there on the scene as he gave you the Lebanese lowdown.

Rivera had his faults, but these rumors were not true. Mindful of his reputation as *20/20* was being organized in 1978, Rivera made a commitment to clean up his image and tone down his rhetoric. He persuaded Charlie Thompson. They agreed that as long as Rivera was interested in doing honest, hard-hitting report-ing, Thompson would work with him. But if Rivera began substi-tuting hype for substance, then Thompson would jump ship. The pair worked together as a team for more than seven years, and

The Death of Elvis

Thompson always believed Geraldo Rivera kept his end of their bargain.

In the summer of 1979, Rivera was just as worried as Thompson about the future of *20/20*. To succeed in a weekly prime-time slot, the show needed good ratings and high visibility pieces. Rivera and Thompson had just finished and aired such a provocative broadcast about the death of billionaire recluse Howard Hughes. Hughes had become addicted to drugs and before his death had been financially manipulated by his staff. For *20/20* the Hughes piece was a huge ratings success.

Flying back to the East Coast and analyzing the Hughes piece, Rivera and Thompson began plugging other celebrity names into the mystery-death formula. Near the top was Elvis Presley, but there were problems. In 1978, the previous summer, Rivera had aired a piece on Elvis. Turned out by a producer other than Thompson, it focused on the seedy commercialism that had blossomed across the street from Graceland. Thompson thought it was superficial, an easy grab of cheap trinkets, hucksters, and gawking fans. And he wondered why it ignored the unresolved controversy about Elvis's death.

―――

Before Thompson flew to Memphis in mid-July 1979, he searched out every book he could find about Elvis Presley. With two exceptions—the bodyguard book and an obscure entourage memoir called *Portrait of a Friend* by Marty Lacker—Thompson regarded them as a waste of time. With skimpy secondary sources and a city hostile to tough journalistic inquiry, he wondered if he could dig up enough material for a standard fifteen-minute spot. He was fired up when his plane landed in Memphis.

The gray stucco bungalow where Thompson made his first stop was the home of James P. Cole, the other coauthor of this book. Jim Cole was (and is) Thompson's brother-in-law. But before Thompson married Cole's sister Betty, the two had been fraternity brothers, drinking buddies, and journalistic cronies, although they never had collaborated formally on a story. Cole also was a *Commercial Appeal* veteran, having talked his way onto the staff without any journalism experience during the Christmas holidays in 1969. Lots of old hands were taking vacation or compensatory time, and the paper was shorthanded. "At least you can type," the metro editor growled after Cole signed on at the payroll office. Until the middle of 1977, about two months before Elvis's death, Cole worked as a reporter on general assignment, the police beat, and the courthouse beat, then as an assistant metro editor. He earned a reputation there as one of the paper's better wordsmiths, but with a penchant stretching the limits of the newspaper's dogmatic style book. After the arrival of Michael Grehl as editor in 1976, Cole grew weary of the sort of arbitrary management that was suspicious of investigative reporters as empire builders and in the same vein regarded staff members as interchangeable parts. Cole resigned in June of 1977, two months before Elvis's death, and was working as a freelance writer when Charlie Thompson showed up.

By temperament Cole was calmer and less confrontational than his brother-in-law and more inclined to give up on a story that wasn't panning out. As for the idea of looking into the Elvis autopsy two years after the fact, Cole was unimpressed. He was chummy with Francisco. And despite a couple of conversations with Beth Tamke about the Elvis story, Cole was willing to give the medical examiner the benefit of the doubt. As a gentle put-down of Thompson's preliminary investigation, Cole tried to steer him toward the latest outlandish scheme to capitalize on Elvis. A man who ran a laundry near Cole's house had bought up all the inch-long ceramic tiles that lined the inside of the Memorial Park mausoleum where Elvis and Gladys Presley had been buried until the bodies were moved to the grounds at Graceland. The laundry executive was selling the tiles individually through the classifieds in fan magazines. And there was the question of refunds on $15 tickets to the Elvis concerts scheduled for August 27 and 28, 1977, at the Mid-South Coliseum in Memphis. (In October 1989 the unclaimed property division of the Tennessee State Treasury announced that it would pay a $43.52 refund for each ticket.)

Thompson wasn't to be distracted. He wanted to look through probate court records and other public files for clues. Cole promised to call Tamke and check for leads that might be worth pursuing.

————

At the Shelby County court house Thompson made his way into the clerk's office and looked up the file number for Elvis Presley's probated will and estate. He could have just asked. It was kept separately from the other files and under lock and key. The clerk handed him a sheaf of bound papers about three inches thick and directed him to a desk where lawyers routinely reviewed court pleadings.

Thompson began plowing through pages, taking notes as he read. On page six of the estate's accounting ledger, he found ten separate notations concerning "Nichopoulos mortgage note collection." He thought that might be important, since he knew that Nichopoulos was Elvis's physician. He also considered it irregular for a doctor to be indebted to a patient in the six-figure range. Thumbing through the file, he saw notation after notation of payments of more than $10,000 that went to "the Medical Group (services on tours)." This also might be important, he decided, especially since he had been told that the Medical Group was actually Nichopoulos's medical partnership. Flipping through several pages more, Thompson saw that there was more information than he could fit on his legal pad. He wrote out a check to the probate court clerk to have the whole file copied.

While waiting, Thompson walked up one flight of stairs and around to the other side of the courthouse hall to the circuit court clerk's office. Contract disputes, including heaps of divorces and insurance suits, were filed here. Scanning for "Presley" in the reference dockets for the past few years, Thompson quickly located a suit filed by Dr. Nichopoulos, Joe Esposito, and a third plaintiff named Michael McMahon against Elvis for more than $100,000 in damages. It was filed several months before he died and ended quietly in a settlement disclosing few details.

The suit claimed Elvis reneged on a twofold promise—to invest in a racquetball club the three men were building in Mem-

phis and to allow the venture partners to use Elvis's name to promote the club. "What the hell kind of relationship did this doctor
have with his patient, anyway?" Thompson asked himself. "He
borrows big bucks of money from Elvis; he gets paid a lot for
treating him, and then he sues him? Something's not right."
Thompson had that suit copied and headed back to probate court
where the other copies were waiting. He foresaw the need for considerably more document research in the days ahead and maybe
the clues he needed to sell ABC on a story. But for now he was
itching to check out the morgue at *The Commercial Appeal.*

Thompson took the lobby elevator to the third floor and
asked to speak to Mike Grehl, who had been the newspaper's managing editor when Thompson was covering the police station years
earlier. Unlike Cole, Thompson liked Grehl and thought most
newsmen took Grehl's brusque manner too seriously.

"What the hell you in town for, troublemaker?" Grehl
teased.

"Elvis Presley," Thompson answered. "What killed him?"

"His ticker quit," Grehl said.

"Ticker quit, but why? Were drugs involved?"

"Find out for yourself," Grehl answered. "You still know
your way around the morgue, I guess." Thompson nodded as Grehl
pointed the way.

Glen Allen had retired, and Thompson introduced himself
to the replacement clerk. He asked for the Presley files and spent
the balance of the afternoon going through about twenty-odd envelopes and copying many of the old clippings. He spotted little to
excite his interest. He wondered about "the shit files" and if there
was one on Elvis. But the new clerk was an unknown factor, and
Thompson hated to ask, "Got anything really good on him in the
shit files?"

While the library was new, some of the furniture wasn't,
particularly the green plywood cabinet with the large padlock in
place. That's where the files used to be stored. Glen Allen used to
keep the key.

Thompson took an oblique approach. "I'm through with
these envelopes. Are there any more files?"

"Yep, in there," the clerk said, pointing to the green cabinet. He would need to find E. B. Blackburn, the paper's metro editor, for permission to open the files. The clerk left and returned with Blackburn, a short, dapper man who wore a bow tie and kept his hair cut in a flattop.

Blackburn greeted Thompson and unlocked the files. He made some small talk about how much the paper had changed since Thompson had worked there. Then he left with the clerk. Thompson was alone with the files.

Thumbing through the material, he found a plain white envelope. He opened it and pulled out what looked to him to be several lab reports. He began jotting notes down on a yellow legal pad. The first report was from Methodist Hospital and concerned a patient named Ethel Moore. It was a drug screen dated August 16, 1977, and ordered by a Dr. Sexton from Baptist Hospital. Ethel had tested positively in four drug categories. The second report was for E. A. Presley and was a chemical analysis done at the University of Tennessee Medical School laboratory on August 17, 1977. It showed that Elvis had six categories of drugs in his body. The last report contained five pages prepared by Bio-Science Laboratories in Van Nuys, California. It named a lot of drugs, contained a lot of numbers with curious symbols, and defined therapeutic and toxic ranges on a chart. Thompson had stumbled onto Tamke's surreptitious evidence. She had been permitted to summarize the Bio-Science report. But the chart, which drew the toxicology research together, had never appeared in *The Commercial Appeal*. Neither had any direct comment from forensic specialists who could explain what it meant.

Thompson knew he had to get copies of these reports and fast, before they were locked up again. He stuffed them in his shirt and headed up a floor to a copy machine he found in the newspaper's promotion department. The woman who ran the office remembered him. Trying to appear nonchalant, Thompson asked her if he could copy about ten pages. "No problem," she said and inquired about his family.

Returning to the morgue, Thompson put the lab reports back in their envelope and closed up the "shit files." He thanked the morgue clerk and left. On his way out, though, Thompson stopped in the newsroom at Beth Tamke's desk. He asked why the newspaper hadn't taken full advantage of the reports. Tamke was stunned. He shouldn't have been allowed to see the reports, she said.

Thompson headed directly to Baptist Hospital, an unscheduled stop. He wasn't a chemist and needed a better understanding of the lab reports. He parked his car in a lot near the hospital, entered the massive complex, and asked a receptionist to page an old friend who now was a resident at the hospital and a relative of a doctor on the Harvey team that tried to bring Elvis back from the dead.

Thompson persuaded his friend to follow him to the parking lot. When they reached the rental car, Thompson opened the trunk. They huddled in the semi-darkness of the trunk as Thompson retrieved his documents and asked for an interpretation. There was silence for several minutes.

"Well?" Thompson asked.

"Well, Jesus H. Christ, it's obvious," Thompson's impromptu consultant said. "The son of a bitch died of drugs." Then he paused. "Who was this guy anyway?"

"Elvis Presley," Thompson answered. On this trip to Memphis, he had heard all he wanted to hear.

VIII

IRRESPONSIBLE
PEOPLE

WITH THE CORNERSTONE of a full-scale investigation locked in the trunk of his rental car, Charlie Thompson began to map plans as he drove from Baptist Hospital to Jim Cole's house. He saw his first objective as verifying the toxicology reports he found in the newspaper morgue. If authentic, he must talk to the scientists who had originated them, then to disinterested experts who might or might not lend support to the findings.

The investigation also should focus on Elvis's habits, Thompson thought. Did he often take drugs? If so, what type and from what source? And where was the paper trail? His experience as an investigative reporter had taught him that when it came to drug abuse, tracking down prescription medicine might run afoul of a lot of confidentiality laws but was heaps easier than street drugs, where frequently the only records were needle tracks.

Hence the question of manpower emerged as his most pressing problem, particularly with his deadline, August 16, 1979, a few short weeks away. In just one trip to the court house and the newspaper, Thompson had compiled enough raw clues to keep him busy from then till next week, maybe longer.

Answering his front doorbell, Cole could sense Thompson's excitement by the impatient way he bustled into the house. In rapid-fire fashion Thompson explained what he had—secret documents, preliminary verification that the official line on Elvis might not be correct, and most of all the makings of a story.

"Jim, I've got to have some help. ABC will pay you a per diem plus expenses."

"Starting when?" Cole asked.

"Starting now," Thompson said. "We've got to verify these documents. And you've seen the list of names I got out of the Elvis books. We've got to track these people down—cover everything that moves to do this story right."

Cole could appreciate the way Thompson was attacking the subject. This wasn't going to be a haphazard, just-get-the-right-sound-bite TV spot. This was going to be an investigation from the ground up, and Cole suddenly was pleased to be part of it.

Around the dining room table, Thompson and Cole hovered over their notebooks, jotting down names in a growing Elvis "Who's Who," phone numbers, schematics of what information they had and what they hoped to get and when.

Around five o'clock the telephone rang in the old butler's pantry connecting the dining room and the kitchen. Cole answered it. E. B. Blackburn, metro editor at *The Commercial Appeal,* was on the line. "Jim, is your worthless brother-in-law there?" Blackburn asked. Looking puzzled, Cole handed the phone to Thompson.

Blackburn wanted to know if Thompson had found copies of the toxicological reports in the morgue files. Thompson told him that he had. Blackburn wasn't pleased and said that the reports were confidential. "Please destroy the copies you took," Blackburn said as more of a demand than request.

"Why? Are the reports authentic?" Thompson asked.

"Absolutely real," the newspaper editor replied and insisted that Thompson destroy his copies. Thompson rolled his eyes and gave Cole a dumbfounded look. Next he heard the sound of paper tearing on Blackburn's end of the line. "Here, I'm tearing up my copies right now. You do the same," Blackburn said.

"Not a chance, Blackie," Thompson answered. "I'm going to check these reports out to see if they're real."

Blackburn insisted that Thompson was wasting his time. He swore that Elvis Presley didn't die of drugs. The medical examiner had straightened everything out. The newspaper had been through all the toxicology reports two years before and couldn't prove anything. Then Blackburn changed his approach and made a strange appeal. He called on Thompson's civic pride as native Memphian not to use the reports to damage the image of Elvis and the city itself. "If you do the story, you will bring all the irresponsible people from *The New York Times* and the BBC into town," the editor said.

For one of the few instances in his life, Thompson was speechless. He thought to himself, "If he thinks those folks are irresponsible, Jesus, what does that make me?"

Blackburn interrupted his thoughts. "You'll do it then? You'll tear up the reports?"

"I can't do that, Blackie. I'm sorry. I'm going to follow this story wherever it takes me," Thompson answered. They hung up.

"What did he want?" Cole asked. As Thompson repeated the conversation, the humor hit both of them—a couple of "irresponsible people" who used to work for *The Commercial Appeal.*

Thompson put in a call to Geraldo, who was on the West Coast, and figured that in striking a nerve with Blackburn he had a strong signal that the tox reports were for real.

The next morning Thompson express-mailed a copy of the reports to Rivera. He picked Cole up and they set off for the library at the University of Tennessee Medical School. It was time for a crash course in forensic toxicology.

———

Bio-Science, the southern California lab employed by Baptist Hospital to help complete Elvis's autopsy, estimated that his codeine level was 1.08 micrograms per milliliter of blood. The lab said the codeine level found in his kidneys was 2.3 micrograms, and it found the codeine level in his liver was 1.6 micrograms. The toxic level for codeine is 1.6 micrograms, with death in documented cases occurring as low as 1.2 micrograms. In the blood alone, Elvis's codeine level was ten times the recommended therapeutic level. It was twenty-three times that level in his kidneys and sixteen times that level in his liver.

Thumbing through several texts, Thompson and Cole learned that codeine is a narcotic analgesic or painkiller that acts directly on the central nervous system. It's used to relieve mild to moderate pain or to suppress coughing. The medical texts warned that combining codeine with other drugs, especially other central nervous system depressants, was quite dangerous. An overdose of codeine combined with other narcotics could bring on a collapse of the circulatory system, impaired breathing, cardiac arrest, and death.

Bio-Science had also found small traces of morphine in his bloodstream. Morphine, the books said, is used to manufacture codeine and turns up as the body metabolizes it. The lab also found the following in serum samples:

- Toxic levels of methaqualone, or Quaaludes, in Elvis's system. This is a sedative-hypnotic drug. The books said care should be used when combining Quaaludes with other sedatives, analgesics, or psychotropic drugs. This could produce shock and respiratory arrest.
- Concentrations of metabolized diazepam, or Valium, that were at the upper limits of therapeutic levels. Valium, a sedative-hypnotic, is prescribed to treat symptoms of anxiety, and sometimes muscle spasms, convulsions, seizures, or alcohol withdrawal. It interacts with a number of other drugs and should not be taken with alcohol, other sedative drugs, or central nervous system depressants. The books warned that this drug had the potential for abuse and must be used with caution.
- Concentrations of ethinimate, or Valmid, higher than recommended therapeutic levels. *The Physicians' Desk Reference,* a widely used authority on drugs, warned that combining this sedative-hypnotic with other central nervous

system depressants will increase the hazards of these drugs.

- Ethchlorvynol, or Placidyl, in concentrations above therapeutic levels and in a gray area regarded as on the borderline of the toxic level. The medical books warned that combining this sedative-hypnotic with central nervous system depressants could cause severe problems.
- Pentobarbital concentrations nearly toxic. Additionally, butabarbital levels were within the therapeutic range, and phenobarbital levels were below therapeutic. These barbiturates are used as hypnotics for treating anxiety and stress. They are central nervous system depressants. All the books Thompson and Cole consulted warned that barbiturates must not be used along with other central nervous system depressants or severe consequences would result.
- And finally, small traces of chloropheniramine, an over-the-counter antihistamine taken by cold and hay fever sufferers, were found in the entertainer's body.

The two reporters kept a running tally of the major drugs found in Elvis's system. As they finished their library research, they consulted their tally sheet and discovered that Elvis was toxic or near toxic for four drugs—codeine, Quaaludes, Placidyl, and pentobarbital. He was well over the therapeutic range for two others—Valium and Valmid. All put together, they were looking at a combination of near-lethal dosages of two central nervous system depressants—codeine and the barbiturates—with dangerous amounts of four sedative-hypnotic drugs—Quaaludes, Valium, Valmid, and Placidyl.

Thompson looked at the totals and asked, "What kind of a doctor would prescribe this kind of crap?"

More to the point, what kind of medical-legal investigator could ignore such compelling evidence?

———

Jerry Thomas Francisco became medical examiner for Memphis and Shelby County in 1961, when Tennessee began phasing out coroners, who might be funeral directors, and replacing them with medical doctors. Over a period of time Francisco's office was handling upwards of 3,000 cases annually while he was developing a cozy relationship with prosecutors, name recognition as an expert witness, and a reputation both inside and outside his profession as a forensic pathologist with a strong suit in politics and a weak one in science.

For example, officially on April 4, 1968, Dr. Martin Luther King, Jr., died of a gunshot whose trajectory matched that of a sniper aiming about 100 yards away from the back window of a boarding house. With the guilty plea of James Earl Ray, this medical-legal conclusion never was tested or defended in open court. Yet its foundation is shaky, as a team of three medical examiners reported in 1979 to the House of Representatives Select Committee on Assassinations. Even in a case of this magnitude, Jerry Francisco chose to cut corners.

Because Francisco failed to make thorough dissection of the fatal wound, the panel of experts was unable to confirm that a sniper fired the shot from the boarding house window. The shot could have come from a clump of bushes at street level where two witnesses, including Dr. King's chauffeur, noted movement immediately after hearing gunfire. "Such a distinction may have no importance to the survivability of Dr. King," the medical examiner team reported, "but accurate documentation of all injuries is desirable in all homicidal deaths in anticipation of issues known or unknown to arise later and to permit others to independently review the findings."

Francisco explained that he chose not to dissect the entire track of the wound out of deference to the King family because a complete dissection would have mutilated King's body unnecessarily. This is the same Jerry Francisco who in 1985 was rebuked by members of the Shelby County commission for putting slides of King's wounds on display in his medical school classes at the University of Tennessee.

Earlier in his career, Francisco supplied pivotal testimony in the spectacular trial and conviction of Louis Montesi, a Memphis grocery store executive with a history of alcoholism and volatile behavior. Officially, Francisco ruled that Montesi's wife died of a gunshot wound, but more damning, that underneath her fingernail was a residue of human skin consistent with scratches on Louis Montesi's neck.

Because Louis Montesi had such a long record as a reprobate, detectives figured they had their man. They failed to lift fingerprints at the Montesi home where the shooting happened or to make a thorough search for the murder weapon. Hence the prime exhibit in the trial was the skin sample, which Francisco linked to the neck scratches.

Dr. Milton Helpern, chief medical examiner for New York City, characterized the Montesi prosecution as "a real travesty of science." Helpern testified that Francisco's sample was nothing more than "gunk." Further, Dr. Robert Hausman, medical examiner in San Antonio, said the sample could have been dandruff but more likely was "southern fried chicken," the main course at the Montesi dinner table before the killing. Ultimately, the homicide charges against Montesi were dropped.

Inside the medical examiner's office, Francisco is a hands-off kind of pathologist. He's not up to his elbows with a scalpel autopsying bodies. If present in the autopsy room at all, Francisco more likely would be checking off the blocks on a form he developed years ago to run corpses through the morgue on an assembly line—a medical examiner's answer to painting by numbers. Instead of making notes of his findings, Francisco would assign number values—1, 2, 3, or 4—to various areas on an anatomical chart. Later on, a secretary in the medical examiner's office would look at the numbered chart and write out a detailed description of the autopsy findings. A "2" on the chart's thyroid section, for example, would become, "The follicles are regular and uniform. Their colloid content is normal and without significant color change." Or a "1" over in the heart section would become, "The myocardial fibers are well preserved. There is no cellular inflammatory reaction present. The cross-striations are prominent." This down-and-dirty method of preparing autopsy reports allowed Francisco to complete in a few minutes what it took a pathologist making individualized notes an hour to finish.

On the witness stand, Francisco usually has a pair of gold-rimmed reading glasses perched on his nose and keeps his knees primly together as he rests an autopsy folder in his lap, referring to it as needed. Although he rarely participated in an autopsy himself, Francisco seldom let that fact slip to the jury or for that matter to the prosecutors. DAs consider him a dream witness, never backing down once his opinions were stated.

Eric Muirhead, Baptist Hospital's chief pathologist, recalled one of Francisco's stellar performances in a civil case. Muirhead testified for a life insurance company that a policy holder, whose coronary arteries were narrowed to pinpoints, had died naturally of a quite predictable heart attack. But when the man collapsed, his head struck a desktop. In Francisco's view, the cause of death was a blow to the head. And Francisco's testimony resulted in a judgment against the insurance company.

"Jerry," Muirhead said afterward, "there's not a pathology textbook on any shelf that will support what you said. And he said, 'Eric, you just don't know how to play the game.' "

———

Returning to Cole's house from research in the medical library, Thompson telephoned Bio-Science and set up an interview for Geraldo with Dr. Raymond Kelly, the lab director, for the following week.

"When we undertake to do this sort of analysis," Kelly told Rivera, "we do it in the most thorough and conclusive way we possibly can, and we don't rush ourselves. We utilize every analytical technique we have available. And that includes some of the most sophisticated methods anywhere in the country."

"How important was the Elvis Presley case?" Rivera asked.

"That is the most important medical-legal case we ever had. And so we, if anything, exercised even more care in the analysis of those specimens than we would normally exercise," the lab director said.

"How do you respond then to the criticism of Dr. Francisco

and others that the results found here at Bio-Science could be discounted?" Rivera asked.

"That doesn't seem reasonable to me at all. I think that the person making that statement just couldn't be familiar with the way we approach these kinds of samples," Kelly replied.

At that, Rivera showed Kelly copies of the reports that his producer had found in *The Commercial Appeal* morgue and asked him how confident he was that the numbers found in the reports accurately represented the drug levels found in Elvis's body at the time of his death.

"I'm sure beyond a reasonable doubt. I understand the thoroughness that was done. Based upon the care at which those samples were done, I am sure beyond a reasonable doubt that those are the correct numbers," he answered.

Now Rivera was convinced that the reports were authentic. He called Thompson in Memphis, summarized the interview, and read him the on-camera stand-up he planned on taping in front of Bio-Science. It read: "Despite the contention by many of the officials in Memphis that Elvis Presley died of natural causes, that contention is disputed by scientific evidence uncovered here at the Bio-Science Laboratories near Los Angeles. According to the findings of Bio-Science, at the time of his death, Elvis Presley was apparently abusing many different drugs."

Back in Memphis, Thompson and Cole visited the Shelby County Medical Examiner's Office and asked Dr. Francisco if he foresaw any problems in giving them a copy of Elvis's autopsy. Francisco laughed and handed them copies of a two-page report of medical investigation and a public relations release he passed out at his October 21, 1977, press conference. He told them that if they wanted to keep this public relations packet, it would cost them five dollars. The autopsy? Well, that was still private, the medical examiner said, not part of his official records. But since he had relied on it to make an official ruling, shouldn't it be in the file? No, it was a confidential medical record and would remain secret, unless of course some court told him otherwise. They could sue him.

Francisco's offhand suggestion, as the day wore on, warmed up to Thompson. Obviously there was a serious medical disagreement here—more than just a difference in making a judgment call. Placing Francisco under oath perhaps would make him more forthcoming than he had been a few moments before. The lawsuit question needed more research.

At the time of Elvis's death, a politician by the name of Jim Rout was the Shelby County coroner. The coroner's job was a constitutional office later abolished, but in 1977 somebody had to sign the paperwork as coroner even though a professionally trained medical examiner handled the real functions of postmortem investigations. Still, state law allowed the coroner to convene an inquest, if he believed the medical examiner was not investigating a case satisfactorily.

Rout, a tall, slender, red-headed man in his mid-thirties, had considered doing just that in Elvis Presley's case. As a teenager, Rout once saw Elvis cruising his neighborhood on a motorcycle. He had watched Elvis perform and thought of himself as an ardent Presley fan. Hence as an official and as a fan, Rout asked Jerry Francisco for more information about Elvis's death after the official ruling was announced, and Francisco had provided Rout the same public relations packet that he had given to Thompson and Cole two years later. Nothing more. In fact, Rout wasn't happy to find that his press packet was buried in a thick stack of other complete and fully documented autopsies.

"I just wasn't satisfied at the time with what I received in the way of obtaining documentation," Rout said. Because the case nagged him, Rout agreed to ask the county attorney for a formal written opinion on the legality of Jerry Francisco's refusal to make the autopsy public.

On another front, Thompson and Cole were in contact with Maurice Elliott, the executive vice president at Baptist Hospital. Elliott had arranged for them to meet with Drs. Eric Muirhead and Harold Sexton. Quickly Thompson got down to cases. Not only had he obtained the toxicology reports, he also had verified them with Bio-Science. Elliott and the doctors broke out in smiles. "They damned near applauded," Cole said later. "It was obvious then and there that we were going to get a lot of under-the-table, backdoor help from these people."

Elliott confirmed there was a strong difference of opinion between the Baptist Hospital doctors and Jerry Francisco. He said the hospital would like to release a copy of the autopsy, yet the hospital's lawyers had warned that this might violate doctor-patient confidentiality.

"But he's dead," Thompson exploded. "The confidentiality died with him."

Elliott turned palms up and shrugged, as if to say, "I know it's stupid, but that's what our attorneys tell us." At that, Thompson surprised Cole by promising to sue Jerry Francisco. "Good," said Harold Sexton. "I hope you win."

—————

That night Thompson convened a legal planning session in the home of his old friend, Mike Pleasants. Pleasants, a tall, dark-haired, and imposing trial lawyer, bore a striking resemblance to Gregory Peck and had the same steady demeanor as well. His father had been mayor of Memphis during the heyday of "Boss" Crump, and Pleasants was now a partner in one of Memphis's most prestigious law firms.

Thompson mentioned that he was looking for outside experts to counter Francisco's opinion and asked Pleasants for his suggestions. Pleasants tossed him a copy of a magazine published by the American Trial Lawyers' Association and told him to check the back of it for ads placed there by forensic experts. Thompson found one that interested him.

Pleasants suggested removing all identification of Elvis Presley from the toxicology reports to run a blind test. Thompson thought that was a good idea, and the next day he sent the reports to Dr. Matthew Ellenhorn, a clinical pharmacologist and internist in Beverly Hills, California. After he had given Ellenhorn a few days, Thompson called and set up an on-camera interview with Rivera.

At the outset of the interview in Ellenhorn's office, Rivera prefaced his first question, "Doctor, you know that we have not identified the person involved here." Ellenhorn nodded. Then Rivera fired away. "But given these laboratory analyses, characterize, if you can, the cause of death?"

"It's my impression from the laboratory analyses, which I was given, that the cause of death was an overdose of codeine and methaqualone, which is also known as Quaaludes. There were other drugs that were found at death also. All of which were depressants to the brain and all of which could have added to the respiratory depression, inability to breathe. And that probably resulted in his ultimate death.

"The drugs found in the bloodstream indicate that the patient had at least about eight different types of drugs, such as barbiturates, Placidyl, Valmid, phenobarbital and pentobarbital, which is a barbiturate, a short-acting barbiturate. These were not by themselves individually present in serious dosage, but they were all present. So therefore, being present at the same time is very unusual. It indicates that this individual was really into drugs, and really into drugs quite heavily."

Rivera asked Ellenhorn just how certain he was about the cause of death. "Based on reasonable medical probability, the dose levels, the drug levels that were found in the bloodstream at the time of death indicate definite fatal levels. These had been reported before in the medical literature, and the levels also observed in the kidneys and in the liver are also compatible with levels found in fatal cases. So that I'm reasonably certain that this was the cause of death."

"Was this person an addict, Doctor?" Rivera asked.

"I would say that this person probably was physically and psychologically dependent on the drugs he was taking. Taking this many drugs indicates a habit pattern of dependence on drugs," Ellenhorn said.

"Why would a person be using these downers?" Rivera asked.

"Well, an individual uses downers for many reasons," Ellenhorn replied. "With this many downers taken at one time, one looks for a person who is either taking uppers like amphetamines or other drugs that cause a stimulating effect on the body, or a person who is under tremendous tension, or is tremendously active in his job. Has irregular hours and is hyped up, going at about 160 miles an hour within himself constantly, and needs something in order to bring him down in order to get to sleep. And what hap-

109

pens is this cycle starts. Tremendous activity, the need to get to sleep, the need to get some rest. Irregular hours, a little more hyperactivity, a little more drugs to get him down, and pretty soon he's in a really vicious cycle. And in this vicious cycle we find experimenting with every kind of drugs, something to give him rest, to give him relief, to give him a little escape from the reality of the life which he leads.

"It's a tragedy, but it's a tragedy that's repeated in hospitals all over the United States. Every emergency room physician has seen this kind of thing. And as long as these people have access to drugs—and they may have access to drugs through legitimate channels through doctors—you're going to see this kind of thing."

Inasmuch as Ellenhorn had been a practicing pharmacologist for more than thirty years, Rivera asked his opinion of Bio-Science Laboratories. He told Rivera that Bio-Science was one of the most reputable laboratories in the United States.

Rivera then asked, "Assuming the doctor who prescribed that medication was the same doctor and assuming that he prescribed it within a short period of time, prior to his death, how would you describe that?"

"I would characterize this doctor as having poor judgment. I would characterize the doctor as perhaps being overcome by the importance of the individual he was giving the prescriptions to," Ellenhorn answered.

Rivera told him that the reports he had analyzed belonged to Elvis Presley. "You don't say!" Ellenhorn said with genuine surprise.

Rivera called Thompson and summarized the interview. The reporter and the producer decided they wanted to show the reports to a forensic pathologist who had a reputation in the medicolegal community greater than Jerry Francisco's. They picked Dr. Cyril Wecht, a board-certified forensic pathologist. Wecht, who was coroner of Allegheny County in Pittsburgh, Pennsylvania, had written textbooks on forensic pathology and had served as an expert witness to the U.S. House of Representatives committee that looked into the Kennedy assassination.

Wecht studied the materials sent him by Thompson and then was interviewed. He was asked what killed Elvis. "I believe that Mr. Presley died as the result of a combined drug effect. Various drugs, all of which are known to be central nervous system depressants, collectively caused his heart and lungs to be depressed. The brain controls the activities of the heart and lungs involuntarily. When the brain is depressed by multiple drugs, such as happened in this case, in my opinion, the heart and the lungs will not function properly."

What specifically were the culprit drugs?

"There were several drugs involved here. The principal offender in this case was codeine, which is a pain reliever, but which is known to have a central nervous system depressant effect. Other drugs included Valium, a tranquilizer; Valmid, a sedative; Placidyl, a sedative; phenobarbital, a sedative; and butabarbital, a sedative. It's incredible really that all these drugs should have been given to the patient simultaneously."

How would Wecht have labeled the cause of death, if he had been officially in charge of the case rather than Jerry Francisco?

"I do not believe, based upon the postmortem levels of these various drugs, that it was a suicide. It seems almost definite that it was an accidental death," he said.

In what way did the drug levels reflect on the type of medical care that Elvis was receiving?

"If one physician prescribed all these drugs, then it was below acceptable standards of care. I would consider this to have been poor, unacceptable, and potentially dangerous medical care," Wecht said. "If the drugs had been prescribed by two or more physicians, then I would say that each physician was at the very least not sufficiently diligent, and perhaps worse, somewhat negligent in having failed to ascertain what other drug might have been prescribed by other physicians. It is a cardinal concept in medicine that before you prescribe a drug that has a brain depressant effect, you find out whether or not the patient is taking other drugs that might have a similar pharmacological effect. Because, if so, then the second drug might have to be withheld or the dosage schedule might have to be in some way revised."

Did the level of codeine kill Elvis Presley?

"The level was significant by itself. It could have resulted in death. It was at a near-fatal level. On the other hand, if he had been taking it for some time, he would have built up some tolerance. Codeine does not usually produce death by itself, although it can. Most codeine deaths that we see are, as in this case, those situations in which other drugs having a depressant effect upon the brain have also been injected together with codeine. That can result in death."

Were the doctors that were attending to the health of Elvis responsible for his death?

"Looking at this case, if I were to do so, from the standpoint of the view and evaluation for a potential medical malpractice case, that it would be a bona fide case that will require further study and possible legal action," said Wecht, who is also a practicing attorney.

"It was not good medical care and that in a situation resulting in harm or death to a patient, that such an odd array of drugs coming from one physician in particular or two or more could possibly be sufficient foundation for a medical malpractice or professional negligence lawsuit," he added.

Wecht said that Elvis's death was not a typical or classical multi-drug overdose, because you don't have many cases—if any —involving ten different drugs. He described the classic overdose case of someone who combines tranquilizers and alcohol or combines barbiturates, tranquilizers, and alcohol. But no traces of alcohol were found in Elvis. He said that those who support the theory that Elvis had built up a tolerance to these drugs were only speculating and have no basis for saying that. And even if you assume there was some tolerance, with ten drugs involved, you have an overwhelming quantity. You get a cumulative effect, he said. It produces the pharmacological phenomenon known as synergism, which means you get more of a geometric than a simple arithmetic effect when you add one drug to another. One compounds the effect of the next. "In this case, it's like adding two plus two plus two. Only you don't come up with six. You might come up with nine or ten or even fifteen."

Then Wecht outlined his legal analysis of the manner in which Francisco handled the Presley case. "Look at the facts. Here you have a forty-two-year-old man—and let's forget for the moment that he's Elvis Presley. A man is suddenly found dead and you have no reason to suspect any prior life-threatening circumstances. That kind of situation would universally be a medical examiner's or a coroner's case. But what happened? An autopsy was requested by the hospital. I think Dr. Francisco's explanation of his role in the autopsy and why it was not conducted at his office leaves much to be desired and raises questions about whether he acted properly in this situation. I believe the autopsy should have been performed in the medical examiner's office and that he could have recommended that to the district attorney.

"Instead, Dr. Francisco claims he did not want to transport Presley's body across the street from the hospital to his office because a crowd was gathering outside. He tells us that the private autopsy was done under the auspices of the hospital and that he was only there as a consultant. His inconsistencies here are unbelievable. On the one hand, he says it was not a case under the jurisdiction of the medical examiner's office. But while the autopsy was being performed, he held a news conference to give the cause of death. If it were not his case, why did he raise the point about his fearing the gathering crowd and the difficulty in transporting the body to his office? It's inconsistent.

"There are other problems—not only with conclusions drawn from the autopsy but with the procedures employed. For example, the sequence of events following the autopsy—the haste with which Dr. Francisco declared that Presley had died of heart disease—casts doubt on that diagnosis. The microscopic slides from the autopsy would have taken twenty-four or forty-eight hours to get back for study. Similarly, the toxicology results that would indicate whether drugs were involved could not have been received.

"Yet Dr. Francisco immediately held a news conference giving the cause of death as cardiac arrhythmia. Cardiac arrhythmia is something a pathologist cannot see when he is doing an autopsy. There are only two ways he can make that diagnosis—in a live person with a stethoscope held to the chest and with an electrocardiogram. When you examine someone after death, nothing will tell you he had ventricular fibrillation when he died. For Dr. Francisco to be giving such a diagnosis when he had no infor-

113

mation about his condition immediately prior to death and without the benefit of microscopic sections and toxicologic analyses is incredible."

Wecht also quarreled with two points that Francisco stressed in his ruling—that the size of Elvis's heart was twice what it should have been and that the coronary arteries were sixty percent clogged. He said Elvis's heart weighed 520 grams, which was not twice the normal size of about 400 grams for someone Elvis's weight. He said a narrowing of 60 percent in the arteries isn't unusual in a forty-two-year-old man.

Wecht's analysis had the reporters' heads spinning. They knew now that they had to redouble their efforts to get the autopsy.

Back in Memphis, Jim Rout called Cole and reported that the opinion from the county attorney was ready. The autopsy was a private document, it concluded. Cole and Thompson weren't surprised. And Mike Pleasants had completed his research to challenge the official line. Pleasants had decided to file suit in the form of a writ of mandamus, a complaint that a public official was not performing his public duties and should be commanded by the courts to do so—in this instance, to make Elvis's autopsy public. Cole and Thompson both would be listed as complainants or "relators," as the moving parties are known in this type of action. The defendants were Jerry Francisco and Hugh Stanton, Jr., district attorney for Shelby County.

Thompson and Cole signed the lawsuit, but Pleasants said he would be unable to file it until Cole, a resident of Shelby County, went through a necessary scenario. Cole met with Francisco the next morning and made a formal demand for the autopsy. Again the medical examiner said it wasn't in his files and wasn't for him to turn over. From a factual standpoint, the lawsuit now was on a firm footing.

Thompson met Cole at Pleasants's plush legal office, coincidentally, Suite 2020 in the First National (later First Tennessee) Bank Building that overlooked the Mississippi River.

"You really sure you want to do this, Charlie?" Pleasants asked. "Sure do. Sue the bastard," Thompson replied.

IX

DR. FEELGOOD

AFTER THE LAWSUIT to obtain Elvis Presley's autopsy was
filed, Thompson, Cole, and Pleasants's law firm were in-
undated with tipsters claiming to have hot information
about how Elvis died. Most of these people were either
crackpots or marginal loonies. But some provided leads to valid
information—enough at least to where Thompson believed he
needed more help, particularly in checking leads outside Memphis.

Hence Thompson enlisted Danny Goldfarb, a former New
York probation officer, public defender and, before either job, Geraldo Rivera's law school roommate. Goldfarb, who had just
turned thirty-five, looked more like a male model in a chic magazine than a product of the New York criminal justice system.
Standing over six feet with a lean frame, sleepy eyes, and a mop of
black hair, Goldfarb was the hippest-looking member of the *20/20*
team and later would turn over some important rocks on the West
Coast. But Cole, for one, wondered in the early going how anybody would want to tell anything to Danny Goldfarb. He wore his
shirts open almost to the navel, sported lots of jewelry, and
pounded the pavement in open-toed sandals.

By background Goldfarb had been a probation officer and,

116

after law school, a public defender. In the seven years he was a New York City PD, Goldfarb claimed the only people he met were liars, cheats, perverts, murderers, robbers, thieves, arsonists, and drug dealers. "And they were all my clients," he said ruefully. "The criminal court system was an absolute sewer."

Thompson assigned Goldfarb to check out an anonymous letter. It was typewritten neatly and mailed to Mike Pleasants's law office. It read: "In 1976 a Memphis physician, Dr. Lawrence Wruble, was called in consultation by Dr. Nichopoulos on account of Elvis's liver ailments. Dr. Wruble is a gastroenterologist. After examining Elvis, Dr. Wruble requested that all drugs be discontinued as he felt that Elvis's main trouble was overuse of drugs. Dr. Nichopoulos refused this request, and Dr. Wruble was taken off the case."

Goldfarb attempted to talk with Dr. Wruble, but the physician declined, citing a possible breach of doctor/patient confidentiality. Later in a public forum Dr. Wruble would testify that the information contained in this letter was essentially correct and that Elvis Presley was addicted to narcotics.

The anonymous letter also said: "Mrs. Marian Cocke was Elvis's private nurse for several years, and she too should know how many drugs were prescribed and administered. She now is employed in Baptist Hospital." This was the same Mrs. Cocke who was summoned to the emergency room on the afternoon of Elvis's death to take custody of his gold chain, pendant, and pajama bottoms.

Mrs. Cocke first met Elvis in 1975, when he came to Baptist Hospital to dry out from drugs. A mother-hen type, Mrs. Cocke ingratiated herself to Elvis and continued to work for him as a nurse at Graceland after his hospital stay. If anybody should know about Elvis's drug problems during the final two years of his life, it should be Mrs. Marian J. Cocke. She had just written and published a slender volume, entitled *I Called Him Babe: Elvis Presley's Nurse Remembers*. Thompson bought the book, finished it an hour later, and concluded that what Mrs. Cocke remembered in print was with rare exception not what he really wanted to find out about Elvis. The book was a saccharine tribute to Elvis, his sweet personality and largesse to Mrs. Cocke—he gave her a new car and what she described as a "fabulous mink." Naturally, it skirted Elvis's drug abuse as if it were leprosy. And it had this comment about his death: "The coroner's report stated that Elvis died of a heart attack and that he had an enlarged heart. This was no surprise to me. Elvis had the biggest heart of anyone I've ever known. He was both generous and compassionate, and his love for people was tremendous. Thus this seems the appropriate way for him to have gone. In my opinion, he had one other fatal illness—loneliness."

Goldfarb and Cole read the book, too. In his quick read, Cole discovered that he had gone to college with Mrs. Cocke's younger brother. With something to lead with, he volunteered to call her and set up an interview. He telephoned her and explained in general terms that *20/20* was doing an anniversary piece on Elvis. Mrs. Cocke agreed to see them.

As the threesome found their way to Mrs. Cocke's midtown apartment a few nights later, Thompson warned Goldfarb to behave while Cole applied the soft soap leading up to the serious questions. He looked at Goldfarb's silk shirt, which was open down to his navel, and told him to button it up.

The interview exceeded Goldfarb's worst fears. Mrs. Cocke's apartment was as orderly as a German place setting. The color scheme was pastel, the patterns mostly floral, and the living room furniture so spotless as to seem rarely used. It became apparent to all three that Mrs. Cocke's favorite subjects to the exclusion of everything else were her family and her absolute adoration of Elvis Presley.

Then there were Liz and Honeybunch. Mrs. Cocke owned two chihuahuas and called them "her girls." Goldfarb and Thompson never got the dogs' names straight, but as Cole made small talk about Mrs. Cocke's brother Joe, it became clear that one of "the girls" had hemorrhoid problems or swollen glands. Continually it dragged its bottom across the deep shag carpeting in search of relief. Thompson was trying to pay attention to the dialogue and make mental notes when he noticed Goldfarb had his sandals on and ought to trim his toenails. Then Thompson attached more significance to the sandals as either Liz or Honeybunch dragged her little butt closer and closer to Goldfarb's right foot. Thompson winced and looked away as the dog settled its bottom on Goldfarb's big toe and began rubbing the inflamed area. "Please, God, don't let him kick the little bastard," Thompson prayed and watched in horror as Goldfarb lifted his foot for a drop kick. Thompson began making cutting signs across his throat as he heard Cole get to serious business.

"Mrs. Cocke, now that almost two years have gone by," Cole asked, "do you believe in retrospect that there were drugs coming into Graceland from other doctors and that they were being abused?"

"Now, boys," Mrs. Cocke said, "I thought we weren't going to talk about drugs."

"But Mrs. Cocke, you wrote about drugs in your book," Cole persisted. "Elvis had a sleeping problem he was taking pills for, high blood pressure, and a colon problem he was taking codeine tablets for, and he was puffy because he ate a lot of salty food."

Elvis was taking a lot of medication, Mrs. Cocke admitted, and he took another painkiller instead of codeine because it didn't agree with him. But it was all prescribed by Dr. Nick.

Slowly, Goldfarb uncocked his foot, slipped it under his chair, and sat up straight. Thompson let out a breath of air. Cole could see this interview wasn't going any further. Almost in unison the three reporters said, "Thank you very much, Mrs. Cocke."

As they rode down the elevator from Mrs. Cocke's apartment, Thompson clumped Goldfarb on the back and said, "You're really a pro. I would have killed that dog."

"God, what could I do? Geraldo's not going to believe this one, Charlie," Goldfarb answered.

———

One area where Mrs. Cocke had been less than forthright was the source of drugs, which Elvis presumably had been swallowing by the handful. In his extensive reading of the Elvis literature, Thompson had come across the name John O'Grady. Known as "the Big O" during the 1950s, O'Grady was sergeant in charge of the Los Angeles Police Department's narcotics unit and was the scourge of drug dealers, musicians, actors, and addicts who plied their trade and mellowed out on drugs along Los Angeles's Sunset Strip. After retirement O'Grady became a private detective.

Elvis's attorney, E. Gregory Hookstratten, brought O'Grady into Elvis's life in 1969 to investigate a Los Angeles waitress named Pat Parker. Parker had brought a paternity suit, which Elvis's attorneys successfully defended with O'Grady's help. O'Grady ran polygraph tests on Elvis and Parker, arranged blood tests, and conducted background investigations of all witnesses in the case. In the process, the colorful former narc got to know Elvis well. And he suspected his famous client was playing around with heavy-duty drugs from the time Elvis got up from an office conference to use the bathroom and walked straight into a wall. During the polygraph tests, O'Grady recalled, Elvis's pulse and breathing rates were well below normal, an indication that he was taking downers, either opiates or barbiturates.

With more than 2,500 drug busts in his police career, O'Grady knew the score on Elvis and decided to help. He believed that if Elvis became interested in meeting policemen and collecting badges, it might discourage him from abusing narcotics. Actually it had just the opposite effect. In public Elvis became a vociferous opponent of drug abuse, an avid police groupie and frenetic collector of police badges. But in private he used those badges and police associations to camouflage and to abet his drug dealings. How could anyone suspect such a proponent of law and order, such a good friend of narcotics officers, and such a rabid opponent of drug dealers of being a junkie himself? John O'Grady found this monumental hypocrisy on Elvis's part to be profoundly unsettling. Still he continued to do jobs for the singer. O'Grady conducted many investigations involving battery suits brought against Elvis by people who claimed they were badly beaten by his bodyguards, other paternity actions, and investigations involving the loyalty and honesty of the many hangers-on who surrounded Elvis.

What began to worry Hookstratten and Vernon Presley above all was Elvis's growing dependency on drugs, particularly when he loaded up on pills and blew an engagement at Lake Tahoe. They observed Elvis's hefty physique and his chronic slur-

120

Elvis Presley was very much a virile family man when these photographs were taken. *(AP/Wide World Photos)*

By 1977, however, even Elvis's most ardent fans could hardly overlook his double chin and expanding paunch. His abuse of drugs and its toll on his digestive system were still well-kept secrets. *(AP/Wide World Photos)*

Joe Esposito (left) and Al Strada, pictured at Baptist Hospital on August 16, 1977, were among the first to discover Elvis's body. *(Mississippi Valley Collection/Memphis State University)*

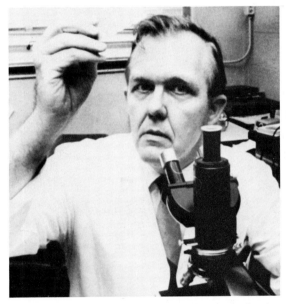

Dan Warlick, the medical examiner's investigator, found solid evidence of Elvis's drug problems, but he was ignored. *(Courtesy of Dan Warlick)*

Dr. Jerry T. Francisco, Shelby County Medical Examiner, oversaw the autopsy procedure, but after the results were in, Dr. Francisco regarded himself merely as a consultant. *(Mississippi Valley Collection/Memphis State University)*

Maurice Elliott, Baptist Hospital's administrative vice president, was expected to cover for Elvis. In stalling the press about Elvis's death, Elliott said the entertainer was suffering from "respiratory distress." *(Courtesy of Maurice Elliott)*

(DP AUG 2 2 '77

1. Victim's Last Name, First & Middle		Sex	Race	Age	2. Agency I.D. No.	Yr.	Mo.	Day	Number
Presley, Elvis Aaron		M	W	42	TN-MPD-0000	77	08	16	2793

3. Residence Address	4. Residence Phone	5. Business Address	6. Business Phone
3764 Elvis Presley Blvd.			

7. Offense	Code	Dist.	Meter	8. Person Arrested	Sex	Race	Age
DOA	8'00"						

9. Location of Occurrence (Street Number)	Code	10. Date & Time of Occurrence	Code	11. Date & Time Police Arrived
3764 Elvis Presley Blvd.	101	8-16-77 530am – 1430		8-16-77 1430

12.	License Number	State	Year	Vehicle Identification Number (Vin)

Vehicle	Year	Make	Body Style	Color	Value	Damage, Decals
	Other Outstanding Characteristics					

13. Reporting Officer	Emp. Num.	Reporting Officer	Emp. Num.	Car No.	14. Date & Time phoned to R.C.	15. Prop. Recpt. #
Peel	6543	Millican	5180	2741	8-16-77 1856	

16. Property Taken		Value		Property Taken		Value	
cd	Item	Taken	Recovered	cd	Item	Taken	Recovered
01	Currency			05	Office Equipment		
02	Jewelry			06	T.V., Radio & Camera		
03	Clothing & Furs			07	Firearms		
04	Motor Vehicles			08	Household Goods		
4a.	Autos			09	Consumable Goods		
4b.	Trucks or Buses			10	Livestock		
4c.	Miscellaneous			15	Miscellaneous		
17. Narrative					TOTAL		

The above subject was brought to the Baptist Hospital after being found unconscious in the upstairs bedroom of his home. The subject was transported by Fire Department Ambulance and was DOA at the Baptist Hospital. Homicide and the Medical Examiner office did make the scene at the Hospital and at 3764 Elvis Presley Blvd.

8/16/77 Info. from Fire Dept. Disp. – Amb #6 arrived at Graceland at 2:33pm – arrived at Baptist Hosp. 2:56pm

3:40pm Chief Molnar advised that Elvis Presley was at Baptist E.R. – had expired. Body transp. by F.D.A. from Graceland to Baptist. M

3:45pm Lt. Mc + Peel to Baptist Hosp.

4:00pm Dr. Francisco advised of situation

4:10pm Info. from Mc. at hosp.:
Came to hosp. as John Doe later ID by Dr. Nichopoulos + body guard Esposito as E.P. Body in Baptist Hosp. Morgue. Dr. Nichopoulos came to hosp. with vict. Vict. appeared to have been setting on commode + lunged forward. Had gone to bathroom to read. Dr. Nich. left hosp. in route to get autopsy papers at Graceland. Wouldn't give cause of death.

The cover page of the Memphis Police Department report was short on information, but Sgt. John Peel, who visited Graceland, was taking thorough notes. At the request of Dr. Francisco's office, however, Memphis homicide detectives were called off the case.

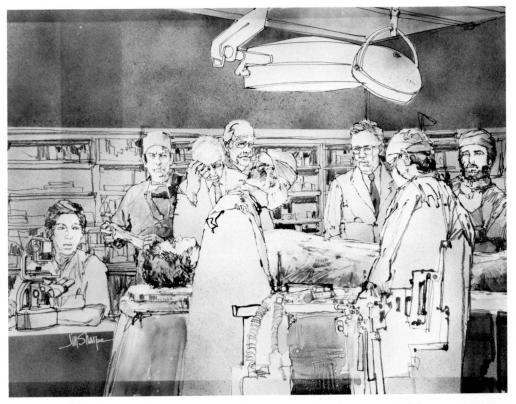

No photographs of the autopsy procedure were taken, but many of those present regarded this drawing, commissioned two years later by ABC's *20/20*, as a good reconstruction of the setting. *(Drawing by Jim Sharpe)*

Dr. Harold Sexton, Baptist Hospital's point man in the investigation of Elvis's death, worked behind the scenes to make the autopsy records public. Sexton died in 1988. *(Courtesy of James P. Cole)*

Beth Tamke, the tart-tongued medical reporter for *The Memphis Commercial Appeal*, knew quickly that she was onto a big story, but her editors disagreed. *(Courtesy of Beth Tamke)*

Ultimately Elvis's body was transferred to the grounds of Graceland Mansion, and Vernon Presley was content to keep the results of the Baptist Hospital autopsy a secret. *(AP/Wide World Photos)*

ring of words and believed he would die if they failed to act. They told John O'Grady to investigate and to determine just where and from whom Elvis was getting his drugs. Hookstratten and Vernon Presley were doubtful that Elvis could be persuaded to give up drugs voluntarily. They were more confident that if O'Grady could discover Elvis's drug sources, then they could bring pressure to bear and dry them up.

Assisting O'Grady in this investigation was another private detective, Jack Kelly, who had formerly headed the Los Angeles office of the federal Drug Enforcement Administration. The two ex-narcs were able to identify three physicians and a dentist as Elvis's main drug sources. However, they dismissed Dr. George Nichopoulos as a candidate because Vernon Presley vouched for him as a reputable doctor. The detectives discovered that a high percentage of the drugs were not prescribed in Elvis's name, but were written in the names of members of his entourage or in the names of their wives. One doctor went so far as to write Elvis a prescription in the name of his young daughter, Lisa Marie. Many of these bogus prescriptions were filled at the Landmark Pharmacy in Las Vegas, directly in sight of the Hilton International, where Elvis lived and played his engagements.

The two hard-boiled, tough-talking detectives confronted the medical culprits with their evidence and told Hookstratten and Vernon that none of their targets pleaded innocent. They then took their investigative report to state and federal narcotics agencies. But no action ever resulted.

Obviously John O'Grady was a major source of information about Elvis and his drug habits, and Charlie Thompson wanted an interview for the show that was taking shape on Elvis's death. Danny Goldfarb was assigned to contact O'Grady and to interview him and Jack Kelly.

In short order Goldfarb managed to get through to O'Grady and caught the next plane from Memphis to L.A. Goldfarb rendezvoused with Rivera and a camera crew and interviewed O'Grady the next day. Burly, white-haired, and superconfident of his opinions, O'Grady wasn't mincing words. He had also taken the initiative by inviting Jack Kelly to attend the interview.

Up front O'Grady told the *20/20* crew that Elvis was a

121

"medical addict" and that the doctors who wrote the prescriptions were largely responsible for his death at age forty-two.

"Being around Presley, I observed that he couldn't sleep," O'Grady said. "He'd stay in his room three or four days with his eyes open and awake. The drugs created such a ravaging effect upon his body that he couldn't sleep. He couldn't perform. He was constantly tired. Constantly. Doctors know, and we both know, what drugs will do."

Instead of continuing to write prescriptions, the doctors should have hospitalized Elvis for drug addiction, O'Grady said. "I think a doctor is obligated to take action in a situation like that or to abandon the patient by giving him notice. I don't think they should take his money and lavish gifts in return for writing prescriptions."

Were others besides doctors responsible for what happened to Elvis? Rivera asked.

"I not only place it on the doctors, but I place it on the people around him, too," O'Grady said. "They contributed to it. I think people like Colonel Tom Parker should not have allowed him to work when they became aware of his problems. If you notice the disintegration of Elvis Presley in the last three or four years—his weight problem, he almost collapsed on his last concert when he came off the stage.

"What are we talking about? We're talking about a money machine. They should have taken action. Allegedly they loved him. Everybody. Every time you read an article, they say, 'I was devoted to Elvis. The greatest man that ever lived.' You can't be devoted, take his money and watch him kill himself," O'Grady said.

O'Grady described Colonel Parker, Elvis's longtime manager, as "a rude, crude son of a bitch." He termed all the members of Elvis's entourage "ignorant shit kickers," with the exception of Joe Esposito. O'Grady said that Esposito "viewed his work for Elvis as a job and nothing more." The others, O'Grady said, stood back and "watched him commit suicide or watched him be murdered."

"Aren't you going too far using these powerful terms?" asked Rivera.

"Eventually drugs are going to kill you," O'Grady replied. "You can't beat drugs. They knew that. All of these people were fully aware of that. They know they were also being used. They were afraid for their jobs."

To illustrate, O'Grady recounted taking his family to the Sahara Hotel in Las Vegas in May of 1976 to watch Elvis perform. "It was a bad experience. I felt so strongly for him, I cried. He was fat. He had locomotive attacks where he couldn't walk. He forgot the words to his songs. I went backstage and looked at him, and I really thought he was going to die that night.

"Upon my return to Los Angeles I went to his attorney, Hookstratten, and he arranged between the two of us to get him in Scripps Medical Clinic on a confidential basis, the whole bit. But how were we going to do it? Well, the only person I know that has any power with Elvis was his ex-wife, Priscilla Presley. I told her what I thought. She agreed to help me. And she did. She went to Elvis, brought it up, what we were going to do. I have to say this, he told us all to drop dead."

"What about the men around Elvis, what did they do about his drug problem?" Rivera asked.

"In 1974, I told each and every one of them that they were violating the law by allowing prescriptions to be cashed in their names. As far as I was concerned this was a conspiracy under the law, state or federal law. They all agreed to cease and desist," O'Grady answered. He added his doubts that any of the aides were able to keep their promise very long if they wanted to continue working for Elvis. "Parker knew about the drugs and didn't care a bit as long as it didn't affect his pocketbook. And it was absurd for Vernon to say he didn't know. I delivered a copy of the investigation we did concerning the drugs to him. That was a long time before Elvis died."

"Why do you believe the doctors wrote the prescriptions?" Rivera asked.

"Well, any doctor, medical doctor, who would arbitrarily overprescribe narcotics is doing it for one of two reasons. He's doing it for money, or he's mesmerized, but a doctor shouldn't be mesmerized. A doctor should do exactly what he's supposed to do. This is not a general indictment of the medical profession. We're talking about a very, very small percentage. They were well paid for what they had done for Presley. Some of them were given great gifts of magnitudes that are hard to conceive for the average person. For what? The minute a doctor accepts a gift from a patient, he's just prostituted himself to the patient. So I think anytime a doctor screws up that way, he makes a bad mistake. And if he made it with my son, I would have killed him."

Rivera asked O'Grady, was there any chance the physicians failed to notice that Elvis was abusing drugs?

"Either they'd have to be a retarded alligator not to notice that or a totally incompetent medical doctor," he shot back. O'Grady then noted that the dentist identified in his investigation, Dr. Max Shapiro, admitted in the press that he had written prescriptions for Elvis in the names of entourage members. "He said he did it to protect Elvis's privacy. They all knew what was going on. Every one of them knew, and they knew it was illegal."

O'Grady said in the months before Elvis died the singer worried that his drug habits would be revealed in a book that his former bodyguards were writing. The detective said he went to Red and Sonny West and Dave Hebler and offered them money to give up the project. But the former bodyguards were bitter at Elvis for being fired and refused to stop writing the book. As Elvis had expected, the book, which was published two weeks before his death, contained numerous references to his drug abuse.

Did the former bodyguards tell the truth about Elvis's problems with drugs? Rivera asked. "Of course," the detective answered.

———

Rivera then turned to Jack Kelly. "What kind of drugs did your investigation reveal?" Rivera asked.

"You name it. All kinds of drugs," Kelly answered.

"Did he have what you call an open pipeline?"

"Yes," Kelly said.

"Did he get whatever he wanted?"

"He got whatever he wanted and when he wanted it. Most

of the doctors that I found were only too anxious to give drugs to him."

"Why?"

"For a variety of reasons. For one thing, there are doctors, who through carelessness or irresponsibility, get their patients addicted. Doctors who do it for monetary gain. And there are doctors, dentists, who do it because they're star struck. You find that out here, particularly in Hollywood. And unfortunately, Elvis was a victim of all three," Kelly said.

"What about Max Shapiro?"

"Max Shapiro was a source of supply for Elvis. Unquestionably."

"You're sure about that?"

"Yes, I'm positive."

"How, tell me?"

"Well, I don't think it's any secret. Max prescribed, over-prescribed drugs for different people in show business. He—Max, I would credit to be one of the ones who supplies it because he's star struck. I really don't believe Shapiro was making any money on it."

"Did you ever talk to Elvis about his drug abuse?"

"Yes, I talked to him—I guess it was in 1975. And at that time, both John O'Grady and myself warned him if he continued using drugs, as perniciously as he was, he was going to kill himself."

"How did Elvis respond when you told him that he was going to kill himself, if he continued using drugs?" Rivera asked.

"Elvis didn't feel that he was addicted. Elvis had a lot of pain, and a lot of medical problems, legitimate medical problems, where he needed drugs. And he didn't feel that he was addicted at all. But you know it only takes a week to ten days for a doctor to addict a patient."

"Was Elvis a medical addict?"

"Yes, I would say he was. I don't believe there's any question about it."

"Do you think that these various doctors and dentists, who you describe, contributed in a meaningful way, to his ultimate demise or death?"

"I feel that the doctors and dentists who prescribed drugs in such quantity to Elvis contributed directly to his death."

"Do you feel that Max Shapiro was one of these?"

"I know that Max was supplying Elvis with drugs. Addictive drugs. I reported Max to the Drug Enforcement Agency on two occasions, and I reported him to the state on another occasion because I felt the man had to be stopped. But he wasn't," Kelly said.

Rivera ended the interview and told Danny Goldfarb to find Shapiro, who had never been reluctant to talk to the press about Elvis. In fact, Shapiro often bragged that Elvis helped him marry his present wife and that he had educated Elvis about the use of drugs.

———

In early 1977, Elvis was vacationing in Palm Springs, California, with Ginger Alden and her sister Rosemary when Shapiro, who liked to be called "Dr. Max," dropped in for an extended visit. His fiancée Suzanne was with him. Shapiro, who maintained an office in Beverly Hills and another in Las Vegas, had a reputation in Hollywood as "Dr. Feelgood." In addition to Elvis, Shapiro had a number of other famous patients, including top movie and rock stars and moguls in the motion picture and entertainment industries. He frequently made house calls, normally carrying his black bag loaded with prescription drugs.

Dr. Max claimed to have designed an artificial heart and had talked to Elvis about the possibility of the singer financing a prototype. In return, Shapiro said he would give Elvis one of his mechanical hearts for his father, Vernon, and another one for Ginger's mother.

During his Palm Springs visit, Shapiro told Elvis that he had been planning on marrying his fiancée soon and had gone so far as to take out a marriage license. Elvis suggested that Max and Suzanne go through with the ceremony right then and there. Elvis persuaded his hairdresser, Larry Geller, who had a minister's license, to perform the ceremony. Ginger Alden would be maid of honor. Elvis called a jeweler and bought rings for the ceremony. He also provided flowers and music. The marriage was quite a scene, according to Shapiro and others in attendance.

After Elvis's death, Shapiro filed a $15,000 claim against the Presley estate for unpaid dental work for a musician whom Elvis had befriended. The probate court in Memphis looked at Shapiro's documentation and denied the claim.

The day after interviewing O'Grady and Kelly, Goldfarb reached Dr. Max in his Beverly Hills office and made an appointment. The next morning Goldfarb was ushered into Shapiro's office and met one of the strangest characters west of the waiting room at the Manhattan PD office. A small, slight man in his late fifties, Shapiro wore thick eyeglasses and a crudely tinted hairpiece that looked as though a black cat had crawled onto his head and died. It slipped from side to side as Shapiro's behavior became animated. Dr. Max was oblivious of the roving hairpiece, but it drove Goldfarb to distraction.

Apart from Shapiro's zany appearance, Goldfarb noticed peculiarities that jarred him even more. As he glanced around the office, he didn't see a sign of a dental chair or a trace of standard dental equipment. Shapiro explained that he didn't need regular equipment in his practice. Even for a blasé native New Yorker like Goldfarb, that sounded downright weird. He had heard that Shapiro made house calls, but he didn't believe it was actually true.

"I've never heard of a dentist who did that," Goldfarb said incredulously.

"Yes, I think I'm about the only one that does that," Shapiro proudly said. He was a medical big shot, he insisted, and bragged to Goldfarb that many of his patients were celebrities. He listed rock superstars, popular singers, and the heads of several Hollywood studios as examples of his celebrity clientele.

"And you go to some of these celebrities' homes in the middle of the night?" Goldfarb asked.

"Yes," Shapiro answered.

"And you perform dental procedures?"

"Yes. Sometimes. Not only for celebrities. I've gone to areas in the ghettos to blacks and to the slums," the dentist answered.

The Death of Elvis

Goldfarb could just imagine Dr. Max hotfooting it down to Watts with a bag loaded with drugs in the middle of the night. He scratched his head over what he was hearing and believed if he could get Shapiro talking about his favorite subject, narcotics, then it would not be too difficult to introduce Elvis into their conversation.

"This three-hour time zone change from New York to Los Angeles is killing me," Goldfarb said. Dr. Max nodded. "I can't sleep. I'm tired. This is killing me. Do you have anything that would help me sleep?"

At that, Shapiro reached into his desk and brought out two round white pills stamped "Rorer 714." "Try these Quaaludes. They ought to do the trick," Shapiro said breezily, handing the pills to the ex-cop. Goldfarb was flabbergasted. "I come here to investigate this guy for being a pill roller. He knows that, and he hands me Quaaludes. Incredible!"

Shapiro told Goldfarb that federal narcotics agents had given him a lot of trouble about the way he handed out pills—the kind of attention he regarded as persecution not only of himself but also of his method of treating patients. "They're just not scientists," he complained.

Given his experience with Shapiro and the Quaaludes, Goldfarb could just bet the narcs were all over this little guy. He hoped they didn't come knocking down the dentist's door while he was sitting here with the Quaaludes nesting in his pocket. "Wouldn't that be the shits," he told Thompson and Cole later. "I get the evidence in my pocket and get busted for illegally obtaining it."

Goldfarb picked up a batch of prescription forms already filled out and lying on the top of Shapiro's desk. He thumbed through them and read the drugs from each script out loud, "Percodan . . . Percodan—40 tablets . . . Percodan—35 tablets . . . Percodan—35 tablets . . . Demerol . . . Demerol . . . Percodan . . . Percodan . . . Demerol . . . Percodan . . . Percodan . . . Percodan . . . and Percodan . . ."

Goldfarb knew Percodan and Demerol were powerful central nervous system depressants that were used for patients suffering moderate to severe pain. He also knew both medications were highly addictive. "Did Elvis retain you, Doctor, because you prescribe things like Percodan and Demerol in a liberal manner?" Goldfarb asked.

"No, I don't think so," Shapiro answered and said that when he first met Elvis he had performed a root canal on him. He claimed he had given Elvis a copy of the *Physicians' Desk Reference* so that he could read up on drugs and their interactions with other drugs. He said that he and Elvis used to stay up all night talking about drugs and what they could do. "I'm not sure if I gave him his basic education, but I always discussed it with him. I always did try to make him knowledgeable. He was always careful about what he was taking, except that if a doctor gave it to him, he would take it without question. That was his nature. He just did what a doctor told him to do."

He told Goldfarb that he often wrote Elvis's prescriptions in the names of other members of the Presley entourage. "It was to preserve his privacy. And that's done here all the time."

Goldfarb asked the dentist if he could bring back Geraldo Rivera and a camera crew the next day and tape an interview with him. Shapiro consented. Then Goldfarb asked one more question.

"How do you respond to being called a 'Dr. Feelgood'?"

" 'Dr. Painless' would be all right," Shapiro answered.

X

THE ENTOURAGE
REVISITED

EVEN THOUGH Goldfarb had recorded his encounter with "Dr. Painless" secretly, Geraldo Rivera was scarcely prepared for the interview the next day. He looked at the skewed wig, remembered Goldfarb's account of the Quaaludes, and thought, "Where do I start?" Dead silence prevailed before Rivera blurted out, "How do you feel about being called 'Dr. Feelgood'?"

Shapiro blinked several times through his thick glasses and answered, " 'Dr. Low Pain' would be all right. . . . If I worked on a patient, they would never have pain. That is one of my very, very strong attitudes. I would . . . I myself am afraid of pain, and I understand what a patient goes through. I have been lied to by doctors. They tell me things wouldn't hurt, and they treated me, and it did hurt."

Suzanne Shapiro, who appeared thirty years younger than her husband, wafted in during the interview and seemed under the influence of something. She talked in a disconnected way about the thrill of marrying Dr. Max at Elvis's Palm Springs home. "He was a gentle man, very nice and peaceful. He was thin when I saw him, but afterwards, I understand, he blew up and got very fat.

When I saw him he was quite thin." Then she went off in a monologue about Elvis's "inner healing power."

Zany answers from Shapiro and his wife were giving Rivera a headache, so he called a halt to the questioning and parked
himself, Goldfarb, and the camera crew outside the office. A few
minutes later, the dentist emerged, carrying his black bag. Rivera
advanced toward him with the camera crew in tow.

"Is this the case that you take with you on your house
calls?" he asked. Shapiro denied it was. He said it was the bag he
normally carried around to treat his wife, Suzanne, and claimed she
required at least three kinds of drugs a day administered by him at
regular intervals.

"You wouldn't let me peek inside there would you?"

Shapiro refused, clutching his bag. "No, because I have
narcotics in there now. I don't like to have it opened. I don't like
people to know I carry these things because I've been robbed."

"What kinds of narcotics are in there?" Rivera demanded.

"There's Demerol. Demerol I think is the only one in there
now."

"Can we go in private and see what's in there?" Rivera
persisted.

Again Shapiro refused. Rivera asked the dentist if he came
to Shapiro's office and requested Quaaludes and was not a patient,
would Shapiro give him any Quaaludes.

"I wouldn't give them to you," Shapiro snapped.

"Then why Danny Goldfarb?" Rivera asked, pointing to
his investigator.

Shapiro said because Goldfarb was apprehensive, working
hard, not sleeping for days. "So I gave him a Quaalude. One or
two."

"But is that the way dentists generally operate?" Rivera
shot back.

"No, I wouldn't give it to him, normally, but simply because I felt he was telling the truth, and . . . I've never given it to
anybody else."

"You're so believing you just happened to believe Daniel?"
Rivera exclaimed. "And if you went to a studio, and there was a

musician, or if Elvis asked you, you wouldn't believe him the way you believed Daniel?"

"I don't give out pills at all, except under prescription or only to patients directly. Everyone has a record in my office," Shapiro answered.

"Was Goldfarb an exception?" Rivera asked.

"Not quite," Shapiro replied, claiming that Goldfarb wanted him to take care of his teeth before he gave him the Quaaludes. "I don't have a chart on him, but . . ."

"Dan, did he take care of your teeth?"

"No," Goldfarb replied.

―――――

Goldfarb's next stop was Las Vegas, where he was assigned to check out Elias Farad Ghanem, a forty-year-old Palestinian Arab who held passports of both Israeli and Lebanese origins. Dr. Ghanem was one of Elvis's regular physicians when he was playing Las Vegas. Interviewed on ABC's special the night of the death, Ghanem said, "Elvis was never a drug taker, and he never took drinks at all. The only thing he took was sleeping pills, just to sleep, just like everybody else, I guess, who was in his field. But I have never known Elvis to take any hard drugs whatsoever."

In Las Vegas, Goldfarb contacted some local narcotics officers who had been recommended by his former colleagues in the New York Police Department. Las Vegas officers identified the Landmark Pharmacy across from the Hilton as the place where most of the prescriptions that went to Elvis were filled.

Ghanem was a swarthy, baby-faced man who had been born in what became Haifa, Israel. He became house doctor for the Hilton (formerly the International) in 1966 and was a partner in an emergency room franchise at the Sunset Hotel in Vegas. In addition, from 1974 to 1978 Ghanem owned Jet Avia, an airplane leasing firm which had a $300,000 annual contract with one of the casinos to fly gamblers into the city.

To accommodate Elvis as a patient, Ghanem designed and built an extra room on top of his luxurious home to remove him from the grinding hotel routine. Elvis liked this hideaway during his continuing efforts to lose weight.

In efforts to contact Ghanem, Goldfarb spun his wheels. He left message after message at the doctor's office. ABC was doing a story on Elvis, Goldfarb said, and Dr. Ghanem probably would be mentioned. Would he be willing to do an interview? Through office intermediaries, Ghanem agreed. But when Goldfarb showed up, a receptionist told him the doctor had left town. To verify that line, Goldfarb had someone else call Ghanem's office and identify himself as a sick guest at the Hilton. Ghanem, the ally learned, was very much in town and agreed to make a sick call at the hotel. The direct approach wasn't working with Ghanem and he was to remain an unknown figure in the *20/20* investigation. Headway wouldn't be until later in Memphis as old members of Elvis's entourage began to reemerge.

―――――

One of the first was Marty Lacker, an Elvis buddy from high school and best man at his wedding. In June 1979, a month before Thompson began nosing around Memphis, Lacker published a book entitled *Elvis: Portrait of a Friend.* Lacker admitted waging his own battle with drug addiction and identified Dr. Nichopoulos as his source. Further, with refreshing candor Lacker said Elvis was hooked, too, and he pointed the finger of blame for much of Elvis's addiction in Nichopoulos's direction.

"I am not a medical doctor, nor was I at Graceland when Elvis died, or present at the autopsy," Lacker wrote. "I do not know the cause of Elvis Presley's death, but I do know that Elvis had a drug problem! That's a direct and honest statement by someone who was as close to him for over twenty years as any human being in this world. More important, it is a statement by someone who shared the same drug problem with him."

Lacker also blamed Dr. Max Shapiro for recklessly giving narcotics to Elvis. Citing an example, Lacker said he called Shapiro from Memphis and arranged a quick flight to Las Vegas to pick up a prescription that Elvis wanted Shapiro to write. "I called Shapiro and told him Elvis needed some pills, either Empirin [with] codeine or Demerol, and asked him if I could pick up the prescription when I got out there. He said yes. So I flew to Los Angeles, where I met Sonny [West] and the two of us went on to Vegas. After completing our business there, we went by Shapiro's office and picked up the prescription, which I later had filled."

Lacker's book, published in Memphis, received little or no attention. But Charlie Thompson spotted it as an important breakthrough for *20/20*. Unlike Elvis's former bodyguards, Lacker had no ax to grind with Elvis and was considered a credible source by most members of Elvis's inner circle.

Lacker was fifteen when he moved to Memphis from New York in 1952. To students at Humes High School, he talked and dressed funny. Not surprisingly, he was an outsider who struck up a friendship with a loner named Elvis. Lacker also knew two other students who later would play major roles in Elvis's personal life and career, Red West and George Klein. Lacker played football with West and was involved in high school politics with Klein.

Lacker, who became fat and bald as he aged, would seem to be an unlikely member of Elvis's southern good-ole-boy fraternity of employees, relatives, and hangers-on. Lacker was a Northerner, born and raised in New York City, but then again so was Joe Esposito, who hailed from Chicago. Lacker was Jewish, but then so were George Klein and Alan Fortas, another Memphian who for twenty years was an off-and-on Presley entourage member. But what set Lacker apart from the other members of Elvis's rat pack was his sensitivity, insight, and reluctance to harm another human being needlessly. He remained different from the loud, crude, obnoxious, often violent people who measured their friendship with Elvis in terms of the good times and the next gift.

Lacker began working for Elvis on a full-time basis in 1961. Before that he had served a hitch in the army and had worked for several southern radio stations as a disc jockey. Lacker, his wife Patsy, and their children had lived with Elvis at Graceland for several years. In 1963 Elvis made Lacker foreman of his operation. He held that job until the middle of 1967, when Colonel Parker demoted him. From that point on Lacker worked for Elvis on a part-time basis and had started his own music publishing and promotion business. When Lacker's business fell on hard times and he became seriously addicted to drugs, Elvis helped him financially.

Against that backdrop and given his reflective nature, Lacker's admission that both he and his old friend had wrecked their lives with drugs was a wrenching experience. Lacker shared authorship of the book, printed by Wimmer Brothers Books of Memphis, with his wife Patsy, and Leslie S. Smith, a professional writer. Each wrote a segment of the three-part book.

Patsy Lacker, the mother of two girls and a boy, vented her frustration on Elvis for his cavalier treatment of women, especially women married to members of his "Memphis Mafia." She said that Elvis viewed "wife" as a four-letter word that carried the same crude connotation as any other base profanity or barnyard obscenity. But Patsy Lacker reserved most of her scorn for Dr. Nichopoulos. She blamed him for supplying the pills that addicted her husband and nearly destroyed her family. And she claimed the Memphis internist practiced the same kind of medicine on Elvis.

"I went to Graceland to see Nichopoulos and told him to stop the drugs," Patsy Lacker wrote. "I told him I was going to report them all if anything happened to Marty. I begged and threatened, and Dr. Nichopoulos laughed at me. I'm only sorry now that I was too afraid to carry out the threats. There were thousands of pills, and I mean thousands. I don't know how many Elvis took a day, or if they led to his death, but I do know that he went downhill just as Marty did."

Leslie Smith did his homework in researching his portion of the book. He interviewed Dave Hebler and Red and Sonny West and obtained details about where and from whom Elvis obtained his drugs—details not specified in their book. The former bodyguards told Smith that Elvis frequently used cocaine and other illegal drugs as well as prescription medicine.

But Smith's real coup came when he obtained certified copies of prescriptions that Nichopoulos wrote for Marty Lacker and that Lacker had filled at Kessler's Pharmacy in Memphis over a forty-six-month period. The list Smith compiled consisted of 6,464 Placidyls, 3,204 Darvon, 1,508 Hycomine, 708 Empirin Codeine #3, 500 Dalmane, 400 Valium, 216 Darvocet, 200 Valmid, and other assorted pills that totaled 13,291 pills in roughly 1,300 days, or an average of ten pills per day.

Smith showed the long list to Sonny West and asked him to comment. West was amazed that Marty took 6,464 Placidyls in four years and survived and added this comment: "In four years? I'll bet you I didn't get more than 500 from Nick in four years. But I'll tell you, Marty was really hooked on them. But if he did that for Marty, if Marty used that many, you'll find out on Elvis that the volume will be much higher. The Placidyl and Darvon will be much higher. The Valium will be much higher, those are the things that I know Elvis used a lot."

Leslie Smith tried to find out how many pills Dr. Nichopoulos prescribed to Elvis, but he was unsuccessful. The doctor wouldn't talk to him, and he had no means of uncovering Elvis's prescriptions on his own. Still, the Lackers and Les Smith had raised some questions that cried out for answers.

Thompson tracked down Marty Lacker and arranged an interview. After looking at Lacker's prescriptions, the producer wished there were some way to come up with similar documentation on Elvis. He knew those prescription records would remove all doubt that Elvis had abused drugs.

When Thompson met Marty Lacker, he discovered a wrecked human being who was pulling himself back together and rebuilding his life. The bearded Lacker had put on even more weight and had less hair than when his picture was taken for his book jacket. During this and subsequent interviews Thompson noticed that Lacker's hands shook, that his voice frequently trembled, and that he was uncomfortable talking about Elvis's problems and his own.

"I wish I had never had anything to do with that damned book!" Lacker told Thompson.

"Why? Isn't what you, Patsy, and Leslie Smith wrote true?" Thompson asked.

"It's all too true, and that's why I wish I never had anything to do with it," Lacker replied. His look was unmistakably sad.

But Lacker loosened up. He told Thompson that in 1976 when medical authorities reviewed what Dr. Nichopoulos had prescribed for him—more than 13,000 pills in less than four years—they were astonished. Then they asked Lacker's drug rehabilitation counselor, who had furnished the records, if Lacker were still alive. Told that he had barely survived, the officials asked the drug counselor if Lacker was still an addict and were amazed to learn that Lacker had managed to withdraw from the pills on his own. "So the next question they asked was if I was in a mental institution, and the counselor said, 'No, thank God!' "

"It was that bad, Marty?" Thompson asked.

"Sure, it was," he answered. Lacker said he had received a lot of complaints and verbal abuse from other former members of Elvis's inner circle and from Presley fans for highlighting Elvis's drug problems and for mentioning Dr. Nichopoulos's role in that addiction. But he said he was so confident about the veracity of his book that he didn't take out any liability insurance against defamation suits. "Why? The book is true," Lacker explained. "So much has been written about Elvis since he has died that people really didn't know what to believe. You had books and things written by people that claimed to have been as close to him as they could be, and they weren't."

Lacker traced Elvis's drug problems to the early 1960s when he was making movies. "He took appetite suppressants, because he always had a weight problem, especially doing the movies. As you know, a camera will pick up one, two, three, four pounds whatever and make it look even greater. And so he took appetite suppressants."

When did that lead to the taking of sleeping pills, the downers?

"Well, because he was a hyper person anyway. He had so much energy that later on, you know, he just needed something to unwind, to put him to sleep. So, you know, he was prescribed some sleeping pills."

At what point did he begin to take more than the prescribed amount?

"Oh, I guess somewhere around 1975. Something like that."

What about Vernon? Didn't Vernon ever try to stop him?

"To my knowledge, no."

Did his girlfriend Linda Thompson try to stop him?

"Yeah. I guess she talked to him for a while about it. You know, I really don't know, she wouldn't do that around anybody else if she did. But, I'm sure she had, you know, some concern. Because Linda loved Elvis very much. She really cared for him."

Thompson asked Lacker if he had any hard feelings against Nichopoulos or against any of the other doctors who had over-prescribed to him or to Elvis. Lacker shook his head and said that he bore no hard feelings.

"Then who is the bad guy in all this?" Thompson asked.

"It was probably the guy who invented all that stuff, you know. Because I'm sure in a lot of cases it's used, you know, to help people, but there ought to be more control over it," Lacker replied, nearly breaking down and crying.

Before Thompson left, Lacker mentioned that there might be another Elvis book in the writing stage. Dick Grob, Elvis's former chief of security at Graceland, was in the process of writing a book. Lacker said he didn't know much about it, but Grob was still around Memphis. "Watch out for Grob. He's gotten kind of spooky, seeing all kinds of conspiracies in things," Lacker said.

There wasn't any love lost between Lacker and Grob. Lacker said Grob had called him "Judas Iscariot" to a group of fans after the publication of *Elvis: Portrait of a Friend.* Later on Grob would say of Lacker to a similar group, "With friends like that, who needs enemies."

Thompson thanked Lacker for the tip and asked where he could find Dick Grob. Lacker gave him Grob's last known telephone number and home address. But the number was disconnected. Grob had moved to a new home in suburban East Memphis. His new number was unlisted, so Jim Cole called in a favor from a dependable police contact. In about thirty minutes Cole had the new number and also learned that Grob had recently opened an office as a private detective. Cole called Grob on his new unlisted number and left a message on his answering machine. Then Thompson and Cole drove to Grob's new address. It was in one of the city's most fashionable neighborhoods, an odd place for a private detective to be living. After repeated bell-ringing and knocking, nobody answered the front door. Thompson left a calling card with Cole's telephone number written on it.

———

The next day Grob called Cole's house. His voice was deep, measured, and direct. "Spooky," Cole thought to himself as he arranged a meeting. Grob suggested a midafternoon time at Denny's restaurant on Summer Avenue, a thoroughfare north of Grob's house. Thompson and Cole were sitting in a booth next to the front window sipping coffee when Grob strolled in wearing jeans and a T-shirt. The restaurant was short on customers at that hour, and Grob didn't have to be a detective to pick out Thompson and Cole as the two newsmen who wanted to see him. Grob was tall, rangy, and shifty eyed. He wore a mustache that seemed to accentuate his slight, Dorothy Kilgallen–type chin and hadn't shaved that day as if to suggest from the outset that this meeting was an imposition.

After exchanging some stilted pleasantries, it was clear enough to Cole that the vibes between Thompson and Grob were clashing. Charlie Thompson hardly came across as a producer doing a puff piece on Elvis. And Dick Grob was mindful that any new and substantial story on Elvis would necessarily be unflattering.

Grob had been a part of the Air Force Academy's first graduating class and had served as a fighter pilot, flying McDonnell F-101 Voodoos. After leaving the military, he had signed on the Palm Springs, California, police department and held the rank of sergeant when he first started running errands for Elvis, the sometime resident celebrity, in 1969. As he did for Dr. Max Shapiro, Elvis paid for Grob's wedding. He also gave Grob and his wife, Marilyn, a new car as a wedding gift.

In the two years since Elvis's death, Grob had teamed up with Charlie Hodge, Elvis's rhythm guitarist, and they were regular speakers singing Elvis's praises on the fan club circuit. Grob was also helping Hodge write and edit an Elvis fan magazine, and the pair had opened a garish Elvis souvenir and trinket shop across the

139

street from Graceland. All in all, Grob was going through some pretty hardscrabble times trying to cash in long term on Elvis's memory. However, when he showed up to meet with Thompson and Cole, he was playing the role of hard-ball former cop, veteran fighter jock, and know-it-all, tough ex-security chief. In return, Thompson was treating Grob like a washed-up has-been, whose life had been put in reverse two years earlier.

In Grob's stated view, *20/20* was wasting its time in Memphis. There was nothing new to report on Elvis for the moment; however, he was in fact writing a book on Elvis's death—a narrative based on his in-house investigation. Like everybody else, Grob said, *20/20* would have to wait on the book for any new information about Elvis. At that, Thompson and Grob began quarreling across the table, all but ignoring Cole, who was trying vainly to learn more about Grob's book.

Injecting cajolery into the confrontation, Cole allowed as how Grob seemed to be everywhere countering intrusive reporters. "Like that reporter Ken Lefoli from Toronto," Cole suggested. Lefoli, despite his first-person posturings, had written the best one-shot story on the death, called "The Last Days of Elvis Presley," for *The Toronto Star,* a year after the fact. In covering a heap of ground, Lefoli had attempted to talk to Dr. Les Hofman, the dentist who had treated Elvis just before the death. Instead of talking to Hofman, though, Lefoli got a phone call at his hotel from Dick Grob, whom he recognized as Graceland's security chief. For Lefoli, it was a neat episode illustrating the intricate stone wall that Memphis had built around Elvis.

"Yeah, that guy was obnoxious," Grob said, with just the hint of a smile. Well, he hadn't really met obnoxious yet, Cole thought as he eyed Thompson, who had regained his composure and bitten his tongue.

With all the garbage that had been written about Elvis, Cole asked, how was Grob's book going to be different? It was going to be a clinical, no-nonsense book, "like a good, straightforward police investigation," Grob answered.

Assuming Grob could write such a book, what were his sources? This was what worried Cole the most. After all, Grob was an insider who at least to a point had had the confidence of Vernon

Presley. He posed a real threat to upstaging the *20/20* investiga-tion. So Cole plunged forward with the $64 question. "Do you have the autopsy report?"

"I have access to it," Grob answered and with a smug grin added that he wasn't at liberty to discuss any details.

Cole took a different approach. If Grob in fact was writing a book and could prove it, Cole said, then *20/20* might be willing to plug it on national TV. In exchange Grob must agree to an on-camera interview with no strings attached. But before Grob could reply, Cole kept up the banter. He and Thompson had been talking to members of the entourage and had heard so many tales about phantom books that they had quit paying attention to them.

Grob bridled at the suggestion that his book was a smoke-screen. "I'm writing it with a guy named Dan Mingori, and I've already copyrighted a summary. That's all I'm telling you guys. End of interview." With that, Grob got up and left. But he hadn't seen the last of Charlie Thompson.

———

Without mentioning his book title, Grob had disclosed just enough to give Thompson the leverage to acquire the copyrighted summary. Thompson frequently worked in Washington with a free-lance reporter named David Rothman, a bookwormish whiz at finding obscure documents in D.C. Thompson telephoned Roth-man to run a check on two prospective authors—Dick Grob and Dan Mingori—and directed him to the federal office in Virginia that handled copyrighted material. Naturally, Thompson wanted a copy of every page that Rothman could uncover. Rothman dropped everything. Within hours he called Thompson back. He had located the material, but he couldn't see it or make a copy of it unless it was requested as part of a legal proceeding. Thompson smiled. "No problem," he said.

Rothman jotted down a Memphis phone number that Thompson gave him and listened to further instructions. He was to return to the copyright office the next morning at 10:00 A.M. and was to call the Memphis number collect.

That night Thompson and Cole met with attorney Mike Pleasants to figure out how to make Grob's copyrighted material a part of their Elvis autopsy lawsuit. "I guess we really have to take Grob's deposition," Pleasants said, "since he claims to have a copy of Elvis's autopsy. We need to know how he got it, so requesting his material from the U.S. Copyright Office is certainly legitimate and proper."

The contents of Copyright No. TXu 18-490 amazed them. On page five, for example, Grob and Mingori's version of events surrounding Elvis's death had Grob in command of operations, removing the body from the morgue and carrying with him some sort of court order protecting the Elvis autopsy record from outsiders.

Pleasants had asked his junior partner, Chuck Harrell, who was assigned to work on the autopsy suit, to go through Grob's manuscript. Harrell, who had the dapper looks of an old-time Mississippi riverboat gambler, even down to his mustache, and a poker face to match, was puzzled. Harrell ran his hand through his black hair and observed, "First of all, there was no autopsy document prepared before the middle of October 1977, and yet Grob claims to have a court order giving him custody of the autopsy on August 16, 1977. Secondly, our research shows that there was no such court order. This looks like it was all made up."

The working title of Grob's manuscript was *The Elvis Conspiracy.* In weaving a narrative supporting that theme, Grob cast Ginger Alden as his central character. He portrayed her as a cold-hearted girlfriend out to capitalize on Elvis, either in life or death. Grob claimed that Elvis was about to dump Ginger, wasn't taking her on the upcoming tour, and actually had plans to take along another girlfriend named Alicia Kerwin. Aware of Elvis's disaffection, Grob said, Ginger was entirely capable of revenge.

Writing with Mingori's assistance in the third person and frequently referring to himself as "Dick," Grob asserted that Ginger had opened negotiations for selling her exclusive story to *The National Enquirer* before she alerted anyone at Graceland that Elvis was out cold on the bathroom floor. Grob's primary source for this claim was James Kirk, a free-lance reporter/photographer who was on assignment for *The National Enquirer* on the day Elvis died. According to Grob's account, Kirk received a telephone call at approximately 11:30 A.M. from a familiar female voice. Her message was for Kirk to stand by for an important telephone call from Graceland, Grob's account claimed. Although the caller didn't identify herself, Kirk told Grob he had spoken to Ginger on several occasions previously and recognized her voice. According to Grob's account, Ginger was beginning to peddle her story a full three hours before calling downstairs that Elvis was in trouble.

Grob wrote that he investigated further to see if he could find some circumstantial evidence to verify Kirk's account. He claimed to have found it in interviews with Joe Esposito, Al Strada, and Charlie Hodge—all of whom reported that Ginger looked fresh, all showered, dressed, and made up when they raced upstairs. Grob also said he learned from two maids on duty that they heard the shower running upstairs at a time when Elvis must have been unconscious on the bathroom floor. Asking why Ginger would be so disloyal to Elvis, Grob said that obviously the answer was money.

Pleasants then flipped to the last page of the synopsis. In the last paragraph he found Grob's thesis. Grob contended that the autopsy proved once and for all that Elvis had only a few months to live beyond August 1977 anyway and would have died more painfully from bone cancer.

Thompson, Cole, and their lawyers were stunned. Where did this theory come from? There was utterly no hint of cancer in any of the material that they had read or from any information they had gleaned in interviews. Putting all that together with the kind of Elvis hustler Grob had become, the idea of impending death by bone cancer seemed preposterous.

"But suppose this guy's right?" asked Pleasants, ever the skeptic. "What then?"

Indeed. Thompson and Cole began putting their heads together. They had to find a way to a medical insider who could confirm or deny if the autopsy turned up cancer. They went looking for that one source, and their luck was holding. They found two.

XI

THE CANCER QUESTION

Dɪᴄᴋ Gʀᴏʙ's copyrighted claim that Elvis was dying from incurable bone cancer was like a booby trap set to obliterate the story that the *20/20* team now had spent weeks putting together. Toxicology reports verified on the West Coast pointed to a drug death. Supporting evidence from old members of Elvis's entourage was beginning to take shape. Yet what did all that matter if in fact cancer had been diagnosed and Elvis was being doped up to make his last days as comfortable as possible? What if Dick Grob had the real story?

In his attic office one night in August 1979, Jim Cole eyed the telephone on his desk and gulped. Taking the direct approach that might well alienate not just one but several sources of information, Cole dialed the home number of a pathologist on the Baptist Hospital autopsy team.

The pathologist came on the line. First, Cole apologized for the irregular nature of his call, then explained the extraordinary circumstances prompting it. He wasn't going to ask the pathologist to violate any confidences but thought there might be some latitude in discussing what *wasn't* in the autopsy.

144

Cole heard the pathologist say a noncommittal "Uh huh." So he continued talking.

From all appearances, Cole said, the toxicology was the key to the Elvis postmortem. But what if there was some disease process—Jerry Francisco said heart problems and now there was a new hypothesis—that would prove embarrassing if *20/20* went on national television saying Elvis Presley died of drugs?

There was a long silence. Cole expected a brush-off. But the doctor began an explanation of how thorough the autopsy had been, how it had been checked, rechecked and, if the truth were told, overchecked by top consultants around the country. Occasionally, Cole interjected a question, and the doctor began to loosen up.

The new hypothesis, Cole said, was Grob's bone cancer story. Could there be any substance to it? Again there was tingling silence, then a chuckle.

"No. There's no truth to that," the pathologist said, adding that he had a vague recollection of a bone cancer rumor, along with ones about lupus and other rare diseases.

During the autopsy, Cole's source went on to explain, Dr. James Holbert extracted bone marrow samples and later had tested them extensively. "There was no bone cancer. There was no cancer anywhere. There's no truth to that story at all," the pathologist said.

Where did Grob come up with his information about cancer? Surely, not out of thin air? Cole's source didn't have the answer but did offer a suggestion. "It might be important to ask who would benefit by diverting attention from the tox reports."

Of course, Thompson was equally relieved that the bone cancer scare was over. But mainly, as was always the case whenever he was misled, Thompson fumed. He sure did look forward to the day when he could confront Dick Grob on camera. And he wondered if Grob was as far off base with his allegations about Ginger calmly applying makeup with a dead body in her midst and the Stanley brothers zonked out and derelict of duty.

———

The Death of Elvis

Sidetracked only temporarily from their plans, Thompson and Cole chose for the time being to work separately on the investigation. Cole's assignment was to dig up financial and other background on Dr. George Nichopoulos in anticipation of obtaining an interview. Thompson, meanwhile, tried to find a way to hurdle one of the story's biggest stumbling blocks. Getting through to a member of the autopsy team for direction and background over the telephone was one thing. But Thompson wanted somebody who was there on camera and interviewed about the official ruling and what really happened. Already he had a full list of those present. Were they all still working for Baptist Hospital? If not, where were they?

Thompson contacted one of the medical sources he had developed since returning to Memphis—one likely to know where Thompson's best chances lay. "You go see Dr. Noel Florendo," the source suggested. "He's a pathologist who participated in the autopsy. He operated the electron microscope and did other things during the autopsy. He's a smart fellow, who knows just about everything that went on. He's left Baptist Hospital and is now working at Doctors Hospital." But don't call, Thompson's source added, just drop in and say you've already done an extensive interview with Dr. Eric Muirhead. "Which is true," the source said. "Only you don't have to tell Noel that Dr. Muirhead was under orders not to tell you anything of any importance."

Thompson headed to Doctors Hospital, the same hospital where Nichopoulos was reached on the afternoon of Elvis's death. It was a come-lately facility in Memphis and ranked a distant fourth in public recognition behind Baptist, Methodist, and St. Joseph hospitals. On the day Thompson showed up, Florendo was working as a specialist of Methodist Hospital's Duckworth Laboratory, which was performing pathological services under contract to Doctors Hospital.

Florendo was in the lab and greeted Thompson in a friendly manner. Thompson repeated just what his source had instructed him to say. He mentioned Dr. Muirhead and then asked Florendo for an on-camera interview. While not exactly thrilled by the prospect, Florendo was agreeable. Thompson then summoned the closest videotape camera crew he could locate—a free-lance crew based near Atlanta.

———

At ten the next morning Thompson, Geraldo, and the camera crew showed up at Doctors Hospital for the interview. With Geraldo was his younger brother, Craig Rivera, an assistant producer at *20/20* who was considered something of a jinx. Quickly they set up their camera in Dr. Florendo's laboratory and began to roll. "Not a hitch so far," Thompson thought, but as Geraldo Rivera asked his first question, trouble started.

Lewis Bailey, the cameraman, signalled Thompson to stop the interview. The camera had just shorted out. They had no picture, no sound. Thompson, Bailey, and the sound technician went back to the crew's van to see if they could find a way to repair the camera. At that point, the sky turned dark, and it began to rain furiously. It was steamy inside the van with the windows rolled up. The tension was nearly as thick as the humidity.

"Can you fix that damned thing, Lewis?" Thompson demanded.

"I can jury-rig it and keep it operating for about a half an hour," Bailey said. "Keep the interview short and to the point." As he finished making hasty repairs on the camera, the rain stopped. Back inside the lab Bailey repositioned the camera on his tripod and told Rivera they could begin again. "Keep it short and sweet," Thompson whispered in Rivera's ear. "The camera's liable to blow up at any time." Rivera nodded.

"Dr. Florendo, in your medical judgment, was there any evidence that Elvis Presley died of a heart attack?" he asked.

"There was no gross evidence of a heart attack," the pathologist answered.

Was he surprised by Dr. Jerry Francisco's announcement on the night of the autopsy that Elvis died of cardiac arrhythmia?

"Personally, yes. I was surprised."

"What is cardiac arrhythmia?"

"Cardiac arrhythmia is best explained as an irregularity in

147

the heartbeat, sufficiently irregular enough to cause death." And in Elvis Presley's case? Florendo said that he could not find enough evidence to substantiate cardiac arrhythmia.

So Elvis didn't die of a heart attack?

"In my opinion, I did not see any evidence of a heart attack, morphologically."

"Morphologically, meaning?"

"Meaning there was no gross evidence of a heart attack."

"I understand that you agree with Dr. Muirhead's conclusions?"

Florendo nodded.

"And those conclusions being?"

"Polypharmacy. That Elvis Presley died of the interaction of several drugs."

Florendo told Rivera that on the night of Elvis's autopsy there was a consensus by all doctors who participated that Jerry Francisco would tell the press only that Elvis had died of unknown causes. They were angry when Francisco broke his word to them. Later, after all the lab work had come in, and the diagnosis of polypharmacy had been made by Dr. Muirhead and his staff, Dr. Florendo said he "was surprised and shocked" that Dr. Francisco insisted that drugs played no role in Elvis's death.

Rivera told Florendo that he found it amazing and incredible that this information had not yet been made public. "How they can perpetuate this myth is beyond me, really," he said. Florendo agreed.

"Thank you, Doctor. You can't imagine how much help you've just given us," Thompson said as they left.

Just outside the hospital, Geraldo Rivera exclaimed, "What a coup! What a score! Way to go, Chazbo!" They took the tape back to the van and rigged up a monitor to make sure that the camera had not failed during the interview. The tape played back perfectly. The sound and picture were both of good quality.

"Craig, hand carry this tape back to New York and guard it with your life," Geraldo said. "And if anything happens to it, I'll personally kill you." Craig put the tape with his gear from the hotel and headed for the airport.

That afternoon Geraldo Rivera and Thompson brainstormed other aspects of the investigation. There wasn't any progress on interviewing Dr. Nichopoulos, who wasn't returning phone calls. The lawsuit was going slowly, but Mike Pleasants was scheduling depositions. However, with the Florendo interview—direct confirmation from the inside that the official ruling contradicted what the Baptist Hospital autopsy had found—Thompson and Rivera believed they had the makings of a good broadcast. They were on an emotional high when Rivera caught a nonstop to Los Angeles late that afternoon. But by the next morning both of them were coming unglued.

Badly shaken and upset, Geraldo telephoned Thompson in Memphis. "I hate to tell you this, but Craig went out last night and lost the Florendo tapes. He can't find them."

Thompson exploded. "I'll kill the fucker! He's dead! I'm on the next plane to New York. Even though he's your brother, I hope you've fired him."

"I told him to offer a reward, to look everywhere, and to find that tape no matter what it cost," Rivera said. "There's no sense in you flying up there. If we can't find them, then you've got to figure out something else."

Thompson knew he had pushed his luck far enough with Florendo, who sooner or later, probably sooner, would mention the on-camera interview to Dr. Muirhead or others at Baptist Hospital. "If he does that," Thompson said, "then we're out of action."

Rivera told Thompson to calm down and do nothing drastic for twenty-four hours. "I'll call you back just as soon as I hear anything from Craig."

Thompson spent a miserable day in his hotel room. He didn't have the heart to tell Lewis Bailey and Jim Cole about the lost tape. About 5:00 P.M. that same day, Rivera telephoned Thompson again. Craig had found the missing tapes, he said.

"It cost him some money, and he refuses to tell me where he found them, but they're safe and have been duplicated," Rivera said.

Thompson was dumbfounded, but relieved that another crisis was over.

The Death of Elvis

To help flesh out the business side of Elvis's life, Thompson began pursuing a courthouse lead he had found on the first day of his investigation. He located Michael McMahon, a Memphis real estate developer and bond salesman, who had formed a partnership with Elvis, Nichopoulos, and Joe Esposito to set up a group for franchising racquetball clubs around the country. The idea apparently originated with Nichopoulos, who considered himself an expert in the sport. The physician had persuaded Elvis to take it up and to build a private racquetball court at Graceland for exercise.

The joint venture was named Presley Center Courts, Inc., and its plans called for establishing at least fifty of the courts around the country. The partnership had planned on having a contractor build the first two courts in Memphis and Nashville, Tennessee, for about $1 million and then leasing them back from the contractor at a rate of about $12,000 per month each. Elvis was supposed to contribute $1.3 million in exchange for 25 percent of the deal.

Colonel Tom Parker first objected to the deal because Elvis was lending his name to the venture. Parker, who had not been consulted in advance, would receive no compensation. But beyond Parker's criticism, the venture was undercapitalized and began to go broke during its first year of operation. When the contractor had difficulty getting paid, he went to Elvis, who pulled out of the deal, leaving McMahon, Nichopoulos, and Esposito financially stranded. To protect their own interests, the threesome hired attorneys and sued Elvis.

McMahon was a dark-haired, stocky man of about medium height, who was in his early forties. He had been associated in the business deal with Elvis from the beginning of 1975 through the early part of 1977. And he knew about Elvis and drugs. "I think that drugs were the biggest part of Elvis Presley's life the last two and a half years I knew him," McMahon told Thompson.

Just before their business relationship blew up, McMahon recalled, he met with Elvis and Colonel Parker in Lake Tahoe. The racquetball venture seemed to be on a smooth track. But a few weeks later, McMahon said, Elvis called him at home late one night and had Joe Esposito on the line, too. "Elvis was just completely incoherent and irrational to the point where he was accusing me of different things—illegal things. And then he told me he was going to kill me, and I said to him, 'Well, Elvis, are you all right? What's wrong?' " McMahon said.

"Then I got mad, and he threatened my life again. He told me he didn't want anything to do with me or Dr. Nichopoulos or anybody that's involved in the business anymore, that we were doing him dirty as far as stealing money from him."

After the stormy call, McMahon contacted Dr. Nichopoulos and asked what had gotten into Elvis all of a sudden. According to McMahon, Nichopoulos told him: "When he takes a certain drug, he gets very paranoid. The drug will wear off and after it does, everything will be fine again."

But it wasn't, and the partnership dissolved. McMahon recalled being in Nichopoulos's office discussing the lawsuit against Elvis. Because of it, Elvis had fired Nichopoulos and refused to allow him to travel on concert tours. Instead, Elvis was relying on Dr. Elias Ghanem, the Las Vegas physician. During the discussion, McMahon said, a call came into Dr. Nichopoulos from his nurse, Tish Henley. Although Elvis had banned Nichopoulos from the tours, he still allowed Nurse Henley on the concert circuit. McMahon said Tish Henley was worried that Elvis was receiving bad medical care. "She was very concerned that Dr. Ghanem was giving him different injections of some type of drug substance and that the needles were dirty. And they were really concerned about the hepatitis problem."

Then within moments, McMahon said, Colonel Parker called Nichopoulos. "He begged him to come back and get with Elvis, because they were really concerned about the shows that he was doing." Shortly after these calls, Elvis fell apart on tour and had to be hospitalized and detoxified for drugs.

McMahon said Elvis was in terrible physical condition during the years he knew him. He estimated Elvis's weight at between 240 and 255 pounds. He said Elvis's bodyguards described him as a "zombie." Elvis had no muscle tone, McMahon said, and "was just a block of blubber."

Did the bodyguards or other people around Elvis attempt to manipulate him, knowing that certain drugs would make him respond in certain ways?

The Death of Elvis

"I would say that was absolutely true," McMahon told Thompson. "Just knowing the different mood that a certain drug would create after he took it, they would know how to approach him at different times about what they wanted. When Elvis was generous to people, that was when he was on uppers." According to the developer, Presley hangers-on often bragged that they received expensive cars and other presents from Elvis when he took uppers. "And then a lot of the people he'd buy the cars for would go out the next day and sell them," McMahon said.

Thompson had already made several unsuccessful attempts to see Nichopoulos. The doctor flatly refused to see him. McMahon still maintained a social relationship with the doctor and his family. He said Nichopoulos was worried that the Dilaudid prescription he had written for Elvis just hours before his death would be discovered. Thompson knew that Dilaudid often was called "drugstore heroin." It's much stronger than heroin and can give an addict a high from three to six hours. According to Red and Sonny West, Dilaudid, which was normally prescribed for terminally ill cancer patients, was Elvis's favorite drug.

According to McMahon, Nichopoulos wrote the last prescription and gave it to Ricky Stanley, Elvis's stepbrother, who took it to the Baptist Hospital pharmacy and had it filled. Nichopoulos claimed that the Baptist Hospital pathologists who participated in Elvis's autopsy were unaware of this prescription.

Thompson was puzzled. He rummaged through his briefcase and located the toxicology reports on Elvis. Dilaudid wasn't listed. Could they have missed it? Later Thompson asked one of his friends at Baptist Hospital to comb the pharmacy's records and see if there really was a final Dilaudid prescription. McMahon's information checked out. Nichopoulos had written a Dilaudid on August 16, 1977, and had it filled in the all-night pharmacy at Baptist Hospital. The pharmacist who had filled it was W. S. Nash, who retired shortly after Elvis's death. Thompson's source provided Nash's last known address.

Thompson jumped into his rental car and drove to that East Memphis address, where he found a real estate sign marked "Sold" in the front yard. He knocked at the front door and discovered the house was vacant. He copied the real estate agent's name and phone number off the sign and found the nearest telephone booth. Real estate agents are usually the most accessible people in the world, and this one was no exception. She told Thompson she didn't know where Mr. Nash had moved but gave him the phone number of the pharmacist's son, Jesse.

Thompson called Jesse Nash and explained why he was looking for his father. Jesse Nash said his father was in poor health and now was living in Madisonville, Kentucky. That Dilaudid prescription, Jesse Nash said, had been troubling his father ever since he filled it and it might do him some good to talk it out. Jesse Nash called his brother, Douglas, who owned a men's store in Madisonville and asked him to set up an interview with their father. Quickly Thompson collected Lewis Bailey, his sound technician, and camera equipment, and chartered a plane to Madisonville. Thompson and the crew flew there, rented a car at the small airport, and drove to the men's store, located near the town square. Douglas Nash took them to his father's modest ground floor garden-style apartment.

W. S. Nash was a small, slender man in his early seventies, frail and in poor health. He told Thompson he was the only night pharmacist on duty in the early morning hours of August 16, 1977. Then he began a narrative that obviously had run through his mind many times before.

"About 2:30 A.M., a young man came in with a prescription to be filled. The prescription was from Dr. George Nichopoulos for Elvis Presley. It was for six Dilaudid tablets, four milligrams," he said. The young man, whom Thompson identified for him as Ricky Stanley, paid for the prescription and left. "There were no unusual circumstances of any kind. It was a simple, straightforward transaction."

Thompson noticed Nash grip his leather armchair tightly as he recalled details with remarkable precision.

"Well, it didn't mean too much at the time. It was only the next day, the next afternoon, I heard on TV that Elvis had died,

153

and then it kind of shook me up, because I knew that in the past he had taken numerous drugs. So it just kind of shook me up. I pictured myself as the person dispensing the fatal dose that killed him. Even though the possibility is that had that been the only drug he had taken, it probably wouldn't have killed him, but in combination with others, it would have killed him.

"It was almost like you got in your car and backed out of the driveway and one of your children, a toddler, was behind the car. And you didn't see him. You ran over him and you squished him. It was an accident you couldn't help, but there was no way that accident wouldn't tear you up emotionally. It did tear me up. I suffered nightmares, I guess, for two months afterwards. In fact, I was right on the point of going to a psychiatrist, because it was beginning to get out of hand."

Behind the camera Lewis Bailey's tough countenance rarely betrayed any emotion, but on this day he was fighting back tears. And so was Thompson, who assured Nash that he didn't believe the pharmacist had done anything wrong.

Nash wasn't persuaded. "It just was the simple fact that I gave him the fatal dose, even though it was legal, and I had no reason not to."

Thompson tried to change the subject. "What do you normally prescribe Dilaudid for?" he asked.

"It's an opium derivative. It's given for extreme pain, but it's not unusual for dentists to prescribe it for an abscessed tooth, which is extremely painful," Nash answered. Thompson remembered that Elvis visited his dentist, Dr. Lester Hofman, during the early morning hours of August 16, 1977. If he had an abscessed tooth, then Lester Hofman, not George Nichopoulos, would have written the prescription, he thought. "If you took the Dilaudid, two or three capsules of four milligram strength in combination with other drugs, like Percodan, Quaaludes, or codeine, would it have any effect on you?" Thompson asked.

"Oh, yes, they tend to become more toxic as you combine them than by taking any one of them by themselves," Nash answered, explaining that this was known as a synergistic reaction.

Did Nash ever consider not filling the prescription for Elvis? "No, I took him [Dr. Nichopoulos] at his word that Elvis had an abscessed tooth, or an extreme toothache, and that Elvis would take the pills according to directions."

"But Dr. Nichopoulos isn't a dentist?" Thompson asked. "Wasn't that a little unusual?"

"Not if it were an abscessed tooth, or a man in extreme pain. At two-thirty in the morning, it would certainly be very difficult for him to find a dentist, and he was constantly in motion. He might have been going out of town and would need some Dilaudid and would try to contact a dentist in another town."

Thompson didn't have the heart to tell Nash that no more than an hour after Elvis left his dentist, who seemed always at Presley's beck and call, he contacted his doctor for Dilaudid for his teeth. Nash said he had filled many of Nichopoulos's prescriptions for Elvis and couldn't understand why Nichopoulos had not warned Elvis about the dangers of combining potent prescription medicines. If Nash felt guilty about giving Elvis the prescription for Dilaudid, why didn't Nichopoulos feel guilty about writing this prescription?

"The difference is just a personality makeup, I guess," Nash said. "I'm just a sensitive sort of person. The idea of maybe being the instrument that caused anybody pain or discomfort, or killing him or anything like that, is almost unbearable to me."

"If you personally knew that Elvis Presley was taking other drugs, would you have given him the Dilaudid?"

"If I knew that he had taken any drugs in the last twenty-four hours, and if I knew what the drug was and in what quantity, then the answer is 'No.' "

Thompson read off the list of drugs Bio-Science found in Elvis's system. What did the retired pharmacist think about all those drugs?

"It would be extremely stupid for a person to take them, and even worse for a person to prescribe them. And if I had anything to do with it, he wouldn't have gotten them. I simply would have refused to fill the prescriptions had I had those exact figures in front of me. There would be no way in the world I would have filled them."

Thompson concluded the interview, not wanting to disturb the old man any further. The crew packed up the camera gear in record time, thanking Nash for talking with them, and drove back to the airport. As the plane was leaving the runway, Thompson asked Lewis Bailey to critique the interview. Bailey was a licensed pharmacist who would don a white coat and fill prescriptions when free-lance camera assignments were slack.

"I'm having a hard time doing that, Charlie," Bailey replied. "I know you got the right questions and answers on tape. But that man was so sad, so full of guilt that he didn't deserve, that I'm having a hard time concentrating on anything but his sadness."

"Why didn't they find the Dilaudid in Elvis's system, Lewis?" Thompson asked.

"I don't know. You've got to ask Ricky Stanley," Bailey said. "Maybe he didn't give it to Elvis? Maybe he took it himself? Maybe he took the Dilaudid, and it didn't get in his system? Did they analyze the stomach contents? The Dilaudid could be there undigested."

Thompson said he didn't know if the stomach contents had been analyzed or not. "Are they important, Lewis?"

"Very important. He could have died with a lot of pills in his stomach that hadn't been absorbed into his system. If I were you, Charlie, I'd find out if they analyzed the stomach contents. If they had, I'd find out what they discovered. If they didn't, then I'd find out why not."

"It's so nice to have a pharmacist for a cameraman, Lewis," Thompson said as he stretched his legs and looked out at the lush West Tennessee farmland on the way back to Memphis.

"There's another distinct possibility, Charlie," Bailey said as an afterthought.

"About what?"

"About why they didn't find Dilaudid. Drug screens can often miss a substance when the technicians running them don't know what to look for. If they suspect somebody has taken Valium, then they have a better chance of screening properly and locating it. If they don't know that there is Dilaudid in the system, then they might not find it. I've been told by experts that Dilaudid is a hard drug to locate."

156

XII

SUSPICIOUS MINDS

THE COMMAND blaring from the hospital's intercom system was startling to everyone who heard it. "Harvey team to the emergency room. Stat!" Doctors, nurses, and technicians, clad in green surgical scrub suits, raced down the hallways with little regard for anyone or anything that stood in their way, as the strident command was repeated several times. Geraldo Rivera, Charlie Thompson, and a camera crew were standing in Baptist Hospital's emergency room in early August of 1979, interviewing the hospital's spokesman, Maurice Elliott, when the pandemonium erupted around them.

As they watched, a team of fire department emergency medical technicians wheeled in a male patient on a stretcher. A nurse quickly motioned to the firemen and directed them to bring the patient into an operating room that was now abuzz with excitement and activity. "Maurice, can we tape this?" Thompson asked. Elliott nodded his approval, and Thompson bustled his camera crew into the operating room to capture the action on videotape.

The man on the operating table had suffered a severe heart attack, and the medical team, which specialized in cardiac- and respiratory-arrest cases, was now fighting the clock and the odds in a frantic effort to revive him. The surgeons performed a thoracotomy and attempted to massage the patient's heart. They administered Epinephrine, sodium bicarbonate, Isuprel, and a solution of 5 percent dextrose dissolved in water. They forced a tube down the patient's throat to drain the stomach contents to keep him from vomiting and aspirating. Scopes around the room were connected to the patient and monitored his vital signs. They would give the team the first signals that their efforts either were failing or were paying off.

The pale green screens of the scopes began to spike, showing that the patient's heart was beginning to beat. The pace and tempo of the team quickened even more. "Come on, sucker, live!" the lead surgeon exclaimed. Other members picked up his plea, uttering their own words of encouragement that, taken together, began to sound like a mass prayer or a chant. Suddenly, the patient's chest began to heave, and he started to breathe on his own. Applause and cheers broke out in the cramped and crowded operating theater. Unlike Elvis Presley, who was pronounced dead in this very room two years before, this patient lived.

After the patient was removed to the hospital's intensive care unit, Elliott, Rivera, and Thompson entered the operating suite. Elliott told the team members, several of whom had been involved in the hopeless attempt to revive Elvis on August 16, 1977, that they were free to talk to Rivera. The television correspondent asked a doctor, who had been on Elvis's Harvey team, what the singer's physical state was when he was brought into this room in 1977.

"I would say dead," the surgeon replied. "Most people are warm. He was cold. He looked like he'd been that way for some time." The doctor said he had held out absolutely no hope that the Harvey team stood a chance of reviving Elvis. "He was very cold, very blue. He was obviously very dead when we got him."

Then unexpectedly Rivera asked, "What happened to Elvis's stomach contents?" The doctor seemed puzzled and dumbfounded. "That was something those on the Harvey team never paid attention to," he answered with obvious irritation.

When Rivera first entered the operating room, he had observed a nurse flushing out a plastic surgical bottle in a sink. He asked her what she had thrown away. "Stomach contents," she said.

"Do you always throw them away?" he asked.

"Yes," the nurse replied.

After questioning the surgeon, Rivera turned to that same nurse and asked if she knew what happened to Elvis's stomach contents. She turned out to be a nurse on the Harvey team and had functioned in that same capacity on the day of Presley's death.

"I don't know," she answered. "They're not usually sent to the laboratory to be analyzed."

"Why not?" Rivera wondered.

"That's the least of your problems. You don't think of an autopsy when you're on the Harvey team, you know, because we're interested in getting the heart of the patient beating again," she answered.

"Did anyone request that you save those samples in the case of Elvis Presley?" Rivera asked.

"Not to my knowledge," she replied.

"So it's reasonable to assume that they were flushed at some point?"

"Yes," she answered. "Our purpose is to resuscitate the person, you know. We're trying to prevent an autopsy. We're not worried about what they might find in an autopsy and saving things then for a later autopsy."

Rivera said it might be important to preserve the stomach contents, especially if they contained undissolved narcotics or poison.

The nurse was unmoved. "Everything we draw, everything that's taken from the patient, blood, whether it be for chemical evaluation, whether it be for arterial oxygen, pH, or the stomach contents, whatever, it's for immediate use. I never considered saving gastric contents for analysis. On a Harvey team patient you don't worry about that."

At that point Elliott intervened, mindful that Rivera had accidentally stumbled on an important, and heretofore unpublicized, aspect of the Presley case. He suggested that Rivera ask the question about Elvis's missing stomach contents of Dr. Harold

Sexton and his boss, Dr. Eric Muirhead. Both pathologists were scheduled to give depositions in the court case that ABC had filed to make Elvis's autopsy a public record. If Sexton were asked under oath about the stomach contents, Elliott said, he would tell ABC's attorneys what Rivera had already surmised—that the Harvey team had thrown out Elvis's stomach contents. Further, Elliott confided, the Baptist Hospital pathologists considered their loss to be quite a blow to their investigation.

Geraldo reviewed the list of those present in the surgical suite when the Harvey team worked on the body of Elvis Presley. He remembered that Dr. George Nichopoulos had arrived with the body and had remained with it until it was taken away to the hospital's morgue. Rivera had failed to ask the Harvey team nurse if anybody had ordered her to throw away the stomach contents. He doubted that she would remember such an order. Or if she did, he doubted she would confess the truth to him. The nurse had made the flushing sound like such a routine procedure. But Rivera never was one to mince words. "Do you suppose that Dr. Nichopoulos insured the stomach contents were thrown away by either ordering it done or doing it himself?"

Thompson and Elliott were taken aback. Thompson, remembering what Mike McMahon, the real estate developer, had told him about the last prescription written for Elvis, broke the silence. "Mike McMahon told me that Nichopoulos was surprised that the Baptist Hospital pathologists didn't find the Dilaudid in Elvis's system. What about it, Maurice?"

"Have your lawyers ask Dr. Sexton. Maybe he knows. If that doesn't work, then ask Dr. Nichopoulos," Elliott answered.

"Every time we learn more, we just get more questions to ask," Thompson said. But the ABC team was elated to turn up some real evidence on a day essentially written off for taking mundane pictures around the hospital.

Thompson didn't have anything or anybody lined up for the rest of the day, but an idea popped into his head. He and Cole had interviewed Ginger Alden several times, and she was eager to meet Rivera. Thompson thought it was about time to introduce Rivera, who fancied himself as a lady's man, to the woman who slept in Elvis's bed on the day he died.

160

Ginger Alden, like a number of other young women who dated Elvis Presley, was first introduced to "the King" by George Klein, a longtime Memphis disc jockey. In early 1977 Klein had served a sixty-day federal sentence in the Shelby County jail for mail fraud. He had been convicted of faking audience listenership surveys with inflated numbers to boost advertising revenue. Elvis tried to intervene on his old high school chum's behalf. He attempted and failed to keep Klein out of jail by calling President Jimmy Carter personally and asking for clemency. Elvis's call to the White House got no further than Chip Carter, the President's son.

Klein first met Elvis when they were students at Humes High School in Memphis in the early 1950s. Klein was elected president of Elvis's senior class. The small, dark-haired and sloe-eyed Klein introduced Nichopoulos to Elvis. Klein's wife, Barbara, worked as a receptionist for Nichopoulos, and Elvis had served as Klein's best man when he married Barbara in Elvis's Imperial Suite at the Las Vegas Hilton.

George Klein enjoyed being known as Elvis's matchmaker. He often said the only woman that Elvis had dated for any time without a Klein introduction was Priscilla Beaulieu Presley. He was the matchmaker for Linda Thompson, whom he invited to a movie theater that Elvis had rented after hours. Linda lived with Elvis for more than four years, splitting up with him during the first week of November 1976.

Klein spotted Ginger Alden, called her two weeks after Linda's departure, and asked if she was interested in meeting Elvis. Ginger was twenty at the time. According to Ginger's mother, Jo LaVern Alden, Ginger had been hanging around Graceland from the time she could barely walk. For her own part, Mrs. Alden was a strident Elvis fan. When Ginger was a tyke, Mrs. Alden dragged her down to Graceland where they waited outside the wrought-iron gates, which were fashioned into an oversized music staff, just hoping for a glimpse of Elvis as he rode his horse or golf cart around the spacious grounds. But the highlight in the Alden family's early relationship with Elvis took place at the Mid-South

161

Fairgrounds, where Elvis patted Ginger, then five years old, on the head and took her riding with him on the Pippin, the fairgrounds' venerable roller coaster.

That roller coaster ride made a profound impression on Ginger, who told George Klein that she would be delighted to meet Elvis Presley. When Ginger first visited inside Graceland, she was accompanied by her two sisters, Rosemary and Terry. Terry had just been selected as the new Miss Tennessee, and might have been a more likely replacement for Linda Thompson, a past Miss Tennessee Universe. But there is no accounting for tastes, and Elvis picked Ginger, who held the less prestigious titles of Miss Mid-South and Miss Traffic Safety. Still, Ginger was a pretty girl with a stunning face. When she first met Elvis in 1976, she wore her hair dark and teased. She put on more makeup than her natural good looks required, and this gave her an appearance much like Priscilla Presley's during the 1960s. After Elvis died, Ginger allowed the normal honey color of her hair to grow out, scraped off some of the excess makeup that Elvis seemed so fond of, and cultivated a more wholesome appearance.

On that first visit as a Graceland guest, Ginger waited for about four hours downstairs and was entertained by some of Elvis's flunkies. While she was cooling her heels, George Klein told her that Elvis was upstairs in the mansion practicing karate. Finally she was told to go upstairs, where she met Elvis and spent the night. Ginger always insisted that Elvis was a "perfect gentleman" that night, but she never elaborated. The next night Elvis took Ginger to Las Vegas, and shortly after that she joined him in San Francisco on tour. That trip took on the trappings of a farce. Elvis had scheduled one last fling with Linda Thompson in San Francisco, but he had planned that Linda would be out of town by the time that Ginger showed up. Somehow his plans went haywire. When Ginger arrived, Linda was still in the hotel suite Elvis had hoped to share with Ginger. For two days, he had to shift Ginger from room to room to keep her out of Linda's way. Somehow Ginger never discovered what was going on and continued her affair with Elvis none the wiser.

In return, Elvis took an active interest in the Alden family's welfare. When Ginger's grandfather died in Harrison, Arkansas, in

January 1977, Elvis paid for the funeral, which he attended. A few months later Ginger's parents divorced. Ginger's father was a retired career army sergeant who had been present when Elvis was inducted into the army in 1958. Elvis paid for the divorce and, according to Mrs. Alden, also promised to pay off the house note on the Alden home. Elvis died before he could do that, and Mrs. Alden sued the Presley estate for breach of contract. Ultimately she lost her suit.

In January 1977 Elvis proposed to Ginger. He popped the question, as Ginger recalled it, in the upstairs bathroom where he was to die seven months later. For the engagement Elvis gave Ginger a $70,000 diamond ring, but they set no wedding date. Shortly after their betrothal, Elvis and Ginger argued over a trip to Nashville where Elvis was scheduled to make several recordings. Contrary to the shy and passive manner that Elvis had come to expect from her, Ginger refused to go. Elvis said she had no choice. And at that, Ginger stalked out of Graceland, saying she was going home to her mother and sisters. According to several witnesses, Elvis followed her out of the mansion and into the night and in a rage fired a pistol over her head several times. Gunfire didn't change Ginger's mind, though, and Elvis went to Nashville by himself. Apparently that uproarious argument so unsettled Elvis that he blew the three-day recording session. Accomplishing nothing in Nashville, he left for Memphis to be with Ginger.

On the surface, Elvis and Ginger were still bent on marriage, but that first argument opened a rift that widened as time went on. Elvis began making disparaging remarks about Ginger to his cronies and then began dating others on the side. Shortly before Elvis's death, Dick Grob said Presley told him that he was unhappy with Ginger and stated, "There's going to be a change in the air." The security man, who disliked Ginger, said Elvis was angry that Ginger often refused to stay with him when he needed her. Grob said Elvis once let the air out of the tires on Ginger's car to keep her from leaving him. Grob insisted to anybody who would listen that Elvis didn't plan on taking Ginger on the out-of-town concert tour that was scheduled to begin on the day he died. Further, Grob said Elvis had no real intention of marrying Ginger and that she knew it.

The Death of Elvis

According to David Stanley, Elvis was jealous of Ginger's independence and asked his stepbrothers to keep an eye on her when she ran errands around Memphis. David also recalled that Ginger was bored with the drug scene at Graceland and disliked Elvis's daily habit of "getting zonked out of his mind." Apparently David's fondness for Ginger started another round of nasty rumors in the strange, extended Presley household. Vernon Presley, the Stanley brothers' stepfather, asked David if he were having an affair with Ginger. David denied romancing Ginger, and that answer seemed to satisfy Vernon. Nonetheless, David wasn't sure if Vernon had asked the question for himself or for Elvis.

After Elvis's death, Ginger was a handy scapegoat. Nearly all the Graceland regulars, led by Dick Grob and Dr. Nichopoulos's son Dean, were openly critical that Ginger should have been far more alert to Elvis's well-being. And as Marty Lacker's wife, Patsy, recalled in *Elvis: Portrait of a Friend,* during Elvis's funeral service Ginger sat with a mirror in her hand, fixing her eyelashes and hair. Other Presley regulars took offense at the behavior of Ginger's mother, Jo LaVern Alden, at the cemetery after the funeral service. They claimed that Mrs. Alden was standing outside the mausoleum pointing out celebrities to Ginger and regarded the ceremony as an opportunity to see and be seen.

But topping all the abuse was Ginger's presumed deal to sell her story to *The National Enquirer,* which Dick Grob accused her of arranging in advance of calling for help while Elvis lay dead or dying in the bathroom. By the summer of 1979 Ginger Alden was Number One on the unpopularity chart among the gaggle of Presley relatives, hangers-on, and good ol' boys, who fiercely guarded the purity of Elvis's reputation. For example, Vester Presley, Elvis's uncle and gatekeeper at Graceland, was quoted in the Memphis newspapers as saying that Ginger was no longer welcome at the mansion. Uncle Vester later denied making that statement.

When Geraldo and the ABC crew arrived at the modest Alden homestead in East Memphis, Ginger was dressed to the hilt and acted quite the southern belle. Jo LaVern bustled about providing iced tea and chatting incessantly. Mother and daughter were eager to show Rivera a large garish picture of Elvis painted on black velvet. Jo LaVern said the painting would be a terrific backdrop for Ginger's interview. And at this point, Rivera was willing to put up with a little unsolicited stage management.

Once the camera and lights were set up, Rivera told Ginger he wanted to begin the interview with questions about the night preceding Elvis's death. In a singsong voice, Ginger began recounting her trip with Elvis to the dentist. Ginger said that after returning from the dentist Elvis wanted to play racquetball. "So I said fine. Then he asked me to call his maid to come and make his bed. So I did. At that time Elvis went into more detail about our wedding than he had gone into at any time ever before."

Among those plans, Ginger confided, was Elvis's intention to announce the wedding publicly when he returned to Memphis from the road tour and performed a concert in Memphis on August 27.

Continuing her account, Ginger said that she, Elvis, his cousin Billy Smith, and Billy's wife, Jo, played racquetball. "And Elvis seemed to be, you know, in a really good mood." It was about 6:00 A.M. The sun was coming up when they finished their game. Ginger said Elvis played the piano for her—the one set up in the lounge area of the racquetball building—and sang spirituals.

Ginger remembered being sleepy when she and Elvis went upstairs to the master bedroom, but Elvis complained about not being able to sleep. "And I remember Ricky Stanley brought up medication for him to take at that time." Then she recalled seeing Elvis going to the bathroom and saying he was going to read. "I said to him, 'Don't fall asleep.' And he said, 'I won't.' And he walked to the bathroom, and that is the last time I saw Elvis."

"How did you discover the body?" Rivera asked.

Her answer was hard to follow. Apparently, when Ginger woke up sometime between 1:00 and 2:00 P.M., she discovered that Elvis had not come back to bed. But before looking for him, Ginger telephoned a friend who was going on tour with her and asked her buddy if she was packing. That didn't make much sense to anybody who listened to it, but it more or less fit into the muddled chain of events that Ginger strung together for Rivera. After this trivial telephone conversation, Ginger decided it was time to see what really happened to Elvis, so she went to the door of the bathroom and knocked.

"And Elvis didn't answer. And that is when I opened the door, and I found Elvis." The first thing that she thought about was "medication." She didn't call it drugs. "I believe Ricky Stanley had sent up . . . some more medication for Elvis to take, because always before a tour, Elvis was so keyed up he just couldn't sleep."

Ginger's account wasn't adding up. If she had been asleep and Elvis had been in the bathroom the whole time, how would Ginger know about Ricky Stanley bringing up another packet of "medication" for Elvis?

"And so when I went in immediately, I saw him. I thought Elvis would fall asleep different times. The medication would hit him all of a sudden, and he would fall asleep. In fact, I have seen him fall asleep in an upright position.

"And I walked in, and I looked at him for a second, and I thought, 'Oh, he has hit his head.' But I knew immediately when I turned his head over. I knew I had never seen him look that way before. So I immediately went into a state of shock, and I felt for a few minutes that the furtherest thing from my mind was that Elvis was dead."

At that point, Ginger said, she picked up the phone and called downstairs for help. "And I was trying to stay calm, because in my heart I just kept on telling myself Elvis is just really all right. Something bad is wrong, but it is not death by any means."

The maid reported that Ricky Stanley had just gone off duty and said she was sending up bodyguard Al Strada to help. It was then about 2:00 P.M. When Strada walked into the bathroom, Ginger said, "Al, I think something is really wrong with Elvis." Strada looked at Elvis, and according to Ginger, "I don't even think Al, at that time, thought, you know, death or anything like that." Suddenly, Joe Esposito ran into the bathroom. "And Joe was kind of slapping Elvis, and saying certain things, and then I think it must have just hit Joe, and he said . . ."

Ginger didn't finish her sentence. Apparently she meant that Joe Esposito decided Elvis was dead.

So far in her account, Ginger hadn't mentioned taking a shower or fixing her hair or applying makeup before going into the master bathroom to check on Elvis. But just about everybody who saw her that day as she stood over Elvis's body said she was perfectly dressed and made up and had her hair neatly in place.

Continuing her story, Ginger said Esposito called for an ambulance and tried to reach Nichopoulos. "And at that time, we were working and working with Elvis, and they phoned Mr. [Vernon] Presley. I believe he was at the office at that time. Mr. Presley came up with his fiancée, Sandy [Miller]. And we all worked with Elvis."

Rivera asked, "Mouth-to-mouth resuscitation?"

Ginger didn't answer his question, but said, "Sandy and Charlie Hodge and we were working with him when the ambulance arrived, and that is when they took Elvis."

Rivera got back to the "medication" issue, asking what kind of pills Ricky Stanley brought to Elvis. Ginger wasn't exactly sure. "It was packets like. I believe a lot of them were tranquilizers. Just anything to, you know, just really relieve the pressure on his . . . I guess the tension and be able to put him to sleep. I don't specifically know of the name of the . . . what was in it."

Rivera asked if Percodan was one of the drugs Elvis took. Ginger said maybe. As one who probably knew Elvis better "than anyone on earth," Rivera said with an application of soft soap, it was very important for her to disclose how many of "these pills" Elvis was taking "toward the end of his life."

But Ginger sidestepped the invitation. "Elvis was in no way heavily into drugs," she said. "No drug scene at all. Elvis I think sometimes thought he needed them more than he really did. And he was not taking them like so many of these trashy papers and certain people have come out and said, you know, that he was constantly . . . that he was a drug addict. By no means. Because it was prescribed medication to my knowledge. But if Elvis ever took anything other than prescribed [medication] I don't know about it."

Thompson didn't believe her. But Rivera wasn't frazzled. "How often did he take those little packets marked 'sleep'?"

Again Ginger was vague. She said Elvis took more of them at the beginning of a tour than at the end.

"Did you suspect he was in ill health?" Rivera asked.

"Elvis had glaucoma, and I stayed many nights keeping

167

patches on his eyes and working with his eyes a lot. And he went to the hospital at one time for intestinal flu." Actually, the hospital visit that Ginger mentioned was for drug detoxification.

"Why are Elvis's former associates and relatives trying to belittle your relationship with Elvis now?" Rivera asked.

Ginger said most of the people who were attacking her were really not Elvis's friends, they were simply interested in drawing their paychecks from him.

With that opening, Rivera brought up Dick Grob's copyrighted synopsis of *The Elvis Conspiracy*. Did she, as Grob asserted, discover the body before she reported it, and did she prepare herself "in some stately way by getting dressed to meet the public, to meet the press?"

"I think that is the most ridiculous thing I have ever heard. I totally don't understand Dick Grob at all. But I think there are a lot of other people that don't either. And it's one of the most horrible things I have ever heard." Ginger's eyes were flashing, but she offered no explanation about her well-groomed appearance when help came from downstairs. Ginger had an explanation about why Elvis had lain on the bathroom floor so long without notice. Under normal bodyguard procedures, nothing like this should have happened. Elvis often spent hour after hour in the bathroom and typically during these protracted episodes one of the bodyguards would stay with him.

"Whoever was on duty was supposed to have been in Elvis's bathroom," Ginger said. "There was a bed, like a lounge area in the back, so they should have been in there."

In truth, Ricky Stanley was on duty during that particular shift, and Ginger now was reporting him absent from his assigned post. As she continued to talk with Rivera, Ginger began to shift the finger of suspicion to others close to Elvis and hint darkly that they might be guilty of some foul play resulting in his death. Ginger thought Elvis had some pretty strange people working for him, and maybe some of them might have benefited by his death. That came out of left field and took Rivera aback.

"You mean you think that somebody could have in some way caused his death? Had something to do with his death?"

"Yes, I don't completely rule that out. I would have to find out a lot more things in the future," she said, warming to the idea of getting even with some of her detractors.

"Do you think that may be something that he took. Maybe one of those packets that this Stanley fellow brought up?" Rivera asked.

"It could have been," Ginger answered. But she offered no details. Rivera and Ginger then went through a list of people surrounding Elvis who she said might stand to gain by Elvis's death. They quickly eliminated Ginger from their suspect list, as she had inherited absolutely nothing from Elvis. She had witnessed Elvis's will, and Tennessee law prohibits a witness to a will from inheriting anything. She didn't know about the law, but Rivera told her about it. She seemed relieved.

Ginger said Vernon Presley also entertained the notion of murder and had asked if she had seen anybody whom she didn't recognize go upstairs on the morning that Elvis died. Ginger told Vernon that she had been asleep and had seen nothing. She insisted she had maintained a close relationship with Vernon after Elvis's death and denied that she had ever been ordered to stay away from Graceland.

Shaking her head, Ginger said Elvis had never complained of any kind of heart trouble and voiced her doubts about Dr. Jerry Francisco's ruling that he had died of a heart attack. Rivera read her the list of drugs that Bio-Science had discovered in Elvis's body. It didn't faze her. Quite often Elvis took a variety of drugs to go to sleep, she said, and Placidyl and Quaalude were two that he took regularly. She also told Rivera that Elvis probably did take Dilaudid the morning he died.

While continuing to insist that Elvis was no drug abuser, Ginger recalled on one occasion how she refused to fly with Elvis to Las Vegas to pick up a supply of drugs. Dr. Nichopoulos didn't approve of these drug forays, Ginger said, and she knew that Dr. Nichopoulos's resident nurse at Graceland, Tish Henley, often withheld drugs from Elvis. "Tish many times would empty out capsules and just put, you know, sugar or something in, so Elvis actually wasn't taking what he thought he was."

"Did Elvis use Nichopoulos's need for money as a bargaining chip to get more drugs from the doctor?" Rivera asked. Ginger thought that might be a real possibility.

As the interview was winding down, Rivera then asked Ginger one of the all-time sappy questions, "How do you feel about the fact that for the rest of your life you will in all probability always be identified as Elvis Presley's fiancée or the woman who Elvis Presley was going to marry?"

"I think that is very nice," Ginger answered with a sweet smile. "I hope people will remember me for that."

At that point, Ginger's mother interjected herself into the interview. She told Rivera about talks she had with Vernon Presley after Elvis's death. Vernon was going through various theories and scenarios insinuating that his son had been the victim of foul play. Mrs. Alden said Vernon told her "there is a shot that can be given that will not show up in the bloodstream. I had never heard of it, and I still don't know what he was talking about. But he said there is a shot that can be given," she said.

At the time of Elvis's death, Mrs. Alden worked for the Internal Revenue Service's regional office in Memphis. She was on the job when Ginger called her about 2:00 P.M. That would have been close to the time Ginger called downstairs at Graceland for help. And perhaps that was the second phone call that Ginger made before she went to look for Elvis. During that 2:00 P.M. call, Mrs. Alden said Ginger told her about Elvis not being able to sleep and going into the bathroom to read eight hours earlier.

"And so she said, 'I am going to check on him,'" Mrs. Alden told Rivera. "And about thirty minutes later, she called me, and she was hysterical. And I said, 'Ginger, what in the world is wrong?' And she said, 'Momma, I think something has happened to Elvis.'"

Mrs. Alden said she left work and was driving home when she heard an announcement on the radio confirming Elvis's death. Jo Alden drove to Graceland with another daughter, Rosemary, to calm Ginger down and to pick up her granddaughter, Amber, who had spent the night at the mansion as a guest of Elvis's daughter, Lisa Marie. Mrs. Alden stayed at Graceland about an hour and said she "brought Ginger home still in a state of shock."

Now Rivera began to sniff out some inconsistencies.

Wasn't it strange, he asked Ginger, that she would be able to sleep for eight hours—from 6:00 A.M. until 2:00 P.M.—and not discover that Elvis had failed to come to bed?

"I hadn't had any sleep the night before," Ginger said. Rivera toughened up. "According to the doctors he died about 9:00 A.M. Rigor mortis had set in, so he was stiff. And he also had turned blue. Does that fit your recollection?"

"Oh, yes, Elvis looked very bad."

"Was he fully clothed?"

"Yes, he had pajamas on."

Thompson started shaking his head, but Rivera signaled him to be still. Rivera knew that Ginger was telling a fib on this point.

Quickly the discussion shifted to Ginger's career. She had done some modeling and was planning on acting in a grade B film entitled *Autumn Mist*. Ginger said she was supposed to sing ten songs in the film. "They are supposed to have a lot of different songs for me to look through. I think I will do a little country and western and then kind of switch over to pop/rock or something quickly."

"How would Elvis react to your business career?" Rivera asked.

"My show business? Elvis I don't think really cared for people being in show business. And one time he made the statement he didn't want me to grow to like Los Angeles. He said, 'Sending you to Los Angeles is like sending pizza to a hungry lion.'

"I think under the circumstances now that Elvis would be exceptionally proud. I think he would, you know, I don't think I could go to work in a clothing store or something. I would feel a little strange, I guess," she said.

Later, sitting around Rivera's hotel suite, Thompson unloaded on the correspondent. "You got some nice emotional material, but you also got a crock of horseshit from that broad. I just hope you know it."

"You're not buying Dick Grob's theories are you, Charlie?" Rivera asked.

"I don't like Grob, and I know he's lying about the cancer part of his story. But I learned a long time ago that just because

171

somebody is lying about part of their story, that doesn't mean they're lying about all of it," Thompson answered.

"She admitted making at least two phone calls before going to look for him, and she never explained how she got dressed up before calling for help," Cole said. "This is new stuff, and it doesn't add."

"I want to track down this *National Enquirer* guy, Jim Kirk," Thompson said, "the one Grob says that Ginger called, and who showed up at Graceland before the ambulance came. And I want to reinterview Ginger before we air this piece."

"Suspicious minds," Rivera said. "I'm surrounded by suspicious minds."

"That's what we get paid to be," Thompson said.

XIII

PRESERVING PRESLEYMANIA

THE OVERDRESSED CROWD stood respectfully and waited. The ceremonies were about to begin at Elvis Presley's refurbished birthplace in Tupelo, Mississippi. It was mid-August 1979. Everybody was suffering mightily from the torrid heat, which enveloped the scene like a wool greatcoat. Rivulets of sweat beaded on foreheads, rolled down faces, collected under armpits, spread across backs, and eventually soaked and wilted the finery donned for this grand occasion in Lee County history.

Some who had gathered began wobbling, an early sign of heat prostration, while ambulances waited just outside the crowd's perimeter to pick up sunstroke victims. Even though these were the Presley faithful or Tupelo boosters or both, given the intensity of the blazing sun, the full range of speech-making and music from the band, this was a physical ordeal. It was really a shame. The upper-crust women of Tupelo had labored long and hard to clean up Elvis's birthplace and transform it into what looked like a cozy dollhouse—a far cry from the crude shack it had been when Elvis was born inside on January 8, 1935.

Adding to the romance of Elvis's life, these socially conscious house refurbishers had painted the bare outside board walls an immaculate white, hung dainty wallpaper on the rough-hewn wooden interior, installed lace curtains at the windows, and filled the house full of possessions that the Presleys could never have afforded when they lived there. As an incentive for waiting out the speech-makers dedicating Elvis's birthplace as a national shrine, the organizers planned on opening the house for its first public tours.

The house had been built just after Gladys Presley discovered she was pregnant in 1934. Gladys and Vernon Presley had been married the year before up the road in Pontotoc County, Mississippi. Both were native Mississippians from desperately poor families. They had falsified their ages on their marriage license. Gladys claimed to be nineteen but was really twenty-one. Vernon claimed to be twenty-two but was really only seventeen.

Vernon had borrowed $180 as a home construction loan from a dairy and hog farmer he worked for. And Vernon's father owned the lot. It was located in East Tupelo, outside the city limits of Tupelo. With help from his father and brother, Vernon built the two-room cabin, a typical southern "shotgun shack," which derives its monicker from a simple floorplan. All the rooms and door frames line up one behind the other, so that a shotgun could be fired through the front door and out the back without hitting anything but stray gnats and mosquitos.

Elvis's mother was attended in her early morning delivery at home by Dr. William Robert Hunt, who later collected a $15 delivery fee from welfare. Thirty-five minutes before Elvis's birth, his mother delivered a stillborn identical twin. She planned to name this child Jesse Garon Presley. She named her live son Elvis Aron Presley, deliberately misspelling his middle name to maintain a twinlike consistency. Elvis later had the spelling legally changed to Aaron.

Two years after Elvis's birth, Vernon Presley was indicted for forging a check. In June 1938 he was taken to Mississippi's infamous Parchman Penitentiary, where he remained until January 4, 1941. After Vernon's conviction, Orville Bean, the man who loaned Vernon the $180 to build his home—and the same man whom Vernon attempted to swindle with his check-forging scheme

—evicted Elvis and his mother. Gladys and her son moved next door to live with Vernon's parents, and she supported herself during her husband's incarceration by working as a seamstress and a laundress.

As a convicted felon, Vernon was exempt from the draft during World War II. He spent most of the war working in a defense plant in Memphis, 100 miles northwest of Tupelo, and sent money back to his small family in Mississippi. In 1946 Vernon moved back to Tupelo, landed a job driving a truck for a wholesale grocery company, and found a place for his family to live inside the city limits. Still times were tough for the Presleys. For the next two and a half years the family lived in a series of rental houses in Tupelo's poorest white neighborhoods—one of them next to a slaughterhouse. During this period Vernon was earning $22.50 a week and going broke. In September 1948 the family packed their few belongings into a beat-up 1937 Plymouth and headed up U.S. Highway 78 for Memphis and maybe a change of luck.

Yet if Tupelo had been hard on Elvis and his family, you wouldn't have known it by listening to the speeches from politicians who glorified the town on this August day as they dedicated Elvis's birthplace as a national landmark.

Charlie Thompson, Geraldo Rivera, and a camera crew were in the crowd, suffering from the heat like everyone else. It was the second mid-August in a row that they had been in Tupelo, Mississippi. The summer before they had taped a number of violent confrontations between the Ku Klux Klan, the Socialist Workers' Party, and the Tupelo Police Department.

Thompson and Rivera had vowed never to return to Tupelo, but here they were. There really wasn't much choice. This dedication ceremony was an ideal opportunity to gain access to some of Elvis's cronies on camera. Many had refused to meet or to talk with *20/20* about Elvis. So Thompson, Rivera, and their camera crew made the most of public ceremonies like this one.

As Thompson scanned the crowd, he spotted the very person he hoped would be here—Dick Grob. He signaled Bob Brandon, his cameraman, and Phil Lauter, his soundman, and vectored them and Rivera in Grob's direction. Rivera pursued the lanky security man like a mongoose. He didn't wait to see if the camera crew had equipment in place before firing off his first question.

"I understand you have a copyrighted report coming out soon. What's the title?" Rivera asked.

"I have no comment on it," replied Grob, who hadn't lost any of his distaste for news people.

Rivera was undeterred. "We've heard the title is *The Elvis Conspiracy*. Is that true?"

"I have no comment on it," Grob said, his voice becoming more emphatic.

"Well, let's be frank with each other," Rivera said. "In your report, a synopsis of which we have seen, you alleged that you had access to certain autopsy reports and to certain people. Is that true?"

Again Grob had no comment. Rivera lobbed a verbal hardball. And the tape kept rolling.

"Would you have a comment if I were to tell you that there are people who said that you are a liar? And that you had no access to those reports and that you are trying to capitalize on his death?"

Grob's face was flushed. He was boiling now. But he clung to his rote "No comment" answer.

"Are you an exploiter of Elvis Presley's death?" Rivera said, directly challenging Grob's loyalty and respect for his deceased boss.

Grob's slow burn looked on the verge of exploding, but he mouthed his "No comment" line for the fifth time.

Rivera backed off a bit and asked when *The Elvis Conspiracy* would be published. Still no comment.

Rivera then turned to Charlie Hodge and boomed, "What do you think Elvis would say about Mr. Grob here writing something called *The Elvis Conspiracy*, wherein he alleges that there is a conspiracy whereby Elvis died by negligence, it seems almost criminal negligence?"

"Oh, I don't think that Dick could write a book of that nature," Hodge replied innocently.

Rivera abruptly turned to Grob. "Oh, do you know, Dick, that we have the report in our possession and that it is being introduced into evidence in our lawsuit?"

Again Grob's face became flushed. He rolled his fists into balls, but restrained himself with another "No comment."

"Are you having a good time?" Rivera asked, observing Grob's clenched fists.

"I was having an excellent time until you came here," Grob replied.

Rivera stuck out his chin, daring Grob to throw a punch, and said, "The feeling is mutual."

Over his shoulder, Rivera told the camera crew to pack up the equipment and "haul ass out of Tupelo before the cops get their hands on your producer."

———

Later that week Thompson, Rivera, and the camera crew continued their quest for former Presley entourage members. They were standing in the back of an auditorium at Memphis State University videotaping a series of dull remembrances by some of Elvis's "closest friends."

Charlie Hodge was at the microphone, telling about how Elvis once split his pants on stage during a concert. It was not a very funny story, and even the die-hard and uncritical Elvis fans in the audience had a hard time being polite as Hodge droned on in a dreary, annoying monotone. The ABC crew finally became bored and restless. They drifted out of the auditorium to wait for Hodge and the other former entourage members to emerge.

As Hodge strolled out, Rivera walked up to him and began rapidly firing a series of questions. The correspondent hoped that with Grob nowhere in sight, the tiny Alabamian might provide some straight answers. Although Hodge was emotionally fragile and easy to browbeat, Rivera found him tight-lipped about drug abuse, either his own or that of his best friend, Elvis Presley. For years Hodge had been fighting a personal battle with the bottle and pills but with only limited success.

"Was Elvis a drug abuser?" Rivera asked as Hodge made his way across Central Avenue to a lot where his car was parked. "Are those stories true?"

177

"If he did it, he never did it in front of me," Hodge answered.

"Really, Charlie?" Rivera said with a touch of sarcasm.

"I don't have to lie," Hodge shot back. "I don't have any reason to. Why would I?"

"It could be argued that you make your living because of Elvis's reputation, and you would never do anything to besmirch your friend's reputation. That is a natural thing—to be protective," said Rivera, answering his own question.

Hodge, who along with Joe Esposito was known to be the direct pipeline to Colonel Tom Parker out of Elvis's camp, swore that if he ever wrote a book about Elvis it would all be positive. "I won't get into anything personal with Elvis. According to whether it was his will, his life-style, anything that was personal. Now if other people want to tell of Elvis's personal life, they can. But he was my friend and things he told me in confidence, I'm going to keep that way."

Rivera saw an opening and pounced. "So even if there was involvement with narcotics or anything you wouldn't tell me, would you, Charlie?"

"I didn't know about any, other than what was prescribed by his physician for glaucoma and hypertension," Hodge said. Later investigations would show that Elvis frequently had prescriptions for narcotics written in Hodge's name and that Hodge personally picked up these bogus prescriptions for Elvis.

Rivera then shifted to Dick Grob's book.

"To my knowledge it is not out, is it?" Hodge wavered.

"Not yet, but do you have any connection with it?" Rivera asked.

"I would like to reserve comment until I know more about it and talk to Dick [Grob] or somebody," Hodge mumbled.

"But are you connected with that at all?" Rivera persisted.

"Am I connected? No. But I would like to talk to Dick and see what he has to say. So far someone told me that there are fourteen books out [about Elvis]. So what I may do is wait until I am about fifty and then get all those books and sit down somewhere and read them and have a few laughs, about where the people lie," Hodge said.

178

Actually, Charlie Hodge did wait several years to write his book. He published it in 1985, just as he turned fifty. Coauthored by Charles Goodman, a Memphis newspaperman, *Me 'n Elvis,* not to be confused with Priscilla Presley's *Elvis and Me,* was that sticky sweet memoir Hodge said it would be six years earlier. Although Dick Grob was not associated with Hodge's book, it contained the fabricated story about Elvis's suffering from terminal bone cancer. Hodge wasn't letting medical truth interfere with his defense of Elvis. "After his death," the Hodge book states, "they found that he had already suffered three heart attacks. His heart was severely damaged. Even then one side was now twice as big as it should have been. His liver problem was severe and deteriorating, the same as his mother's had been not long before she died."

Finally Rivera asked Hodge if he believed that Red and Sonny West, Dave Hebler, and Marty and Patsy Lacker were all lying about Elvis's drug problems just to sell their books?

"Well, it could be my ignorance, so to speak. Because again, I never pried into Elvis's private life or his private business. And I'm not going to now," Hodge said.

═════

The next day Rivera, Thompson, and the crew were standing in a cow pasture located near Bull Frog Corner just across the Mississippi state line and the Memphis city limits. A huge white painted concrete cross dominated the field. Clustered around the base of the cross were the same gaggle of Elvis's groupies that the *20/20* team had been tailing all week.

After the speech-making, Presley's buddies were scheduled to light "an eternal flame" under the cross to remind everybody that Elvis had once owned this land and had used this field as a getaway ranch. Elvis bought it in the late 1960s, paying a local farmer $530,000 for it. He called it the Circle G Ranch. Elvis converted it into a kind of redneck commune, purchasing six mobile homes for his band of merry men, so they could stay with him on the ranch and ride horses, shoot guns, and generally raise unfettered hell. To outfit the ranch further, Elvis went on a truck-buying

179

binge. He spent so much money equipping his whole contingent with sparkling, brand-new pickup trucks that he nearly drove his penny-pinching father, Vernon, crazy with worry about how to pay for the extravagances. Elvis spent more than $500,000 on the trucks, horses, trailers, tractors, and assorted supplies in a few short months. He came very close to spending himself into bankruptcy and finally had to sell the ranch to avert such unfavorable publicity.

After Elvis's death, a group of local real estate developers tried to turn the ranch into a tourist attraction like Graceland. As part of the hype, the developers promised to keep the flame burning as long as the tourists came to the ranch and spent money. The flame flickered and went out in the early 1980s.

As the not-so-eternal flame was being dedicated, Thompson tapped Rivera on the shoulder and pointed out Billy Smith, Elvis's favorite cousin. Rivera and the crew walked gingerly around the crowd—careful to sidestep the profusion of pasture patties littering the field.

Elvis had been protective of Billy Smith, who had been a regular companion and stabilizing force for years. Billy took care of Elvis's wardrobe, but in a larger sense he lent Elvis a refreshing, down-to-earth perspective on life. Billy and his wife, Jo, lived in a house trailer behind Graceland mansion, and they had played racquetball with Elvis the morning he died. Billy was short, unassuming, and athletic, but made sure Elvis won his share of the racquetball games.

According to several Presley insiders, Elvis had promised to take care of Billy Smith and Charlie Hodge in his will, bequeathing both of them enough money to insure they could spend the rest of their lives without working. But if there ever was such a promise, it was broken when Elvis signed a will a few months before his death. After it was probated, both men found out there were no bequests to them. Billy returned to his old job at Illinois Central Railroad.

Billy owned a large collection of Elvis memorabilia, and he enjoyed talking about it to fans who came to view it. But he had steadfastly refused to disclose any personal details of his famous cousin's life to the press.

Over the years, though, Billy was exposed to some harrowing experiences that made the dangers of drug abuse impossible to forget. In 1962, for example, he came very close to witnessing the drug death of one of his and Elvis's cousins, Gene Smith. That year Billy and Gene were accompanying Elvis on a long drive in a mobile home. Gene had been taking amphetamines to stay awake for the three days it took to make the trip. Gene finished his allotted time as driver. He retired to the back of the vehicle to get some much needed sleep, but the drugs wouldn't let him doze off. He complained to Elvis, who gave him a 100-milligram dose of Demerol, a potent downer. And it laid Gene out cold. Later, when Billy went back to check on Gene, he noticed his cousin's shallow breathing and then detected a faint heart beat.

Memories were still fresh in Billy's mind about Gene's brother, Junior Smith, another Elvis sidekick in the early days who had died in his bed, probably from a drug overdose. Billy was the one who discovered that Junior was dead.

Billy yelled at Elvis to stop the vehicle so that they could get help for Gene. Elvis was unhappy about stopping, and groused about doing it, but he gave in. Gene was slapped back to consciousness and for the next three hours Elvis, Billy, and Joe Esposito took turns walking him up and down the highway. Finally he was able to shake off the effects of the Demerol.

Stationing himself at Billy's side, Rivera introduced himself and asked what he knew about Dick Grob's book. Only rumors, Billy said, nothing more. "Rumor to me is just that. It goes in one ear and out the other. Today is really not a good day as far as I'm concerned to talk about it. This is supposed to be a happy occasion. I would like to end it on that note."

Grob's book proposal, Rivera persisted, was alleging criminal negligence in the death of Elvis. "What are your own personal feelings?" he asked.

"Oh, if it had me in it, I might object. But if it don't have me in it, it's his problem," Billy replied.

Rivera saw the pointlessness of asking Billy any more questions, so he thanked him and walked off.

The next four interviews that Rivera attempted—with

181

George Klein, Al Strada, Dean Nichopoulos, and Richard Davis—
were also zeroes.

Klein, Elvis's disc jockey friend who moonlighted at Memphis nightspots with his turntables and collection of hit records from the 1950s, was the first to escape an interview. A week or so earlier at a midtown watering hole, Thompson and Cole had caught Klein's act—"GK, your DJ. It's the Geeker in your speaker." Somewhere between Frankie Lyman and the Teenagers and Alvin Cash and the Crawlers, Klein waved a bottle of pills over his head, identifying them as "Rorer 714." He claimed that Elvis had taken pills from this very bottle on the day he died.

Checking later with a pharmacist about Rorer 714, Cole found out they were Quaaludes (methaqualone), which showed up in high concentrations on the Bio-Science toxicology report. Inasmuch as George Klein's wife, Barbara, worked for Dr. Nichopoulos, the plastic bottle at Trader Dick's could have been the real McCoy. Thompson wanted to get his hands on the bottle, so he unleashed Rivera. But Klein saw the ABC crew headed his way and scooted off to the safety and security of his automobile. Rivera quit pursuing him. The day was too hot for those kinds of games.

Next Thompson pointed out Al Strada. He had been the first person to arrive at Elvis's bathroom after Ginger Alden called for help on the day of Elvis' death. Strada also had told the fire department paramedics that Elvis had died of a drug overdose. Strada noticed Thompson pointing at him and instantly bolted.

Thompson then spotted Dean Nichopoulos, Dr. Nick's son and a flunky for Elvis. He had castigated Ginger for causing Elvis's death, claiming she had not properly monitored his drug intake. While Thompson briefed Rivera on these lesser lights in the Elvis entourage, young Nichopoulos followed Strada's example and left. "Damn!" Rivera exclaimed. "We're going to empty this place out at this rate. Got anybody else?"

Thompson was running out of targets, but he finally observed a likely suspect. He was Richard Davis, a former Presley employee, who had been quoted in the Lackers' book as admitting he had been an active participant in Elvis's daily abuse of drugs. "Sure, I was part of the drug scene. Day in and day out there were pills. They were a part of our way of life, easy to get and easy to take," Davis was quoted as saying in the Lacker book. But Davis wasn't willing to repeat that line or any other line for ABC. As soon as Davis was aware that he was the focus of Thompson's attention, he left.

By this time it was apparent to both Thompson and Rivera that they were wasting their time at the eternal flame.

———

Mike Pleasants and Chuck Harrell, *20/20*'s attorneys, were busy laying a solid foundation for the Elvis broadcast while finding new evidence compromising the secrecy of the autopsy. Backed by subpoena power, Pleasants and Harrell had set up depositions for five key witnesses to the events of August 16, 1977. Many of their questions during these interviews under oath were necessarily dry and technical—aimed at scoring legal debating points. However, the two attorneys were just as wound up as their reporter clients in establishing the facts surrounding Elvis's death. And with rare exception, the information was fair game for broadcasting.

Three of the witnesses, Maurice Elliott and Drs. Eric Muirhead and Harold Sexton, all associated with Baptist Hospital, were deposed on August 24, 1979. Under court guidelines established for the depositions, witnesses were free to discuss the events of Elvis's death but with one prohibition—they weren't allowed to reveal any technical medical information. For example, Dr. Sexton could say he took blood samples and sent them off to Bio-Science for testing, but he couldn't say the tests were positive for Quaaludes.

Elliott, the hospital's executive vice president, established details happening around the hospital on the day of the death. He also was present when the autopsy report was presented to Vernon Presley two months later. In keeping with the ground rules, Elliott stopped short of revealing the results, but he could say that Dr. Francisco voiced his agreement with those results and surprised Baptist Hospital officials when he changed his mind a few days later.

This information reinforced the interview with Dr. Noel

Florendo, who as a participant in the autopsy had stated that Dr. Muirhead and the other hospital pathologists determined that Elvis died from the fatal interaction of depressant drugs.

Depositions from Drs. Muirhead and Sexton confirmed that the best evidence for finding cause of death—the stomach contents—had been washed down the drain in the hospital emergency room. And as experienced pathologists, they testified that Elvis's death had all the trappings of a medical examiner's case, one that they approached with the utmost caution.

From a factual, who-did-what-where-and-when standpoint, the most useful testimony came from Dan Warlick, who no longer was Dr. Francisco's chief investigator. The position had been eliminated—for budget reasons, Dr. Francisco said. And Warlick really didn't disagree. He wanted to enroll in law school.

Appearing in Pleasants's law office on August 30, Warlick related how that note scrawled with initials— "EP, OD? DOA, BMH"—first involved him in the Elvis case. Warlick seemed willing to disclose full details of Elvis's autopsy, which he had observed firsthand. But these days Warlick was in the middle of law school at Memphis State University and on the side he was working as a paralegal for attorney James Cox, one of the city's top plaintiff lawyers in medical malpractice cases. Cox took it upon himself to represent Warlick in the deposition and refused to allow these details to come out.

Nonetheless, Warlick filled in many gaps in the factual narrative that *20/20*'s attorneys were compiling for the lawsuit and for the upcoming broadcast. And then there were the photographs. Warlick told Chuck Harrell, who was doing the questioning, that he had definitely taken photographs of Elvis's bathroom. What had become of them? Warlick supposed they were in Dr. Francisco's file.

With that answer there were raised eyebrows around the conference table and a tacit question: Why hadn't Thompson and Cole seen these photos when they asked Dr. Francisco for the file? Nobody knew, but you could bet the photos would be brought up again.

More than once, Warlick testified, he tried to give Francisco a complete briefing, photos included, about what he found at

Graceland, but the medical examiner's attention was elsewhere. "He [Francisco] just listened to what I had to say, and I suppose he shook his head. I don't remember him asking any specific questions."

A week later, on September 4 and 5, Pleasants and Harrell tackled their toughest witness, Dr. Francisco. The narrow, poorly lighted office was cramped and uncomfortable for the visitors, who somehow had the feeling that they weren't welcome.

Pleasants led the questioning. Letting up only occasionally to stretch his long, basketball legs, the soft-spoken attorney remained unruffled throughout as he probed the peculiar logic of the answers he was hearing.

Had anyone, Pleasants asked, told the medical examiner that Elvis had died of a drug overdose?

"Oh, maybe 25 percent of the newspaper reporters that called this office asked the question, 'Had I read the book that had just been published that alleged that he was a drug user?'" Francisco replied.

But what about prior to his going into the autopsy room? Did he learn that his office had received information that Elvis was suspected of dying of a drug overdose?

"The newspaper reporters, television reporters, journalists from Washington, Chicago, in their deluge of calls to this office commonly asked that question, did I know that, that somebody else in a book had alleged that," Francisco answered.

Unsatisfied with Francisco's evasion, Pleasants persisted. "This deluge of calls, when did this take place?"

"Well, it began to take place that evening and continued for eight weeks," the medical examiner replied.

Pleasants bore in with the "EP DOA" note that had been handed to Dan Warlick. "Were you aware that information was being circulated in your office?"

"Well, the office is hardly big enough to apply the term 'circulate within the office,'" Francisco observed. "The community of Memphis is big enough that certainly the term 'circulate' is a very common term, and there were all sorts of rumors circulating within Memphis, as I assume over the rest of the country, ranging all the way from the fact that Elvis Presley had lupus erythematosus disseminatus to Chagas' disease. You know, these are rumors, and we can't deal in rumors. We always have to consider all possibilities, but we can't deal in rumors."

The circumlocution notwithstanding, Pleasants asked with greater detail, "Were you aware that Lieutenant Sam McCachren of the Memphis Police Department was the source of the information received by Mr. Warlick that I have just described to you?"

"No, because I always consider every death of a relatively young individual as the possibility either exists, or somebody will raise the question, 'Are drugs involved?' It's just like every traffic accident that I investigate; I always consider the possibility, 'Is alcohol involved?' Even though sometimes it proves not to be the case, it always is considered. It's somewhat akin to an instruction—that I'm dangling from the top of the Empire State Building with a mountain-climbing harness, and you're standing at the parapet, and you yell out the instructions, 'Be careful.' The fact that you yelled out the instruction 'Be careful' comes under the category of wasted words, because I already know I'm supposed to be careful."

"Well, Doctor," Pleasants asked, "if in fact your office received information from Lieutenant Sam McCachren of the Memphis Police Department homicide division that there was a suspicion by their office that Elvis Presley died of a drug overdose, isn't that a significant factor in your evaluation of the circumstances of the course of the investigation?"

"Certainly," Francisco replied.

If Francisco had been advised of the possibility that Elvis had died of an overdose, why didn't he notify the prosecutor about it?

"Well, because the possibility of a drug overdose is not a suspicion of felonious cause," Francisco replied.

"So until you have established that there was a drug overdose, you would not bother to notify the attorney general, even though you know that a drug overdose can be a result of a felonious crime," Pleasants asked.

"Every death of every person in Shelby County, every person, can be considered a felonious cause if you stretch the definition of felonious cause to what a next-door neighbor might think or say to another next-door neighbor."

"How would you determine whether or not an overdose was a felonious act?"

"By investigation," Francisco shot back.

"Fair enough," Pleasants said, and asked him what sort of evidence would lead the medical examiner to conclude that a drug overdose was associated with a felonious act.

"Oh, a witness that said somebody gave somebody a medicine, or a witness that said somebody injected somebody with something, or a witness that says that they thought they were taking tea, and somebody gave them arsenic," Francisco answered.

"So in your opinion," Pleasants asked, "the administration by someone of an excess quantity of drugs of whatever kind to a person who died might be a felonious act?"

"Sure," Francisco said.

Well, did the medical examiner's office ascertain during the course of this investigation whether or not such circumstances ever occurred with respect to Elvis Presley?

"Yes," Francisco said.

"What was that information?" Pleasants demanded.

"We have no information on that," Francisco said.

"You have no information as to whether or not Mr. Presley was supplied with drugs in excess of a normal, usual quantity?" Pleasants asked.

"That's right," Francisco assured him.

But where did Francisco get his information? He told Pleasants he got it from the Memphis Police Department. Did Francisco or anybody working for him make any independent investigation of Elvis's use of drugs?

"Other than the discussion with physicians or other professionals, none," the medical examiner replied.

Well, what physicians or professionals did Francisco discuss this subject with?

"Personal physicians that had been seeing or treating him in the past."

187

"That would include Dr. George Nichopoulos, right?"

"Yes."

"And what did Dr. Nichopoulos advise you was the use or misuse of drugs by Mr. Presley?"

"He didn't advise that there was a misuse of drugs," Francisco said. That answer didn't surprise Pleasants or anybody else sitting in the room. Nichopoulos would have been nuts to tell the medical examiner that Elvis was a heavy-duty drug abuser. The medical examiner then admitted that Nichopoulos had informed him of some drugs that Elvis was taking, but Francisco had neglected to itemize them in his report.

Pleasants then shifted his questioning to the news conference Francisco held in October 1977. The medical examiner announced he had consulted two independent toxicologists before ruling that drugs played no part in Elvis's death.

"Who are they, sir?"

Francisco conferred in whispers with his attorney and was advised he must identify the two toxicologists. "Brian Finkle and Robert Blanke," he answered reluctantly. Then Pleasants established that Finkle was a toxicologist at the University of Utah and Blanke at the Medical College of Virginia. Francisco said he had provided neither with copies of Elvis's autopsy report. And Pleasants asked how these outside experts could have come to any conclusion.

"Just a telephone conversation in which I discussed with them the findings and asked their advice," Francisco said. "And I'm not even sure they were aware of the case which I was referring to, because this is done commonly with cases to be investigated, that I will call someone to seek their advice without giving them the detail of which case I'm calling about."

The names of these two scientists became important clues and later would lead *20/20* to several undercurrents of controversy in the forensic community.

Drawing from Francisco's press release from October 1977, Pleasants asked Francisco how he determined that "only drugs prescribed by his doctor" were found in Elvis's body. "Did you make any effort to verify through consultation with pharmacies or otherwise the truth of what they [Dr. Nichopoulos and others] told you?"

"No," Francisco admitted.

What did he mean when he said he found no "illicit" drugs in Elvis's body?

"Cocaine, heroin, things of that nature, Schedule One," Francisco explained.

Did he ever consider that Schedule Two drugs, such as Dilaudid, Percodan, Demerol, and Quaaludes, could be "illicit" drugs?

"Oh, yes, they could be," he conceded.

"Do you know whether or not Dr. Nichopoulos or others prescribed Schedule Two drugs for Elvis Presley?"

"I don't recall," Francisco said.

Pleasants moved on, asking if Francisco considered the analysis of stomach contents important in suspected drug overdose cases.

"Sometimes."

When were they not important?

"When the cause of death is obvious," Francisco said.

"Was the cause of death so obvious in this case as to eliminate any consideration of the possibility of death by drug overdose?"

"No, not at the original phase of it," Francisco said.

"Doctor, to refresh your recollection about the stomach contents, do you recall making a statement to a representative of the press on or about August 26, 1977, to the effect that Mr. Presley's stomach had not been pumped during efforts to revive the singer?"

"Vaguely," Francisco answered.

Pleasants then read him a story in *The Commercial Appeal* by Beth Tamke which quoted Francisco as saying Elvis's stomach contained "nothing identifiable" at the time of the autopsy. The story also quoted Francisco as saying that Elvis's stomach had not been pumped during resuscitation efforts. "Do you recall that interview, and can you now testify whether or not your statements at that time were accurate," Pleasants asked.

"No, I cannot," Francisco said.

Pleasants wrapped up the deposition by asking Francisco to produce Warlick's photos of the death scene.

Francisco said the pictures had apparently disappeared from his files.

Finally Pleasants asked for a copy of the autopsy, and again Francisco said he had returned his copy to Baptist Hospital.

Pleasants was exhausted by his two-day ordeal of extracting information from Francisco. "It wasn't like pulling teeth; it was more like pulling toe bones," Pleasants said later. Rather than end the deposition, though, Pleasants adjourned it, reserving an opportunity to talk to the medical examiner again.

On yet a third front that August, Jim Cole was looking for possible leads on drug prescriptions written for Elvis, but he was having little success. As a long shot, he visited the local office of the federal Drug Enforcement Administration to see if they had ever conducted any drug audits of Memphis area pharmacies or physicians. Gayle Ruhl, the agent in charge of the Memphis DEA office, told him that catching illegal dope dealers was a more pressing assignment for federal narcs than nailing doctors who doubled as pill rollers. If DEA hadn't done any audits, had there been any local or state agencies that had audited the drugstores or the doctors, Cole asked. The federal man shook his head and told Cole that he seriously doubted that any agency was involved in that line of work.

Cole kept sifting. Thumbing through one especially thick file of probate records, Cole discovered an obscure item that immediately caught his attention. It was a bill for $142 from The Prescription House, and it was dated the day before Elvis died. Cole was familiar with The Prescription House. From time to time he had stopped in to have a prescription filled for his family. Prices might be higher than at Walgreens, but for Cole the location was convenient. In addition, it was located directly across the street from the offices of Dr. Nichopoulos.

Cole was acquainted with Jack Kirsch, the owner of the

pharmacy, and felt reasonably sure that Kirsch would talk to him. Running out another fly ball, Cole bundled up the probate records that contained the $142 drug bill and headed to The Prescription House. It turned out to be one of the most important decisions that Cole or anybody else made during the *20/20* investigation. As a result of the visit, Cole would find that important clue leading to a treasure trove of drug records and an avalanche of proof that Elvis Presley was indeed a medical drug addict.

XIV

THE PHARMACY

For passersby on Madison Avenue the bars of the window guard obscured the stenciled letters spelling out The Prescription House. The pharmacy would have been easy to miss except for a tall blue-and-white sign that showed signs of age at the edge of the sidewalk. The interior of The Prescription House scarcely lent itself to a large volume of over-the-counter sales. You didn't find piped-in music or disposable diapers or cosmetics or mixers for Saturday night, just drugs. A vintage Coke machine and ceiling-high shelves crammed with bottles and boxes of nonprescription elixirs and remedies hemmed in the customer area and could turn two people into a crowd. There in front of a foam-rubber two-seater couch was a marred coffee table looking for more shins to bruise.

But from that small location Jack Kirsch carried on a hefty business among middle-aged and elderly Memphis midtowners making up a large percentage of the tenants in high-rise apartment buildings in the area. These residents were within a short ride to the city's medical center. And many of them depended on Kirsch for everything from digitalis to rarefied dermatological ointments for hiding age spots.

The Pharmacy

Kirsch's pharmacy also happened to be directly across the street from the Medical Group, touted as the largest internal medicine clinic in Tennessee, and the office of Dr. George C. Nichopoulos.

Jim Cole was no stranger to The Prescription House or to Jack Kirsch. He had gone to high school with Kirsch's younger brother, Joe. In the early 1970s Cole and his wife had lived in one of those high rises. Several years had gone by since Cole had seen Kirsch. But in August 1979 Cole had a prescription for his youngest child and strolled into The Prescription House to have it filled, to renew acquaintances with Kirsch, and perhaps to talk a bit about Elvis Presley.

A young woman at the cash register asked if she could help. Cole gave her the prescription and asked for Jack. As a good customer, he began loading up on a supply of Bufferin, Outgro, and Mennen Speed-Stick.

A few minutes later Kirsch hopped off his high perch in front of a typewriter and stepped into the front room. He looked the same as ever—trim, wiry, confident, smartly dressed in a blue-green pharmacist's smock.

"Hi, Jack. I'm Jim Cole. Remember me?"

Kirsch's face was a blank.

"I used to work at the newspaper." No better. "You might remember my wife, Sara Jane."

"Yes, yes, Sara Jane. Yeah, now I remember you. You went to school with Joe, didn't you. It's been a while."

And it had. Cole half expected Kirsch to ask where he was filling his prescriptions these days. But the conversation trailed off into how're-the-kids banter and how Cole was claiming the pharmacy's last bottle of Amoxicillin. The timing, Cole judged, was poor for bringing up probate court records and Elvis. Better just to make contact, chum it up some, and call later.

Cole did notice a peculiar sign, however. It was visible through the passageway leading back to Kirsch's high stool and declared that The Prescription House no longer stocked Schedule II drugs. Cole asked about it.

"I got burglarized a few months ago," Kirsch explained. "I'm not laying my life on the line for some junkie. I'll tell the world I don't have any Quaaludes and amphetamines. I don't need 'em."

Cole complimented Kirsch on his price for antibiotics, which was a few pennies below Super D, settled up with his MasterCharge card and left with his sack. The contact had been affable enough, but Cole wondered how it would become when he pressed Kirsch about somebody else's business, particularly when that somebody was Elvis Presley.

―――――――

Later that afternoon Cole voiced that concern at his home, where he rendezvoused with Charlie Thompson. "Call him back," Thompson said. "We're less than two weeks away from airtime, and we've got to know what we've got on our hands. If Kirsch talks, then there's no telling how much work we'll have to do. If he doesn't talk, then you know he has something to hide."

Cole picked up the telephone. "Jack, this is Jim Cole again. Listen, I didn't have much chance in the store to tell you this, but I'm working with ABC News on a story about Elvis Presley. And I ran across something in the probate court records that interested me. The Presley estate paid you $142 for a purchase made the day before Elvis's death, and I was wondering if you could tell me what it was for."

God, what a mouthful, Cole said to himself as the words kept tumbling out. The question could have been smoother.

"It was for all kinds of things," Kirsch answered. He scarcely hesitated. Kirsch explained that Dr. Nick routinely picked up a large quantity of supplies whenever he was going on tour with Elvis. It included drugs, sure, but most of it was for an array of pharmaceuticals, everything from corn plasters to eyewash, like a first-aid kit for Dr. Nick. He treated not just Elvis but the entourage as well whenever there was a tour.

Then Kirsch got chummy, congratulating Cole on landing a network assignment. He asked what kind of story ABC was doing but cautioned, "I'll be glad to help. Just leave me out of it."

Cole, seeing no reason to be coy, said the story revolved

around the last few months of Elvis's life, the controversy over how he died, and, it followed, Dr. Nichopoulos.

Kirsch said he knew a lot about Dr. Nichopoulos. "You can check it out, just don't quote me."

"That's what I'm looking for, Jack. I need somebody to bounce a few leads off of. I'm interested in finding out where Elvis and his crowd filled their 'scrips,' who wrote them, in what quantities, that sort of thing."

Kirsch mentioned the names of several drugstores near Graceland where he believed most of the prescriptions were filled. As an afterthought, he said he was on the outs with Dr. Nichopoulos and the other doctors in the Medical Group. Kirsch had backed out of a deal to relocate his pharmacy in the Professional Building, a six-story marble-and-glass office building recently completed next door to the Medical Group's clinic. Kirsch said he had been in favor of the move until the doctors decided he should pay far more rent than originally agreed. The fallout was bitter.

"When I backed out, their [the Medical Group's] patients stopped coming in here," Kirsch said. "I know what's going on. Instead of giving the patients a prescription and letting them fill them where they want, they are phoning them into the apothecary they've set up over in the building. I get people wandering in here by mistake asking for their prescription."

What Kirsch began relaying to Cole jibed with what Charlie Thompson was hearing from Mike McMahon, the real estate developer involved with Dr. Nichopoulos in the racquetball venture. McMahon said the Professional Building was the brainchild of Dr. Walter K. Hoffman, one of Dr. Nichopoulos's partners. It was intended as an all-purpose medical facility capable of handling the problem of about any patient who walked in the door. It was financed on a cost-plus basis in the early 1970s at an estimated cost of $30 a square foot. Then in 1974 construction costs rose dramatically—up to nearly $50 a square foot. To finish construction the doctors in the Medical Group pulled hard on their line of credit at Union Planters National Bank of Memphis. The result was a high-risk venture whose success depended on rents much higher than originally projected.

On the leasing end, the Professional Building was a flop.

Too far from the medical center and well away from the growing office markets, it attracted few tenants. Soon the doctors ran into trouble scraping up monthly payments ranging above $30,000. McMahon believed that in 1977, the year of Elvis's death, the bank put the Medical Group into receivership to gain control of the clinic's cash flow. Kirsch, who never met McMahon, told Cole the same story.

"Check it out," Kirsch became fond of saying. "What I'm telling you is the truth."

The tips from McMahon and Kirsch sent Cole to the office of Mid-South Title Company with attorney Allen Wade, an associate in Mike Pleasants's law firm. He and Cole plowed through a pile of tract books tracing a dry history of transactions documenting how the Professional Building came to be.

The Medical Group formed three different partnerships to buy property along Madison Avenue where the office building would be constructed. One parcel had been the site of Jimmy Webb's Bar and Grill, one of Cole's favorite watering holes back in his college days.

Wade checked out a stack of microfilm slides connected to the building and began flipping them onto a title company projector. Each financial document bore a series of doctors' signatures, and Dr. Nichopoulos's appeared on them all. The slides kept going —a loan here, an additional loan there, an extension of payment, a further extension, new modifications, more collateral, more money. A cash register at the bank kept ringing in Wade's ears.

"Whew," he exclaimed. "Cole, let's you and me form ourselves a corporation and go over there and get some of that money."

The Medical Group acquired the necessary property, including a parcel on a side street to build a parking lot, for $135,000. Union Planters lent that sum and the doctors paid it back promptly. Then in November 1973 the doctors borrowed $3.5 million as a construction loan. Contractors were on the job in 1974 when the economy went into a tailspin. The documents reflected the downturn in the form of new loans, extensions delaying the first payment, and modifications upping the ante of the Medical Group's liability.

196

By 1975 the project was in danger of collapse. Like a poker player hoping to draw a fifth diamond for a flush, the group sought and received an additional $1.2 million to stay in the game. The doctors' payments now ranged above $37,000 a month, and they had delayed making the first one.

By 1976 UP Bank officials became wary of their investment as it then stood. They demanded and received additional collateral from the group under a new security agreement. By its terms the Medical Group pledged its accounts receivable to support the project. The doctors agreed to provide complete financial statements and collection data to the bank on request. And finally the agreement authorized the bank to take over those receivables and apply them to the doctors' debt if they defaulted.

Moreover, the title company records showed UP Bank had pumped $5.5 million into six stories of marble in a poor location for medical specialists and at over-market rental rates—in other words, a white elephant.

The property records also indicated that the building was tied up in more than one lawsuit. Three involved construction companies and material suppliers. But a fourth, a chancery court case, showed UP Bank squaring off against the Medical Group itself.

A few days later Cole visited the chancery clerk's office, an old haunt. In digging up background material on old Memphis families, Cole had put his hands on original documents as much as 150 years old in chancery court and was convinced that very little had been lost in the interim. The UP Bank/Medical Group case was a snap to find. Cole planked the case file on a massive oak table set aside for researchers and began reading.

The suit was an eye-opener. The Medical Group's bubble burst on August 1, 1976. On that date the doctors failed to make their long-deferred first payment, and the loan went into default. The bank filed suit to enforce its security agreement and sought a court order forcing the Medical Group to place all its assets in an escrow account. The doctors objected.

Negotiations for a settlement dragged into 1977 but without success. Then on April 14 of that year the bank obtained a court order placing the Medical Group in receivership. The action cut the doctors off from all sources of income.

"Nick had to go to the receiver before he could buy a tank of gas to make his rounds," McMahon said.

And the lawsuit confirmed it. From top to bottom the receiver took over the financial operations at the clinic, paying the salaries of the clinic's employees, the telephone bills, the insurance premiums, the notes on equipment and, as McMahon said, the auto expenses. The bank's stranglehold over the doctors lasted for two months. Then the group hired new lawyers and without any explanation in the court record they settled the lawsuit.

"They [the Medical Group] made a deal with the devil," said Kirsch.

The pharmacist was referring to Doctors Hospital, a proprietary facility in southeast Memphis and the roosting spot for many doctors who had been booted off the staffs of the city's more prominent hospitals. Almost since its inception Doctors Hospital had been plagued financially. Early in 1979, Cole recalled, the hospital had made a pitch to Shelby County to be bought out and become a public facility. But against opposition from key county officials, who put a sharp pencil to the hospital's financial condition, the proponents abruptly withdrew from the scheme.

Cole got on the phone to Jim Rout, the former coroner who had questioned Dr. Francisco's actions in the Presley case and who now held the elected post of county commissioner. Rout was chairman of the commission's hospital committee.

"Do you still have the Doctors Hospital proposal to go public?" Cole asked.

"Not in my office, but I can get my hands on it," Rout said. And did.

The proposal was about 100 pages long. It contained the hospital's bylaws, several pages of graphs, an audit by Ernst & Ernst, a medical staff listing, an accreditation statement, an appraisal of the hospital's worth, and, of particular significance to Cole, a feasibility study arguing why the hospital should become a public facility.

A subsection entitled "Forecasted Utilization" was like the piece of a jigsaw puzzle that had been kicked under the dining room table. It provided a breakdown of the physicians on the medical staff, plus their contribution to the hospital's total admissions going back to 1977. In relationship to the other documents Cole had found, it explained why UP Bank had been willing to drop its lawsuit against the Medical Group.

In the first quarter of 1979 there were fifty-one physicians who were admitting patients to Doctors Hospital. Of that fifty-one, there were ten physicians who accounted for a whopping 78 percent of total admissions. Five of the ten were internists in the Medical Group, and one of them was Dr. Nichopoulos. In fact, the Medical Group contributed nearly 40 percent of total admissions. Doctors Hospital was proud of that association, and its proposal for a county buy-out explained the dollars and cents of it.

In May of 1977, at about the time the Medical Group was settling the bank suit, Dr. Nichopoulos and his associates entered into a five-year management contract with Doctors Hospital, doing business as "the Madison Company," to take over the business affairs at the clinic and also to manage the Professional Building. After the ink was dry on this contract, the number of admissions provided by the Medical Group declined at Baptist Hospital. But at Doctors Hospital the figures began skyrocketing.

As the proposal spelled out, the Medical Group was responsible for 26,000 patient days spent in all the county's hospitals in 1977, about one in four going to Doctors Hospital. In 1978, after settlement of the bank suit, the Medical Group was sending almost half its patients to Doctors Hospital and in the first quarter of 1979 more than half.

"For all practical purposes it was a business deal," said Maurice Elliott, executive vice president at Baptist Hospital at the time. "Those patients weren't being sent down there because Doctors Hospital offered better care."

Said Tharon Lee, then chief administrative officer at Doctors Hospital, "They [the Medical Group] are better physicians than they are businessmen."

The pitch to the county disclosed an additional aspect of the cozy relationship between the Medical Group and Doctors Hospital. One would expect a hospital to house its accounting department in the same facility as its patients. Not so at Doctors

Hospital. The Ernst & Ernst audit showed the hospital was renting two floors for its bookkeepers several miles across town in—where else?—the Professional Building, the Medical Group's white elephant. The rent was listed at $12,500 a month or roughly one-third of the monthly payment to UP Bank.

It all fit. Low-grade hospital bails Medical Group out with bank. Group begins sending patients to hospital in droves. Hospital in turn rents space from group. Even so, there was no telling how many patients were being hospitalized when they could have been treated on an out-patient basis.

At a more personal level, Nichopoulos definitely was in dire financial trouble during the last months of Elvis's life. Most of it revolved around the building fiasco, but the Nichopoulos family's new custom-built house on the eastern outskirts of Memphis was also eating a hole in his pocket.

Further digging into Nichopoulos's and the Medical Group's finances later would show just what an important patient Elvis Presley was. From 1970 through the middle part of 1977, Elvis's personal loans to Nichopoulos totaled $275,000—that's over and above a new Mercedes and gifts of jewelry. Payments for medical services rendered during that same period were more than $76,000 with an additional $147,000 going to the Medical Group to cover for Dr. Nichopoulos while he was away on tour.

After Charlie Thompson learned of the Professional Building's importance, he racked his brain for a way to get into it with a camera and without attracting attention. A couple of blocks east of the building, Thompson noticed a teenager unloading a linen cart at the Mercury Valet Cleaners. He struck up a conversation and found out the young employee attended Catholic High School right around the corner, Thompson's old school.

"I just told him I was an old alum," Thompson explained to Cole later on, "and that for twenty bucks I'd like to borrow his cart and some dirty linen. He let me have it but refused the $20."

Bob Brandon, Thompson's cameraman, loaded his prized Ikegami in the cart, covered it with sheets and towels, and wheeled the rig down the street and through the front door of the Professional Building. They proceeded to take it from floor to floor and shot footage of expensive vacant space.

Kirsch was delighted that his leads were pointing to useful documents. "Like I've been saying, what I'm telling you is the truth."

Then he dropped another tip, almost incidentally. "Did you know," he asked Cole, "that the state is doing an audit of Memphis drugstores? They've been in here a couple of times already, looking through old prescriptions."

———

Kirsch wasn't sure which agency was conducting the audit but it had something to do with "healing arts" and wasn't the state board that governed pharmacy licenses. With that lead, Cole telephoned the number for information in Nashville and asked for the healing arts board.

Kirsch didn't have a name that Cole could ask for, so when a receptionist answered at the Nashville office, Cole said he wanted to speak to the chief investigator. Actually the chief investigator was an administrator named Jack Fosbinder, and by training he wasn't a cop but a lawyer. The healing arts board, Fosbinder explained, was the state licensing agency for physicians and some allied medical professionals. Historically, the board had issued licenses to medical school graduates and done little to police the profession. But these days, Fosbinder said, the board was taking its follow-up duties more seriously.

As luck would have it, Cole found out early in this conversation—the first of what turned out to be many—that Fosbinder had been a student of Professor Sara T. Cole at Memphis State University Law School. And Professor Cole, who ran the law library and taught legal research and writing, was Jim Cole's wife.

With that fortuitous introduction Cole felt easier about explaining himself. He wanted to know more about this audit and its aims. Fosbinder explained that field investigators in Tennessee's four largest cities—Memphis, Nashville, Knoxville, and Chattanooga—were pulling prescriptions for Schedule II drugs, the heaviest-duty legal medicines—and recording raw data for new computer equipment that Tennessee state government had purchased and was anxious to use. The basic data included the patient's name, type of drug, quantity, and doctor's name. Feeding all that information into a data base, the healing arts board was attempting to detect patterns of overprescribing in the computer readouts or, put in the crass vernacular, "to pick off the pill rollers."

After hearing Fosbinder's rundown, Cole explained that he was working on a story about Elvis and had pretty good information to suggest that Dr. Nichopoulos was quick to pull out a prescription pad. As an example, he cited Marty Lacker's book and the long list of drugs Dr. Nichopoulos was said to have prescribed.

"He's in our top five in Memphis," Fosbinder said.

"What's your time frame?" Cole asked.

"The first six months of this year," Fosbinder said, meaning January through June 1979.

"Well, why don't you go back to the first seven months of 1977 and check out Elvis and his entourage," Cole suggested.

Given his limited manpower—only one field investigator in Memphis—Fosbinder said he would need some direction to expand the audit. Locations of pharmacies where the prescriptions were filled would be helpful. And, of course, he would need the names of those in the entourage.

Cole promised to supply that help in exchange for an agreement. "If my help results in any sort of civil or criminal action, then I want *20/20* to get a break on the story."

Fosbinder explained that he couldn't control access to a complaint once it was filed as a public record. However, he wouldn't be out of bounds in alerting Cole that an action had just been filed. And he could see to it that an action was filed at an oddball time where unsuspecting reporters might miss it for several days.

With that, Cole and Fosbinder struck a bargain. They also sewed the seeds of later accusations that the healing arts board was acting as a cat's-paw for *20/20*. In truth, the board had its own investigation under way—one that was paralleling *20/20*'s work on Elvis. When asked later about the relationship, Cole told local reporters it was like a good citizen telling the police where he thought a body might be buried.

Because of the promising leads that were turning up early

in August, Thompson and Rivera persuaded ABC executives to scrap the idea of running a fifteen-minute piece on the anniversary of the death. Instead, the Elvis story was being considered for the fall, maybe even the *20/20* opener scheduled for September 13.

From mid-August, Cole began seeing a lot of Joe Dughman, a young Nashville attorney who handled most of the healing arts board's trial work, and Steve Bilsky, a recent law school graduate who was the board's field investigator in Memphis. Frequently they met in Cole's dining room.

First, Cole pointed out all the signals the *20/20* team had picked up in interviews, medical documents, and the Presley literature about drug abuse around Graceland, and he supplied Dughman and Bilsky with a "Who's Who" in the Elvis entourage. Then with some behind-the-scenes help from Jack Kirsch he identified pharmacies, primarily in the Whitehaven area near Graceland, where prescriptions to Elvis and the entourage might have been filled.

But after this meeting and later ones, Dughman's and Bilsky's legwork at the pharmacies wasn't picking up anything that resembled a trail of drugs leading to Graceland. Cole couldn't figure out why. He kept asking Kirsch for other pharmacies. Still there was no breakthrough. He tried additional names, including "John Burroughs," one of Elvis' favorite aliases. Still no luck. Cole was becoming exasperated, particularly as September drew near.

Nonetheless, Dughman and Bilsky were eager to continue their investigation. They worked by themselves but called on Cole regularly to check out leads and to monitor *20/20*'s progress. They kept saying he was providing them with useful information. Cole didn't tell them everything, though. After all, he had confidential sources to protect.

XV

DRUG WATCHERS

As THE SUMMER of 1977 approached, the bodyguard/ valets at Graceland began making forecasts about exactly when Elvis would die. His demand for drugs had become so unremitting and the occasions when he had come within a razor's edge of overdosing so alarmingly frequent that a routine was established to watch Elvis day and night. "There was two or three of us that pinpointed a date," noted David Stanley, Elvis's stepbrother, who was twenty-three when he gave an inside look at Graceland to Geraldo Rivera two years after the death. "Well, I missed about two days—we weren't betting, but we were all sitting around with deep concern. One of us said, 'Hey, man, he just can't go on like this!' One guy said, 'five months or six months." I said, 'two and a half or three months.' And he was obvious. Elvis was obvious. No human being could take that abuse."

David and his brothers, Ricky and Billy, became Elvis's stepbrothers when their mother, Dee Stanley, married Vernon Presley in 1960. Vernon met Dee, then the wife of army Sergeant William Stanley, when Elvis was serving in the army and was stationed in Germany. By 1977 Vernon and Dee were no longer living together; he had filed for divorce when Elvis died. At one time all three Stanley brothers had worked for Elvis as bodyguards, valets, and general flunkies, starting these jobs when they were impressionable young teenagers. Elvis was hardly a wholesome influence, purchasing them the favors of Las Vegas prostitutes and introducing them to drugs. Elvis's senior bodyguards, especially Red and Sonny West, set a roughneck macho image, carrying pistols and freely using their fists and gun butts to beat anyone they suspected of threatening Elvis. Not surprisingly, the Stanleys were converted into unschooled brats, who experienced frequent run-ins with the law and other Memphis toughs and bullyboys. Elvis always bailed the rowdy brothers out of these scrapes and found ways to cover up their misdeeds. Of the three, only Billy Stanley permanently deserted Elvis's fold. He became soured and disillusioned after discovering Elvis was having an affair with his eighteen-year-old bride, Ann.

Ricky and David, who freely admitted having serious drug problems while in Elvis's service, were still on the payroll when the time of death they had been trying to predict finally came. In fact, Ricky was supposed to be on duty during those critical morning hours monitoring Elvis's drug intake and physical condition on a regular basis. David was scheduled to relieve his brother and to perform these same functions. But both brothers were out-of-pocket when Elvis dropped to his bathroom floor and died.

David Stanley had immeasurably cleaned up his appearance in the two years since leaving Graceland. In Dallas, where the *20/20* interview took place, he told Rivera that by the spring of 1977 nearly every member of the Presley entourage had become convinced that Elvis's drug addiction was going to kill him in the near future. At that time Elvis was scheduled to perform at the Louisiana State University Coliseum in Baton Rouge, but he was so incapacitated by drugs that he couldn't get out of bed. "He canceled that tour, that night. We only had three cities left, and that's when I looked at him and I said, 'Hey, man, you're copping out. You're copping out, you're going down. You're fading out, and you don't give a damn, you could care less. I can't save you, nobody can save you. Whatever you're doing, you're doing it your way,' " David recalled.

The Death of Elvis

Road manager Joe Esposito conferred with David and Elvis and scrapped the rest of the tour. He had Elvis flown back to Baptist Hospital in Memphis where he would be admitted for "fatigue." David had to make the cancellation announcement to the packed crowd at LSU. The audience roundly booed and jeered at the announcement and hurled insults and paper cups at him. Other bodyguards and local police officers surrounded David and formed a cluster of protection as they shuffled their way through the buzzing crowd.

Back in Memphis after the short-circuited tour, David was so angry about the scene in Baton Rouge—not to mention the futility of knowing it might be repeated somewhere else—that he took his .357 magnum pistol and blasted holes in the ceiling of his apartment. Then took a baseball bat and smashed an expensive aquarium that he owned.

On an earlier occasion when Elvis had overdosed, David said he confronted Dr. Nichopoulos and threatened "to kick your butt, if you think I'm going to let you kill Elvis." Vernon Presley, meanwhile, was taking Elvis's drug abuse in stride, David said. "Elvis needs those drugs," he recalled Vernon saying when the question of Elvis's pharmacy bills came up.

"Did he think of himself as something other than a normal human being?" Rivera asked.

"He tried not to, but every now and then he would get to a point where he would sit down and try to realize that he was a mortal man," David said. "And then again, with that kind of magnetism, charisma, that he had, he kind of took it to the limit."

David believed Elvis had a death wish. "He was just burnt out," said David, who would later become a fundamentalist Christian minister. "In what he had done, he had done just about everything he thought he could do."

Did that mean that Elvis's death was a suicide? Rivera asked. David said emphatically that it wasn't.

"What was your personal physical shape just prior to Elvis's death?" Rivera asked.

In a word David told Rivera his emotional state was rotten. He was arguing constantly with his wife, Angie. He was taking more and more drugs and was strung out on them when Elvis died.

Earlier that same week Elvis had attempted to reconcile David and Angie. He summoned them up to his bedroom, invited them to seat themselves cross-legged with him and Charlie Hodge and form some sort of ritualistic circle there on his mammoth bed. Looking like a fat swami in a long emerald-green, gold-trimmed robe, Elvis joined hands with the couple and began praying for them. Bowing his head, he intoned, "God, let's keep these two together!"

"He was really concerned," David said. "He could really see hurt, and I was hurting bad. I wasn't totally flipped out, I was doing more drugs than I usually did. I asked Elvis himself, 'God, give me something 'cause I'm going through some pretty heavy times.' "

Through a Schedule II haze, David regarded Elvis at the time as a demigod or latter-day prophet with a pipeline to some drugstore in the sky. Elvis quoted passages of Scripture, prayed, and then asked Hodge and Angie to leave the room. After they had gone, David remembered Elvis looking at him and announcing: "Though it appears like she wants to stay, I've got the answer from God Himself. She'll leave."

"Two days later she was gone," David said. "The next day, he died."

"What kinds of drugs was Elvis taking regularly?" Rivera asked.

"There was three packages, little packages," David said, ticking off Elvis's routine nightly drug intake. "Pack 1, pack 2, and pack 3 were all downers. Quaaludes, Placidyl, Valmid, he started with that. He would wake up in the middle of the night, and he would take pack 2, basically the same, but a little more. And he'd wake up again and take pack 3, which would be the final one, which was even a little more strong. But in between those times, he was into Demerol."

"Was he a pill freak, a real junkie?" Rivera interjected.

"I wouldn't say he was hooked on downs. I just think he got on drugs to see how far he could push himself. He pushed himself pretty far, to see how far he could go. Finally, he pushed himself too far."

Reconstructing the morning of August 16, David said his

207

brother Ricky, who had the earlier shift, was under instructions not to disturb Elvis during the hours he was in the bathroom. When David came on duty about noon that day, Ricky passed on those instructions, telling him not to check on Elvis until 4:00 P.M. "I said, 'Okay,' and I went downstairs, started shooting pool with a friend of mine," David said. "And then I heard this commotion and everything, and I went upstairs, and I see Elvis laying there dead, and it kind of hit me."

Since then David always has wondered if Elvis had issued the "do not disturb" order because he planned to overdose himself. That would explain why the Stanley brothers departed from the normal pattern of monitoring Elvis. But there might be more sinister reasons.

David said that when he first saw Ricky on August 16, he looked bad, unhealthy. David asked his brother if he had experienced a bad drug trip. Ricky muttered that he had had a harried night, said he was going off to get some sleep, and didn't offer any further explanation for his disheveled appearance.

A point David failed to clear up in his interview with Rivera involved his unexplained disappearance from Graceland right after the body was discovered. Sam Thompson and several other Graceland employees saw David driving out of the estate at a high rate of speed. There was someone else in David's car, but the witnesses couldn't tell whether that person was a man or a woman. In his book, *Elvis, We Love You Tender,* which David wrote in 1980 with his mother and brothers, he claimed the person in his car was named Mark. He said he had smuggled Mark into Graceland and was playing pool with him when Ginger Alden called for help. Mark was not authorized to be at Graceland, and as soon as the crisis began, according to David's book, he knew he had to remove his unauthorized guest as quickly as possible. He claimed he was driving Mark home when he stopped and yelled out to Sam Thompson that Elvis was dead.

However, in another book, *Life with Elvis,* which David wrote by himself and published in 1986, he changed his story, dropped Mark entirely from his scenario, and identified the mysterious passenger in his car as Elvis's cousin, Billy Smith. In this later version, he claimed to be driving Billy to Baptist Hospital. Neither of David's accounts of his activities on the day of Elvis's death have satisfied several former Presley employees. They have openly speculated David's friend Mark was either a female with whom David was dallying or was a male with whom he was sharing dope during the time he was supposed to be alert and frequently monitoring Elvis.

In September 1989, ten years after telling Rivera that Elvis "wouldn't deliberately kill himself, but he pushed himself too far," David dramatically altered and embroidered his account. He announced to the London *Daily Mirror* that he was planning yet another book about Elvis's death. The London tabloid quoted David as saying, "I was one of the first to find him. And not only was he dead, but it was by his own hand. I know, because I helped destroy the evidence that pointed to a suicide."

David's third account emerged in 1990, not as a book but as a collaborative article in *Life* magazine. It's rife with factual errors and contradictions. For openers, David was one of the *last* of the Graceland regulars to arrive at the death scene, and whatever physical evidence of suicide that David "helped destroy" is carefully omitted from the *Life* article. On a television interview later David would argue that as the paramedics were treating Elvis, he picked up empty envelopes that had contained Elvis's pills and quietly stuffed them into his pocket. This claim is hardly consistent with accounts from other entourage members who recall that David, like Al Strada, blurted out to the paramedics that Elvis had "OD'd." Sam Thompson, probably the most reliable witness of the events at Graceland, had David speeding down the driveway with Mark or Billy Smith or whomever at the time when the cleanup of Elvis's master bedroom and bathroom took place. In accounts from others, David is most notable for his unexplained absence.

More convincing than his belated picture of Elvis coolly plotting suicide are David's memories of Elvis's bombastic behavior toward the end, as told during his long interview with Geraldo Rivera in 1979. During a stay in Los Angeles, for example, Elvis couldn't reach one of the normally compliant physicians who kept him well stocked in drugs. "He jumped up on the table, and he pulled out a gun, and he said, 'I'll buy the goddamned drugstore if I have to. I'm going to get what I want. People have got to realize either they're with me or against me.' " Elvis apparently was quite serious about buying his own drugstore. He actually had Red and Sonny West price a Bel-Air, California, pharmacy and came close to purchasing it before his manager, Colonel Tom Parker, was able to talk him out of it.

As Elvis's drug overdoses became more frequent, David said the bodyguards had to watch him closely during mealtimes. To keep Elvis from choking to death, they often had to clear his mouth of the food when he lapsed into a coma. "Elvis looked like a pin cushion, you know," David added with a wry, twisted smile. He found it hard to believe that the autopsy pathologists had not reported finding any needle marks on Elvis's buttocks, especially since he routinely had himself injected there with liquid Demerol three or four times a night. David termed Jerry Francisco's findings that drugs played "no significant role" in Elvis's death a "mind-blower."

Rivera suddenly grew solemn, adopting a prosecutorial tone and manner: "Listen to me. It's very important. You person-ally witnessed Elvis Presley taking drugs on many, many occa-sions, almost daily?"

Every time he was on duty with Elvis, at least three days a week, David swore.

"Every time you were on duty?" Rivera asked.

"Yes, every time. Every day. Last two years of Elvis's life, it was every day."

Rivera leaped back to an earlier topic in the interview that David had raised. Did he notice that Elvis's condition was deterio-rating to the extent that he was going to die? And if so, did he talk about it?

"We always talked about it. We were concerned—we knew he was going to die," David answered. "We didn't think. We knew it. Me and some of the guys would sit around and say, 'Hey, he hasn't got long.' It was like a fantasy to see how far—almost as if he wanted to die—and come back, just to see the other side. And it all goes back to a spiritual thing. I think Elvis's death was so spiri-tual because he wanted to know, but he was going about it totally the wrong way."

"What about Ginger Alden?" Rivera asked.

"Ginger Alden had a very rough position. She came into this thing overnight," David replied. "We got a nineteen-, twenty-year-old girl—young, beautiful woman, and she was put in a position where she'd say, 'God, I don't know what is going on.' Elvis used to get upset because she wouldn't talk to him. Well, hell, she didn't know what to say. She saw this going on nightly. And she even attempted to stay away from it."

Could she have stopped him from taking drugs?

"No. Nobody could stop Elvis. Not his father, not the Colonel [Parker], not [Joe] Esposito, not me, not Ricky, not anybody."

According to David, what most distressed Elvis in the last few months of his life was the news that his old-time friends and bodyguards, Red and Sonny West and Dave Hebler, were writing their book about him, which would reveal to his adoring fans some of his drug problems and violent episodes from his strange lifestyle. David recalled how Elvis went out of control late one night in Los Angeles over the upcoming bodyguard book. He picked up a machine gun and announced that he planned to murder the three men, David said.

David reconstructed the madness of Elvis's heavily armed search for his three former friends, telling about an insane 140-mile-an-hour late-night ride down the Santa Monica Freeway in a Ferrari, as the singer headed to a spot where he believed he could find and kill the Wests and Hebler. David pleaded with Elvis to give up his angry vengeance, but had no success, so he attempted to play mind games. "I said, 'Elvis, if we do this, and I get arrested, I've got to have a color television and a refrigerator in my jail cell,'" David recalled. "That would do him out as a psychological thing, to make him laugh or do something, anything to change his attitude. And he didn't laugh at all, he just told me to shut up." Next David attempted heavier stuff, asking Elvis if he got arrested for committing the three murders, who would take care of his young daughter, Lisa Marie. "Well, he just threw up his hands, locked the brakes up, and he broke down on my shoulder and started crying, saying, 'You're right.'"

Before concluding with Rivera, David helped line up an interview with his brother Ricky, who was living in Florida. But he had something to say about the official ruling that Elvis died of a heart attack. "I believe that Elvis overdosed. Elvis took too much. And his aides weren't there. By his own self will, he didn't want us there. He said, 'We don't want anybody upstairs tonight.'"

"Was it suicide, do you think?" Rivera asked a second time.

"I don't think it was suicide," David answered. "I think . . . I'm confused . . . I think he wouldn't deliberately kill himself, but he pushed himself too far. So that makes me believe that he knew he was going to kick out. Whether it's suicidal or not, I can't say."

———

That night after he flew back to Memphis from Dallas, Rivera called Ginger Alden and scheduled another interview for the next day. When Rivera, Charlie Thompson, and the camera crew arrived at Ginger's home, it was apparent that both Ginger and her mother were more nervous than the first time around. Ginger began recapitulating Elvis's last hours in her singsong style. She was careful again to highlight that she and Elvis had discussed their wedding plans on the day he died. But early in her interview, she introduced something new—that she had been taking Quaaludes that day and that the pills threw her for a loop. Ginger had been suffering from menstrual cramps, so Elvis summoned Graceland's resident nurse, Tish Henley, to the master bedroom to bring her some Quaaludes. During the same time nurse Tish was giving Ginger the Quaaludes, Ricky Stanley came up and gave Elvis his first packet of medication. This was about 6:30 A.M. Ginger professed to be a novice at taking Quaaludes, and the pills plunged her into a deep sleep shortly after she took them.

Elvis managed to wake her briefly at about 8:00 A.M., saying he was restless and couldn't sleep. Ricky was again summoned and fetched Elvis's second packet. That explanation from Ginger cleaned up one problem created by her last interview. In this version she at least explained how she knew Ricky brought up the second pill packet.

Elvis woke her up a third time—she was vague about when —saying again that he couldn't sleep and headed toward his bathroom, "taking a book on psychic energy." Again Ginger insisted that she slept until about 2:00 P.M. and remembered calling her mother after she woke up. But she neglected to mention the call she had earlier told Rivera she made to her friend, who was scheduled to accompany her on the concert tour. She also didn't explain how she came to be so well groomed and dressed before she knocked on Elvis's bathroom door, opened it, and found him dead on the floor.

"All the documentary evidence we've been able to gather," Rivera confided, "shows he was in a pretty bad way during the last nine months of his life." Could she have stopped him from his rampant drug-taking?

"I tried on different occasions to stop Elvis, when I saw him take something that I felt he shouldn't be taking or taking too much of something, and on the different times, he would say that I didn't understand it, and he needed them," she said. Her faint voice was beginning to crack with emotion. "When I first started dating Elvis, I'd just turned twenty, and no one ever told me anything about what to expect. I had to learn everything on my own."

Rivera attempted more questions—her personal awareness of drug abuse, the availability of drugs at Graceland, and her exact knowledge about which doctors supplied drugs to Elvis. But he just drew blank stares and inconsequential answers. Rivera believed Ginger now had volunteered everything that she was willing to tell him.

During the drive downtown to conduct interviews with several county officials, Thompson and Rivera discussed what Ginger had just told them. "Do you believe her now?" Rivera asked.

"Partially. I don't think she could handle his drug abuse," Thompson answered. "But I think Dick Grob is right about her making some phone calls and getting cleaned up. She doesn't want to admit that she got up earlier than she said she did, but I don't believe she found him, left him on the floor, fixed herself up, and then calmly phoned the *National Enquirer* and cut a deal."

Thompson said he still planned on tracking down Jim Kirk, the free-lancer for the *Enquirer,* who claimed Ginger tipped him off about Elvis's death before she called for help. "I don't believe that story, but I want to check it out just the same."

Rivera said he felt sorry for Ginger and considered Dick Grob or anybody else who said bad things about her to be liars. Thompson and Rivera agreed to disagree.

———

The next scheduled interview was with Dr. Vasco Smith, a black dentist, civil rights veteran, and member of what was then called the Shelby County Court, the county's legislative branch. Smith had been an Elvis fan and was an abiding critic of Jerry Francisco, primarily because of the medical examiner's stance on police brutality complaints. In one case that sparked an outcry from Smith, a suspect was beaten during an arrest and thrown handcuffed and bleeding into a patrol car. He later died from aspirating blood. Some medical examiners, such as Dr. Robert Stivers of Atlanta, would classify that death as "homicidal." Francisco, however, regarded this type of death as "accidental," giving the benefit of the doubt to the police department and earning the enmity of politicians like Vasco Smith.

The secrecy of evidence associated with Elvis's case threw up a red flag for Smith, and a few years later he would go into high dudgeon over Francisco's classroom display of autopsy slides in which the body of Dr. Martin Luther King, Jr., could be identified.

Standing with Smith in the county court chambers, Rivera asked him to characterize the quality of the official investigation of Elvis's death. "It was surrounded with mystery and contradictions," he replied. "But I did not concern myself too much as a member of county government until it became apparent to me that there was a cover-up, generally approved by county government and others concerned. When I read in the paper that a toxicological report has revealed the presence of at least ten drugs in the body of Elvis, but they also concluded this was not related to his death, I immediately became concerned and asked for a copy of this toxicological report." Smith said Francisco denied having the report and was backed up by the county. "It became apparent to me that there was collusion to hide the facts by the county attorney, the county attorney general, the county medical examiner, as well as the county coroner. This I resent very much."

Next Rivera turned to Steve Cohen, another county court member. Asked why the whole story about Elvis's death hadn't emerged, Cohen said, "I think that he was the number one public figure in the city of Memphis. He is at present the number one commercial attraction that the city of Memphis has. . . . The Elvis mystique completely pervades the Memphis area, and if there are individuals who are so concerned with the mystique that they do not care to know the truth, then I feel that somewhere along the way someone has to take it upon himself to see that the truth is brought out."

Doubtful that any official investigation would be launched two years after the fact, the *20/20* team had a couple of local politicians voicing concern about the unanswered questions in Elvis's death and declaring that there had been a cover-up.

Outside the county building, Thompson and Cole compared notes on tasks remaining for the day. Thompson, Rivera, and the camera crew were heading for Francisco's office to attempt to interview him. After that stop, they planned to visit Graceland to take some shots and then to drive to Nichopoulos's home for more footage. Cole, meanwhile, was preoccupied with his documents and with the healing arts investigators, who seemed to be making little headway finding prescriptions written for Elvis. About noon, shortly after Cole walked in the front door of his house, the telephone rang. It was Steve Bilsky, the healing arts investigator who had been wearing his fingers out at Memphis pharmacies. What the state investigator had to say shocked and excited Cole and ultimately sent him into a frenzy. "We finally found what we've been looking for," Bilsky said matter-of-factly. Where? Cole wanted to know. Bilsky refused to say. The evidence was solid, though, and there was a complaint that had been filed quietly in Nashville, the investigator said.

Bilsky said his associates, Jack Fosbinder and Joe Dughman, were in Memphis and—in accordance with the original agreement with *20/20*—could meet for an interview that afternoon. Bilsky and Cole agreed on 2:30 P.M. at some office space the agency was leasing in the medical center.

Then Cole's mind drew a blank. Where in hell did Charlie say he and Geraldo were going? He didn't have the foggiest notion. What if Thompson didn't check in? The healing arts interviews might have to be done later in Nashville. What if some state official pulled rank and disallowed any interviews? Cole's mind raced as he watched a silent telephone and hoped Thompson would check in. "Come on, Charlie. Call, dammit!"

Within an hour of pacing and cursing, the phone jingled and Thompson's voice came on the line. Before he could ask what was going on, Cole exploded with the news. He relayed the gist of what Bilsky had told him. He gave Thompson directions to the office where the interview would be held. And foremost, they could assume they had the missing element the *20/20* story desperately needed—an official paper link between Nichopoulos and the prescriptions that he had written en masse for Elvis Presley.

———————

Shortly before 2:30 P.M., Thompson drove up to a concrete and glass high-rise apartment building near the intersection of Washington and Manassas. A decade earlier the building had been a favorite for singles of the about-to-be-professional types, but by 1979 the crime rate in the medical center area had soared while both occupancy and rental rates declined. Retailers were hard to find for the ground-floor space, but a lowball government lease beats vacant space. Thompson was convinced that Cole had given him a bum address. But behind the glass door leading off the lobby and down a hallway with ratty carpeting and saggy wall covering, Steve Bilsky and employees of other obscure Tennessee agencies labored under discolored drop ceilings.

Cole pulled into the parking lot and eased Thompson's mind about the location. Bilsky must have spotted the *20/20* crew through the window. He popped his head out of the lobby doorway and motioned to them to follow. Inside were Jack Fosbinder and Joe Dughman, both sitting behind a long, fold-out table piled

Dr. Jerry Francisco and his two assistants, Dr. James S. Bell (left) and Dr. Charles Harlan (right), were steadfast in their opinion that Elvis died only from heart trouble. *(Mississippi Valley Collection/Memphis State University)*

The following materials were identified in the urine or confirmed to be present in the blood at concentrations reported as less than the toxic or lethal levels:

Ethinamate
Methaqualone
Codeine
Meperidine
Chlorpheniramine
Barbiturates

The urine was screened for the following materials, which, except those listed above, were not demonstrated to be present:

Amitriptyline	Doxepin	Methaqualone
Amphetamine	Ethinamate	Morphine
Barbiturates	Flurazepam	Pentazocine
Chlordiazepoxide	Glutethimide	Phencyclidine
Chlorpheniramine	Hydroxyzine	Phenmetrazine
Cocaine	Imipramine	Phenothiazines
Codeine	Meperidine	Placidyl
Desipramine	Meprobamate	Procaine
Diazepam	Methadone	Propoxyphene
Dilaudid	Methamphetamine	Quinine
		Salicylates

Other forensic experts regarded the medical examiner's drug tests as superficial and, in some instances, erroneous. Above all, there were no numerical quantities.

Dr. Norman Weissman, chief toxicologist at Bio-Science Laboratories, was stunned by the case of "Ethel Moore," the code name for Elvis. *(Courtesy of Dr. Norman Weissman)*

DATE SHIPPED	SHIPPER'S REFERENCE NUMBER	CHARGES—CHECK ONE		AIRBILL NUMBER
NOV 3, '77		PREPAID / COLLECT / OTHER [X] See Bill To		3661079

SHIPPER
Harold Sexton, M.D.
STREET
899 Madison Ave.
CITY
Memphis,
STATE Tenn.   ZIP CODE 38146

CONSIGNEE R.E.Orynich
(Bio-Science Laboratories)
STREET
7600 Tyrone Ave.
CITY
Van Nuys,
STATE CALIFORNIA   ZIP CODE 91405

AIRBORNE
AIRBORNE FREIGHT CORPORATION
190 QUEEN ANNE AVE. NORTH
P.O. BOX 662
SEATTLE, WASHINGTON 98111

BILL TO:
(IF OTHER THAN SHIPPER OR CONSIGNEE)
Pathology, Baptist Memorial Hospital
899 Madison Ave.,Memphis, Tenn. 38146

PIECES	DESCRIPTION OF PIECES AND CONTENTS	WEIGHT
1	Medical Specimen packed in DRY ICE	17 lbs

SHIPPER SHOULD COMPLETE EVERY THING WITHIN THE BOLD RED LINE.

NON NEGOTIABLE AIRBILL SUBJECT TO CONDITIONS SET FORTH ON REVERSE SIDE HEREOF.
SPECIAL SERVICE REQUESTED: [ ] NOTIFY ON ARRIVAL (INC'L NAME & PHONE NO.) [ ] HOLD AT AIRPORT FOR PICK UP

DELIVER ONLY TO R.E.ORYNICH

UNLESS A GREATER VALUE IS DECLARED HEREIN THE SHIPPER AGREES AND DECLARES THAT THE VALUE OF THE PROPERTY IS RELEASED TO AN AMOUNT NOT EXCEEDING $50 (DOLLARS) FOR ANY SHIPMENT OF 100 POUNDS OR LESS AND NOT EXCEEDING 50¢ (CENTS) PER POUND FOR ANY SHIPMENT WEIGHING IN EXCESS OF 100 POUNDS.

SHIPPER'S SIGNATURE
X Harold Sexton M.D.

DECLARED VALUE: CARRIAGE None   DECLARED VALUE: INSURANCE None

SHIPPER'S C.O.D.

RECEIVED BY AFC AT: [X] SHIPPER'S DOOR [ ] AIRBORNE TERMINAL   NO. P/U THIS STOP   DIMENSIONS   X   X   =

FORWARDER'S SIGNATURE
X

DATE REC'D AFC 11/3/77   TIME REC'D AFC 1330   3661079

To expedite movement, shipment may be diverted to motor or other carrier as per tariff rule unless shipper gives other instructions hereon.

SHIPPER'S COPY   202 FIV REV.,7-76

Dr. Harold Sexton was sending large packages of samples to California for thorough testing.

After Elvis's death, Dick Grob (with mustache) and Charlie Hodge opened a souvenir shop across from Graceland and were regular speakers to Elvis fan clubs. Meanwhile, Marty Lacker (right), once one of Elvis's closest friends, was writing a book detailing his own struggle with drug abuse and decision to leave the entourage. *(Mississippi Valley Collection/Memphis State University)*

Marian Cocke, Elvis's nurse, wrote her memoirs, too, and donated a plaque to Baptist Hospital. It was stolen. *(Mississippi Valley Collection/Memphis State University)*

Ginger Alden, the girlfriend who found Elvis's body, was subjected to ridicule afterward from some entourage members, particularly Dick Grob, who was writing his own secret account of how Elvis died. *(AP/Wide World Photos)*

(Courtesy of Sam Thompson)

(Courtesy of Linda Thompson)

Two Graceland survivors who established new careers were brother and sister. Sam Thompson, a Graceland bodyguard and later a Memphis judge, once pondered how to deal with Elvis's death if it happened outside Memphis. His sister, Linda Thompson, was Elvis's onetime girlfriend and later became a television star. Linda, years after leaving Elvis, provided an important clue about what really happened.

Dr. George C. Nichopoulos, Elvis's physician in Memphis, was stunned by overprescribing charges first heard from ABC correspondent Geraldo Rivera. In a shot from that confrontation, Dr. Nichopoulos is belatedly removing a clip-on microphone. *(Courtesy of ABC)*

Elvis was also a patient of Dr. Elias Ghanem's (left), a celebrity doctor in Las Vegas, and Max Shapiro's (above), a dentist who answered to the title "Dr. Painless." *(AP/Wide World Photos for Ghanem; Courtesy of ABC News for Shapiro)*

Among those experts who challenged the official ruling were Dr. Eric Muirhead (top left), chief pathologist at Baptist Hospital; Robert Cravey (top right), chief forensic toxicologist for the Orange County, California, Sheriff's Department; Dr. George Lundberg (below left), then chairman of the pathology department at the University of California at Davis; and Dr. John R. Feegel (below right), associate medical examiner of Fulton County (Atlanta), Georgia.

In view of the lack of significant pathology to explain death, and considering the vast number of sedative-hypnotic and analgesic drugs found in concentrations ranging primarily from therapeutic to toxic, the combined effect of these drugs in combination must be considered. These findings would be consistant with coma and certainly could have proved fatal.

Cravey, who conducted a blind test that verified the startling results at Bio-Science Laboratories, had no doubt about how Elvis died.

CONCLUSION

The table below lists blood therapeutic and toxic levels for those drugs identified.

	Serum Level Found	Therapeutic Levels	Toxic Levels
codeine	1.08 μg/ml	0.09-0.117 μg/ml	1.6-5.6 μg,
morphine	0.03 μg/ml	- - - - -	0.05-3.0 μg,
methaqualone	6.0 μg/ml	0.9-8.0 μg/ml	>5 μg/ml
diazepam	0.02 μg/ml	0.1-1 μg/ml	3-14 μg/ml
diazepam metabolite	0.302 μg/ml	0.02-0.5 μg/ml	1-7 μg/ml
ethinamate	10-20 μg/ml	0.5-11.7 μg/ml	- - - -
ethchlorvynal	5-10 μg/ml	0.5-7.0 μg/ml	>20 μg/ml
pentobarbital	3.4 μg/ml	1-4 μg/ml	>5 μg/ml
butabarbital	11.0 μg/ml	10-14 μg/ml	>30 μg/ml
phenobarbital	5.0 μg/ml	15-35 μg/ml	>40 μg/ml

Diazepam, methaqualone, phenobarbital, pentobarbital, butabarbital, ethchlorvynol and ethinamate are below or within their respective therapeutic ranges. Codeine was present at a level approximately ten times those concentrations found therapeutically. In view of polypharmacy aspects, this case must be looked at in terms of the cumulative pharmacological effect of the drugs identified by this report.

RONALD E. ORYNICH, Ph.D.
Director
Department of Toxicology and
    Emergency Services

NORMAN WEISSMAN, Ph.D.
Senior Research Scientist
Toxicology Research and
    Development Group
Research Department

In a preliminary report, Bio-Science provided a table of toxic ranges showing where Elvis's intake was in the danger zones. Drs. Orynich and Weissman were particularly alarmed by the high concentration of codeine.

high with law books, photocopies of prescriptions, and scatterings of legal-size paper. After a round of introductions and handshakes, Dughman passed out copies of the administrative complaint that the state had just filed against Dr. Nichopoulos earlier that day in Nashville.

Glancing through the seven-page-long document, the reporters counted eleven other patients, listed alphabetically, whom Dr. Nichopoulos was accused of overmedicating. They recognized three of the patients—Art Baldwin, a local topless club owner turned government informant; rock 'n' roll singer Jerry Lee Lewis; and Chrissy Nichopoulos, the doctor's own daughter. Reaching the bottom of the third page, they read the name of Elvis Presley.

The list of the numbers and kinds of drugs that Dr. Nichopoulos had supplied to Elvis from January 20, 1977, until August 16, 1977, was mind-numbing. It continued from the bottom of the complaint's third page through two more legal-size pages. The drugs went on and on—Biphetamine, Dexedrine, Dilaudid, Amytal, Quaalude, Percodan, Carbrital, Placidyl, Demerol, cocaine hydrochloride. On August 15, 1977, the day before Elvis's death, Nichopoulos had written him prescriptions for 100 Percodans, 20 cc's of liquid Dilaudid, 50 Dilaudid tablets, 112 Amytal pills, 150 Quaaludes, 178 Dexedrine, and 100 Biphetamine tablets. And on the morning of his death, the doctor had written Elvis another prescription for six Dilaudid tablets, just as Mike. McMahon and Mr. Nash said he did. The ABC men attempted to run a quick tally of the total number of pills and injections that Nichopoulos had prescribed for Elvis, but they were too excited to do the math.

After Elvis's long entry there were the names of four more patients whom the state alleged Nichopoulos had overmedicated. This brought the total number of patients to sixteen. But none of these last four names rang any bells for the television reporters. Cameraman Bob Brandon and soundman Phil Lauter, *20/20*'s Texas crew, signaled that they had their gear in place and were ready to begin the interview.

Dughman began by formally stating the charges. "The State of Tennessee has issued charges against Dr. Nichopoulos for a law that concerns his license to practice medicine in the State of Tennessee. That is, we have charged him with unprofessional con-

217

duct, gross incompetence, gross ignorance, gross negligence, and gross malpractice concerning his dispensing of narcotic substances. Specifically we have charged him with dispensing, prescribing, and issuing narcotic and control substances not in good faith to relieve pain and not for legitimate medical reasons."

Elvis Presley "was issued more Schedule Two uppers, downers, and amphetamines than any individual I have seen," Dughman said. "Looking at this one doctor [Nichopoulos] and this patient [Elvis], this is the worst case of overprescribing, or indiscriminate prescribing, that I have ever seen in my time as an investigator in the State of Tennessee."

Did Dughman have any totals on Elvis for the seven-month period before the death? Rivera asked.

"Just pills, no injectables, approximately 5,300 pills. That includes ups, downs, and painkillers," Dughman replied. Later, the healing arts board would backtrack on its legwork, discover other prescriptions, and change that figure to approximately 12,000 pills in the last twenty months of Elvis's life.

Were there any medical reasons that could possibly justify that kind of overprescribing? None that he could think of, the state investigator replied. Would this mean that Elvis was abusing drugs? Dughman cracked up on that one. That was a safe assumption, to say the least, he said with a grin.

Rivera turned to Bilsky and asked about the prescriptions written on August 15, 1977.

"He prescribed a variety of drugs common on the streets. The ups, downs, pain pills," Bilsky said, "to be specific, Percodan and Dilaudid, both in pill form and injectable. Amytal, which is a sleeping-hypnotic sleeping pill, Quaaludes, Dexedrine in two different strengths. Dexedrine is an amphetamine. A total of approximately six hundred pills."

Six hundred pills in one day. Nobody in the room could believe that figure. But here it was on paper, in black and white, in an official document. Would any criminal charges be forthcoming? Bilsky said his office was sending a copy of the complaint to the federal narcs and the local prosecutor.

Then Bilsky dropped a thunderbolt on Jim Cole. Where were most of Elvis's prescriptions filled? The Prescription House.

And by Jack Kirsch, Cole's deep background source, who had been pointing his finger at other pharmacies. No wonder Bilsky and Dughman had been spinning their wheels finding the locus focus of Elvis's prescriptions.

Dughman said the healing arts board didn't govern pharmacists but added that the Nichopoulos complaint would be sent to the board that did. He cautioned against broadcasting any of the complaint's details until Nichopoulos had been formally served. That would happen the next day.

Rivera promised to keep the complaint under wraps, but he told Dughman that their next scheduled stop was Nichopoulos's office, where there was a glimmer of hope for that interview he and Thompson had been trying to arrange for weeks.

———

The afternoon was another scorcher. It was September 6, 1979, and summer wasn't letting go. Jim Cole, Charlie Thompson, Bob Brandon, and Phil Lauter were feeling every degree of the debilitating heat as they waited on the asphalt parking lot behind Dr. Nichopoulos's low-slung medical office. Geraldo Rivera was inside the building, attempting to persuade the white-haired doctor to commit unwitting suicide on camera. Thompson wasn't optimistic about Rivera's chances. Just another fly ball to run out, particularly since this marked the seventh time in the past two months that the producer had participated in similar attempts. Nichopoulos had always rebuffed them, and Thompson had grown weary of spending hours hanging out in this same parking lot, hoping to get a shot of the doctor coming out the door, scrambling into the gold Mercedes convertible Elvis had given him, and driving off.

And there was a potentially dangerous aspect to frequenting the lot too often. An employee of the Medical Group owned two large, fierce-looking Doberman pinschers. Every time Thompson had seen those dogs so far, they had been on a leash. But the black handyman who acted as a part-time chauffeur for some of the doctors in the Medical Group had teased Thompson that those dogs just might get loose someday. Literally, the producer was watching his ass.

After a half-hour wait, Thompson saw Rivera emerge from the building. He yelled, "Bring in the camera." Thompson walked up to him and asked, "How did you do it?"

"I told Nichopoulos he basically had a choice," Rivera said. "He could either sit down and talk to me like a gentleman, or I would wait outside his office and stick a microphone in his face and he could say, 'No comment.' "

The whole production team trooped into the building behind Rivera. Icy glares from nurses and receptionists greeted them as they walked down a narrow hall and into Nichopoulos's small office. The doctor was sitting behind a desk wearing a white medical smock. At his back hung a bas-relief of a Greek physician treating a patient. Thompson looked at Nichopoulos's stark white, flyaway hair and pristine coat, both set off by a brown-tanned countenance. Gold and diamond rings gleamed on his fingers.

Brandon and Lauter set up their taping equipment without any cues and were ready to shoot. Thompson and Cole sat on the floor silently and distantly flanking Rivera, who took the seat across the desk from the doctor. Brandon signaled to Rivera that he was rolling, and the correspondent began.

"May I call you Dr. Nick?" Rivera inquired politely. Nichopoulos acquiesced. "Dr. Nick, how did you and Elvis get together?" It was a mushy beginning but seemed to defuse some of the thick tension that blanketed the room.

Nichopoulos said he had a phone call from Elvis one Sunday when the entertainer couldn't get in touch with his regular physician. "He wanted me to come out and check him before he was leaving for California," he said. That was twelve or thirteen years earlier, Nichopoulos guessed.

At what point in Nichopoulos's relationship with Elvis— Rivera hesitated, then plunged—did the singer begin to have a drug problem?

It was as though Rivera had put a live hand grenade on Dr. Nick's desk. The doctor didn't like the question or its tone but didn't know quite what to do about it.

Finally Nichopoulos retorted that he couldn't answer for the "obvious reasons that it's confidential and personal."

Well, Rivera continued, did he ever counsel Elvis against taking drugs?

"I can't answer that," Nichopoulos pouted. The tension began mounting again, and Rivera eased off.

Was the doctor/patient relationship the only one he and Elvis shared?

No, the doctor answered, they played sports together, and after Vernon became ill, he acted as Elvis's father. "And there were other times when I may have played the role of his brother, relatives, his sister, friend, and companion. So we had these types of relationships." Sister? Obviously Nichopoulos was a bundle of nerves beneath a calm exterior. Elvis found emotional strength in their association, and "the majority of the time" he provided Elvis with straight answers, the doctor said.

Did the fact that Elvis was such a legend in his own time affect the doctor's medical judgment?

"Never," the doctor asserted.

Did Elvis ever play his emotional "you're either for me or against me" routine on the doctor?

"Sometimes," the physician admitted.

Did his financial dependence on Elvis affect his medical judgment?

"I was never financially dependent on Elvis," Nichopoulos countered.

"But you owed him large sums of money?" Rivera argued.

"No," the doctor insisted emphatically.

"Isn't it a fact that you owed well, according to the records, over two hundred thousand dollars on your home and at least several tens of thousands of dollars more than that in various loans?" Rivera persisted.

The doctor answered that Rivera had brought up a subject that he didn't want to discuss. He maintained the house loan was a business deal "and not a donation and not something else, and is money that I am paying back to the estate."

Rivera now began toying with a large legal-size folder, which contained the state's complaint against Nichopoulos. He didn't open it, but he raised it so that Nichopoulos could get a glimpse. Then he got down to cases.

"The records indicate that especially in the last year of his life, you prescribed certain medications to Elvis Presley in quite extraordinary large amounts. Why?"

Nichopoulos shuddered. "I can't comment on that, and I don't believe it is true."

Rivera waved the folder like a bloody shirt. "Well, the records we have, Doctor, and I will say this as gently as I possibly can, indicate that from January 20, 1977, until August 16, 1977, the day he died, you prescribed to Elvis Presley, and the prescriptions are all signed by you, over five thousand Schedule Two narcotics and/or amphetamines. It comes out to something like twenty-five per day."

Nichopoulos was silent and stunned. Rivera then pulled out a scrap of paper from his folder. It was about the size of a prescription form.

"I don't believe that," the doctor answered belatedly, his voice breaking.

"Well, is it something you would like to refresh your recollection or something that you deny?"

"I deny it," Nichopoulos said as a half-question, half-reply. Cole, sitting to Nichopoulos's right, later said he was sure the doctor believed Rivera was holding an actual prescription. "In fact, I think he believes to this day that we brought stolen prescriptions with us to the interview. He never asked Geraldo if the piece of paper was a prescription. If he had I don't think Geraldo would have lied about it. But Geraldo did ask the questions with great authority and insistence. I can see how Nichopoulos could have had the impression that we had some prescriptions with us."

Rivera paused, let the atmosphere percolate and then demanded: "Make a statement as unequivocal as you can then, Doctor."

"I have nothing else to say but . . ."

"But you deny that you prescribed large amounts of narcotics to Elvis Presley in the last year of his life?" Rivera interrupted. "To wit, over five thousand Schedule Two narcotics and amphetamines?"

"I don't have any comment," Nichopoulos said.

"According to the records, they include Dilaudid, which is a morphine-type drug; included Placidyl; they included barbiturates; they included uppers, downers, painkillers for which the people we have asked indicate there was no acceptable medical rationale."

Nichopoulos appeared lost, dazed, and said he didn't have an answer.

Rivera wasn't satisfied. Why had Nichopoulos prescribed all of those drugs in that short period of time?

"I think you didn't understand me. I said that I don't think that I did," the doctor replied.

"You don't think that you did?" Rivera asked, emphasizing "think."

"I know I didn't," the doctor said.

"You are absolutely stating that you did not? And with the documentation made very clear to you, you still deny it?" Rivera demanded, waving the folder again.

"Yes," Nichopoulos insisted.

"Maybe there has been some mistake, perhaps?"

"Could be. I have forged prescriptions [meaning, perhaps, he had seen where patients had forged prescriptions]. I don't think that he would forge prescriptions, but I am sure that there must be an error somewhere."

"Do you think that if we have prescriptions for fifty-three hundred pills, Schedule Two, they would be forged, or a great many of what we had would be forged?"

Nichopoulos said he didn't know.

Did he remember that he wrote a Dilaudid prescription for Elvis on the day he died? "What was the rationale for that?"

"He told me that he had been to the dentist and that the dentist had given him some, I think codeine, that he had a lot of pain, and it wasn't helping him. And that he was leaving for a tour the next day and that he needed to get some sleep. And he couldn't sleep because he was having pain."

But wasn't Dilaudid an extremely strong narcotic analgesic?

"It depends on the individual," Nichopoulos said. (Dilaudid is an extremely strong narcotic analgesic regardless of the individual and drug tolerance doesn't change the chemical makeup and potency of the drug.)

Rivera continued. Didn't he prescribe six Dilaudid tablets, 4 milligrams each? Nichopoulos said he had. But why did Elvis need such strong stuff? According to Rivera, the records from Dr. Lester Hofman, the dentist who treated Elvis in the early morning hours of August 16, 1977, showed that Elvis had only had two teeth filled and his teeth cleaned.

Nichopoulos said he wasn't sure what was done that night "other than he went to the dentist and he was having some pain."

But why Dilaudid? Why give somebody with a minor toothache a drug normally reserved for terminal cancer patients in unbearable pain?

Nichopoulos quizzed Rivera about what he would have given Elvis. Rivera conceded that he was not a doctor, but reminded Nichopoulos that there was a whole range of analgesics, beginning with aspirin, which would have been much more appropriate to prescribe for Elvis's toothache than Dilaudid.

And besides, why had the doctor prescribed Demerol, Placidyl, and a multitude of barbiturates for Elvis that same night that he had given him Dilaudid?

"Because he was having a problem. I knew that he went to the doctor, because they called me from the doctor's office," Nichopoulos said, meaning "dentist."

Rivera sorted through this confusion and asked why the dentist didn't prescribe Dilaudid.

"Well, because he can't prescribe. I don't think they can prescribe Dilaudid." As an afterthought, Nichopoulos noted, "He still had twelve the next day."

Nichopoulos's meaning was clear. On the day Elvis died, the doctor had checked Elvis's drug supply and found twelve Dilaudid tablets, even though the pharmacy records show he prescribed six on the early morning hours of August 16. Since someone had cleaned up Elvis's bathroom and whisked away all the drugs before outside investigators arrived, there was no way to verify Nichopoulos's claim about the Dilaudid, Elvis's favorite downer.

Rivera returned to the 600 pills that Nichopoulos had prescribed for Elvis the day before he died?

"What do you mean six hundred pills?" Nichopoulos shot back.

"Six hundred pills of various narcotic substances were prescribed to Elvis Presley, and you signed the prescription on August fifteenth," Rivera insisted.

"No, that's not true," Nichopoulos replied with conviction.

Was it a smaller number?

Nichopoulos didn't answer, then asked, "Let me make a statement, okay? You have been patient, and I have been patient, and I have got a lot of work yet to do. And as far as I'm concerned, the interview is closed."

Rivera tried to ask another question, but Nichopoulos began fiddling with the small microphone clipped to his smock. "I don't want to hear it. When you came in here today, you said that I can make a statement that I wasn't going to make any comments. And we have already passed that manyfold."

"May I ask one question? One general question?" Rivera persisted. "Do you have any regrets?"

"No regrets," Nichopoulos mumbled and laid the microphone on his desk. The room was silent, but Bob Brandon had spotted a memento hanging on the wall beside the door. Before breaking down his gear, Brandon turned his camera and shot an autographed photograph inscribed "To my good friend and physician, Dr. Nick. Elvis Presley."

Thompson and Cole slowly stood up and helped pack up the equipment.

XVI

IN THE CAN

CHARLIE THOMPSON had been stewing ever since finding out that Jack Kirsch had supplied most of the drugs during the last seven months of Elvis's life. Kirsch had been misleading Jim Cole, who in turn had been misdirecting the state investigators away from The Prescription House.

Thompson fumed as he dropped the heavy sound case he had carried from the Nichopoulos interview on the tailgate of the camera crew's rented station wagon. He wiped sweat off his forehead, glanced across Madison Avenue to the pint-size building that housed Jack Kirsch's pharmacy and saw that it was still open, even though it was now well after 6:00 P.M. "Okay, let's go across the street and get Kirsch."

That prospect upset Cole. He liked Kirsch. Despite the bum leads, Cole thought, where would the story be if Kirsch hadn't tipped him off about the audit? He believed *20/20* owed Kirsch more than an ambush interview and a nasty, maybe unnecessary, confrontation. He took off across Madison and hollered over his shoulder to Thompson, "I'm going to tell him what's going on." The store was empty of customers, and knowing he had maybe a short minute, Cole got Kirsch to the front counter. "I know I said I'd keep you out of this, Jack, but we've found out that most of the prescriptions for Elvis were filled right here," Cole said. "Geraldo and a camera crew are coming over here right now to get your comments."

"What, on camera?" Kirsch exclaimed. "Uh-uh, no way." Then the pharmacist looked out the window and saw Thompson coming across the street in a brisk jog with Rivera and the camera crew not far behind. As Thompson yanked open the pharmacy door and stalked in, Kirsch bolted for the back part of the store. Kirsch had met Thompson once before, recognized him as the producer, and didn't like the look of fury on his face.

Kirsch scampered back to the sanctuary of a bathroom in the rear of the store. Thompson was right behind him. Cole threw up his hands and from the front counter listened to the exchange of words. Once in the john, Kirsch locked the door and prepared himself to outlast Thompson, who now was pounding on the restroom's flimsy door and cursing. "Go away, please go away," Kirsch moaned from within.

Thompson raised a booted foot and was ready to kick in the door when Rivera appeared in the hallway. He put a restraining hand on Thompson's shoulder and told him to calm down. Then Rivera knocked on the bathroom door and began coaxing Kirsch out. "Jack, let's not be childish about it. Now come on out here. Come on, Jack." But Kirsch refused to budge. "Don't you think," Rivera said with a broad grin, "that this is a shitty place to do an interview?"

That brought guffaws all around. Then Rivera signaled to Bob Brandon, who was waiting at the other end of the hall, to begin rolling his videotape for a stand-up. "This is the drugstore where the investigators discovered that all those prescriptions were filled," the correspondent intoned. Still hiding in the loo, Kirsch overheard what Rivera was saying and offered to come out if Rivera could guarantee his safety.

"All right, come out now. Otherwise we will do it this way," Rivera promised. "We will do it one way or the other. Okay. Now we will do it like gentlemen."

"Wait just a second," Kirsch pleaded. He finally crept out of the bathroom, glancing nervously in Thompson's direction.

Thompson glared back. Cole was waiting out by the front counter when Kirsch reappeared with the others and set up for the interview. Rivera wasn't wasting any time or risking another escape.

"Between January 20, 1977, and August 16, 1977, in the period of seven months, you filled prescriptions for Elvis Presley, for fifty-three hundred pills, most of them Schedule Two, that is narcotics, Quaaludes, etc., all the barbiturates, and Demerol. Could you tell me what went through your mind when you continually saw these prescriptions by Dr. Nichopoulos and made out to Elvis Presley?"

All the color drained from Kirsch's face. "I don't know where you are getting your figures. And I don't know that they are accurate."

Rivera was still carrying the legal folder, which he had just used so effectively as a prop in Dr. Nick's interview. He bandied it about now and gave Kirsch the impression that he had the goods. "There are obviously a lot of prescriptions, Jack. Let's not play games. Tell me what you thought when you saw these?"

Kirsch admitted there were quite a few prescriptions but said he had no qualms about filling them because either Dr. Nichopoulos or his nurse personally picked them up.

Did he ever question what was going on?

"My job is to fill prescriptions, sir. You know, and if a licensed physician comes in with the prescription, you know, that's my job to fill prescriptions. And, yes, possibly in my own mind I questioned this thing. But I never questioned the doctor."

What about what happened to Elvis Presley? "Do you have any regrets?" Rivera asked.

"I fill prescriptions. I didn't give the drugs to the patient. I gave the prescriptions to the doctor. No, I don't have any regrets," Kirsch said.

"You were just following orders?" Rivera asked.

"I was just following orders," Kirsch repeated. "I really didn't think they were going to Elvis."

Thompson interjected, "My God, it is a violation of federal law. You didn't think they were going to Elvis? You had to know who they were going to. Haven't you read the code?"

Kirsch was speechless.

Rivera jumped back in. "If you didn't think they were going to Elvis, who did you think they were going to?"

"Oh, I had no idea," Kirsch answered. "I was giving them
as I say, to the physician."

Thompson couldn't restrain himself. "And you never had a
second thought about where the drugs were going? You never had
a second thought as to how destructive they would be?"

"I was giving these drugs to a physician that I had confidence in," Kirsch retorted.

"Do you still?" Rivera asked.

Kirsch nodded. "In fact, he [Nichopoulos] is a fine physician. There are a lot of good things that he has done."

"And if he came in," Rivera asked, "and said, 'I want six
hundred assorted pills, Dilaudids, Placidyls, Amytals, Seconal,
Demerol, every barbiturate known to man,' you would fill the prescription and not have a second thought about it?"

Kirsch shook his head. "At this point, no, probably not.
No, sir."

Rivera, Thompson, and Cole looked at one another, then at
the camera crew. What else was there to ask or say? Even Charlie
Thompson's anger was spent.

———

Later that night Thompson and Rivera drew up a work
schedule for the next few days. It was then Thursday, September
6, 1979, and they were supposed to broadcast this piece one week
from this night. Considering the huge news breaks they had just
obtained exclusively—the state charges against Nichopoulos, their
interview with him and then with Kirsch—they couldn't safely
hold this material and postpone the broadcast. Sooner or later some
other news organization would learn about the state charges, and
20/20 would lose its scoop.

Hence Thompson and Rivera decided to tape stand-ups in
the morning with Brandon and Lauter. Then Rivera would line up
a second crew and fly to Florida to interview Ricky Stanley.

Thompson and Cole would stay in Memphis and use Brandon and Lauter to clean up any shooting that was still required. By Saturday, Thompson and Rivera would be in New York, working with their executive producer, Av Westin, and shaping their raw footage into a complete broadcast. Cole would remain in Memphis to backstop them on details and to monitor developments on the scene.

Thompson and Rivera telephoned Westin, a bright, articulate, and creative executive, and described what they had. As a working title, Rivera suggested, "The Elvis Cover-Up." Westin told them he was willing to gamble and turn this piece into an hour-long show if their videotape was near as good as they swore it was. Considering that Thursday, September 13, was *20/20*'s season opener in a regularly scheduled prime-time slot, Westin was sticking his neck out. If he locked himself into the Elvis show and Thompson and Rivera delivered a dud, *20/20* might be a goner.

On Friday morning, Thompson and Rivera were standing on the steps of the Shelby County Courthouse, a quadrangular stone building with imposing columns in classical Greek tradition. With the building as a backdrop, they were preparing to tape a series of on-camera stand-ups that would introduce, summarize, and conclude various segments in the hour-long broadcast. Phil Lauter attached a wireless microphone to Rivera, who would have freedom to roam outside the court house without wires trailing along like a leash. Brandon had his Ikegami mounted on a tripod and motioned to Rivera to begin.

"The official investigation of the death of Elvis Presley, at least insofar as we have been able to determine," Rivera began, "must rank among the worst, most unprofessional investigations of this type ever made. For whatever reason or motive, essentially no real effort was ever made to truly unearth the circumstances of Elvis Presley's death. It seems almost as if the city of Memphis itself just did not care to know the truth about the death of its most prominent citizen."

It was a smooth take, but Brandon wanted a backup. Rivera breezed through the script again. Then the crew set up to record a number of assertions about the story. These would be taped at different focal lengths of the camera and shot from different vantage points around the court house. Their aim was to vary the background while Rivera was talking. These breaks also overcame the need for Rivera to memorize long passages of script. Thompson wasn't allowing Rivera to ad-lib any lines.

"Consider, if you will, the following points," Rivera continued.

"Item: No real police investigation was ever made. At nine in the evening on the same day Elvis died, before it was medically or scientifically possible to know for sure why or how he died, the Memphis police declared this case closed.

"Item: Dan Warlick was the man in charge of the medical examiner's investigation. Dr. Jerry T. Francisco, his boss, claimed Warlick had made an extensive search for drugs at Elvis's home, Graceland. In fact, Warlick admitted to us that he had never searched the house trailer of Graceland's resident nurse, the house trailer where all the drugs were kept.

"Item: Elvis's stomach contents were destroyed without ever having been analyzed.

"Item: There has never been a coroner's inquest.

"Item: The Shelby County district attorney was never officially notified or asked to determine if there were any violations of criminal law.

"Item: No attempts were made, even after the toxicological reports were completed, to find out where Elvis had been getting all those drugs.

"Item: All the photographs taken of the death scene, all the notes of the medical examiner's investigation, and all of the toxicological reports allegedly prepared by the medical examiner are missing from the official files.

"Item: Officials of the county government believe there has been a cover-up."

There at the sidewalk, Brandon set up a video monitor to satisfy everybody on the team that they had a clean tape. It was stunning.

The Death of Elvis

Ricky Stanley, who was twenty-five in 1979, had inherited the light blond hair and fair complexion of his mother, Dee. His neat appearance, when Rivera met him for the interview, belied a recent past of hard living, drug taking, and keeping up with Elvis Presley. And Ricky kept pace as an unbridled, all-purpose substance abuser. Ricky recalled visions of himself smoking marijuana, swallowing downers and hallucinogens, snorting long lines of cocaine, and washing it all down with bourbon or tequila. He was an alcoholic by the time he was nineteen. He became addicted to heroin, and in 1975 he was arrested for obtaining drugs from the Methodist Hospital pharmacy in Memphis with a forged prescription. The charges were later reduced to malicious mischief. He paid a $50 fine and got a six-month suspended sentence. All added up, Ricky had been busted on drug charges five different times by 1977.

In 1979 Ricky was living in the Florida panhandle. In the two years since Elvis's death, Ricky had transformed himself from a dissolute doper, drunkard, and loud-mouthed tough to an even-tempered, clean-cut ministerial student. It had been quite a battle, and to Ricky's mind it wasn't all over. He feared slipping back to his old habits and relied on memories of Elvis's miserable death to walk the straight and narrow.

Rivera informed Ricky of the recent and still unannounced state charges against Nichopoulos.

"I'm not surprised in the least," Ricky said.

"Why not?"

"Well, you know Dr. Nichopoulos gave Elvis quite a bit of medication over the years, and if anybody was investigating, they'd find out that it would be illegal—there was so much medication given." Then Ricky rattled off some of the drugs that Dr. Nick normally administered to Elvis on a daily basis—Quaaludes, Demerol, morphine, barbiturates.

Were these essentially drugs "to make you feel good?" Rivera asked.

"Oh, for sure."

Was Dr. Nick a "Dr. Feelgood"?

"Dr. Nichopoulos? I would say so. You know Dr. Nick was with him and worked with him for a long time, and it got to where he even traveled with him. I knew it would be just a matter of time before it came out."

Doubling back over ground he had covered with Ricky's brother and with Ginger Alden, Rivera asked about those early morning hours of the day Elvis died.

Ricky said he saw Elvis about 4:00 A.M. when he brought him his first packet of pills. He had picked up the last Dilaudid prescription at Dr. Nichopoulos's house about 3:00 A.M. and had taken it to the Baptist Hospital Pharmacy to be filled. And from there?

"Well, I went back to Elvis's house and went upstairs and gave it to him, talked with him for a moment, and left," Ricky said. This meant that Elvis had the Dilaudid available to take with his first regular packet of pills. As best as Ricky could remember, Elvis did just that. This conflicted with Dr. Nichopoulos's assertion that he found all the Dilaudid tablets he had prescribed in Elvis's bathroom. And Ricky's recollection also was at odds with the toxicology tests, which had found no traces of Dilaudid in Elvis's system.

Ricky recalled that when Elvis took the Dilaudid he "seemed to be kind of tired at that time. Elvis looked like he was on the brink of tears, almost anytime."

Ricky said he received another phone call from Elvis about 5:30 to 6:00 A.M. asking for a second drug packet. Ricky's timing was about two hours different from Ginger Alden's, who said Ricky brought the first packet up about 6:30 A.M. and the second one about 8:00 A.M.

During the second trip upstairs, Ricky said he talked with Elvis briefly. "Elvis looked at me and said, 'Rick, if I need you, I'll give you a call.' And he damn near said he didn't want to be disturbed. So I just left and went down to my own room. That was the last time I saw him."

What was in that second packet of pills? A variety of sleeping pills—Quaaludes, barbiturates, Seconal, Placidyl, Valmid, Valium, and, as Ricky remembered, "a couple of Demerol tablets."

Was that common? Rivera asked.

"Yes, it was."

"It happened every night that you were on duty?"

"Oh, yeah, every night I was on duty. Elvis had a serious

drug problem. The reason I can say that is because I used to have a drug problem. I would say it was very bad, and we knew if it continued, that something like this would happen. We knew it would just be a matter of time."

Had anything like this happened before, a really serious overdose?

"He'd collapsed several times from too much medication. It got to the point that part of the job was watching him like a male nurse. Just watching him, helping him, if he needed any help."

What was the real reason that Elvis checked himself into Baptist Hospital in April 1977. Fatigue? Intestinal flu?

"No, that wasn't the real reason, Geraldo. Elvis went in the hospital to dry out. Elvis had a drug problem. He went in several times to dry out, because of drugs, because of the variety of medications he was taking."

Was he surprised that Elvis's drug problems and their role in his death had been covered up for so long?

"Yes, it is amazing, but you see a lot of amazing things have gone on with Elvis Presley that people will never know. It didn't surprise me. I figured within a matter of time, it was all going to come out."

Ricky already had mentioned Nichopoulos, but what about the other doctors and dentists? Did Ricky know Dr. Max Shapiro, the dentist from Los Angeles?

"Oh, yeah, I know the man, I know who he is, I know him very well. Max gave Elvis all the things that he wanted. He was like the rest of all the doctors, just gave him the medication he wanted. Volunteered it."

What about Dr. Elias Ghanem of Las Vegas?

"Well, Elias was no different from the rest. No, Elias did the same thing. Now I'll say Elias to me did seem like he cared for Elvis. But you know, after a while he fell into it like the rest of them, just giving him whatever he wanted, whenever he wanted it."

Were there any doctors who said "No" to Elvis?

"No, there were no doctors, Geraldo, that said 'No' to Elvis. They all gave him whatever he wanted, anytime he wanted

234

it, and there wasn't anybody that ever said 'No' to Elvis Presley that I've been around. Especially doctors."

Where did all the codeine in Elvis's system come from?

Ricky didn't know. He thought that it had been prescribed by Dr. Lester Hofman, the dentist that Elvis had seen early in the morning of his last day.

Did Ricky bring Elvis the last drugs he took the morning he died? Ricky thought so, but later evidence would show that he was mistaken. Later that morning, Elvis tried to contact Ricky for more drugs. Unable to find Ricky, he called on someone else to bring him another packet of pills. That information would have shot holes in Ricky's contention that Elvis didn't want him around. But at the time Rivera was interviewing Ricky, this new information hadn't surfaced.

Rivera and the rest of the *20/20* crew were also unaware at this point that next to Elvis's huge padded toilet was an intercom system with a toggle switch. It was well within reach when Elvis was stricken. If it were working, then it was possible for Elvis to have thrown the switch when he went into distress and called for help over the intercom.

Rivera, nonetheless, had nailed down several points that were critical to the upcoming broadcast. He had first-hand confirmation of the large numbers of drugs Elvis had taken hours before his death. He had confirmed the actual depths of Elvis's addiction. And he had an eyewitness naming names of doctors who gave Elvis prescription drugs for no apparent legitimate medical purpose. All put together, Rivera's quick trip to Florida was valuable for the upcoming broadcast less than a week away.

———

On Saturday morning in New York, Thompson and Rivera met with Av Westin, *20/20*'s executive producer. They screened the Dughman and Bilsky interviews plus the confrontations with Nichopoulos and Kirsch. Westin was impressed with the material and gave them thumbs up for the whole show the following Thursday night. "Let's go for broke," Westin said, and assigned the pair a half dozen assistants who would work with them around the clock for the next five days.

Westin was curious about whether the complaint against Nichopoulos would remain under wraps until airtime. Thompson and Rivera thought the chances were good. The healing arts people were keeping quiet and Nichopoulos wasn't likely to be holding any press conferences.

On Monday afternoon, September 10, Rivera and Thompson were overhauling the script when a production assistant interrupted them. A lawyer named Ken Masterson from Memphis was on the phone and said he represented Nichopoulos. Thompson and Rivera took the call together. Nichopoulos shouldn't have been interviewed without an attorney present, Masterson said. "We're not the cops or the FBI," Thompson replied. "We don't have to read somebody their Miranda rights before we interview them."

How would they like to interview Dr. Nichopoulos again? Masterson asked.

That would be fine, Thompson said. When?

The sooner the better, Masterson said, but with some conditions.

"Like what?" Rivera demanded suspiciously.

"You have to throw away the first interview, and I have to be present at the second and be able to tell the doctor which questions that he can answer," Masterson said.

"Like hell we do," Thompson said. "We'll agree to reinterview him, but we reserve the right to use both interviews."

In that case, no deal, Masterson said.

From their perch in the catbird seat, Thompson and Rivera told the attorney that any further discussion was pointless. They thanked him for calling and rang off.

By lunchtime Tuesday, two days before airtime, they were exhausted from viewing tape, editing interviews, and double-checking factual details by long distance with Cole in Memphis. Needing to stretch their legs and take a breather, Thompson and Rivera went for a walk down Columbus Avenue. The sun was out, and they took longer than intended. On the way back as they neared the production facility, Rivera's younger brother, Craig, came flying up to them and shouted, "You guys have got trouble on your hands. The Nichopoulos story just broke on the wires."

Thompson and Rivera were devastated. They raced to their office to make a damage assessment. After several frantic calls, Thompson began piecing together how the story broke. He learned that whispers among secretaries in the Tennessee Department of Public Health had become too rampant over five days. Word of the Nichopoulos complaint found its way to a reporter for Nashville's afternoon newspaper, *The Banner.* With a screamer of a headline, it had published the story in its early afternoon editions. The wire services had picked it up with additional comments from the healing arts board.

Av Westin was quicker to put this turn of events in the right perspective. "You guys just got a million bucks worth of free promos," he said. Years later, Thompson, Cole, and Rivera would be chagrined at the suggestion that *20/20* deliberately leaked the story to boost the ratings.

Westin ordered up a short news item for that night's evening news show. He also suggested that Thompson return to Memphis, handle any more unforeseen surprises, and update with Rivera any late developments right up until airtime.

The wire services were quoting Shelby County Attorney General Hugh Stanton, Jr., as saying that he had opened a criminal investigation into Nichopoulos. Weeks earlier, *20/20* had talked with the attorney general about looking into the Elvis death and the Graceland drug scene. Stanton had been cordial but threw up his hands. "I can't go against my medical examiner," he had said.

———

Right up until airtime Thursday night, in both Memphis and New York there was a "hang-loose" attitude about updates. But with a few minor adjustments, the show really had been "in the can," ready for airing a day earlier.

The show began with a kaleidoscope of images from Elvis's career—from the svelte hip-swiveler in ducktails to a blimpy character in a bejeweled jumpsuit. Rivera recounted Elvis's last day, starting with the late-night trip to the dentist. Ginger Alden appeared, voicing the events of those last hours. There was Ricky and the sleep packets, Ginger waking up dreamlike from time to time calling "Elvis?" to no response.

Then there was the body and stark reality. Ginger mentioned the book on "psychic energy." But Dan Warlick, the investigator for the medical examiner's office, brought matters into focus —the "EP DOA" note, Elvis's body tinged with deep blue, and the early signs of rigor mortis. There was the dead weight, probably 250 pounds of it, felt by the paramedics as they loaded the body on their stretcher, the frantic ride to Baptist Hospital, and the futile resuscitation efforts.

The autopsy, Rivera said, revealed no clear cause of death. Although the heart was enlarged, "serious heart disease was still years away for Elvis Presley." And that was why Jerry Francisco's announcement about "cardiac arrhythmia" was so surprising.

After commercials, Rivera reappeared and identified the key figure in the mystery surrounding Elvis's death as Dr. Francisco. Even though this was a medical examiner's case, Francisco had withheld the evidence contained in the autopsy and kept it off the public record. Hence ABC had filed suit. "Our motives are simple," Rivera said. "Based on the evidence you are about to see, we believe there has been a cover-up."

Rivera outlined the disagreements between the Baptist Hospital autopsy team and Francisco. Then he introduced Dr. Noel Florendo, who said there was no evidence that Elvis suffered a heart attack. Florendo agreed with Dr. Eric Muirhead's conclusions that Elvis died of the interaction of several drugs.

Then Rivera revealed the Bio-Science toxicology report and its remarkable drug list. It was strong evidence, the best available since Elvis's stomach contents had been dumped down the drain in the emergency room.

Next came a taped replay of Jerry Francisco's October 1977 press conference, where he discounted the drug findings and ascribed Elvis's death entirely to heart disease. Then came the experts who challenged Francisco's official ruling—Dr. Raymond Kelly of Bio-Science Laboratories; Dr. Matthew Ellenhorn, who backed Bio-Science in a blind test; and Dr. Cyril Wecht, the Pittsburgh coroner and forensic pathologist, who stated flatly that drugs killed Elvis.

Establishing the circumstances for all this drug taking, the broadcast shifted to David and Ricky Stanley. Nobody could stop Elvis, they said. It was a matter of time before he overdosed. Then Ricky detailed how he picked up the last Dilaudid prescription at Dr. Nick's house and had it filled at Baptist Hospital. W. S. Nash, the grief-stricken retired pharmacist, said he believed he helped kill Elvis by filling that Dilaudid prescription. Sharp-eyed viewers would have wondered why Dilaudid didn't show up in the toxicology reports.

John O'Grady, the retired Los Angeles narc and private detective, opened the final half hour. O'Grady said that doctors contributed primarily to Elvis's death. Talking ridiculously tough, O'Grady said a doctor would have to be "a retarded alligator" not to notice Elvis's drug addiction.

Jack Kelly, the former DEA officer and O'Grady's sidekick, identified Dr. Max Shapiro as a willing if not exuberant source of drugs. For proof there was Dr. Max's boffo performance as "Dr. Painless," the dentist who makes house calls.

Ricky Stanley confirmed that Dr. Max was a steady supplier of drugs to Elvis, and he also pointed his finger at Dr. Elias Ghanem of Las Vegas. Rivera reran an interview with Ghanem that was taped on the night that Elvis died. In it, Ghanem denied that Elvis was a drug taker. But given what the *20/20* viewers had just seen, the denial was unconvincing.

This set the stage for Nichopoulos. He denied everything, and his denials were broadcast over the screen as the long list of drugs from the healing arts complaint rolled on and on and on. Then investigators Joe Dughman and Steve Bilsky appeared to state that the Elvis case was the worst case of overprescribing they had ever seen.

Elvis's old buddy, Marty Lacker, came on and told about his own addiction to drugs—drugs he had obtained from Nichopoulos.

And Rivera returned to the taped Nichopoulos interview. "Why would you prescribe that amount of drugs in that limited period of time?"

"I think you didn't understand me. I said I don't think that I did," said Nichopoulos in desperation.

Nichopoulos's tangled finances and his debts to Elvis were detailed. Then the white-haired doctor said he had "no regrets" about his treatment of Elvis.

Next up was Jack Kirsch and his lame excuses for filling so many of the questionable prescriptions. "I was following orders," Kirsch said.

The final segment consisted of the stand-ups that Rivera had recorded at the Memphis court house. It summarized the evidence supporting the broadcast's central theme—that the cause and real circumstances of Elvis's death had been covered up.

Rivera closed the broadcast with these words: "Reporting this story has been a melancholy personal experience for me, because I wanted it not to be true. For the last two years, I have made it a point to ignore the rumors of Elvis's drug abuse, and I even got angry at the people telling the stories. But they were right. It was true. By the end of his life, Elvis Presley had become a medical addict."

As the credits were rolling, Mike Pleasants turned to Thompson. "I think you proved beyond a shadow of a doubt three of your four major points. One, Elvis was an addict. Two, his system was full of drugs when he died. Three, he got those drugs from his doctors. Point number four is where your evidence is weak. Did anything else but drugs kill him?"

There was Florendo and sources that couldn't be identified who were on the inside of the autopsy, Cole reminded him.

"I understand that," Pleasants said. "But I'm betting that Jerry Francisco comes back at you and claims that because you haven't seen the whole autopsy, you don't know what you're talking about."

Unbeknownst to anyone at the Cole household, Francisco was planning a press conference for the next day. And Pleasants had anticipated the counterattack.

XVII

REACTIONS AND UNDERCURRENTS

"THE ELVIS COVER-UP" was the most watched public affairs broadcast on network television that season. Almost 17 million households viewed the program, according to the Nielsen ratings, and overall it ranked fourth
behind *Charlie's Angels, The Love Boat,* and *Three's Company.* It was four
slots higher than *60 Minutes* on CBS, *20/20*'s primary competitor
and a perennial Top Ten program. Executive producer Av Westin
had rolled the dice and now was raking in the blue chips; *20/20*
won ABC's regular 10:00 P.M. slot on Thursday nights and kept it
for years to come.

Immediately after the broadcast and well into the following day, viewers swamped the network's switchboards with telephone calls. Callers asked for more information about Elvis's
death. They requested transcripts of the broadcast. In some instances, they offered tips about how and where *20/20* could uncover more information about Presley's drug addiction. Surprisingly, most calls were positive and laudatory. A few were from
distressed, die-hard Elvis fans who threatened to murder Geraldo
Rivera or, as one young woman wrote in, to wish that Geraldo
needed drugs and would "have to do without."

The Death of Elvis

Newspaper reviews for the most part were favorable, and many competing news organizations phoned ABC and requested follow-up material on Nichopoulos. The show spawned a round of magazine articles focusing either on Nichopoulos or the Stanley book, *Elvis, We Love You Tender,* which appeared a few weeks after the broadcast.

The show's instant success made many members of *20/20*'s production staff giddy, and several of them were quick to pick up the telephone and call Charlie Thompson in Memphis to pass on the good news. But Thompson wasn't listening. He was in the middle of a crisis—the first challenge to the show's findings and credibility.

Jerry Francisco emerged the morning after the broadcast and called a press conference to answer *20/20.* Thompson was unaware of Francisco's planned rebuttal until after the conference had begun. He showed up at the tail end of it.

Francisco was seated calmly in front of a packed mob of Memphis print and television reporters saying he never covered anything up. With the medical examiner were his two assistants— James S. Bell and Charles Harlan—who had nothing to say but who kept nodding as Francisco made his points. Bell had penciled out "EP, OD? DOA, BMH" when the medical examiner's office was first notified of the death, and for all practical purposes ducked any further participation in the investigation until Francisco saw the need for cosigners on his ruling. Harlan played even less of a role and later would complain that he had no direct contact with Francisco's outside consultants, who presumably were ruling out drugs as a factor in the death. Absent and out of town was Dr. David Stafford, the chemist transformed by Francisco into a forensic toxicologist whose testing had been so superficial and confusing in the Presley case.

Francisco opened his attack on *20/20* by saying that neither the recent state charges against George Nichopoulos nor anything that ABC had broadcast the night before had changed his mind in the slightest about how Elvis died. "And consequently, we see no reason to modify our opinion that we originally gave that Elvis Presley died as a result of heart disease, and drugs did not cause or contribute to his death."

That was the sum total of Francisco's prepared remarks. Certainly Bell and Harlan had none. And at that the medical examiner was ready for questions. Francisco always was more comfortable fielding questions than taking a theme and running with it. This abrupt shift in format and Francisco's tone stunned the reporters, who were slow to respond. At last, one reporter found his tongue. He asked how Francisco could possibly disagree with the findings of the Baptist Hospital pathologists who had actually performed the autopsy?

The medical examiner said he was not concerned about differences of opinion, although obviously he was. Why else had he staged this news conference? "It is the role of the forensic pathologist that whatever you say, somebody is going to disagree with you." And he added that such medical disagreements were in direct proportion to the prominence of the deceased.

Then he began taking swipes at clinical pathologists whom he regarded as unqualified to determine causes of death. In particular, he attacked the credentials of Dr. Noel Florendo, the member of the Baptist Hospital autopsy team who appeared on the broadcast. Clinical pathologists, Francisco said, were accustomed to seeing fatal heart disease develop over a period of time from an infarct, that is, an area of dead heart tissue, while forensic pathologists were more likely to see evidence of sudden death by heart attack.

Of course, Francisco didn't explain—and the reporters were too poorly informed to ask about—the small hemorrhages that covered Elvis's upper torso, indicating that death wasn't really so sudden. The medical examiner also sidestepped the microscopic slides, dozens of them, that beyond any doubt convinced Eric Muirhead, Florendo's mentor, that Elvis was years away from serious heart problems.

"ABC submitted some data to independent pathologists, who concluded a drug death had taken place," a print reporter said. "What additional data did you operate from that would lead you to differ with those forensic pathologists?"

Francisco rubbed his chin and said he had to speculate, because he didn't really know what ABC had presented to their experts. Obviously, he said, they didn't submit a copy of the au-

243

topsy, since ABC was currently suing him to get it. Hence ABC's experts probably had less data than that available to the Shelby County Medical Examiner's Office. That appeared to contradict Francisco's deposition wherein he denied keeping any autopsy data.

"What was your additional data?" a reporter asked.

Francisco rattled off a long list: the autopsy report (which he swore he didn't have); the laboratory results (all of which contradicted him); the death scene itself (which he had never visited); Elvis's prior medical history (which showed Demerol addiction, methadone treatments, and telltale symptoms of drug abuse); electrocardiograms, pulmonary functions studies, and laboratory tests (all of which demonstrated Elvis suffered side effects from his drug addiction). Francisco ended his list by stressing, "All of that data which I feel reasonably certain they did not have access to and consequently, would have a limited perspective of the cause of death."

Throughout the press conference Francisco would employ the plural in referring to "our ruling" or "our opinion." Finally a television reporter demanded, "You are saying, 'Our decision' again. Who is that?"

Francisco made an expansive gesture to his two understudies and replied, "That would be Dr. Bell, Dr. Harlan, Dr. Stafford, and myself." Significantly, Francisco said nothing of any independent toxicologists, as he did in the press conference held two years earlier. Having revealed the identity of his two outside consultants—Dr. Robert Blanke of the Medical College of Virginia and Dr. Brian Finkle of the University of Utah—he was wary of claiming they supported his ruling.

"Why do you call Elvis's death a sudden death as opposed to a drug death?" a reporter asked.

Because, Francisco replied, in drug deaths the victim is usually found in "a position of comfort," in a bed or on a couch, not on the floor of a bathroom in an awkward position. That must have been news to experienced forensic toxicologists who had seen drug victims in all sorts of contorted positions and states of shock.

"Well, what about the combination of sedatives and codeine?" another reporter asked.

Codeine would only be significant if all the drugs were at the toxic level, Francisco said. He described the sedatives as being at therapeutic levels and said they typically would be prescribed to a heart patient.

If any of the reporters had checked a copy of the Bio-Science report, which at this point had been published by several newspapers and both wire services, they would have discovered how far off the medical examiner was in his drug analysis. Codeine was detected at ten times greater than a therapeutic dose with methaqualone (Quaalude), to cite one other example, within a toxic range.

If Francisco really was correct about how Elvis died, a reporter demanded, then why was the district attorney now investigating Nichopoulos in connection with Elvis's death? "Doesn't that make you wonder a bit about your findings?"

No, Francisco insisted, because he and the district attorney agreed "there is no medical evidence to support the conclusion of criminal homicide on the part of Dr. Nichopoulos."

What about the contents of Elvis's stomach? a reporter asked.

Francisco said he understood there were no contents to be analyzed. Even if they hadn't been thrown away, the medical examiner added, they would be "immaterial."

"The contents of the stomach, medically speaking, are outside the body. Only when the contents of the stomach have been absorbed into the body do they become a factor." Again, this must have been another shocker to forensic toxicologists, who regard stomach contents as a prime indicator of what the killer substance might be.

Was there a cover-up, as *20/20* had asserted?

"I am not involved and never have been involved in a cover-up," Francisco declared. "I have my own reputation to protect without worrying about somebody else's reputation."

What about exhuming Elvis's body? "I can say from a medical standpoint it would be a waste of effort," Francisco said.

With all the evidence about drug abuse that was presented the previous night, "You can still say unequivocally that drugs did not cause Elvis Presley's death?" a reporter asked.

"If he took all of the drugs that are mentioned as having been prescribed," Francisco hypothesized, "and took them all at one time, it clearly would have been enough to cause death. But the point is that he didn't take that quantity of drugs. . . . Obviously he did not take that level, because those findings were not present."

As the press conference was closing down with longer pauses between questions, Charlie Thompson slipped into the room out of breath. "Have I missed anything?" he wheezed to Joan Droege, a reporter from WHBQ-TV, the ABC affiliate in Memphis. Droege had been helping Thompson ever since the filing of *20/20*'s autopsy suit.

"Jerry doesn't like you very much, Charlie," Droege said. "Other than that and the fact that he hasn't changed his mind about anything, you haven't missed much. I don't think many of us believed him, but he isn't going to roll over and die. Basically, he's saying that you didn't change anything unless and until you get that autopsy."

After being briefed in more detail, Thompson borrowed a typewriter and hammered out a response to Francisco. Thompson stressed that under oath Francisco had refused to answer many of the same questions he freely discussed at this press conference. He wrote: "Francisco says that what happened inside the autopsy room, the drugs in Elvis's system, and any conversation between members of the autopsy team are privileged information. Considering the press conference that Dr. Francisco held today and the fact that many of the statements made by Dr. Francisco touch on these subjects, I have instructed our attorneys to go to the judge and seek an order to compel Dr. Francisco to answer these questions under oath. If he still refuses, we will seek a contempt citation against him. An official cannot have it both ways—hiding behind the cloak of privilege when he is afraid to talk under oath and convening press conferences on the same subject at other times. Considering the serious questions raised about his performance in our broadcast last night, it is imperative that the public be given free and full access to the autopsy report and that the gag be removed from the doctors at Baptist Hospital, so that they can respond to Dr. Francisco. He is playing a coward's game, and the public has the right to know if we have been deceived by Dr. Francisco."

These were high-sounding words, and Thompson hoped, as he delivered copies to news organizations in Memphis and the wire services, that ABC executives would continue to back him up. For the time being the hefty ratings would allow *20/20*'s investigation to continue. But sooner or later, Thompson suspected his ABC bosses and Rivera would become bored and disenchanted and would begin insisting that he spend his time on other stories. Thompson also knew that his lawsuit was expensive and would cause him no end of trouble with the network's accountants in New York.

But what the hell, Thompson concluded, how many times in your life would you get to work on such a stem-winder of a story? With any kind of luck, he figured he and Jim Cole could wrap it up in a couple more months, a year maximum. They still had plenty of leads to track down. The Nichopoulos charges would keep the Elvis story stirred up. Their credibility and that of *20/20* had survived Francisco's assault by news conference. But Cole and Thompson hardly expected a second assault, one presumably under the banner of the American Medical Association.

———

The two-column headline was uninspired but clear—"Examiner is firm: heart disease fatal to Presley." Above it at the top of page one was a photo of Jerry Francisco in his lab coat leaning casually on a desk against a backdrop of medical books and looking very much the victim of network news. This second attack against *20/20* appeared in the October 12, 1979, issue of *American Medical News,* a weekly newspaper published by the American Medical Association.

Part profile and part polemic, this article contained most of the pitfalls of a one-source story, that source being Jerry Francisco. While the masthead noted that the opinions expressed "are not necessarily endorsed by the AMA," the disclaimer was little defense against the preconceived notions of this story. And ulti-

247

mately, *American Medical News* would be forced to pay in a defamation suit filed by a doctor maligned as part of this effort to discredit *20/20* and "The Elvis Cover-Up."

The reporter, Dennis L. Breo, had access to *20/20's* script and to the records of the *20/20* lawsuit, including depositions that hadn't been filed as public records. He was offered this material but wasn't interested. Instead, Breo chose to rely entirely on Francisco's memory and assertions as well as what looked suspiciously like information that the Shelby County medical examiner lifted selectively from a copy of the Elvis autopsy.

"Wait a minute!" Jim Cole said to himself, as he read Breo's story. How could Francisco recite all these drug levels and organ weights without having a copy of the autopsy? Francisco would say he was relying on old press clippings. Cole and Charlie Thompson didn't believe that dodge, then or later.

Taking Breo's story from a scientific standpoint, the toxicology, as reported, ignored the very existence and crucial importance of toxic ranges in forensic detective work. To Francisco, a drug level was either therapeutic or lethal with no in-between. Hence Breo reported uncritically that because none of the drugs found was in a lethal range, Elvis died of something other than drugs. Instead of codeine being alarmingly high in a toxic range, for example, Breo said it was "one-fifth of the lethal dose." Instead of methaqualone (Quaalude) being well within its toxic range, Breo said it was "near the therapeutic range." Francisco denied the presence of ethchlorvynol (Placidyl), based on the tests conducted under the auspices of Dr. David Stafford, Francisco's protégé at the University of Tennessee lab. Other specialists regarded the University of Tennessee tests as inept.

From the standpoint of personal invective, the *American Medical News* story was shameful. Breo reported that *20/20* paid Dr. Matthew Ellenhorn of Beverly Hills, California, a fee to render an opinion in the Presley case. That was no secret. As the broadcast pointed out, *20/20* took Elvis's toxicology report to Ellenhorn as a blind test. The patient wasn't identified. Ellenhorn's opinion was neither foreordained nor contrived, rather it was aimed at checking the lab work of Bio-Science Laboratories, up or down.

Breo, however, saved most of his venom for Dr. Cyril

Wecht, the forensic pathologist who at the time was coroner of Allegheny County in Pennsylvania. While Wecht was identified by *20/20* as one of the nation's "foremost forensic pathologists," Breo wrote, "it did not mention that he is currently involved in a local controversy." The story then quoted Pittsburgh newspapers as saying Wecht had used his coroner's post for "private financial gain." But what Breo failed to report was that this controversy in Pittsburgh erupted *after* the *20/20* broadcast. Further, in a telephone conversation with Charlie Thompson about the *American Medical News* story, Breo declared that Cyril Wecht was "a medical whore" who would say anything for "a buck or some time on the camera."

In other aspects, Breo anointed himself as a Tennessee lawyer, quick to tell his readers that Elvis's autopsy really was beyond Jerry Francisco's control. "That is the law—then and now," Breo declared. He also employed phantom sources at pivotal points. "Did this list of drugs kill Elvis Presley?" Breo asked toward the end of the story. "Probably not, informed sources say." In another passage he quoted "one physician-toxicologist" as saying, "If the case went to court with the autopsy findings as outlined by Dr. Francisco, the medical examiner would win hands down. If only one choice can be made, heart failure is that choice."

Cole wrote a letter to *American Medical News* detailing the slipshod reporting and asking why Breo had been permitted to unleash such a one-sided attack. The newspaper printed a toned-down version of Cole's letter but never explained why Breo had his hatchet out.

Cyril Wecht fought his own battle. In 1980 he filed suit against the American Medical Association, its officers, *American Medical News,* and Dennis Breo, who in that connection denied calling Wecht "a medical whore." Nine years later, though, the defendants paid Wecht an undisclosed sum to settle the defamation action.

American Medical News never revealed who Breo's "informed sources" were, either. Most likely they were Francisco's in-house cronies. In truth, further work by Thompson and Cole would show that no pathologist or toxicologist outside the employment of the Shelby County Medical Examiner's Office supported Jerry Francisco's ruling. And the two outside toxicologists that Francisco relied on in 1977 had a lot to say about how their opinions had been twisted.

———

Cole found it worthwhile to read and reread what Francisco had stated in his original press release. Regarding toxicologists, it stated that two out of three men agreed with him that "there is no evidence of medication present in the body of Elvis Presley caused or made any significant contribution" to the death. It added that the third toxicologist believed that all drugs found in Elvis's body "were in the therapeutic range and individualy [sic] did not represent an overdose."

One of those agreeing toxicologists was Stafford, Francisco's in-house man. Francisco, during his first round of depositions, reluctantly revealed the names of his outside consultants. By telephone Cole already had contacted the consultants—Dr. Brian Finkle, director of the Center for Human Toxicology at the University of Utah in Salt Lake City, and Dr. Robert Blanke, a toxicologist at the Medical College of Virginia in Richmond.

Late in October, six weeks after the *20/20* broadcast, Cole reached Finkle and had his notebook handy. Finkle spoke in a precise, clipped British accent, and Cole was surprised to hear what he had to say about the Shelby County medical examiner. Yes, he had received a phone call from Francisco, but never regarded himself as an official consultant, as Francisco's press release had indicated.

"We discussed some analytical data," Finkle said of his conversation with Francisco. "He told me his conclusion. I have no basis to agree or disagree with Dr. Francisco."

Finkle outlined the elements of determining a cause of death—an investigation of the circumstances, the medical/pathological investigation, and the laboratory findings. He must be the consultant mentioned in Francisco's press release who took a neutral stance on the cause of death, Cole surmised.

Then Finkle added that several weeks after his conversa-

250

tion with Francisco he did in fact become an official consultant in the Presley case, but through Bio-Science Laboratories. Bio-Science saw a need for a backup opinion in the analysis of some tissue samples. "My sole involvement was through Bio-Science," Finkle said. "I never saw the full report. All I know is my report."

Finkle balked at revealing the results of his report and referred Cole to Bio-Science. Cole knew that was a dead end and tried his inside contact on the Baptist Hospital autopsy team. "Was there anything in Brian Finkle's report," Cole asked, "that contradicted the other tox tests or that would undermine the conclusion that Elvis died of polypharmacy?" The answer was a resounding "No." Finkle, Cole learned, was a whiz at analyzing such samples as liver tissue and had developed a good working relationship with Norm Weissman at Bio-Science. Finkle's role was limited, but his test results were entirely consistent with those at the other labs.

In contrast, Bob Blanke's role in the Presley case was entirely through Francisco and, as Cole was to discover, involved some real professional shenanigans.

By telephone Cole reached Blanke in Richmond. He had done no analysis himself in the Presley case, Blanke said. But yes, Francisco had contacted him, although Elvis's identity wasn't mentioned. "I've known Jerry for several years. What I know about the case was what he conveyed to me. The levels he relayed—there were a large number of them—some of the levels were quite high. Based on that information, I told Jerry he had a drug-related death."

What? Cole was astounded when Blanke mentioned his letter. After Francisco's press conference and Beth Tamke's coverage of it, the wire services in Memphis picked up the drug levels and reported them. Blanke's newspaper in Richmond carried the story, and it disturbed him in two ways. First, Francisco had failed to mention some of the drugs found while understating the levels of others. Second, Francisco said that he had an outside toxicologist agreeing with him.

"I wrote Jerry and told him that perhaps our conversation had been misinterpreted," Blanke told Cole. And Francisco's response? "I haven't heard back from him."

Blanke's letter to Francisco was dated October 25, 1977. "A

recent article in our local newspaper (photocopy enclosed) disturbed me somewhat since it seemed to be at variance with our telephone discussion of [a] case last week," Blanke wrote. "I realize that the media have a habit of distorting facts, but I am concerned that either I misunderstood what you told me or you misunderstood my opinion."

Then Blanke listed a chart. In the left-hand column he wrote down what Francisco had told him and in the right-hand column what had appeared in the wire service story.

Blanke noted that the news story agreed with their conversation on the codeine and methaqualone (Quaalude) levels found in the bloodstream. He said the pentobarbital level that Francisco gave him was lower than the newspaper's report. Francisco hadn't given him a level for ethinimate (Valmid), which the story reported at a significant level. And on the flip side he was surprised that the news story didn't list diazepam (Valium) at all. Over the telephone Francisco had put the Valium at a level "which could be lethal but certainly would be expected to produce coma."

Blanke described the level of codeine as "much higher than therapeutic," and methaqualone (Quaalude) at "a high therapeutic level," unspecified barbiturates at "the low end of the lethal range," if pentobarbital or "therapeutic" if phenobarbital.

"I qualified my comments that tolerance in a patient would modify my interpretation," Blanke wrote. "However, without hesitation, I believe that all of these drugs combined at the levels described would be consistent with a drug death, even with tolerance to some, and so stated to you.

"Thus, I was surprised that in the quote ascribed to you, it was inferred that two of the toxicologists are of the opinion that these drugs made no significant contributions to the death and that the third stated he did not know. Perhaps the toxicologists giving the opinions described were not the same ones you mentioned to me, and my opinion is not included. Nevertheless, it was startling to see this statement in print, and I felt compelled to write this letter attempting to clarify my verbal opinion."

Who agreed with Jerry Francisco about Elvis's death? Not Finkle. And certainly not Blanke. With the exception of his own staff and in direct contradiction to his own press release, Jerry Francisco was alone in his opinion.

XVIII

UNCOVERING THE COVER-UP

THE TENSION in the large, book-lined, oak-paneled legal office was oppressive. Dr. George C. Nichopoulos had his hands cupped to both ears vainly attempting to decipher instructions from each of his attorneys, Frank Crawford and Ken Masterson. They were whispering simultaneously to him in competing ears.

While Nichopoulos was struggling to understand his attorneys Mike Pleasants, the opposing counsel, sat stoically across the table from Nichopoulos. Pleasants had been grilling the doughy-faced doctor relentlessly until Nichopoulos's attorneys called time out for a huddle. Pleasants was flanked on his left by his junior associate, Chuck Harrell. Dr. John R. Feegel of Atlanta, a forensic pathologist and practicing attorney, was seated on Pleasants's right as an associate counsel in the case. Its aim, of course, was to force the Shelby County medical examiner to disclose the results of Elvis Presley's autopsy, and Nichopoulos's lawyers were irate about being dragged into it. Off to the right some distance from Feegel were the two plaintiffs in the lawsuit, Charlie Thompson and Jim Cole. The last time they had seen Nichopoulos face to face had been unforgettable.

The Death of Elvis

Since that television interview in early September, Nicho-poulos's world had crumbled. The State of Tennessee had filed charges to jerk his medical license. He was under criminal investigation for overprescribing pain pills to Elvis and to a number of other patients. And his reviews were mixed among Presley fans about whether he was Elvis's well-meaning friend or irresponsible foe.

There was no mistaking, though, that at this moment in his life George Nichopoulos would prefer to be somewhere besides the twentieth floor of a downtown Memphis office building where he was being compelled to give more answers to *20/20*. He and his attorneys had gone to great lengths to prevent it. They had filed a motion with the judge assigned to the case, Chancellor D. J. Alissandratos, to quash Mike Pleasants's subpoena. They accused Pleasants and ABC-TV of issuing the subpoena to obtain "information to be used for exploitation of its alleged news value." They complained about abuse of legal process and "an exploitation of this honorable court."

Chancellor Alissandratos recognized that *20/20* had legitimate reasons for deposing Nichopoulos. He kept Pleasants's subpoena in force and ordered Nichopoulos to show up for the deposition. Nichopoulos was somber as a funeral director when he walked into the conference room. He said nothing and avoided eye contact with everyone else at the table as one of his lawyers, Frank Crawford, bickered about John Feegel being there. Civility went downhill from there as Crawford objected to almost every question that Pleasants asked.

After the first half hour, Pleasants had covered little more than Nichopoulos's background. But amid all the interruptions, objections, and whispered conferences at Nichopoulos's end of the table, the *20/20* side had an opportunity to look over a set of interesting documents. Pleasants's subpoena not only had required Nichopoulos to show up but also to bring with him every document in his possession related to Elvis's death. They were four in number, and Nichopoulos turned them over to Pleasants early in the deposition without a squabble.

The first was Elvis's admission form into Baptist Hospital on August 16, 1977. Other than the drugs that had been administered by the Harvey team, it contained no new information. The second was the autopsy permission form that Vernon Presley had signed at Graceland. The third and fourth were showstoppers.

There was a letter written by Dr. Thomas Chesney to Nichopoulos on August 18, 1977, two days after Elvis's death. Chesney was a member of the Baptist Hospital autopsy team. His letter contained the exact weights and diagnoses of Elvis's organs. It demonstrated without a doubt that Elvis didn't die of heart disease. Chesney wrote that blockage of Elvis's coronary arteries was "mild" and blockage of the aorta was "minimal." The letter also showed that none of the other organs were diseased or had contributed to Elvis's death.

The last document provided more evidence of a cover-up in Elvis's death. It was a copy of a death certificate for Elvis that Nichopoulos had attempted to file on August 18, 1977. This was long before any of the quantative toxicological tests had been run by Bio-Science and was more than two full months before Jerry Francisco, the medical examiner, announced an official cause of death. What was written on the certificate contradicted the information from the gross autopsy as reported in Chesney's letter to Nichopoulos. On the death certificate, Nichopoulos listed "Cardiac Arrhythmia, Coronary Artery Disease, and Hypertension and Diabetes Mellitus" as the causes of death. He said the other significant condition he found was a "Fatty Liver."

Feegel, Thompson, and Cole studied these documents and sat stunned as Pleasants and Crawford jousted over the phrasing of another question. They couldn't believe that Nichopoulos would produce such damaging material, even though he had been required by subpoena to do so. During a recess, Feegel coached Pleasants to bear down on Nichopoulos about the death certificate. As Pleasants started that line of questioning, Crawford and his partner, Masterson, sensed danger and began whispering instructions to Nichopoulos in stereo. Nichopoulos looked thoroughly confused when his attorneys signaled Pleasants that he could resume questioning the doctor about the death certificate.

"Why did you fill out a death certificate in this case prior to getting the autopsy report?" Pleasants asked.

255

"I'm not sure why I did," Nichopoulos replied in a dazed fashion.

When did Nichopoulos learn that the health department refused to accept his death certificate for Elvis? The doctor couldn't remember. That was about as far as Pleasants got on that subject when a new round of bickering erupted. Toward the end of the ragged session, Pleasants asked Nichopoulos if he had ever seen the final autopsy. Nichopoulos said he hadn't. Instead, he had been summoned into the office of Dr. Eric Muirhead, chief pathologist at Baptist Hospital. Muirhead told him that Vernon Presley had issued instructions never to give Nichopoulos a copy of the autopsy.

—————

If the efforts to get testimony from Dr. Nick had been rancorous, they were mild compared to the animosity generated in the fight to take Dick Grob's testimony under oath. After the *20/20* broadcast, Grob, former chief of security at Graceland, had been guest speaker at several large meetings of Presley fan clubs. With bitterness and sarcasm he lashed out at Ginger Alden, David and Ricky Stanley, and *20/20* for their portrayal of Elvis's drug dependence and declining health. Grob's harsh remarks appeared in full in fan club newsletters circulated nationwide.

For example, Grob was quoted as saying: "We had Ricky who was the duty aide who was supposed to check on him [Elvis] occasionally, and Ricky was downstairs zonked out of his gourd. I think that possibly everything that could go wrong went wrong that particular night with the system. You had Miss Alden there who obviously woke up and went back to sleep several times. If I was her, and I was to become engaged to Elvis, then I would sure want to know where my intended was. When Elvis went into his bedroom with a female that was supposed to stay there, we assumed that she would kind of take heed, although the other aides would go up periodically and check just to make sure that when he woke up that they would know that he was awake. Ricky failed to do that. David, who came on at noon, was supposed to relieve Ricky, came on and asked the maids if Elvis was up, and they said,

'No,' and David split and went over and probably blew a joint with his friend before he left on the tour."

Grob was right about Ricky Stanley's condition on the morning of August 16, 1977. In August 1989, on the twelfth anniversary of Elvis's death, Ricky claimed in *People* magazine: "If I'd gone back up there [to Elvis's bathroom], I might have found him. But I was abusing drugs too. . . . I think it'd be safe to say I had enough Demerol going through me right then to sedate Whitehaven [the Memphis suburb where Graceland is located]. So instead, I went back to my own room and shot up."

In his broadside against the *20/20* broadcast, Grob was particularly tough on Ginger. Posing rhetorical questions to himself, he asked, "Dick, if you come to my house and use my bathroom, in thirty or forty minutes I'm going to ask you if you're all right. In that time lapse with Ginger between going to bed, and the time she found Elvis's body, where was she? Did the dumb broad stand there and watch him die?" Filling in the answers, Grob said: "I have some possible answers, but nothing from her. I got into it because, first off, the coffin photo [the one taken for *The National Enquirer* by one of Elvis's distant cousins] and then the discussion I had with Vernon. He asked me certain questions, and I said that I would find out about them. So in doing this it came to light that there was a reporter who worked for *The National Enquirer* that had gotten this phone call. Well, I eventually got him to admit that he had received a phone call, but he never would tell me who it was from." Grob was alluding to a phone call he claimed was placed about 11:30 A.M. that morning. In his copyrighted book synopsis, *The Elvis Conspiracy,* Grob claimed that James Kirk, a Memphis freelance reporter for *The National Enquirer,* swore to him that he was certain this phone call came from Ginger Alden and prompted him to go to Graceland at least two and a half hours before Ginger sought help for Elvis. In his book synopsis, Grob wrote that the call proved that Ginger was lying about the time she claimed to have discovered Elvis's body.

In the weeks following the *20/20* broadcast, Charlie Thompson had found James Kirk. He was short, blond, tanned, twenty-six years old, and he spoke with the sort of hip deejay jargon that seemed to match up with stringing for a sheet like *The*

Enquirer. Kirk confidently repeated the story about that morning. He told Thompson that the call from a young woman came in about 12:30 P.M. He believed it was Ginger. He had talked to her several times before. The caller, Kirk said, instructed him to come to Graceland, saying "that something was going on." A second phone call, Kirk said, came in at 2:00 P.M. from the same woman, who ordered him "to come at once and bring money."

Kirk said he had arranged with *The Enquirer* to pay Ginger $105,000 for her exclusive story. But the newspaper, he added, later double-crossed Ginger and cut the payment to $35,000. The reduction resulted from Ginger's interview with *The Commercial Appeal*, which diminished the value of her story, he said.

After talking with Kirk and confirming with a friend in top management at the tabloid's home office that Kirk really had negotiated a deal between Ginger and the newspaper, Thompson confronted Ginger and her mother, Jo LaVern. They admitted having dealings with Kirk and knowing his home telephone number, but both mother and daughter adamantly denied that they had called Kirk with an advance tip about Elvis's death. Ginger was upset that anybody would believe she was brassy enough to try to shake down *The National Enquirer* for money. This inconsistency in testimony posed a dilemma for Thompson. On the one hand, he regarded Kirk as a credible witness, despite his association with a sleazoid publication. In addition, the Aldens had fed Thompson more than his fair share of misleading information. But on the other hand, Thompson believed the Aldens had been truthful when convinced that he had the goods on them. And then there was Jim Cole. He put little stock in what Kirk had to say and wanted more corroboration if this aspect of the story was to be aired.

This quandary persuaded Thompson all the more of the importance of taking Dick Grob's deposition. Attorney Mike Pleasants issued a subpoena for Grob's appearance, and Grob hired an attorney to fight it. "James P. Cole and Charles Thompson are using this particular chancery court for personal gain and are abusing the constitutional rights of many individuals," declared Grob's motion to quash the subpoena. "Richard Grob is the author of a manuscript entitled *The Elvis Conspiracy* and his disclosure of materials contained in said copyrighted manuscript would allow monetary gain for the American Broadcasting Corporation and its executives and other producers of a certain program known as *20/20*. The subpoena issued is clearly an abuse of process."

Pleasants argued in court that since Grob claimed in his book proposal to have access to Elvis's autopsy, the subpoena was fair and proper. Chancellor Alissandratos agreed and ordered Grob to appear in Pleasants's office for sworn testimony. He also ordered Grob to produce at the deposition any documents that he had relating to Elvis's death and autopsy.

Chuck Harrell, Pleasants's junior partner, took Grob's deposition and went straight for the jugular. "Did you ever have access to the autopsy report or laboratory results in regard to the autopsy performed on Mr. Elvis Presley?"

Grob started playing games, asking Harrell to define the word "access."

"Did you ever see it?"

"Yes, I think I saw it."

"Did you ever have possession of it?"

Grob admitted he hadn't.

"Were you ever allowed to read the autopsy report, Mr. Grob?"

"No, sir," Grob replied.

Harrell asked if Grob knew about any of the autopsy's contents.

"No, sir, not factually."

Harrell asked Grob to explain what he meant by "not factually."

"I have never seen the autopsy report; therefore, I don't know what it contains, according to the facts based upon the autopsy report," Grob answered.

"I thought you stated earlier that you had seen it?" Harrell countered.

"I said I saw what I thought to be the autopsy report, sir."

Harrell handed Grob a copy of his copyrighted synopsis, "The Elvis Conspiracy." The attorney read one paragraph:

The Death of Elvis

Grob managed to have the body removed from the morgue. He carried with him the order to protect the autopsy from anyone and everyone.

What was Grob talking about when he said the autopsy was done in the morgue?

"I am referring there, sir, to attempts to steal the autopsy report by many of the news media personnel that were in town at that time," Grob replied.

"Was an autopsy report in existence at that time?" Harrell asked.

"No, sir, not to my knowledge, there wasn't."

"Who instructed you to prevent them from stealing something that didn't exist?" Harrell demanded.

"There were attempts made to . . . said to obtain what information was available," Grob said, stumbling over his thoughts. "In my position, I was not instructed to do so by anyone. Now, it became an automatic thing."

Harrell read the concluding paragraph of Grob's synopsis:

The autopsy proved beyond any shadow of a doubt that he [Elvis] would have been dead in a few short months. His eventual death would have been slow, excruciatingly painful and intolerable to witness. Elvis was dying of bone cancer.

After Harrell finished reading the passage, he paused to let it sink in, then looked purposefully at Grob and asked: "How did you gather that information, Mr. Grob, if you have never seen the autopsy report?"

Grob gulped, then answered: "That's as good an ending to a manuscript as any others."

"Is that ending substantiated in any way upon a factual basis?" Harrell asked.

"Not at the present, to my knowledge. There is a number of speculative items such as that, but . . ."

"Is this a fiction, Mr. Grob?"

"Well, I imagine it's part fiction and part nonfiction, sir."

"All right. Is that part of it fiction that I just read?"

"To my knowledge, since I haven't seen the autopsy report, I can't determine that it is, in fact, factual," Grob said.

"Can anyone else determine whether it is factual or not?" Harrell persisted.

Grob said he presumed the "individuals that conducted the autopsy could make that determination."

"But whether it is factual or not has not been conveyed to you, is that correct?" Harrell said.

"No, sir. As I said, I have not seen the autopsy report."

Had Grob heard whether anyone had obtained access to the autopsy information?

Grob said he had heard that the "ABC News team from *20/20* has made contact with these individuals" who have access to the autopsy information.

Thompson rocked back in his chair, glanced over to where Cole was seated and winked. Chuck Harrell's withering cross-examination had devastated Grob and stripped the manuscript of credibility. Presumably it had spiked the Elvis cancer hoax as well, but it would surface again.

Thompson and Cole hadn't identified the primary source of that phony story. From all indications the cancer yarn originated with George Nichopoulos, who immediately after Elvis's death was trying to ingratiate himself with Vernon Presley. While Grob admitted under oath that it was a concoction, his sidekick Charlie Hodge would resurrect the hoax five years later in his book, *Me 'n Elvis.* Then in early 1989 it popped up again in the memoir of Larry Geller, Elvis's sometime hairdresser and spiritual advisor. Geller cited Charlie Hodge as his source, but nobody cited Grob's deposition.

Harrell called for a break in the deposition to confer with Thompson and Cole. "Ask him about the intercom in the bathroom, Chuck," Thompson suggested. "Was it working? Could Elvis have triggered the intercom and called for help as he was dying?"

Harrell posed the question. Grob said there were two intercom systems in Elvis's bathroom. One was connected to the phone and had to be dialed before it functioned. The second one was a speaker-type system that could be activated with a toggle switch. But Grob said the second one had been inoperative for years.

"In the course of your investigation of the particular scene where Mr. Presley died, that intercom system wasn't on, was it? Did you notice it being on?" Harrell asked.

"Oh, no, it wasn't on. As I said, I don't believe it even worked." If Grob were correct, then Elvis couldn't have triggered the intercom to call for help.

Harrell finished the examination by asking Grob if he knew who had cleaned up Elvis's bathroom and bedroom before the arrival at Graceland of Dan Warlick and the homicide detectives. Grob said he had no idea.

———

Mike Pleasants was taking a crash course in forensic pathology and toxicology from Dr. John Feegel, associate medical examiner in Atlanta and a practicing attorney hired as a scientific consultant. They were preparing for Dr. Jerry Francisco's two assistants, Drs. James Bell and Charles Harlan.

Bell showed up at Pleasants's office with a disheveled suit and loose shirttail and without a lawyer from the county attorney's office. Pleasants wanted to know how Bell first alerted investigator Dan Warlick that Elvis was dead.

"I think I wrote on a note, 'EP is dead,' I think," Bell replied.

"Mr. Warlick has testified that the message written on a piece of paper and handed to him by you was 'EP DOA BMH OD?' " Pleasants said, transposing sets of abbreviations to emphasize OD at the end.

Bell began to nod. He bobbed his head affirmatively and gave everybody a goofy grin.

"Did you convey to Francisco the same suspicion that you conveyed to Mr. Warlick of 'OD?'?" Pleasants asked.

"I could have," Bell replied. "I could not have. I would imagine that he would have probably been thinking the same way I do, because I always think that way. I'm highly suspicious."

As a matter of course, Bell explained, he always viewed each case from the outset in its worst light. Therefore, his initial suspicions in Elvis's death was homicide—right up to a staff meeting he attended the day before Francisco called a press conference to announce that Elvis died naturally of heart problems. What changed his mind so quickly? Reports that Francisco showed him in that staff meeting, Bell said.

But the deputy medical examiner had trouble telling Pleasants and Feegel just where those reports came from and what they contained. And although Bell admitted signing a press release in October 1977 saying that "the toxicology findings have also been discussed with two other toxicologists here in the United States," he confessed that the identities of those two outside toxicologists were a mystery to him.

"Was polypharmacy considered as a cause of death of Elvis Aaron Presley?" Pleasants asked.

"Not by me. It was suggested by someone, but not by me," Bell said.

———

While Jim Bell's suspicious mind was rolling over and playing dead, Charlie Harlan was relying on a bogus medical history of the Presley family. "To my knowledge his mother died at age forty-two of heart disease and diabetes," Harlan said in his deposition that afternoon.

Where did he obtain that knowledge?

"Several TV programs, newspaper accounts, et cetera," Harlan answered.

Pleasants then informed Harlan that Gladys Presley actually died of infectious hepatitis. She was forty-six years old, not forty-two, when she died, and the hepatitis had been aggravated by abuse of alcohol and drugs.

Like Bell, Harlan admitted having no real idea which toxicology charts he had reviewed in determining cause and manner of death.

Did any of the medical texts or references he consulted contain any therapeutic, toxic, or lethal levels for combinations of codeine, Quaaludes, Valium, Valmid, Placidyl, pentobarbital, butabarbital, and phenobarbital?

"To the best of my knowledge there were no references that had all of those materials contained within it within a single person," Harlan replied.

Pleasants then showed Harlan an autopsy of a man named Frederick McDonald, who had died in Memphis in March 1977 from an ethchlorvynol (Placidyl) overdose. Francisco had signed McDonald's autopsy and certified his cause of death as a drug overdose.

"In your opinion are the levels of Placidyl found in the body of Mr. McDonald in the lethal, therapeutic, or toxic range?" Pleasants asked. Even though the Placidyl levels found in McDonald's system were clearly listed on his autopsy, Harlan said he couldn't answer Pleasants's question without checking his sources.

"Do you know whether or not the levels of Placidyl found within Mr. Presley's body were in excess or less than the levels found in Mr. McDonald's body?" Pleasants asked.

"I don't know. I don't recall," Harlan said.

In fact, the levels in McDonald's blood were more than twice those found in Elvis's body. But it was nice to know that the medical examiner's lab had some track record of finding Placidyl. While Francisco's technicians apparently were burning it off with excessive temperatures, every other lab involved in the Presley case was finding Placidyl high in the therapeutic range.

———

On December 14, 1977, the second round of Jerry Francisco's deposition was held in a county government conference room. At long last the medical examiner produced the Polaroid pictures that Dan Warlick had taken of Elvis's bathroom. They showed the black porcelain toilet, the deep red carpeting and what appeared to be a discoloration in that carpeting. Francisco explained that the photos had been in a separate correspondence file regarding the Presley case all along. Why wasn't there just one Presley file? Because the medical examiner thought keeping a correspondence file separate from medical information would be more appropriate.

On the subject of what else might be in the medical examiner's file, Pleasants pulled out a copy of Dennis Breo's story in *American Medical News,* the one where Francisco had reeled off specific drug levels so freely. Just what records had he relied on for this interview?

"Mr. Breo's press clippings. The information was reasonably accurate. I saw no gross discrepancy," Francisco said, meaning no discrepancy between the clippings and the autopsy he still maintained wasn't in the file.

Pleasants showed Francisco a copy of the letter obtained in Richmond from Dr. Robert Blanke. Why was this letter, which complained that Francisco had twisted a consultant's opinion, not kept in the files of the medical examiner's office?

"Well, I don't really know," Francisco replied stiffly, adding that he didn't know what had become of Blanke's letter.

Was Blanke's letter in accordance with Francisco's recollection?

"I can't be precise on any given point, because to be precise on a given point means that I do, in fact, remember, and I don't," Francisco answered.

What about Dr. Brian Finkle? Pleasants asked. Had Francisco talked to the Salt Lake City toxicologist to see if he agreed or disagreed with official ruling opinion about Elvis?

Francisco replied that he hadn't received any correspondence from Finkle. But Finkle, the medical examiner added, supported the conclusion that Elvis's death wasn't drug related; Blanke was the toxicologist who wasn't sure.

Later in the deposition, Francisco insisted that he had never heard the term "polypharmacy." At that Pleasants plopped down, one after the other, four respected scientific journals containing lengthy articles about polypharmacy. Had Francisco heard of any of these scientific papers or journals?

The medical examiner said he hadn't. They could have been made available to him before the official ruling was determined. All of the articles were monographs on which the Baptist

Hospital autopsy team members had relied in reaching their own conclusion about how Elvis died.

For the record, Francisco agreed that Elvis's death became a medical examiner's case when he first learned of its circumstances. Yes, on a death certificate form he would have checked that an autopsy was performed. And yes, he did rely on the autopsy to reach an official conclusion about the cause of death—heart disease —and the manner of death—natural.

On leaving the Francisco deposition, the *20/20* team believed that with each new revelation of missing letters, suppressed reports, and misstated medical opinions, their chances of bringing Elvis's autopsy into the open were improving. And to round out all the circumstances surrounding August 16, 1977, they managed to track down some elusive witnesses and documents.

Sam McCachren, the police lieutenant who had accompanied Dan Warlick to Graceland, had retired and was working as an electrical and plumbing contractor. But when *20/20* found him in Water Valley, Mississippi, where his deposition was taken, McCachren brought his own handwritten notes and official typed reports. If he had known the large quantities of drugs that Nichopoulos had been prescribing, McCachren said, the homicide bureau would have conducted its investigation in an entirely different manner. But as the retired detective's documents showed, Nichopoulos and his nurse, Tish Henley, revealed only partial or misleading information about what Elvis's drug intake had been that day. According to one of McCachren's notes: "We learned from Nurse Henley that to her knowledge Mr. Presley had taken two Valiums, five milligram, and also to her knowledge, he had taken one other pill during the late evening or morning."

Before appearing for his deposition, Homicide Sergeant John C. Peel stopped by the police legal advisor's office for a briefing on what he could and couldn't say. But the legal advisor wasn't there. Peel eyed his watch, saw the hour was getting late, and also saw the department's complete Elvis file on the advisor's desk. So he scooped it up and left for Mike Pleasants's office. During the deposition Peel couldn't think of any good reason why *20/20* shouldn't have copies. Actually, the police file should have been made public two years earlier. But on general police principle— that is, that reporters shouldn't see everything—the Elvis file had been kept secret. While the police file contained no startling reve- lations, it provided an invaluable source of precisely timed events.

Jerry Stauffer, the tobacco-chewing deputy prosecutor who accompanied Dan Warlick and Sam McCachren to Graceland, had become a staff attorney for a local chemical company. He testified that Warlick was quite angry when he learned that Elvis's death scene had been sanitized. Stauffer said there was never any dis- agreement that Francisco should be involved in the investigation and autopsy and that he understood Francisco's involvement would be official as county medical examiner. That testimony con- tradicted Francisco's view that he was merely a consultant to Bap- tist Hospital.

———

By mid-December 1979 Charlie Thompson had been in Memphis on an almost continuous basis since the *20/20* broadcast in September. He began to feel pressure from the ABC accountants in New York and from Geraldo Rivera about the time he was spending in Memphis on a story that they insisted was over. Thompson consulted Av Westin, *20/20*'s executive producer. He explained to Westin that new material in the Elvis case justified a follow-up piece. Westin was impressed. "It sounds like you have some interesting material," Westin said, "and frankly I like follow- ups."

With Westin's backing, Thompson found Rivera more amenable to a second Elvis story. Rivera snapped up the idea and agreed to return to Memphis.

About this time, Thompson started feeling pressure from another source, one that he couldn't control. Mike McMahon, the real estate developer involved with Elvis in the skewed racquetball venture, still maintained ties to the old Presley entourage. Thompson and McMahon had become friends during the thick of the *20/20* investigation that summer, close enough to where McMahon felt compelled to offer some friendly advice. "Charlie, you've stirred up a hornet's nest," McMahon told Thompson that December. "I keep up with some of the people who hung around Elvis. They're mad at you. And I know some of the Greeks who are friends with Dr. Nick. They'd like to see you hurt for what you did."

McMahon took Thompson out to the parking lot. There was a gift in his car, McMahon said. "I know you think you're invincible, and that nobody can hurt you, but you're wrong." McMahon opened the trunk. He pointed to a box and told Thompson to take it. Inside Thompson found a long-barreled .357 magnum stainless-steel pistol and a box of fifty shells.

"What do I want this for, Mike?" Thompson asked.

"For your own protection. Go out and shoot it. Elvis gave it to me. Use it to protect yourself," McMahon said. "Trust me. I know I'm right, and if I'm wrong, you haven't lost anything."

The irony of McMahon's gift wasn't lost on Thompson. Here was a firearm that ought to be mounted on wheels. He had few doubts that it was the sort of outlandish item that would appeal to Elvis. And now it was in his possession for protection against Elvis nuts who were angry about the truth of Elvis's death.

XIX

COD FROM SCANDINAVIA

THE EVIDENCE that Charlie Thompson and Jim Cole uncovered in the fall of 1979 conclusively demonstrated that the cover-up of what really happened to Elvis Presley began as his body began cooling on the thick shag bathroom carpet.

Ulysses Jones, the fire department paramedic, was the first person outside of Elvis's immediate entourage to arrive at the death scene on August 16, 1977. His arrival came minutes after Joe Esposito phoned the fire department for an ambulance. Tracked down after the first *20/20* broadcast, Jones told the ABC reporters what he had been reluctant to discuss publicly two years earlier—how a number of people were vainly attempting to revive an obviously very dead individual, how he was surprised that this obese figure who appeared to be black was really Elvis Presley, and how the dark-haired fellow later identified as Al Strada said, "We think he OD'd."

Under the circumstances, a drug search was out of the question. Jones asked for the medication Elvis was taking, but it never was turned over to him, not by Nichopoulos or anybody else. Jones recalled what the bathroom looked like when he and his partner went back for their equipment. "Everything, everything had been cleaned up, the bed had been made, the rest room and everything had been cleaned up. Our equipment was placed over on the sink in a neat little pile."

From their review of the Memphis police records, Thompson and Cole believed it was clear that Nichopoulos made false and misleading statements to investigating authorities about Elvis's drug problem. The police records had Nichopoulos stating that Elvis had taken some medication—two Valiums and one other pill —in the hours preceding his death. That hardly jibed with the testimony of eyewitnesses, the toxicology reports, and the list of drugs the State of Tennessee claimed Nichopoulos prescribed to Elvis the day before he died. Furthermore, additional information began to emerge suggesting that Nichopoulos may have taken an active role in covering up Elvis's drug abuse.

In his interview with Geraldo Rivera, for example, Nichopoulos was absolutely certain that Elvis had not taken any of the potent Dilaudid pills that he had prescribed just hours before he died. Nichopoulos swore that he accounted for all the Dilaudid pills, which had to mean he had personally inventoried them. But as Thompson and Cole learned from their stack of sworn depositions, Nichopoulos failed to turn over the Dilaudid to Ulysses Jones or to Dan Warlick, the medical examiner's investigator, or to any of the pathologists at Baptist Hospital. He also neglected to mention, much less to hand over, any of the hundreds of narcotic pills and injectables that he had prescribed for Elvis on August 15, 1977. Instead, Nichopoulos merely reported to Dr. Eric Muirhead, the hospital's chief pathologist, that he prescribed "a pain pill" after Elvis's early morning visit to the dentist. Muirhead would remember Nichopoulos's recalcitrance when the toxicology reports came in. And with raised eyebrows Muirhead would question just what role Nichopoulos played in the Baptist Hospital emergency room when Elvis's stomach contents were washed down the drain. There is no evidence, however, that Nichopoulos was responsible for disposing of the stomach contents.

A ghoulish piece to the Elvis drug puzzle surfaced as late as October 1979, when a small notice appeared in the classified advertising section of *The Memphis Commercial Appeal.* The ad offered to sell one of Elvis's last prescription bottles. Cole contacted a young Memphis couple, Randy and Amy McCord, who had placed the ad. The McCords were asking $1,000 for the bottle, but they refused to show it to Cole after he identified himself as a reporter working with ABC News. The couple described the bottle in detail. They knew what drug had been in the bottle, its quantity, and the date that the prescription was filled. It matched one of the bottles that Nichopoulos had prescribed to Elvis on August 15, 1977. Yet the origin and chain of possession of the McCord pill bottle couldn't be verified independently. State investigators couldn't have cared less. Nichopoulos was prepared to admit that he had written the prescriptions. The dispute was whether they were written within the standards of acceptable medical practice.

The mounting evidence of drug abuse surrounding the Graceland scene finally stirred the district attorney general's office in Memphis to look beyond the dockets filled with rapes, robberies, homicides, and burglaries. Hugh W. Stanton, Jr., a DA in the habit of sending white collar cases over to the U.S. Attorney's office, assigned a team of investigators to plow through more than six million drug prescriptions as the first step in seeking criminal indictments against George Nichopoulos. The detectives dubbed their investigation "Operation Dr. Nick." The attorney general moaned to his staff that he wished they had dug into Elvis's death two years earlier. Stanton, a former state legislator, believed in keeping a low profile as a prosecutor and by disposition looked for the line of least resistance. Given the power of his office and his legal mandate to ferret out crime, Stanton often surprised his colleagues whenever an unusual investigation got under way. "Now don't you get me sued," he would caution.

But *20/20*'s broadcast had built a bonfire under Stanton. Certainly the raw evidence for a criminal case was there. "At last," sighed Larry Hutchinson, chief criminal investigator for the attorney general. For two years Hutchinson had pleaded with Stanton to let him investigate Elvis's death. "It was obvious to everybody that drugs were involved," Hutchinson said. "But Stanton was just scared of getting into that case and pissing off Jerry Francisco."

Hutchinson, a burly law enforcement veteran who had grown up in the same North Memphis neighborhood as Elvis, was firmly in charge of the Nichopoulos investigation. He plunged into his new assignment with the intensity of a bear eyeing a mountain stream for his next meal.

If Hugh Stanton was fearful of crossing Jerry Francisco, another Memphis public official was not. Tennessee State Senator Jim White was a former newspaper reporter, and he had no compunction about blistering the medical examiner for sealing the Presley autopsy. White met with Francisco and told him that he was dead wrong about the privacy of the autopsy. "The legislature of Tennessee really intended that the public be fully satisfied that death under these circumstances be public knowledge," White told ABC News. "The autopsy, the medical report, and the toxicological reports should all be public."

With the autopsy suit still in the courts, Francisco refused to talk directly to ABC News. However, late in 1979 he did consent to be interviewed by Joan Droege of Memphis television station WHBQ-TV, and Droege made the videotape of her interview available to Thompson and Cole.

"Since many outside forensic experts have questioned the accuracy of your ruling in the Presley case, would you consider reopening it?" Droege asked the medical examiner.

"Well, there's nothing to reopen," Francisco answered as though the question surprised him. "The charges against Dr. Nichopoulos have absolutely nothing to do with the cause of Elvis's death. There's no relationship."

On December 27, 1979, *20/20* aired its second Elvis broadcast and scored another ratings coup. Geraldo Rivera had returned to Memphis about a week before Christmas and helped Thompson and Cole assemble the show. In their script they reviewed the findings of the first show, reminded the viewers of the state charges of malpractice against Dr. Nichopoulos, and laid out in some detail Nichopoulos's role in concealing Elvis's drug addiction. They revealed that Nichopoulos had attempted to file a false death certificate for Elvis and that it was so blatantly false that even Jerry

Francisco had blocked it. Then they turned to Francisco's handling of the case. They ran the portion of Joan Droege's interview with the medical examiner in which he refused to reopen the case.

During the broadcast Rivera introduced Dr. John Feegel. "Because of the technical nature of this case," Rivera said, *"20/20* has retained the services of Dr. John Feegel. Currently the deputy medical examiner in Atlanta, Dr. Feegel has twenty years' experience in investigating suspicious deaths."

Was the fact that Elvis Presley received 196 prescriptions for over 12,000 pills irrelevant to the cause of Elvis's death, as Jerry Francisco asserted?

"Well, I would have to disagree," Feegel said. "I think that it is relevant and probably very significant."

Would Feegel reopen this case, if he were in Francisco's shoes? "I would open it this very afternoon, if that were something I just learned," the doctor replied.

Rivera theorized that Francisco's refusal to reopen the case could be based on either of two motives. "Either the medical examiner made an innocent mistake, but now refuses to correct it, or he may intentionally have tried to cover up the real reason Elvis Presley died."

Then he outlined some of the evidence the ABC team had accumulated to support its contention that the circumstances of Elvis's death had been covered up. The program took a close look at Jerry Francisco's press release issued in October 1977. It stated that Francisco had consulted two outside toxicologists in the case— one who concluded that "there is no evidence the medication present in the body of Elvis Presley caused or made any significant contribution to his death." This statement was false, Rivera declared. *20/20* had identified both of those toxicologists, interviewed them, and discovered that the press release had twisted what these experts had told Jerry Francisco.

The first expert was Dr. Brian Finkle of the University of Utah. "Dr. Finkle told us that based on the limited information Francisco provided him at the time, he was unable to form any opinion on the cause of death. He told us also that he so informed Dr. Francisco," the correspondent said.

Rivera identified Dr. Robert Blanke of the Medical College

of Virginia as the other expert. Blanke was said to have told Francisco that the drugs found in the body, individually, did not represent an overdose. "That was true. As far as it went," Rivera said. "But what Dr. Francisco neglected to include in his press release was what Dr. Blanke went on to say—that the drugs, taken together, were in fact consistent with a drug death."

Summing up the broadcast, Rivera said: "Because so many people have been at least less than candid, there has never been a definitive official investigation of Elvis Presley's death and of the people and of the practices which may have been in part responsible for that death."

At the end of the piece, *20/20* host Hugh Downs reminded the audience that hearings to determine whether Nichopoulos would lose his medical license were scheduled to begin in Memphis on January 14, 1980. "The criminal investigation of Dr. Nick remains ongoing, and we will keep you posted," Downs promised.

Even though the show was broadcast two days after Christmas, a time when television viewers traditionally abandon their sets, the second Elvis show scored high ratings, nearly as impressive as the first one. Charlie Thompson's and executive producer Av Westin's gamble had paid off again. The accountants were momentarily off Thompson's back, and Rivera was happy, at least for the time being. Westin now gave Thompson the green light for covering the Nichopoulos hearings in January.

━━━━━

During the last weeks of 1979, Dr. George Nichopoulos was occupied with giving sworn testimony before lawyers representing the Tennessee Board of Medical Examiners. His testimony was taken in preparation for those upcoming hearings. During his three-day-long deposition, the doctor and his attorneys began to develop the first prong of Nichopoulos's defense—blame *20/20.* Nichopoulos wouldn't be on trial in the first place, the defense lawyers argued, if the state investigators hadn't conspired with *20/20* to trump up these charges, all of which had reasonable explanations. The more flak directed at the *20/20* reporters and the state investigators, the less flak they expected from the panel of five practicing physicians who would decide just how reasonable and professional Nichopoulos's methods were.

The deposition was held in the offices of Nichopoulos's attorneys in the 100 North Main Building, located on the same intersection as Memphis City Hall, where the hearing would be held in mid-January. Nichopoulos began detailing his personal and professional background and it quickly became clear that he had never been much of a scholar. He grew up in Anniston, Alabama. His father ran a restaurant and is remembered as a hearty promoter and philanthropist who always could be counted on to support a fund drive or bankroll a Little League baseball team.

After graduating from high school, Nichopoulos enrolled in the University of Alabama, but barely finished a semester before dropping out and enlisting in the army for two years. After his discharge from active duty, he completed another year of college at Birmingham Southern University. Nichopoulos didn't explain why he left that school, other than to say that he wanted to play football at another school, which turned out to be the University of the South at Sewanee, Tennessee, a prestigious liberal arts college tucked away in the lower Appalachian Mountains above Chattanooga. He received his B.S. degree in 1951.

After graduation, he went to Vanderbilt University in Nashville, where he worked for about eight months on animal research in the university's department of pharmacology. He was admitted to Vanderbilt Medical School in 1952, was immediately placed on academic probation and lasted one year. Nichopoulos recalled that his grades were bad in biochemistry and physiology, courses he attempted to make up in summer school in Indiana, but failed. Nonetheless, Nichopoulos continued to hang around Vanderbilt for a year, this time working in the university's anatomy department and vainly hoping to slip back into medical school. When he failed to be admitted a second time, Nichopoulos moved to Memphis where for three years he worked at the University of Tennessee Medical School's Department of Clinical Physiology. He attempted to earn a Ph.D., but he came up short by failing to write a dissertation.

In 1956, however, Nichopoulos was readmitted to medical

school at Vanderbilt, where three years later, in 1959, he received his M.D. degree and a medical license. He interned at St. Thomas Hospital in Nashville for one year and completed his three-year residency requirements in internal medicine in 1963. The doctor added that he hadn't taken much postgraduate training since completing his residency.

Rounding out his personal background, the fifty-two-year-old Nichopoulos and his wife, Edna, had two daughters, twenty-two-year-old Chrissy and twenty-year-old Elaine, and a twenty-four-year-old son, Dean. Nichopoulos was charged with overprescribing drugs to Chrissy—a count that the defense lawyers vigorously and unsuccessfully argued should be dropped to avoid embarrassment to the Nichopoulos family. Dean Nichopoulos, as his father explained early in the deposition, was currently employed by the Presley estate. Asked how long Dean had worked there, the doctor muttered, "Too long." Why was that? "Because he didn't go back to school. I guess he started working for Elvis when he was . . . I'm not sure. He was eighteen or nineteen."

On the lighter side, Nichopoulos said he had been married, "seventy-five, a hundred years." "You better strike that," interjected his attorney, Frank Crawford. "Twenty-five years," Nichopoulos corrected.

Did he have any other children? "No, sir. I couldn't admit them if I had them, could I?"

"I wouldn't," Crawford chimed in.

The state's lawyers stared back blankly. This deposition was starting off like a smoker at a Shriners' convention. Handling the questioning for the state was Frank Scanlon, a short, precise deputy attorney general with a reddish-blond beard. Scanlon was ready to turn to more pertinent matters.

Had Nichopoulos, he asked, ever had any complaints lodged against him by any peer review group in any of the hospitals at which he practiced with respect to his handling of his patients?

Nichopoulos glowered. "Not up until this *20/20* thing," he answered darkly. Asked to elaborate, Nichopoulos added, "Apparently something has happened. I think *20/20* went to the administrator of Baptist Hospital and asked them if they were going to review my patients' records there. And this was made public in the paper here."

Had Nichopoulos seen the television program aired on *20/20* on September 13, 1979? "Very much so," he replied. Was his interview with *20/20* taped prior to the broadcast? Nichopoulos confirmed that it was.

Was it taped before Nichopoulos was served with an official complaint by the state? He wasn't sure. "Different people from *20/20* came to me two or three times a day, called me up all day long, sent me all kinds of little letters and notes, and which I talked to them a couple times, told them I was not going to give an interview. And that so some day along in there . . . I don't remember which day it was . . . one of the guys came in, Geraldo, whatever his name is, came in, said . . ."

Scanlon interrupted and told Nichopoulos to slow down. Crawford then objected to Scanlon's interruption. The deposition had gone from hokey to fractious.

Nichopoulos continued, "Geraldo whatever his name is. Okay. Geraldo whatever his name is . . . came in and said that, 'If you'll just say that you won't make a comment, then we'll leave it at that.' And, gosh, that sounded great to me! And so I said, 'Fine. You come back this afternoon after I get through with my practice.' And he expected me to stop whatever I was doing with my patients and take care of him any time he walked in there."

Getting back to the original question, Scanlon said he couldn't understand why Nichopoulos failed to remember if he had been formally served by the state before or after the interview with Rivera.

"That's because you haven't been faced with this crazy guy, and you haven't gone through the frustration of all this. And I just cannot remember the date," Nichopoulos huffed.

Who from *20/20* was in the interview room when it took place?

Nichopoulos said he was by himself "on my side," but that Rivera had two or three people backing him up. He believed one of them was Charlie Thompson. "And the other people there were cameramen, somebody holding a mike, somebody holding a camera, somebody holding batteries. They had little different jobs they were doing."

Had Rivera or Thompson told him what they wanted to talk about?

"Oh, Rivera had given me a list of . . . a number of questions which I have in my office that he was going to ask me. But basically they said that they wanted to get my side of the story of what happened," the doctor said. "As far as Elvis was concerned. About his death."

Why did he do the interview?

"Because they said they weren't going to leave me alone," Nichopoulos replied. "They said they would follow me to the hospital, the parking lot, my home."

Who told him that? Rivera?

"Yeah," the doctor grunted.

Delving into questions that Rivera had asked, Scanlon ran into the objections of defense attorney Crawford, who instructed his client not to answer any more questions about his dealings with *20/20*. Scanlon argued that the questions were relevant to Nichopoulos's apparent defense that *20/20* had manufactured the charges. "If you are going to stipulate that ABC is not going to be any part of this hearing," Scanlon offered, "then I'll drop this line of questioning now."

Crawford refused, then asked, "Is ABC actually working with the state as a party to this case? Is that the reason for these questions?"

Scanlon denied that ABC and the state were working together on the case. He noted that the defense had taken depositions from Jack Fosbinder, Steve Bilsky, and Joe Dughman in an effort to show that there was a conspiracy to bring the charges against Nichopoulos. The state, therefore, was entitled to find out what happened in the interview between Nichopoulos and Rivera.

"Okay. Well, you're accepting then, apparently by your line of questioning, you're accepting the fact that ABC had something to do with the filing of the complaint against Dr. Nichopoulos," Crawford insisted.

"Absolutely not," Scanlon countered.

Nichopoulos sat silently as the two lawyers squabbled. He

certainly was more comfortable hearing arguments about the alleged misdeeds of *20/20* than about the formal complaint he was facing. But his respite ended.

Returning to the Rivera interview, this time without objection, Nichopoulos said that at first he refused to answer any of the correspondent's questions. "And I was ill at ease, and I was PO'd [pissed off], and I just sat there." (Crawford asked the court reporter to delete "PO'd," but it remained in the transcript.)

Nichopoulos continued his narrative, saying that Rivera wanted to know how long he had known Elvis, when he first started treating him, and other background questions. Nichopoulos recalled answering those routine questions, "and then suddenly the whole thing turned around."

In what way? Scanlon asked.

"Well, he [Rivera] just . . . he took the stand as an attorney would, he just started, you know, just started questioning me about the questions of different things that he said he wasn't going to ask me," Nichopoulos replied with a quaver creeping into his voice.

"What did he ask you?" Scanlon asked.

"He took out a folder that he had and showed me a bunch of prescriptions, asked me did I recognize these prescriptions and I said, 'Yeah, they got my signature on them.' And he . . . just went on with this questioning about prescriptions that he had."

Did he remember specifically which prescriptions Rivera had asked him about?

"He showed me the actual prescriptions," Nichopoulos replied.

To whom were the prescriptions written?

"To Elvis." Nichopoulos claimed that the prescriptions that Rivera had shown were typewritten and had been prescribed to Elvis during the month of August 1977. They appeared to be copies that pharmacist Jack Kirsch had received from him. (In point of fact, Rivera never had the actual prescriptions or copies of them.)

Did Rivera tell him that any action would be taken against him by the Board of Medical Examiners?

Nichopoulos was unsure about that point, but he believed that Rivera had implied that the board was indeed after him.

The Death of Elvis

How did the interview end?

"I told him that I wasn't going to answer any more questions, and I put the microphone down," Nichopoulos said.

Did he have any more conversations with Rivera after that?

"No. I showed him the way out," Nichopoulos replied.

———

On the second and third days of his deposition, held late in 1979 and after New Year's Day 1980, Nichopoulos developed an important portion of his defense strategy. Even though he admitted prescribing 12,000 pills and injectables to Elvis during the last twenty months of the singer's life, he insisted they really weren't all intended for Elvis's personal consumption. He conceded that Elvis actually took some of the drugs, but maintained that the bulk of them were intended for other people who accompanied Elvis on his concert tours. This was an important defense. If Elvis had taken all of these drugs himself, his average daily consumption would have been twenty uppers, downers and other narcotic pills during that last twenty-month period of his life. Everybody in Elvis's entourage shared the drugs, Dr. Nick argued, even the shadowy Colonel Tom Parker.

Well, what drugs did Elvis actually take? Scanlon asked.

"He used Dilaudid," Nichopoulos replied. And he also used Demerol and Dexedrine. Nichopoulos was rattling off the drug names too rapidly for Frank Scanlon's notetaking.

"Just a minute, Doctor," the prosecutor pleaded.

But Nichopoulos hardly slackened his pace, and in rapid-fire fashion continued to enumerate Elvis's drugs of choice. "Amytal, Placidyl, Tuinal, Percodan, Dexamyl, Ionamin."

Scanlon was a methodical man, and Nichopoulos was driving him crazy with this roller coaster recitation of uppers and downers. He interrupted again. "Excuse me, Doctor, have you gone through the whole list?"

"Not yet," Nichopoulos answered, adding Biphetamine

and Quaaludes to his list. "I may have omitted something, but I'm sure you'll come back to it. Oh, the Valium."

Nichopoulos attempted to refer to his office records from time to time, but had to admit that they "leave a lot to be desired." Customarily he didn't write down a whole lot on Elvis's medical charts "since so many people had access to the records."

Elvis, whom he never knew to sleep without some sort of pill, was especially fond of Dilaudid, Nichopoulos said. Frequently, though, he said he fooled Elvis by substituting placebos for the potent narcotic. "And I would imagine that 80 percent of the time these were placebos that we gave him."

What did he do with the 80 percent of the real Dilaudid that he prescribed to Elvis and didn't give to him? "Usually threw it away," he said.

If Nichopoulos was really substituting placebos and throwing away 80 percent of the real Dilaudid, why was it necessary for him to keep ordering so much real Dilaudid?

Because Elvis was suspicious, Nichopoulos said. Elvis would double-check the drug bills, and if he didn't see a large sum of money being spent for Dilaudid, he would know that Nichopoulos was pulling a fast one on him—probably substituting sugar pills for the real stuff.

Well, was Elvis addicted to Dilaudid? "Hard to get addicted on placebos," Nichopoulos retorted.

If he didn't actually believe that Elvis was addicted to Dilaudid, why did he claim in letters he wrote to the manufacturer of Dilaudid that Elvis was in fact addicted to the drug? Because, Nichopoulos insisted, that was the only way he could obtain placebos from the company.

"The only way that you could get placebos was to make a false statement about your patient?" interjected Hayes Cooney, another deputy attorney representing the state.

Nichopoulos gamely stuck to his story that the drug company told him the only way he could procure the placebos was by certifying that Elvis was a habitual abuser of pills. Nichopoulos conceded that Elvis was a habitual user of Dilaudid, which he distinguished from being a Dilaudid addict. He also quibbled about whether Elvis was a habitual abuser of pain pills.

281

The Death of Elvis

The state attorneys then began to ask about the other drugs that Nichopoulos admitted prescribing to Elvis on a regular basis. How many of them had he given Elvis? How many had he substituted or thrown away? They started with Demerol, a powerful opiate. Nichopoulos claimed that Demerol tablets were "substituted at times" with phenobarbital, maybe 50 percent of the time. Injectable Demerol was handled in various ways. Sometimes he substituted water for the drug, sometimes he diluted it with saline solution, and sometimes he substituted Elavil or Talwin, two other narcotics and central nervous system depressants.

"Now, Elvis knew a lot about medications, and he would always look at the bottle and watch what I drew up. And if I tried to draw up a half a cc [cubic centimeter], he wanted to know why I'm doing this. So what I'd do, when I'd ask him to turn around and bend over [obviously, Nichopoulos was injecting Elvis in the buttocks], I would squirt out part of it on the floor and give him part of it, so he wouldn't know what he was getting. And sometimes I gave him a full amount of Demerol, depending on what my judgment was at that time, what his problem was."

Nichopoulos estimated that Elvis actually consumed about 80 to 85 percent of the Dexedrine, an amphetamine or upper, and believed Elvis consumed 100 percent of the prescribed Amytal, a sedative-hypnotic barbiturate. He also consumed 100 percent of his Leritine, a narcotic given to those who are allergic to codeine. "Placidyls were used a lot by him and some of the other members in the group, too. It was a good drug for me to use with him initially to put him to sleep," Nichopoulos said. He ticked off the names of Charlie Hodge, Joe Esposito, and Ricky and David Stanley as the other users of Elvis's Placidyl, a potent downer. Elvis used the bulk of the Tuinal, another sedative-hypnotic barbiturate, and also took most of his own Percodans, which were narcotic and opioid analgesics. Nichopoulos thought Elvis consumed most of the Ionamin, an appetite suppressant, and most of the Biphetamines, another upper, either were substituted or flushed without Elvis's knowledge.

"Quaaludes were only rarely used. He didn't care for that. There were other people in the group that used that," Nichopoulos said, listing Jerry Schilling, Red and Sonny West, David and Ricky

Stanley, Joe Esposito, and Elvis's dates. "Valium, he used some, not very much," Nichopoulos said, adding that Elvis's former girl-friend, Linda Thompson, had a fondness for Valium.

That about summed it up, Nichopoulos thought. Then as afterthoughts, he remembered that Elvis liked to take Carbrital, a barbiturate; Parest, methaqualone like Quaaludes; Valmid, another powerful sedative-hypnotic, and Hycomine, a narcotic-based cough suppressant.

Nichopoulos noted that he prepared envelopes of drugs to give Elvis four or five times a day. Elvis had four retainers who took turns acting as valet-for-the-day. These factotums and nurses Tish Henley and Marian Cocke (whose book, *I Called Him Babe,* contended that Elvis wasn't addicted to drugs), and sometimes Elvis's aunt, Delta Mae Biggs, dispensed the drugs to Elvis at Graceland.

At this point, Nichopoulos began to develop his third de-fense. His medical bag, which was stuffed with Elvis's drugs, was stolen twice in 1977, once in April and again in July. The thefts forced him to reorder large quantities of drugs. This was a solid, albeit partial, defense. But unfortunately for Nichopoulos, Shelby County sheriff's deputies recovered one of those stolen bags along with a bit of evidence that would make him squirm later. In addi-tion, a close look at the prescriptions indicated that some of the other patients in question, Jerry Lee Lewis in particular, had altered the dosages and obtained larger numbers than Nichopoulos had intended.

Nichopoulos also noted that he was not the only doctor supplying drugs to Elvis. He identified Elias Ghanem, the Las Vegas doctor, as another physician who had traveled with Elvis on tour and routinely given the entertainer drugs. And Nichopoulos made a passing reference to an acupuncture practitioner, whom he didn't name, who almost killed Elvis with drugs. The acupuncturist, Nichopoulos said, was treating Elvis in California for a strained back. "The acupuncture consisted of multiple injections with a sy-ringe using Novocaine [a pain killer], Demerol, and steroids." After this bizarre treatment, Elvis was flown back from the West Coast for detoxification. "He came back into Memphis in real bad, almost terminal condition," Nichopoulos said. "And at that time, I think he was addicted to Demerol. He was . . . he had too much cortisone [a steroid] and looked to be Cushingoid."

This was in 1973, the first time that Elvis went into detoxification at Baptist Hospital under the care of two Memphis psychiatrists, Dr. David H. Knott and Dr. Robert D. Fink. The two doctors who specialized in treating drug addicts and handled Elvis's case off and on for the next four years with little success. They put him on a methadone maintenance program and were able to wean him off of Demerol for a time. Nichopoulos said that any detoxification that Knott and Fink accomplished was only temporary because Elvis refused to be candid about his drug dependence and didn't like psychiatrists. "He didn't want anybody to know about his problem," Nichopoulos said. In 1975 and again in 1977, Nichopoulos consulted Knott and Fink while Elvis was hospitalized for more drug treatment at Baptist Hospital.

Frank Scanlon was curious about the word "Cushingoid" and asked Nichopoulos to define it. "Cushing's disease is when you have too much cortisone or cortisol in your body," he answered. "Either that your body makes too much from a tumor, or either somebody has taken too much of it. The face gets all blown up, and you get hypertension and draw up a lot of fatty tissues. And a number of systems are affected by it. But when someone talks about Cushingoid, they usually . . . I use this term to mean the way someone looks, their face looks."

"He looked that way toward the end of his life, didn't he?" asked Hayes Cooney.

"Yeah, but it was for different reasons, not because of cortisone," Nichopoulos answered, but failed to specify what actually caused Elvis's face to bloat during the final years of his life.

Was 1973 the first time that the doctor had concrete evidence that Elvis was a drug addict? "To the best I can remember," he answered.

Was Demerol the only drug to which Elvis was addicted? "He took a lot of drugs, but he never had any evidence of drug withdrawal, even though he used large quantities of different medicine at different times," he replied.

Was Nichopoulos sure about Elvis's drug dependence? "Yeah, I think there was a definite drug dependence. He thought there was a drug for everything. . . . If he sprained an ankle, he'd much rather go get an acupuncture and take a chance of getting immediate cure than for me to treat him for a couple of days with anti-inflammatory drugs and bed rest, because he was depending on barbiturates or sedatives or hypnotics for sleep."

Could Elvis sleep without the barbiturates, sedatives, or hypnotics? "I've seen him doze before, but I've never seen him sleep without them," he replied.

Nichopoulos added that he once put Elvis in a "sleep clinic." For three days, Elvis was kept awake to see if he could break himself of the habit of taking drugs to sleep. Nichopoulos said the sleep clinic treatment failed and that Elvis soon returned to his normal practice of ingesting handfuls of barbiturates before going to bed. Nothing that Nichopoulos or Drs. Knott or Fink could do "could really detoxify him totally from the barbiturates."

Did Knott and Fink know how many drugs Nichopoulos was prescribing for Elvis? "Any physician that treated Elvis besides myself knew what was going on. I mean, they knew all the medications that I was prescribing," Nichopoulos answered. He blamed drugs for most of Elvis's health problems, including his gross overweight, his hypertension, and his badly distended colon.

What about his dependence on amphetamines? "I don't think he was ever dependent on amphetamines," Nichopoulos answered. "He was dependent on some drug he got from Sweden that was supposed to cleanse the body."

That sure sounded weird to the attorneys sitting around the conference table, but it got kinkier as Nichopoulos continued. "He never liked to take a bath, and he thought by taking these pills that he didn't have to take a bath. And he wouldn't do without them."

This unexpected subtopic now had all ears in the room perked up. Nobody in the room could believe what they were now hearing. As three full days of questions, answers and hassles were grinding to a close, was Nichopoulos putting them on about some Scandinavian cure?

"Would he take a shower or bath?" Scanlon inquired, arching his eyebrows a notch.

"No."

"Just wouldn't bathe?" Scanlon asked in disbelief.

"No."

"What drug was this?" the attorney persisted, unable to let the subject drop.

"I don't know," Nichopoulos replied. "Something that he had shipped in. It was a bunch of different herbs of some sort. I don't know what they were."

"Do you think there was a physical dependence on that?" Scanlon felt compelled to ask.

"Yeah," Nichopoulos agreed. "Not a physical dependence. I think it was a psychic dependence on it."

At the close of Nichopoulos's deposition, his lawyers provided the state's attorneys with a list of defense witnesses, including Dr. Jerry T. Francisco. Even with the hearing less than two weeks away, Crawford said it wasn't complete, though. There were other potential witnesses the defense had difficulty contacting, he said. One of those would come as a complete surprise to the Baptist Hospital pathologists and to the *20/20* team.

XX

THE HEARING

EARLY IN JANUARY 1980 a message went out over the paging system in the laboratories of the Orange County, California, Sheriff's Department. There was a long-distance telephone call from Memphis for Bob Cravey, the lab director, who padded back from his Bunsen burners and picked up the phone in his spartan office. The caller identified himself as Dr. Harold Sexton. His voice sounded nervous. Haltingly, Sexton explained himself. He was the clinical pathologist who had coordinated the testing in a particular case two years earlier. Bio-Science Laboratories had done the toxicology workup, which turned out to be the guts of an unusual autopsy. Sexton said he understood that Cravey had run his own tests from samples Bio-Science provided and came up with the same results. Cravey said he remembered running those tests. And he should have been surprised when Sexton identified the subject as Elvis Presley. But long ago Cravey had put that ID on the case, even though officially he was supposed to be ignorant of it.

Cravey, an affable character, hadn't lost the lilting accent of his growing-up days in Georgia and put Sexton at ease. Why he oughta have his test tubes padlocked, Cravey declared, if he hadn't been able to figure out that he was backstopping Bio-Science in the Presley case. The timing, the nature of the case—it was, so to speak, a dead giveaway. Cravey and Sexton chatted about how Norm Weissman had hand-delivered the samples, how hours later Cravey jotted down his results on a sheet of paper and handed it to Weissman. No written report, no fanfare, just a favor for his old friend Norm Weissman.

Then Sexton got to the point. Would Cravey be willing to recommit his findings to paper and attest that drugs and drugs alone killed Elvis Presley? Sexton explained that since ABC's broadcasts on the Presley case and with the Nichopoulos hearing coming up, he was under pressure to assemble a juggernaut case about what really killed Elvis Presley. And that meant lining up as much expert opinion as possible. For the record he had an opinion from a distinguished forensic toxicologist, Dr. Irving Sunshine of Case Western Reserve University in Cleveland. While Sunshine didn't do any testing on his own, he analyzed the data in the autopsy and reached the same conclusion as Bio-Science, that is, that the drug levels in combination were consistent with an overdose. Sexton said his boss, Dr. Eric Muirhead, was expected to testify in the Nichopoulos hearings and might need help from other experts, particularly if they had run independent analyses.

Again, Cravey wasn't surprised. He had watched both *20/20* broadcasts, and Jim Cole, then Geraldo Rivera had already interviewed him. "Sexton said he wanted Muirhead to be well prepared for his testimony," Cravey said. "I told Harold that I had gone as far as I could with the case, unless he would agree to show me all of the autopsy results. I had to see them to eliminate any other possible causes of death."

Sexton agreed. On January 9, 1980, the Memphis pathologist showed up in Cravey's office bearing the complete autopsy results. "Harold was really miffed about Jerry Francisco," Cravey recalled. "He couldn't believe that Francisco was saying that Presley had died of heart problems."

After dropping off the slides and documents, Sexton checked into a nearby hotel in Anaheim and waited for Cravey's opinion. That night they met and discussed the case for more than three hours. Cravey's conclusion was unequivocal. Baptist Hospital had reached the only proper conclusion—drugs had certainly killed Elvis Presley. The level of codeine was alarmingly high and alone could have caused death, but in combination with the other drugs it undoubtedly sent Elvis's system on a steep downhill slalom. Cravey added that the only explanation for Jerry Francisco's official ruling was "a cover-up, pure and simple."

"That seemed to take a load off of his mind," Cravey recalled of his extended meeting with Sexton. "I promised to write him a report, and he seemed to relax."

Cravey's report to Sexton states in part:

> In view of the lack of significant pathology to explain death, and considering the vast number of sedative-hypnotic and analgesic drugs found in concentrations ranging primarily from therapeutic to toxic, the combined effect of these drugs in combination must be considered. These findings would be consistent with coma and certainly could have proved fatal.

Even though Sexton seemed relieved, he asked Cravey for more support. Was there any other forensic toxicologist with Cravey's reputation who would be willing to review the autopsy results and render an honest opinion? "I thought immediately of Randy Baselt. He was my student. We've written books together. He's as good as they come," Cravey said.

Dr. Randall C. Baselt was then associate professor and director of clinical toxicology at the University of California at Davis, located near Sacramento. Baselt and Cravey are coauthors of *Courtroom Toxicology,* the definitive textbook on that subject. Baselt, a tall and slender man, began working for Cravey in 1965 and later earned his Ph.D. in pharmacology at the University of Hawaii. He remained there for four years, but stayed in close contact with his mentor over the years. Cravey took personal pride in Randy Baselt's academic and scientific accomplishments and agreed to call him.

Sexton also asked Cravey for the name of a first-rate forensic pathologist who might be willing to look at the Presley autopsy and give him an opinion of the cause of death. "I told him that if he were going north to see Randy Baselt, then he should also see George Lundberg, who was Randy's boss at UC Davis," Cravey said.

George David Lundberg, M.D., was another southern transplant. Hailing from Alabama, Lundberg had studied forensic pathology at the Armed Forces Institute of Pathology (AFIP) in Bethesda, Maryland, and under Dr. Milton Helpern at the New York City Medical Examiner's Office. And the rest of his curriculum vitae leading up to his appointment as professor of pathology at UC Davis showed that he was qualified to fit into Sexton's medical lineup as a cleanup hitter. Later Lundberg would become editor of the prestigious *Journal of the American Medical Association.*

"I told Harold that George was a good guy, as honest as they come, and that I'd call him. I was sure he would help," Cravey recalled. And sure enough, Baselt and Lundberg agreed to meet with Sexton the next day.

"Harold was nervous as a cat. He was really worried about the hearings and was feeling a lot of pressure. He wanted to be right," Baselt recalled. Meeting in a hotel room with Sexton, Baselt and Lundberg first discussed the case with Sexton, then took copies of the autopsy, including test results, and promised to report back as soon as possible.

Baselt concluded that the codeine alone was enough to have killed Elvis. "This amount would in itself be sufficient to produce a coma with severe respiratory depression in most persons." From an overall standpoint, Baselt wrote, "The presence in the blood of this unusual combination of depressant drugs, several of which are present at toxic levels, in the absence of life-threatening postmortem pathology, even allowing for moderate drug tolerance development, leaves no doubt in my mind that death was in all likelihood a direct result of drug use."

Baselt offered two possible explanations for why neither the Bio-Science nor the Orange County drug screens picked up Dilaudid in Elvis's system. One, perhaps Elvis hadn't taken the last prescription that had been written for him. Or two, "If you're not told about someone ingesting Dilaudid, you probably won't find it in a screen," he said.

Lundberg, commenting on other possible causes of Elvis's

death, ruled out cardiac problems. "Elvis clearly had a big heart, but that's not what killed him. Elvis Presley died of drugs, the interaction of drugs. I was amazed and appalled at what had happened in Memphis, by what Jerry Francisco said. Jerry was entitled to his opinion, but he was quite simply wrong."

Sexton had recruited the sort of blue-ribbon backing he had been looking for, but he was in for a rude shock.

⸻

As the days were growing short just before the Nichopoulos hearing, Jim Cole received an unexpected call in his upstairs attic. It was from Harold Sexton. "Do you have any idea," Sexton asked, "why Brian Finkle would be testifying for Dr. Nick in the hearing next week?"

"Finkle," Cole exclaimed. "That doesn't make any sense."

The two discussed Finkle's role in the autopsy. At this point Sexton felt free to disclose that the Utah toxicologist had gone along with the other consultants in the Presley case. Cole added that on two separate occasions—once to himself and then to John Feegel—Finkle had denied supporting Francisco's opinion and contended he didn't have enough information to say how Elvis died. What help Finkle could provide for Nichopoulos's case was mystifying.

Sexton was sure that Finkle would be a witness, though. While meeting in California with Baptist Hospital's other consultants, Sexton had planned to visit Finkle in Salt Lake City, only to be shocked when he contacted Finkle's office.

"I found out Finkle was in Memphis meeting with Buddy Thomason [John J. Thomason, one of Nichopoulos's lawyers]. All I can say is that the chief [meaning Muirhead] is furious," Sexton said. "We never got a written report from Finkle, but he is supposed to be our consultant. If he's waffling on what he told us, then we're entitled to know about it. We feel pretty certain that Francisco's behind this."

Then Sexton asked a favor. From day one, Francisco had harped on the superiority of forensic pathologists and how their

291

clinical counterparts weren't qualified to determine a cause of death. Sexton was aware of *20/20*'s association with John Feegel and asked for some help to line up not just a forensic pathologist but a medical examiner willing to go over the entire autopsy record and render an opinion. Feegel was out, inasmuch as he was signed on as an attorney for *20/20*. But could Cole ask Feegel for some help in finding such an expert?

Cole agreed to help. He also promised to nose around about Brian Finkle and find out what kind of curve he planned to throw in the upcoming hearing.

———

Joe Dughman was becoming exasperated. When he and other officials on the healing arts staff had been deposed by Nichopoulos's lawyers, the Tennessee Attorney General's office entered the case to represent them. Then the attorney general's office offered extra manpower to prosecute the charges against Nichopoulos. In both instances Dughman appreciated the help. But as the healing arts board's staff attorney, he had prosecuted cases without any help from the attorney general. And now with the Nichopoulos hearing less than a week away, the two deputies sent over by the attorney general were outvoting him and dictating to him on trial strategy.

For openers, they weren't interested in ridding the upcoming proceedings of a silly defense, the one arguing that the charges against Nichopoulos were a mere contrivance of ABC News. Plainly enough, the healing arts investigators had been on Nichopoulos's trail a year before *20/20* entered the picture. The evidence, thousands of prescriptions with George Nichopoulos's signature, was clear and irrefutable. For damn sure Geraldo Rivera hadn't written the prescriptions. Indeed, with a few exceptions where it appeared Jerry Lee Lewis had added a zero to some dosages, Nichopoulos's lawyers were ready to stipulate that the evidence was valid. So why not head that preposterous defense off at the pass—in the pretrial conferences where attorneys had an opportunity to streamline the proceedings in advance? That was Joe

292

Dughman's argument. But his colleagues—Frank Scanlon and Hayes Cooney—believed the appropriate time to object would be in the proceeding itself.

What troubled Dughman more, though, was the equivocal attitude within the attorney general's office toward Elvis's autopsy. At first, the three prosecutors as well as William Leech, Tennessee's attorney general, agreed they should be able to review the autopsy and establish the relationship between what Nichopoulos prescribed and what Elvis took. But the prosecution failed to move quickly. Many weeks after the Nichopoulos complaint was filed, the prosecutors discovered that Baptist Hospital had turned the autopsy records over to the chancery court as part of the ABC suit against Francisco. Now the state was forced into a position of having to intervene in ABC's lawsuit to gain access to the records. If any portion of the autopsy was used in the hearing, the prosecutors believed, then for reasons of context the entire record must be introduced. As Attorney General Leech noted in one discussion with the prosecutors, "I personally think that no patient-record privilege exists." Hence the state would have no basis for arguing that the autopsy evidence could be introduced privately or for honoring any sort of protective order from the chancery court to keep the records from becoming public.

All put together, the State of Tennessee would be fighting *20/20*'s battle if the autopsy was going to be used. When this realization struck, Leech moaned and called ABC "a sadistic bunch of bastards." Soon his deputies, Scanlon and Cooney, began finding solace in the idea that what Elvis Presley took just before he died wasn't really an issue and that the case should be confined to what Nichopoulos had prescribed.

Dughman disagreed. He couldn't believe Scanlon and Cooney would cut corners in this case so easily. Obviously, Buddy Thomason and his partner, Frank Crawford, were planning on making a big issue out of Elvis's death in Nichopoulos's defense. Days earlier Thomason and lawyers for the Presley estate entered a court order allowing Nichopoulos access to the autopsy—no doubt with the promise that the State of Tennessee couldn't make, i.e., that the record would remain private. Francisco and his troopers at the Shelby County Medical Examiner's Office were lined up to testify about it, no doubt selectively. Why should they be prosecuting this case blindly without having reviewed the autopsy record? Sure, there was a lot of interest from *20/20* and the general public about the autopsy. But Dughman also believed there was a lot of interest in it as well from the five physicians who would be sitting in judgment of Nichopoulos. They shouldn't be getting their information through Francisco's filter. Dughman was in favor of prying the autopsy loose from the chancery court any way possible, but his colleagues from the attorney general's office postponed making a forthright decision about the autopsy issue. They hoped it would go away.

Most of all, Dughman foresaw a real danger in the Elvis count overshadowing all the others. It was plain enough that Nichopoulos's lawyers would argue that Elvis lived a special life, had special needs, and made special demands on Dr. Nick, who would be portrayed as a quiet, unassuming, and caring physician. That argument wouldn't hold up for, say, Ivan Cook, the tall, skinny patient named in the complaint, who on request kept getting uppers for "weight control" and downers for "insomnia." The less heralded cases, Dughman believed, would be Dr. Nick's undoing, and they wouldn't come to the forefront as readily if there was a tantalizing mystery about what really happened to Elvis.

In secret conversations, which Scanlon and Cooney warned against, Dughman remained in frequent telephone contact with Jim Cole. Dughman kept Cole posted on behind-the-scenes activity and picked Cole's brain for ways to overcome the shortsightedness of his trial colleagues. In exchange, Cole kept Dughman up to date on *20/20*'s latest findings, and that included the news about Brian Finkle. Dughman also drew a blank on what Finkle could contribute to Nichopoulos's defense, but he appreciated knowing what the Utah toxicologist had said to Cole and Feegel. It would come in handy during cross-examination.

Dughman also appreciated Cole's alerting him to little tidbits of information that kept trickling in. The second accounting of the Presley estate, which was filed quietly in probate court during the Christmas holidays, 1979, showed that Nichopoulos was up to date in his loan payments but as of June 26, 1979, still owed the estate $245,807.33. Precision and detail always impressed a panel of doctors. Dughman hoped the prosecution had enough of it to overcome the lamebrained strategy his associates from the attorney general's office had mapped out.

———

Along an oval-shaped oak railing a clatter of metal cassette canisters and sound boxes opened the Nichopoulos hearing on Monday, January 14, 1980. A dozen or more camera crews interlaced with still photographers shifted their tripods and shuffled back and forth to stake out the best vantage point for capturing the witnesses and lawyers in this unusual proceeding.

"This is not a public forum," declared Michael Bramham, the hearing officer appointed by the State of Tennessee to advise the five-man physician panel about the law and to keep order with a gavel. "There will be no disruptions."

The hearing site was the spacious chambers of the Memphis City Council, a 420-seat auditorium capable of handling a large crowd of Elvis fans, Nichopoulos supporters, curiosity seekers and journalists. John J. "Buddy" Thomason, Nichopoulos's combative lead counsel, glared through his thick eyeglasses at the gaggle of cameras just outside the railing. And he objected to the sight. The cameras were blocking out the spectators, he growled, and interfering with a public proceeding. "We've heard nothing but prosecution statements since September thirteenth," Thomason said. "This isn't a hearing, it's a media event."

And so it was, but quickly it settled into a routine that for the next five days was disrupted more by outbursts from the attorneys than by disturbances from the spectators. Bramham read the charges. Dr. Nichopoulos was accused by the Tennessee Board of Medical Examiners, the state's licensing authority, of unprofessional conduct, medical malpractice, and overprescribing dangerous drugs to twenty patients, including Elvis. If found guilty, Nichopoulos could have his medical license revoked or suffer the lesser penalty of a license suspension for a fixed period of time.

Historically these administrative hearings attracted little attention wherever they were held in the state. This one, however, was attracting a heap of attention worldwide, for the picture that would emerge of Elvis Presley, his closely guarded private life, and maybe his secret autopsy.

Opening the proceedings for the prosecution, Frank Scanlon focused on the narrow issue of whether George C. Nichopoulos had violated the public trust by prescribing drugs that were "not appropriate for the treatment of his patients." There would be attempts, Scanlon warned, to lead the case down trails irrelevant to that issue. But the hearing was not for determining whether Nichopoulos was well liked by his patients and friends or whether his intentions were good. Gazing out at the cameras, Scanlon added that the hearing also was "not a public inquest into the cause of anyone's death."

The *20/20* team was reporting the proceedings each night for the network news while assembling more footage for what was expected to be a clincher broadcast on "The Elvis Cover-Up." Rivera was jotting down a few random thoughts for a stand-up, Cole was taking careful notes and coordinating them with what would be a five-day procession of videotapes, and Thompson left himself free to roam the auditorium and duck in and out to confer with Mike Pleasants and John Feegel, ABC's attorneys.

As the hearings were opening on January 14, 1980, Cole and Feegel had lined up Dr. Robert Stivers, medical examiner of Fulton County, Georgia (Atlanta), to meet Harold Sexton's request for yet another expert to review Baptist Hospital's autopsy. In terms of position, function, and background, Stivers was as close a counterpart to Jerry Francisco as could be found. And he went over every scrap of evidence in the Elvis Presley case with Dr. Eric Muirhead.

"Muirhead must have had a hundred slides of the heart alone," Stivers said later. "I looked at every single one of them, all the reports, and came to the same conclusion they did. There was no cardiac pathology. None. Yet here is Eric Muirhead, probably the best cardiac pathologist in the world—he'd written all the texts on the subject—and all of a sudden he's called a damned fool because he didn't recognize a heart attack. It was like somebody took a swipe at his balls, and he didn't know how to react."

Muirhead had met with the prosecutors shortly before the

hearing and had agreed to testify about Baptist Hospital's findings as long as he had clearance from the chancery court to do so. Stivers, as an expert who had testified countless times in court, coached Muirhead on what to expect from and how to deal with hostile and crafty lawyers and how to state an expert opinion precisely. The state's prosecutors, however, hadn't made a move to provide Muirhead with clearance to testify. As they kept reminding Joe Dughman, they weren't going to make an issue of the autopsy in their proof but intended to use Muirhead in rebuttal testimony if the defense raised the issue.

Unmistakably, though, the defense announced that it would do just that. In his opening argument, John Thomason declared, "We will show the autopsy. Elvis Presley did not die a drug death. The largest drug found was codeine, which was not prescribed by Dr. Nichopoulos."

Thomason's assertion about codeine overlooked an irrefutable fact developed by his own witnesses, however. Among a staple of drugs prescribed by Nichopoulos and kept on hand in a house trailer behind Graceland were Empirin with codeine and Tylenol with codeine. Thomason was assuming that the codeine showing up in the toxicology reports came from Elvis's dentist.

Calling its first witnesses, the prosecution began questioning some of Nichopoulos's lesser known patients, those who could be found and officially summoned. Ivan Cook, for example, who identified himself as an antiques dealer and broker of gold and silver, said he had a sleeping problem and liked to keep his weight down. Standing six feet tall, Cook weighed in at 145 pounds—beard, frizzled hair, and all. Since 1975, Nichopoulos had been prescribing him Quaaludes, Preludin, and Sopor—"whenever I wanted it," Cook testified. Art Baldwin, a flamboyant topless-nightclub owner turned government informant, testified about having the same problems—too much weight and sleeplessness—for which Nichopoulos was prescribing uppers and downers. Both Cook and Baldwin said Nichopoulos was a fine doctor. Out in the hallway Baldwin told the local press, "This is the biggest fiasco I've ever seen for the finest man I've ever known. It's called catering to the press."

A parade of ten patients continued through the morning

and into the afternoon. Occasionally one of the doctors on the panel would ask a question, like one put to Alan Fortas, a former member of the Elvis entourage and a longtime Nichopoulos patient. The evidence showed that Fortas had been receiving sizable quantities of Quaalude, Placidyl, and Eskatrol, enough to prompt Dr. Howard Foreman of Nashville to ask, "Are you abusing medicine?" To which Fortas replied, "I'm still alive."

Then the state called its first expert witness. Dr. Raymond Harbison, a pharmacologist at Vanderbilt University, testified that prescribing such drugs as Quaaludes and Eskatrol at the same time was "not medically appropriate." They were pharmacological antagonists, he said, and if prescribed over long periods of time would create a dependence. Looking over the long list of drugs prescribed to Elvis, Harbison described the narcotics alone as "inappropriate unless you're treating a cancer causing severe pain."

Then in a surprise move, the state called Nichopoulos himself. At the defense table, Buddy Thomason exploded. The good doctor had a right not to testify against himself, Thomason argued. Well, he could take the Fifth Amendment, Hayes Cooney shot back from the prosecution table. Besides, Cooney added, Thomason had said himself in the opening statement that Nichopoulos would testify. Yes, Thomason complained, but calling him now would put the proceedings out of their proper order. Countered Cooney, "This prosecution is not going to be run by defense lawyers." Calling Nichopoulos as a state's witness followed a routine in previous medical board hearings. Then the hearing officer, Mike Bramham, ruled that Nichopoulos wasn't being prosecuted as a criminal and would be required to take the witness stand.

At that, Thomason waved at a lone camera mounted on a tripod far on the left side of the auditorium. He knew what it was. The video camera had a long lens and was put there by investigators for Hugh Stanton, Jr., the district attorney general in Memphis. Publicly Stanton had stated that his office was looking into the Nichopoulos matter. Larry Hutchinson, Stanton's chief investigator, wasn't missing this rare opportunity not only to record testimony but also to capture the expressions, moods, and nuances of a prosecution target and his witnesses, all in advance of a grand jury presentation.

Hutchinson also was working in tandem with local authorities in providing security for the Nichopoulos hearings. Memphis police and sheriff's deputies were assigned to the hearing and escorted the physician-panelists to and from their hotel. At one point the hearing was delayed as authorities searched the City Council chambers for a bomb. And unbeknownst to ABC, Hutchinson had enlisted the support of Gayle Ruhl, agent in charge of the local Drug Enforcement Administration (DEA), to provide agents to keep an eye on Rivera, Thompson, and Cole. There had been threats, and Hutchinson was taking them seriously.

During the hearing Hutchinson kept noticing a tall, almost chinless man with a sleepy expression and mustache who appeared to be part of the Nichopoulos crowd and who kept staring at him. Buttonholing Charlie Thompson, Hutchinson found out it was Dick Grob, former chief of security at Graceland. As the hearing progressed, Grob's stares turned into unmistakable gestures. "That son of a bitch was pointing his finger like a gun at me," Hutchinson said later.

When the hearing resumed for its second day, Nichopoulos's attorneys had changed their tune. They would allow their client to testify as part of the state's proof, although Frank Crawford quibbled that the prosecution was employing "a coercive measure that does not speak to fairness, equity, and justice."

For the spectators, Nichopoulos's testimony was an earopener. For those who had heard his deposition weeks earlier, it was a repeat performance. Nichopoulos admitted that his office didn't keep the best records in the world—obviously patients were dropping in without appointments and getting drug refills that weren't noted on the charts—but he always used his best medical judgment and took the time to be compassionate about his patients' particular problems.

Well, sure, interjected Dr. Howard Foreman, the most vocal panelist, but do you prescribe three Preludins a day to a woman who weighs ninety-seven pounds to control her weight? Couldn't she be depressed because of an amphetamine overdose?

"No," Nichopoulos mumbled with his chin on his collar. "The office was going through a lot of changes. It was hard to get a chart up. Patients came in with other patients. I agree that too many drugs were prescribed in a number of cases."

Later, Nichopoulos would explain that one cluster of patients was particularly hard to monitor. This group included Ivan Cook; his twin brother, Drew, who was almost impossible to distinguish; Gail Clifton, Drew Cook's girlfriend and member of "The Clits," an all-female rock band in Memphis; Barry Underberg, like Ivan Cook an antiques and art dealer, who months after the hearing would be found shot to death at his downtown warehouse in what police regarded, but never proved or solved, as a murder over a business dispute; and Barbara Kaplan, Underberg's girlfriend and another skinny patient (five feet four and 107 ½ pounds) who was getting Quaaludes for insomnia and Desoxyn as an appetite suppressant.

The spectators perked up as prosecutors got to the Jerry Lee Lewis case. The pyrotechnic piano player had been hospitalized for drug abuse on several occasions, Nichopoulos testified, and had been counseled by skilled drug rehabilitation psychiatrists. "Their feeling was that Mr. Lewis really couldn't be helped, that I was wasting my time trying to help him," Nichopoulos said. Nonetheless, he persisted in treating Jerry Lee, prescribing uppers and downers to try to control his intake and keep him away from other drug sources. Nichopoulos noted that some of the prescriptions he had written for Lewis had been altered, upping the number of doses. When did he realize this? the prosecution asked. "When I reviewed these allegations," Nichopoulos replied.

Then you could almost hear the fury of ballpoint pen on paper as print reporters listened to Nichopoulos's testimony about Elvis. And naturally the network news tapes were rolling. There was the 1973 crisis, Nichopoulos recalled, with Elvis bloated beyond belief from his Demerol and steroid and acupuncture treatments on the West Coast; how Drs. David Knott and Robert Fink (the same psychiatrists who treated Jerry Lee Lewis) put Elvis on methadone and visited him frequently at Graceland, only to be dismissed as Elvis improved because he didn't like psychiatrists. There was the 1975 detoxification for Elvis's problems with barbiturates and narcotics. And again, this time in April 1977, when Elvis had to cancel the remainder of a tour because of drug abuse and woeful, drug-related gastric problems. Nichopoulos repeatedly pointed out that many of the drugs listed in Elvis's name were for his whole entourage and that he tried to use placebos as often as possible and diluted injectable drugs on many occasions before injecting them into Elvis's rear end. All in all, Nichopoulos was unable to say just what percentage of the drugs listed in the complaint had actually been consumed by Elvis.

There was a drug protocol, Nichopoulos explained, something he wrote out in longhand that established just what Elvis should be given during a twenty-four-hour period while he was on tour. But that document was missing. It had been stolen during one of two thefts of his doctor's bag during the early part of 1977, which also helped account for why he had written so many prescriptions in Elvis's name.

When Elvis wasn't on tour, Nichopoulos said he prepared small packets of drugs and instructed his nurse, Tish Henley, who lived with her husband in a trailer behind Graceland, to dispense them to Elvis at regular intervals. It was all part of a concerted effort to control Elvis's drug intake, to make sure he wouldn't wake up at odd times and take whatever was there on his night table. Alternately Elvis could be very emotional and volatile, then meek, gentle, and compassionate. He was a strong-willed individual, Nichopoulos said, a hard patient to control. And if he suspected that Nichopoulos was tampering with his drug supply, a package would appear from out of town or abruptly Elvis would fly out of Memphis and go where he wanted for what he wanted.

What about Elvis's blood pressure? asked Dr. John V. Dowling, a Memphis cardiologist. It ranged from 180 to 200 systolic (on the high side) over 84 to 88 diastolic (at a median level). What about hypertension? Dowling added. "Borderline," Nichopoulos replied.

What about the money owed to Elvis? Foreman wanted to know. Did it influence Nichopoulos's medical judgment? "No, I don't think it did," Nichopoulos said. "My objective was to help him."

Later in his testimony, Nichopoulos said, "I don't think I would ever get myself in that position again. I'm sure I would do things differently."

"What would you do differently?" Scanlon asked.

"If I had an option, I would get myself out of it."

Rounding out its proof with two more physician experts who rattled off how Nichopoulos's treatment in each case was inappropriate, the prosecution rested its case. A small exchange indicated that Elvis's cardiac condition wasn't really worrisome, but apart from that indirect reference, the prosecution had steered clear of the autopsy.

As an exercise in show over substance, Nichopoulos's attorneys opened their defense with a couple of good-looking women. Shirley Dieu of Los Angeles, road manager Joe Esposito's old girlfriend, testified that Elvis didn't use drugs for "recreational purposes" and that Dr. Nick made a diligent effort to control his intake. The contradiction here, that is, that Nichopoulos wouldn't need to be diligent if Elvis were using drugs responsibly, wasn't lost on anybody paying attention. Then Sheila Caan of Beverly Hills, former wife of actor James Caan, testified that she dated Elvis in 1974 and 1975 and offered a tin echo to Shirley Dieu. Asked if Elvis had a drug problem, Sheila Caan replied, "He did take several medicines, but I know it was not for recreational use. He objected to it." Of course, Ms. Caan wasn't aware of Elvis's 1975 detoxification, which occurred during the time she said she was dating him. "I loved Elvis very much," she told the board. "If Dr. Nick had done anything to hurt him, I wouldn't be here." That brought huzzahs and applause from the Nichopoulos supporters and some gavel pounding from the hearing officer.

Now that the defense had portrayed Dr. Nick as "the doctor you've gotta love," they turned to Dr. Nick, the unwitting victim of a national television conspiracy. They called Joe Dughman from the prosecution table to the witness stand to answer questions about how *20/20* had put him up to bringing these charges against Nichopoulos. Scanlon and Cooney objected to this entire defense strategy as irrelevant. But Mike Bramham, the hearing officer, heaved a sigh. He pointed out to the prosecutors that they had ample opportunity at a pretrial conference on January 7 to enter their objections to any evidence. Bramham told Cole during a break later that he would have thrown the news media defense out if Scanlon and Cooney had objected. But they hadn't. And as hearing officer he had no choice but to allow the defense to proceed.

Dughman denied that there was any conspiracy to cite Nichopoulos and testified that the board had acted independently. He also denied describing Elvis's case as the worst case of overprescribing he had ever seen. Later Dughman would view videotape showing he had made that characterization, which while obviously true by any reasonable standards was technically a violation of legal ethics.

In an effort to show that the standards of medical practice are in a state of flux, Nichopoulos's attorneys called Edward M. Brecher of West Cornwall, Connecticut, a science writer who claimed that cigarettes and alcohol are as bad for your health as Schedule II drugs. Brecher added that the medical profession might be able to do more good for addicts by providing them drugs than by divorcing them from the mainstream of medical care.

Then the defense started calling Elvis's associates. Billy Smith, Elvis's closest cousin, talked about how Elvis might wake up and take anything that was lying around, how Tish Henley took care of the drugs, and how he tried to intercept drugs coming in from out of town. Smith also recounted how he helped dry Elvis's hair at 7:30 A.M., just hours before the death, and how Elvis had sent out for a special prescription in preference to what the dentist had given him for tooth pain. Elvis was alert, Smith said, "in real good spirits." Then Al Strada, one of Elvis's valets, testified about regularly substituting sterile water for injectable drugs and filling drug capsules with Sweet 'N Low to limit Elvis's drug intake. Strada added that he saw a lot of packages filled with drugs coming in with Las Vegas postmarks.

Tish Henley confirmed that she had been in charge of the drugs at Graceland since 1975 and kept them in an overnight bag under lock and key in her trailer. In the early morning hours before Elvis's death, she remembered sending one Dilaudid tablet up to Ginger Alden for menstrual cramps. (Ginger identified the drug as Quaalude.) Then shortly after 8:00 A.M. while she was at work, Tish said she got a call from Delta Biggs, Elvis's aunt, who lived at Graceland. Aunt Delta reported that Elvis was having trouble going to sleep. Tish said she called her husband Tommy at the trailer and had him send Aunt Delta over with two Valmids and a Placidyl placebo. (Nichopoulos noted in his deposition that the only manufacturer's placebo he was able to obtain was for Dilaudid.) Tish said she kept no records of when or how she dispensed drugs to Elvis. But from memory she was able to recite the drugs he took: The sedatives and painkillers were Placidyl, Nembutal, Quaalude, Percodan, Dilaudid, Demerol, Empirin codeine and Tylenol with codeine; the uppers were Dexamyl and Biphetamine.

Dr. Walter K. Hoffman, one of Nichopoulos's associates, tried to take the blame for the poor record keeping at the Medical Group while Imajean Coley, who coordinated those records, testified with charts and graphs that less than 1 percent of Nichopoulos's patients received prescriptions for Schedule II drugs. Of course, as the prosecution was quick to note, the large numbers of prescriptions that weren't written on the patient charts invalidated all this graphic handiwork.

Dr. Lawrence Wruble, a Memphis gastroenterologist, testified that he first treated Elvis in 1973. Elvis had been taking massive amounts of cortisone in Las Vegas, Wruble said, and as a result had a distended colon and no control over his bladder function. Elvis overcame those problems with therapy in 1973, Wruble added, but his continued use of drugs caused ailments to his digestive system. Wruble recalled a counseling session when Elvis said he needed drugs to become excited for a Las Vegas show, then drugs to relax afterward, and was performing twice a night. "I told him if he had to do that to perform, then either he didn't have to perform in Vegas or we wouldn't be taking care of him any longer. He agreed to cut down to one show a night."

On the morning of January 18, the fifth day of the hearing, the state prosecutors finally moved to hash out who could testify about Elvis's autopsy and to what extent. On behalf of the state, Hayes Cooney asked Chancellor D. J. Alissandratos to interpret his court order in the ABC suit that prohibited anyone with Baptist Hospital from revealing medical-technical information contained in Elvis's autopsy. Specifically, Cooney wanted permission to call Dr. Eric Muirhead as a witness. Alissandratos was no help. He said his court order spoke for itself and if anyone violated it, they could be held in contempt. Neither Cooney nor Mike Pleasants, ABC's lawyer, liked what he heard. Without some protection, the hospital wouldn't allow Muirhead to testify. The two lawyers foresaw the worst-case scenario—Francisco and company testifying about their interpretation of the Elvis autopsy with no documentary evidence or expert testimony available to rebut it. Joe Dughman bit his tongue and refrained from telling his cocounsel, "I told you so."

That same morning Jerry Francisco took the witness stand in Nichopoulos's defense. Repeating his controversial ruling, the medical examiner said Elvis died suddenly and unexpectedly. If drugs had killed him, he would have been found in a restful position. When Francisco began discussing how his opinion could be reconciled with the toxicology reports, Cooney objected. The drugs found in Elvis's body were irrelevant. For the defense Buddy Thomason argued that the toxicological evidence needed to be admitted to show how it could be ruled out as a cause of death. Then Thomason pulled the same trick Jerry Francisco concocted for his ABC deposition. Instead of using the autopsy records, why not use Beth Tamke's story in *The Commercial Appeal,* which reported the drug levels?

At that the squabbling inside the oak railing turned into a bombastic free-for-all. Cooney said Thomason's suggestion was preposterous. Newspaper articles were inadequate sources for medical testimony, Cooney argued. Then he added, "Dr. Nichopoulos isn't charged with murdering Elvis Presley."

"Yes, he was charged with murdering Elvis Presley!" Thomason screamed.

Dr. John Burkhart of Knoxville, the courtly president of the board, was stunned. He had underestimated the depths of Thomason's acrimony in the Nichopoulos case. "The board does not wish to deprive the defense of bringing all facts before the board," Burkhart said softly and in marked contrast to Thomason's outburst. "Can't we keep this confined to the levels of drugs?"

Mike Bramham, the hearing officer, seized on Burkhart's suggestion. "Although Dr. Nichopoulos is not charged with overdosing Elvis Presley," Bramham said, "the board feels that testimony as to cause of death and the level of drugs is acceptable."

With that Francisco was allowed to continue, touting forensic pathologists such as himself as the best authorities in determining causes of death. There was no gradual loss of consciousness here, Francisco said. Two toxicologists, Dr. David Stafford at the University of Tennessee and Dr. Brian Finkle, agreed that no drug found in Elvis's blood was at a lethal level. Here again, the medical examiner was making the assumption, perhaps naive but certainly misleading, that an individual drug must be lethal for there to have been an overdose.

But Joe Dughman failed to delve into this critical and fundamental point of toxicology in his cross-examination. Instead he asked Francisco whether his opinion differed from that of the Baptist Hospital pathologists. With that the medical examiner turned up the tempo of his shell game. Pointing to the decorative paneling at the front of the City Council chambers, Francisco replied, "If I said that's not oak and someone else said that's not pine, then the two opinions could be agreeable or they could not."

"Aren't you aware, Doctor, that the conclusions listed on the autopsy are different from yours?" Dughman persisted.

"As far as the factual items are concerned," Francisco said, "I have no problem. The opinions listed are the result of the preparer of the report. I can't determine what the others found."

"But aren't the opinions in the report different from your own?" Dughman asked a third time.

"I'm not real clear exactly what opinion is in that report," Francisco said.

Dr. Edgar Akin of Chattanooga asked the medical examiner if he reassessed his opinion after seeing the list of drugs which Dr. Nichopoulos had prescribed.

"No," Francisco answered.

Then the defense called the wild-card witness—Dr. Brian Finkle, the Utah toxicologist who seemed to be talking out of both sides of his mouth. Was he supporting Jerry Francisco, as his role as defense witness would suggest? Or was he supporting Baptist Hospital, which up until a few weeks earlier had every reason to believe that Finkle's work was consistent with their own?

After giving his qualifications as a forensic toxicologist, Finkle testified that Bio-Science Laboratories contacted him in the fall of 1977 about performing some tests as a part of toxicology workup. Finkle stressed that he did only part of the testing, that related to liver and kidney tissue. About two months earlier, Finkle said he had discussed this same case with Jerry Francisco over the telephone. With that, Buddy Thomason had one of his junior partners turn on the videotape.

Finkle said he remembered viewing the *20/20* broadcast that aired December 27. He added that Dr. John Feegel, who was working as a consultant for ABC, "must have misconstrued my comments." Appearing on the screen to illustrate how ABC had goofed was a typewritten press release in the funny italic type that Thompson, Cole, and Feegel recognized instantly. In highlights the document read:

> It is the considered opinion of all the Forensic Pathologists and 2 of the 3 Toxicologists that there is no evidence the medication present in the body of Elvis Presley caused or made any significant contribution to his death. The third Toxicologist was of the opinion that all medications were in the therapeutic range and individualy [sic] did not represent an overdose.

This wasn't anything that *20/20* had written. It was Jerry Francisco's press release. And apparently nobody at the defense attorney's table was aware of it. Certainly Brian Finkle was confused about the authorship.

"I have no recollection of saying that at all, . . . that about how it made no significant contribution to death," Finkle testified. Then he asked Thomason for a copy of the toxicology report. The defense lawyer backed and filled, saying the report was part of the autopsy and was unavailable.

Asked on cross-examination if his tests confirmed the Bio-Science reports, Finkle answered, "Substantially, yes, except I couldn't find any butabarbital [in the kidney] and couldn't identify an unknown substance."

As Finkle was excused, Thompson, Cole, and Feegel huddled outside in the lobby. Unwittingly, Finkle had called Francisco a liar. And because the defense presentation of Francisco's press release was so clumsy and confusing, Finkle's testimony went over everybody's head. "How're you going to explain that in a ten-second sound bite, Charlie?" John Feegel chuckled.

After the defense showed a few more excerpts from *20/20*'s broadcasts and closed their proof, the prosecutors headed to the chancery court to plead again for Muirhead's testimony. Hayes Cooney argued that the defense had presented testimony about cause of death and drug levels based on the autopsy's contents. "It's not the state's intention to use the autopsy, but Dr. Muirhead is essential to rebut the testimony."

"How can you examine and cross-examine him without the autopsy?" Chancellor Alissandratos demanded.

Before Cooney could answer, Max Shelton, an attorney for Baptist Hospital, said Muirhead could not honor the state's subpoena without an order from the court protecting him from lawsuits by the Presley estate. Shelton added that attorneys for the Presley estate already had put the hospital on notice that Muirhead should not testify.

Alissandratos said indeed there was a need for a protective order and that in this instance the judicial branch of state government had controlling authority over the administrative branch, meaning the Board of Medical Examiners. The chancellor mapped out what he described as "a compromise" that from its inception he must have known was unworkable. He said he would issue an order allowing Muirhead to testify, but that testimony must be given in secret.

Tennessee's open-meetings law is broad in scope. And it was as plain as the noses on Alissandratos's and Nichopoulos's faces that Muirhead wouldn't be able to testify. And so it was. Muirhead was standing in the wings when Mike Bramham, the hearing officer, disallowed Chancellor Alissandratos's so-called compromise.

This outcome was as insane as an episode from *Alice in Wonderland*. There was no rebuttal proof from the state because the shadow of Elvis Presley still loomed large in Memphis, even in the courts of law. A shimmering distortion of the autopsy was revived. The autopsy itself and the proof of what really happened to Elvis were to remain a secret.

The closing arguments—Scanlon for the state, Frank Craw-ford for the defense—echoed the opening statements. Neither the news media nor the Department of Public Health wrote the pre-scriptions in question, Scanlon said. They were Nichopoulos's pre-scriptions for drugs in too great a quantity, over too long a period of time, and in inappropriate combinations. Crawford in contrast spoke of "a true, authentic, sensitive man," not a pill-pusher. He said Joe Dughman "busted a gut to get the complaint filed at ABC's request. He [Dughman] was allowed on the broadcast to proceed to punish a citizen of the state of Tennessee unmercifully without any hearing or trial, without determining the justice of the situation."

The board adjourned for the night and according to that same open-meetings statute, the physicians were not supposed to discuss the case among themselves until the session reopened the next morning, a Saturday.

Minutes before the final session opened, Buddy Thoma-son, looking dapper in his gray overcoat and tweed hat, walked confidently down the aisle to the defense table. Moving around inside the rail in a talkative mood, he seemed to be smelling victory in the air and a monstrous defamation suit against ABC.

In contrast, Thompson and Cole were down in the dumps. The prosecutors had blown their opportunity to lay the Elvis case to rest once and for all. Rivera, no longer interested in the outcome of the hearing, had flown back to New York City. Feegel was back in Atlanta. So much had gone wrong that maybe Nichopoulos would get off after all.

The hearing opened promptly at 8:30 A.M. Bramham read the ground rules of the deliberations. Decisions would be based on a preponderance of the evidence, not beyond a reasonable doubt as in criminal cases. Nichopoulos had stipulated that he wrote the prescriptions. The board had the options of deciding that there had been violations in none of the counts or violations in certain counts or violations in all counts.

On the first charge, accusing Nichopoulos of unprofessional, dishonorable, or unethical conduct, the board quickly voted "Not guilty." Thomason's face lit up.

On the second charge, accusing Nichopoulos of gross incompetence as a medical practitioner, the board again voted "Not guilty."

On the third charge, the overprescribing violation, the board had twenty counts to consider and took them one at a time. In the first case, that of Art Baldwin, the former topless-nightclub operator, the board voted "No." The proceedings were looking grim for *20/20.* Then the board unanimously voted "Guilty" in the Gail Clifton case. Guilty votes were unanimous in the Drew and Ivan Cook cases. As the cases were called alphabetically, there were eight Guilty verdicts, including one for Jerry Lee Lewis, when Elvis's case came up. It was unanimous—Guilty.

Cole looked over at the defense table and saw tears welling up in Buddy Thomason's eyes. The ABC suit he had envisioned had just evaporated.

All put together, Nichopoulos was found guilty on ten counts of overprescribing, to nine patients and to himself. Dr. Charles E. Allen of Johnson City, Tennessee, who had hardly opened his mouth all week, said that the seriousness of the charges required the board to take some sort of punitive action. Dr. Howard Foreman added that Nichopoulos was "not a bad doctor" but had become very careless in some areas. His record keeping was "atrocious" and his willingness to prescribe Schedule II drugs to patients who just dropped in was "inexcusable."

As the deliberations continued, they sounded rehearsed. Ultimately, Dr. John Burkhart, the board president, said he "would feel kindly toward light action." Foreman recommended a brief period of suspension "and an opportunity to reflect." He moved for a three-month suspension of Nichopoulos's license and three years' probation. Foreman's motion was seconded. The vote was unanimous.

310

During the weekend after Thompson had caught an airplane to Washington, Cole put in a call to Dr. Harold Sexton. He was deeply disappointed that the Elvis cover-up still was intact. "As a doctor, I have an obligation to keep the autopsy confidential," Sexton said. "But after I'm gone, my obligation ends."

"What are you getting at, Doc?" Cole asked.

"Well, you know I've got this weak ticker. My enzymes sometimes get out of balance if I'm not careful. Don't be surprised if someday you get something in a plain brown wrapper."

XXI

UNSPEAKABLE CHORES

Six months after the suspension of Dr. George Nichopoulos's medical license, a task force of detectives had
visited 153 Memphis pharmacies and spent 1,090 man-
hours plying through a total of 6,570,175 prescriptions.
The task force was drawn from the federal Drug Enforcement Administration, the Tennessee Bureau of Identification, and the
Memphis and Shelby County Metro Narcotics Squad. Coordinating the work was Larry Hutchinson, Jr., chief investigator for Attorney General Hugh Stanton, Jr. After retrieving the documents
needed for an indictment, the task force spent another 1,120 man-
hours compiling its evidence with the help of two secretaries.
Quite early in this laborious investigation, the detectives learned
they couldn't do without rubber finger- and thumb-protectors,
which aside from salaries were Hutchinson's largest single expen-
diture. He was forced to ask for an additional appropriation to buy
500 more boxes of them. "Everybody used them but me," Hutchinson recalled. "I'm Catholic."

But after months of monotonous, finger-numbing, eye-
straining work, the detectives believed their thoroughness had paid
off. By comparison to the civil complaint resulting in the three-

Colonel Tom Parker, Elvis's longtime manager, rarely missed an opportunity to peddle memorabilia. Pictured here in 1958, Colonel Parker passed out photographs outside the induction center where Elvis entered the army. Later the colonel would observe Elvis's drug problems uncomfortably from a distance. *(AP/Wide World Photos)*

Larry Hutchinson (right), who grew up in Elvis's North Memphis neighborhood, and David McGriff headed the criminal investigation resulting in the indictment of Dr. Nichopoulos. *(Photo by Jim Raines)*

The criminal investigators uncovered a drug protocol in Dr. Nichopoulos's handwriting. It called for immense dosages of uppers and downers for Elvis when he was on tour.

Tish Henley, who lived in a house trailer behind Graceland and dispensed drugs to Elvis on Dr. Nichopoulos's orders, hurries down a courthouse stairway in Memphis with her husband, Tommy, to tell a grand jury about Elvis's habits. *(Mississippi Valley Collection/ Memphis State University)*

Jerry Schilling left the entourage before Elvis died but later became a marketing consultant for the Presley estate. *(Mississippi Valley Collection/ Memphis State University)*

Alicia Kerwin, pictured as a high-school senior three years before she met Elvis, was expected to replace Ginger Alden. However, the inside scene at Graceland alarmed Alicia and she broke off her relationship with Elvis in the summer of 1977. (*Courtesy of Memphis Central High School*)

An elated George Nichopoulos with his family and defense lawyers leaves the Criminal Justice Center in Memphis after his acquittal on criminal malpractice charges in 1981. With Dr. Nichopoulos (from left) are: Tom Dundon, attorney; Chrissy Nichopoulos; Elaine Nichopoulos; James Neal, attorney and former Watergate prosecutor; and Edna Nichopoulos. *(Mississippi Valley Collection/Memphis State University)*

Bio-Science Laboratories
7600 Tyrone Avenue, Van Nuys, California 91405

TABLE 1

DRUGS DETECTED AND CONFIRMED

Drug	Serum μg/ml	Blood μg/ml	Urine	Liver μg/g	Kidney μg/g
Amitriptyline				+	+
Nortriptyline				+	
Codeine	1.08		+	1.6	2.3
Morphine	0.03		+	0.04	0.04
Diazepam	0.02		+		
Diazepam Metabolite	0.30		+		+
Ethinamate	+	5		+	
Ethchlorvynol	7.5	7.4			
Amobarbital[1]	11.0		+	+	
Phenobarbital	5.0		+	+	
Pentobarbital	3.4		+	+	
Methaqualone	6.0			+	+
Meperidine				+	+
Phenyltoloxamine				+	

[1] BSL identified this as butabarbital, CHT as amobarbital. CHT estimated a total of 20 μg/g total barbiturates, in agreement with BSL.

The final toxicology report from Bio-Science Laboratories showed a list of depressant drugs in various degrees of absorption.

Bio-Science Laboratories
7600 Tyrone Avenue, Van Nuys, California 91405

TABLE 2

Drugs Searched for But Not Detected:

Ethanol	Dextromethorphan
Cocaine	Flurazepam
Propoxyphene	Methyprylon
Glutethimide	Methadone
Meprobamate	Methylphenidate
Phentermine	Dilaudid

But Dilaudid, the drug Elvis preferred the most and especially requested just hours before his death, was among those drugs failing to show up on Bio-Science's tests.

I. Toxicologic Studies:

In accordance with interpretations made by our consultants versed in therapeutic and toxic drug levels in body fluids and tissues, and in accordance with our interpretation of results on drug levels and their clinical significance as recorded in the literature, it is our view that death in the case of Baptist Memorial Hospital A77-160 resulted from multiple drug ingestion (commonly known as "polypharmacy"). Of particular note is the combination of codeine, ethchlorvynol and barbiturates detected in body fluids and tissues. The levels in the body fluids and tissues exceed some other known identifiable multiple drug overdose cases where codeine has been implicated.

II. Morphologic Studies:

Several major abnormalities of the cardiovascular system were revealed by the autopsy examination. There was significant cardiac hypertrophy (heart weight 520 gm.) due principally to left ventricular hypertrophy without dilatation. Moderate amounts of coronary atherosclerosis were present in all major coronary arteries. The degree of coronary luminal narrowing was impressive when the subject's age is considered. Study of the intrarenal arterial system demonstrated rather marked arteriolar sclerosis manifested by hyalinization and hyperplastic changes. Obsolete glomeruli and focal atrophy and fibrosis indicated some degree of nephrosclerosis.

The cardiac hypertrophy and renal arteriolarsclerosis and nephrosclerosis result usually from significant hypertension. Coronary atherosclerosis is known to be aggravated by hypertensive disease.

III. Additional Comment:

Clinical studies, conducted earlier, indicated that the subject had α_1 antitrypsin deficiency. This abnormality in the serum was demonstrated on two occasions at Baptist Memorial Hospital and on one occasion by a sample transmitted to the Mayo Clinic. The Mayo Clinic typed the subject as MS.

While the Baptist Hospital pathologists found moderate abnormalities in Elvis's heart, their unanimous conclusion contained in the final page of the secret autopsy was that Elvis died of a multiple drug overdose—polypharmacy.

month license suspension, the criminal task force uncovered evidence strengthening cases involving some of Nichopoulos's patients and replaced weaker counts with brand-new ones. Nonetheless, the Elvis Presley count continued to stand out as the eyepopper of overprescribing.

Hutchinson, a tall, heavyset man with a thick mop of graying hair, intended to devote many more hours to finding out why Elvis ingested so many drugs and whether those drugs had been the cause of his death. Deep down he believed the attorney general's office was more than two years behind schedule on this investigation. As an old-line gumshoe by method, Hutchinson knew he needed background, a crash course on Elvis. And for that he turned to Jim Cole. They had been friends for ten years—ever since Cole began holding down the courthouse beat for *The Commercial Appeal*. More recently he had observed Cole's work on Elvis for *20/20* with interest. With *20/20* now out of the picture except for a lingering civil suit, he asked Cole for some pointers, starting with an Elvis "Who's Who." Cole drew up a long list of names and underscored those most familiar with Elvis's drug problems—Ginger Alden, David and Ricky Stanley, Marty Lacker, and John O'Grady, all of whom had provided information to *20/20*. But there were others who either declined to talk to *20/20* or were otherwise inaccessible —people like Colonel Tom Parker, Joe Esposito, and Dr. Elias Ghanem. Hutchinson's edge here was grand jury subpoena power or the threat of it.

The introductory witness for the criminal investigation, however, was right under Hutchinson's nose, and he was to prove invaluable both for his own credibility and his insights into other witnesses. Sam Thompson, one of Elvis's bodyguards at the time of death, had returned to the Shelby County Sheriff's Department. Thompson hadn't spoken with *20/20,* but on Friday, February 8, 1980, he showed up in his deputy's uniform at room 640 of the Shelby County Administration Building for an interview. Hutchinson and two other detectives were there with their tape recorder. As Thompson sat down, Hutchinson nodded and switched on the recorder. "Reference: George C. Nichopoulos, Criminal Investigative Division Case No. 556," Hutchinson intoned into the microphone.

The Death of Elvis

As the spools of tape turned, Thompson recounted how he had been a Shelby County sheriff's deputy for nearly four years before going to work at Graceland. Elvis paid him $350 a week for being on hand at the mansion and accompanying him on what added up to fourteen concert tours in about 130 cities over a year's time. All that ended with Elvis's death. Thompson, whose sister Linda had been Elvis's girlfriend, was quick to voice his disapproval of Elvis's erratic, often autocratic life-style. "It was more or less a paramilitary organization in terms of command structure. We rarely approached Elvis directly without going through Joe Esposito [the road manager] first." Thompson believed Elvis's wish to insulate himself and withdraw stemmed from drug use and a self-consciousness about his appearance. "I felt like Elvis's health was not going to continue for a great number of years and there wouldn't be a future in that business for me. . . . I began to realize how much weight the man was putting on. At different times his personality or mood would be drastically altered just in a matter of hours, and it just didn't seem like a normal thing that a normal person would be undergoing. He would be extremely excitable and what I would call hopped up."

Thompson remembered a black bag that Elvis always kept handy, a little doctor-type bag containing drugs. (This was probably the same bag with numerous plastic compartments that Dan Warlick, the medical examiner's investigator, found emptied out in Elvis's bathroom on August 16, 1977.)

Thompson said he conferred daily with Dick Grob, Graceland security chief, about Elvis's drug habits, and together they drew up a number of contingency plans in case the entertainer died on a road trip. "We also felt that Elvis was highly irrational. You know, he carried weapons a lot on him. When he was in these excited states and acting erratically—I'm going so far as to say that we were in fear of our lives—we did feel like some due caution needed to be taken." The two security men decided that if Elvis died in a strange city, they would wrap his body in a sheet and smuggle the corpse back to Memphis on Presley's private jet. "I guess we were primarily concerned with the fact that we did not want him, if he was going to expire from any type of drug overdose, for it to reflect directly on him as an individual." They believed they had a better chance of keeping the scandal of drug death a secret in Memphis than in any other city in the United States. "We were always told to deny any abuse of drugs that Elvis was involved in" when the press posed those questions, Thompson said.

The Graceland security officers also had contingency plans in case somebody took a shot at Elvis while he was on the concert stage, or if Vernon Presley died of a heart attack, or if somebody kidnapped Elvis's daughter, Lisa Marie. But concealing signs of the singer's drug abuse was their primary concern, and on road trips the security men had to be especially vigilant to ensure that all empty pill bottles and used syringes were picked up and safely discarded.

Why did he think Elvis's abuse of drugs was so extensive? the investigators asked.

Thompson, who majored in psychology and English at Memphis State University, believed Elvis's inability to mature or to accept growing older was at the bottom of it. "Here he was 'the King of Rock 'n' Roll,' the bad boy, and now all of a sudden he was getting a little heavy, gray, bags under his eyes, over forty. And his ego was very big—as most entertainers' are—and I think he had suffered a great jolt when he lost his wife, Priscilla, and his little girl, Lisa. I think it had irrevocably, really, hurt him psychologically."

Elvis's breakup with Sam's sister, Linda, didn't help his mental state much, either. Elvis's courting of Ginger Alden, who was then a sprightly nineteen while he was a dowdy, declining forty-one, tangled the emotional mess even more. "There seemed to be a strain in terms of keeping up that relationship, which I think is natural with an older man and a young girl like that—her moods and what she wanted to do."

When Thompson first went to work at Graceland, did anyone on the staff inform him Elvis was a drug addict?

"No one likes to say 'drug addict.' It conjures up all kinds of thoughts, of lying in the gutters and buying nickel bags of fixes, and living day to day. No, it wasn't something that I was just blatantly told, that 'Elvis is a drug addict, he is a junkie, we've got to watch him.' It was just the fact that the man was on some type

315

of 'maintenance medication,' and he was taking large amounts of it, and a great variety of it, and we had to be acutely aware of how these [drugs] would change his personality."

Could anybody talk Elvis out of taking such a large quantity of drugs?

"If anybody ever said, 'Elvis, you don't need that, or Elvis, you shouldn't take that,' he became pretty irrational. And he was always a master at turning the tables on you, making you feel very guilty, like you didn't care anything about him, and would try to explain to you that he had this medical problem and that he needed the drugs and that you weren't aware of these things and he was."

Did Sam ever see Dr. Nick dispense drugs to other members of Elvis's entourage?

Charlie Hodge "was always taking these little green capsules they called Placidyl," Thompson replied. "Charlie drank a great deal. He drank every day, every evening. He indicated that he had a lot of trouble sleeping. He said that these Placidyls helped him rest."

Did Thompson think Charlie Hodge was dependent on drugs?

No, he thought Charlie Hodge was dependent on booze. "You know, he was just drinking all the time, and many times would get very drunk. Charlie's personality never changed. He was always a comedian, always in the center of the limelight, and always had to be talking loud and telling jokes. He always had a drink in his hands. You know, somebody like that, it is hard to say if they were under the influence of drugs or just under the influence of a lot of alcohol."

Hutchinson noted that Hodge was on their list of potential witnesses as Thompson fielded another question. Who else in the entourage regularly abused drugs and/or alcohol?

David and Ricky Stanley abused both, Thompson said. "We were aware that they would smoke marijuana in their rooms, they would try to buy it on tours, and we were aware they would take pills, and the Quaaludes they would both take, I remember that terminology. I have seen both of them what I would consider spaced out, you know." The two brothers were such inordinate

316

substance abusers that other entourage members worried that their antics would embarrass Elvis publicly. "So we would from time to time stage, you know, little fake raids on the boys," Thompson recalled, "and advise them the police were on the way up with a search warrant or something of that nature. It would scare them to death, and they would end up throwing all this stuff down the toilet and flushing it. We would use that as leverage. The boys both knew that Dick [Grob] and I were both ex-cops."

If Dr. Nichopoulos refused to provide a drug to Elvis, would the entertainer fly in his personal jet to another city and get the drug from another physician?

"Yeah. Elvis would do that," Thompson replied. "This necessitated some of those midnight flights that I indicated earlier about the Jetstar."

Did Elvis ever try to score street drugs?

"I think that for psychological reasons he clothed his addiction in terms of prescriptions, you know, 'legally' prescribed drugs. I think that way he accepted it [drug dependence]."

Had Thompson heard rumors that Colonel Tom Parker was considering selling Elvis's management contract in 1977?

It was more than a rumor, Thompson said. In either April or May 1977, Parker told him he was going to sell the contract, saying "that Elvis was a lot of trouble—it was getting to be more trouble than it was worth." Drug abuse and its debilitating effect on Elvis's ability to perform before live audiences were the reasons Parker gave for wanting to rid himself of the formerly lucrative Presley contract, Thompson said, although Parker always was closemouthed about who his prospects were. Afterward the Colonel baldly denied ever discussing the contract matter with him, Thompson said. The deputy still appeared to be irked.

Did Parker hold anyone responsible for Elvis's drug addiction?

The doctors who treated Elvis, particularly Dr. George C. Nichopoulos, Thompson replied, and that included Dr. Max Shapiro, the Los Angeles dentist, and Dr. Lester Hofman, the dentist who saw Elvis shortly before the death. "Colonel Parker seemed to have a particular kind of animosity for Dr. Nick and any other doctor. In fact, he was very bold in cursing some of these doctors.

The Colonel just told me that he felt some of these people were responsible for getting Elvis in the situation that he was in taking all these medicines, drugs. You have to forgive my using the word 'medicine'; it was just something that we always said—we were taught to say that."

Why was Colonel Parker so concerned about Elvis's consumption of drugs?

"I think that it was primarily financially motivated, you know. That was his meal ticket," Thompson said.

With such a clean-cut, forthright witness who observed Elvis's last days from the inside, Hutchinson believed this aspect of the investigation was off to a good start. His primary assistant, David McGriff, agreed. Before becoming an investigator with the attorney general's office, McGriff had been a marine, serving in Vietnam, and a District of Columbia cop, pounding a rough, inner-city beat. With that sort of background, McGriff regarded truth as one of life's rare commodities, and he wasn't in the habit of mincing words about liars.

"Of all the people who worked for Elvis, Sam Thompson was the one who spoke the most truth," David McGriff said. "The others were low-life shit heels. All of them were constantly in heat to please Elvis. It was like grade school, where everybody else gravitated around the most popular kid. If Elvis gave one of these guys a new toy, a new car, the others would pout till they got one."

Before Thompson left the interview, he promised to call his sister Linda in Los Angeles and persuade her to speak, to cooperate, with Hutchinson and McGriff. She could give them an earful about Elvis's drug problems.

———

A few days after Thompson's interview, Hutchinson accepted a strange offer of help from an unlikely source, from an old friend of Elvis's who lived in Dallas. Hutchinson received a long-distance telephone call from a person who identified himself as B. J. (for Billy Joe) Thomas. The name didn't connect immediately.

Then it dawned on Hutchinson that this was B. J. Thomas, the singer, the "Raindrops Keep Fallin' on My Head" guy (the theme song of the movie *Butch Cassidy and the Sundance Kid).* Elvis recorded several of B. J. Thomas's hits, "I Just Can't Help Believin'," "It's Only Love," and "Tomorrow Never Comes."

What ever happened to B. J. Thomas after that? Hutchinson asked himself. The hits had quit coming somewhere in the early 1970s. As Thomas freely admitted in his 1978 autobiography entitled *Home Where I Belong,* he developed a serious drug problem during those years. Now Thomas apparently had overcome those problems and was singing and recording gospel music as an evangelical Christian in his native Texas. Elvis had been a B. J. Thomas fan and mentioned him by name in 1970 during a Las Vegas concert, as documented in the movie *Elvis—That's the Way It Is.*

Thomas's point in calling Hutchinson at this stage was that during his days as a drug addict and a friend of Elvis he came to know Dr. George Nichopoulos quite well. He promised to give details of that association if Hutchinson would come to Dallas and interview him in person. It was an intriguing proposal, and Hutchinson persuaded Executive Assistant Attorney General Jewett Miller, who would be lead prosecutor in the Nichopoulos trial, to catch a flight to Texas with him.

Once in Dallas, Thomas told Hutchinson and Miller that among hard-core drug abusers in the music industry, Memphis was known as an easy place to score prescription drugs. In that connection, he added that Dr. Nick had the reputation as a soft touch, a compliant pill roller. When pressed for specific instances—names, places, and circumstances—Thomas became vague and off-hand. Hutchinson and Miller were after hard evidence, not some elusive memories of another entertainer with a past drug problem and doubtful credibility. Furthermore, coming up empty on a trip to Dallas hardly fit into their lean budget on this investigation. And Hugh Stanton, the man at the top, already was looking askance at the cost of sending a team of investigators to the West Coast for interviews.

One strategy of the investigation was to size up witnesses during either personal interviews, as with Sam Thompson, or grand jury appearances. Hutchinson and McGriff often detailed themselves to serving subpoenas. And they vividly remembered a cold morning in February 1980, when they served one at Graceland in exchange for a stack of canceled checks that Elvis had written to Nichopoulos. At the front gate was Vester Presley, Elvis's uncle, who recognized Hutchinson and knew he was seeking evidence to indict Nichopoulos. Uncle Vester, more and more the addled survivor of the Presley clan, smiled brightly and waved the detectives through the gate. He wished them well, saying, "Boys, I'm fer justice."

Hutchinson parked the unmarked cruiser on the circular driveway in front of the mansion. Climbing out of the car, he glanced at the grass next to the asphalt and spotted something that really threw him. Strewn across the lawn were a handful of bright green-and-black Librium capsules. "Goddammit," he swore at Mc-Griff. "They're growing 'em here!"

Apart from the unexplained Librium crop, the trip to Graceland was well worth the detectives' time. The checks they picked up from Patsy Presley Gambill, Elvis's secretary and double-first cousin, turned out to be an evidentiary gold mine. Arranging them in chronological order made it simple to see how Elvis's handwriting had degenerated as his addiction worsened and the number of prescriptions he received increased. The last few signatures on the checks, written to Nichopoulos in the final months of Elvis's life, were a pitiful reminder of his ill health. Appearing as little more than shaky, squiggly lines, the signatures could have been penned by a chimpanzee. Hutchinson and Mc-Griff believed these documents should have a terrific impact on a jury.

High on Hutchinson's list of witnesses was a name that Jim Cole described as "either a bust or a diamond in the rough." Either way, the *20/20* team had regarded James K. Caughley, Jr., Elvis's former valet and wardrobe keeper, as a secondary player too rambunctious to handle in the quick, clean fashion required by television journalism. Ask Caughley a question and his answer would roll on like a runaway freight for the next several minutes. Then once you had brought everything to a halt, you had to wonder if his answer had been responsive. Beyond Caughley's troubles with communicating a cogent thought, he told Charlie Thompson in

January of 1980 that he was writing a book and didn't want to talk to *20/20*.

In the bodyguard book, *Elvis: What Happened?* by Red and Sonny West and Dave Hebler, Caughley was identified under the pseudonym "Fetchum Bill." He was short, stocky, red-faced, slick-haired, and always in motion. The bodyguards scorned Caughley and claimed he had fast-talked his way into Elvis's employment in 1967 when running the concession stand at the Memphian Theater. Elvis often rented the theater for all-night private movie screenings and gorged himself with the greasy repasts that Caughley brought out from behind his popcorn popper/candy counter enclosure.

In the episode accounting for the pseudonym, the bodyguards accused Caughley of forging Elvis's name to checks and stealing several rings, including a $19,000 30-carat sapphire that a casino gave Elvis for setting an attendance record. After becoming aware of Caughley's misdeeds, the bodyguards claimed, Elvis orchestrated a brutal comeuppance. Caughley was scheduled to fly from Las Vegas to Memphis for a brief vacation with his parents and already had left for the airport. Elvis and the bodyguards pursued Caughley to the Las Vegas airport only to find he had boarded his plane. As the bodyguards recounted the story, Elvis stormed onto the airliner moments before takeoff, flashed a federal drug agent's badge that President Nixon had given him, and ordered a startled pilot to surrender Caughley. Manhandling Caughley off the airplane by the scruff of his neck, the bodyguards continued, Elvis acted out his fantasy as "Superfly" or "Dirty Harry" by reading Caughley what passed for his Miranda rights and searching both his person and his suitcase for the missing loot. Elvis came up empty.

Nonetheless, Elvis was riled up. The bodyguards said Elvis shoved Caughley into a waiting sedan and drove into the Nevada desert where he threatened to shoot "Fetchum Bill." The valet's salvation, they added, was his quick argument that his father, the retired cop, was expecting him in Memphis and that if anything happened, the finger of suspicion would point to Elvis. After screaming at the valet that he was fired, Elvis was quoted by the bodyguards as saying, "Go on, 'Fetchum,' go back to Memphis.

The Death of Elvis

Nobody is going to bother you no more. Just keep your mouth shut." At that, as the story goes, Elvis jumped in his car and roared off. The Wests and Hebler never explained how "Fetchum Bill" got out of the desert, only that the last they heard of him he was pumping gas in Memphis.

When Larry Hutchinson talked to him, though, Caughley was working as a salesman for a Memphis brewery. Only indirectly did he refer to his firing, saying, "Red [West] tried to put the facts together."

The investigators discovered that Caughley had a lot to say about Elvis's extravagances. Remembered more as "Hamburger James" than as "Fetchum Bill," Caughley could bend your ear about Elvis's frequent demands at 3:00 A.M. for a plateful of well-done-to-burnt hamburgers on grease-soaked buns. He could tell you about Elvis's insistence on turning a hotel suite into a resting place worthy of a Transylvanian cavern—cold as a tomb and absolutely free of natural sunlight—because at each tour stop Caughley made sure that the windows in his boss's rooms were masked with aluminum foil and that the thermostat was racked down toward 60 degrees.

Caughley referred to himself as "head valet, personal aide, wardrobe detail, errand boy" during the time he worked for Elvis —for about eighteen months during 1967 and 1968 and again for about three years from 1970 to 1973. Two years in the army interrupted his employment. But that last stretch apparently set new limits in the upstairs, downstairs relationships with Elvis, both on tour and at Elvis's homes in Memphis and Beverly Hills. Frequently Elvis would disappear with a new girlfriend for days at a time. Meals would be deposited outside his door. Maids would pick them up, sometimes eaten and sometimes untouched. Suddenly during one such episode that had extended to four days in Beverly Hills, Caughley remembered being buzzed furiously on the intercom. Elvis and his friend were craving Popsicles. "So at four o'clock in the mornin' I'm ridin' through Beverly Hills tryin' to find Popsicles. You know, whatever he's messin' with is changin' his taste buds around, and he'd wipe 'em out in two days' time. He'd just take a big bowl, a huge bowl, and fill all this up with Popsicles, and he'd go upstairs, you know, and he would stay out of it."

322

Despite what gastroenterologists might say later about Elvis's impacted colon, Caughley remembered the incontinence, both bowels and bladder, that sometimes wasn't discovered for days at a time and always was a delicate matter to handle quietly.

Hutchinson stammered at this unexpected relevation. "There's been times that, uh, you had to even, uh, uh, uh, uh, wipe his butt, because he defecated all over himself . . . ?"

"Not him personally," Caughley replied, "but I have had to, uh, to clean up the mess in the bed, flip the mattresses, to turn the mattress, get rid of the sheets or somethin' where it'd be embarrassing if the hotel saw it."

The residue of Caughley's workaday contempt for Elvis was unmistakable, but Hutchinson needed more than war stories. He needed to find out what Caughley could tell him about the state of Elvis's health and his relationship to Nichopoulos.

The physician's nickname within the entourage, Caughley said, was "Needle Nick," but he hastened to add that he didn't believe Nichopoulos was "syringe happy." As the factotum who picked up most of Elvis's many drug prescriptions, Caughley said that during his last three years as valet, Elvis's drug problems worsened and the number of overdoses increased. "Nineteen-seventy-one wasn't a bad year. We had a couple [of overdoses]. Nineteen-seventy-two, it started gettin' a little worse. And at the time, the last nine months with Elvis, we had three ODs; it was unbelievable."

Hutchinson pressed for more details. What led Caughley to believe that Elvis had overdosed? "[He had] hardly any circulation in the body. I mean, hardly any heartbeat. He could not respond to vocal or shaking abuse. I've had ODs before in Vegas where he wouldn't respond—so far out on sleeping pills that I've actually had to sit him in the bed and shake him, slap at him, take a vibrator to the back, you know, try and get him moving, circulating." On this occasion, like others, Nichopoulos was summoned, Caughley said. "Several of the boys got Elvis out of the bedroom, set him up in a chair. Nichopoulos had his bag with him." At that point, Caughley said, Joe Esposito ordered the mere functionaries out of the room while Nichopoulos worked to revive the singer.

Vernon Presley, who from other accounts had kept his distance from his son's drug problems, witnessed some of these over-doses, Caughley said, including a near-fatal one in St. Louis. Did everybody in Elvis's inner circle know how bad his drug addiction was? "Unless they were completely blind or dumb," Caughley replied.

Then he named other doctors who regularly gave Elvis drugs—Dr. Thomas "Flash" Newman of Las Vegas, Dr. Elias Ghanem, also of Las Vegas, and Dr. Max Shapiro of Los Angeles. And when the drugs came in, regardless of the name on a package or pill bottle, everybody knew they were for Elvis?

"Uhm hum," Caughley affirmed.

"And ultimately got delivered to Elvis Presley?" Hutchinson asked.

"Very much so."

"Let me ask you a question, James. You indicated earlier that there were several bad periods between seventy-one and seventy-three?"

"Very much so."

"Okay. During those periods, Elvis Presley was very much involved in the use of narcotics. Is that correct?"

"Yes. His dependency seemed to be growing stronger and stronger. It started showing more openly, and he started . . . Because it seemed like it progressed; it seemed to get worse and worse, like on a graph, as I explained."

"Okay. Now, did you ever have an occasion to observe needle marks on the body of Elvis Presley?"

"Oh, yeah. We used to joke about it. It looked like a pin cushion. His ass looked like a pin cushion."

"And these were from needle marks made by syringes?"

"Sure."

"Is it a fair statement to say that Dr. George Nichopoulos during that time period also observed the same needle marks or track marks?"

"Uhm. If he did any kind of physical examination, or looked at his client, yes. He'd have to see it. If he was nude, he would have to see those. But I cannot [say that Nichopoulos saw them] because I was not in the room."

Later Hutchinson asked if one of Caughley's duties was to pick up the evidence of Elvis's drug use, such as old syringes.

"Very much so," he answered. "Not only dispose of syringes, I also disposed of empty bottles and labels which had names on it, and several times I got mad, because I'd find my name after asking certain doctors not to put my name on a bottle."

By mid-1973, June or July, Caughley said, Nichopoulos summed up Elvis's drug problems with a memorable declaration to the entourage. "You know, I think 'E' [Elvis] is no longer an addict. I think he's a hard addict."

In that connection, Caughley remembered pouring himself a cup of coffee in a mansion that Elvis was renting in Los Angeles on Monovale Drive when the unexpected happened. It was about noon, early in the day for Elvis to be awake. Caughley dropped one saccharine tablet in his coffee but routinely used one and a half. He was breaking another tablet in two when Elvis stumbled into the kitchen and snatched it out of Caughley's hand. "Give me that!" Elvis demanded. Before Caughley could say, "Hey, it's sweet, you know saccharine," Elvis popped the pill in his mouth and swallowed it, believing it was a narcotic substance. "I did what I shouldn't have done. I went in the other room, and fell over on the pool table laughing. . . . The quickest way to get Elvis down on your ass was to start saying something, or showing too much interest in his problem. And you start talking too much, you'd be on the street."

Perhaps the closest call Elvis had to overdosing during those years, Caughley recounted, was in Palm Springs, California. Elvis and his young date, still a teen-ager, were swigging down Hycodan, a habit-forming, narcotic-analgesic cough syrup, from champagne glasses. "I think she was just gullible to anything he did. We almost lost that poor girl," Caughley said. An overdose of Hycodan typically produces deep sleep, slow breathing, a slow pulse, respiratory arrest, flushed and warm skin, and constricted pupils. About 4:00 A.M. both Elvis and his date nodded off from the effects of the drug. Neither one was breathing properly. The bodyguards and Caughley managed to slap Elvis back to consciousness, but they had no luck with the girl. She barely had a pulse, and her eyes were fixed like marbles. Somebody—Caughley couldn't remember who—called a friendly doctor to the house on Chino Road, but the physician said Elvis's date was so close to death that she needed to be taken immediately to the hospital. She was turning blue as an ambulance arrived and picked her up on a stretcher. Elvis wasn't happy about this turn of events. He had argued unsuccessfully with the doctor that his date could be revived with a nice shot of Ritalin, a strong stimulant that has the odd property of calming hyperactive children. But the doctor refused to pay any attention to Elvis.

The entourage planned a cover-up in the event the girl died, Caughley said, and the fall guy would be Charlie Hodge, who apparently was asleep at the time. Hodge, Caughley, and the bodyguards would swear to the authorities that the girl was Hodge's date and that he had gotten her stoned on the narcotic. Other girls in the house, who had come there as dates of other entourage members, were sworn to secrecy. Caughley said that Dick Grob, who was then a sergeant with the Palm Springs Police Department, was asked to help insure that no police investigation of the incident would be made. After the girl was taken to the intensive care unit of a local hospital, Elvis called Colonel Tom Parker, who lived in Palm Springs and wielded considerable influence there, and also enlisted his aid in blocking any official inquiry into the girl's overdose.

At the hospital, meanwhile, the girl's stomach was pumped. She was given injections to overcome the cough syrup's effects, but her life hung in the balance for many hours. Then at 7:00 P.M., after seventeen hours of unconsciousness, she finally came to. Sonny West visited the girl that night and reported that she sprang out of the hospital bed and hissed at him like a wild animal. West was concerned about her, especially after the doctor told him she was suffering from the effects of oxygen deprivation to her brain. Apparently the Hycodan episode resulted in no lasting ill effects, however. The girl and her mother were offered money but refused to take it and kept quiet. The incident didn't see daylight until the bodyguards published their book just before Elvis's death.

Elvis was reckless with firearms, too, Caughley told the investigators. He remembered seeing a stoned Elvis shoot out the light of a chandelier of the penthouse of the Las Vegas Hilton "sitting at the breakfast table with a .22 caliber, $2,000 pistol engraved in gold and black, you know, a semi-automatic shooting iron." And the wild shot in the thirteenth floor Imperial Suite of the Las Vegas Hilton almost was Linda Thompson's undoing. "Linda's in the bathroom, and that goddamn gun went off," Caughley said. "I thought Linda had killed herself." Then spotting Elvis with a smoking .22 caliber Savage revolver in his hand and a small bullet hole in the bathroom wall, Caughley reconstructed what had happened. He yelled for Linda. Still perched on the toilet, the former beauty queen answered that she was alive. Elvis had been shooting at a statue of an owl in the penthouse, but he was bonkers on narcotics, and his aim was erratic. The bullet had gone through the bathroom wall, gouged a hole in a roll of toilet paper next to Linda's knee, and then splintered a mirror on a closet door to shards of glass.

Luckily for Linda, Elvis had only fired once. "I was petrified! How the bullet missed her I don't know, it was a miracle!" Caughley said. "The first thing that went through my mind was they'd had a lovers' quarrel." When Linda was able to pull her clothing together, she stalked into the room where Elvis was sitting and demanded archly, "What in God's name was that?" Red and Sonny West converged on the penthouse and were as upset with Elvis as Caughley and Linda were. But Elvis seemed amused. He was reclining on a sofa facing the bathroom wall, and told Linda, "Hey, now, hon, just don't get excited."

Given this sort of devil-may-care behavior, Caughley was mystified that a woman of Linda Thompson's stability would stick with Elvis as long as she did. "Linda was a lotta help to Elvis."

XXII

THE WESTERN SWING

BEFORE LARRY HUTCHINSON and David McGriff could fly out to California to interview Linda Thompson and other former members of Elvis's "Memphis Mafia" then living on the West Coast, they had to attend to grand jury business in Memphis. McGriff, a slender, angular investigator with thinning, prematurely gray hair, drew the assignment of serving a subpoena on Davada (Dee) Elliot Stanley, Vernon Presley's former wife.

The job turned out to be a revealing experience for McGriff. The detective drove to Dee's high-rise apartment building, located in a fashionable section of East Memphis, took the elevator up, and knocked on her door. Dee had been married to Vernon until 1977, when she obtained a divorce decree from a court in the Dominican Republic. Now, three years later, she was still a perky blue-eyed blonde, but she was showing her fifty-five years. When Dee opened the apartment door, McGriff was thunderstruck. Rather than comporting herself like a middle-aged hausfrau, Dee was decked out like the hookers McGriff used to arrest when he was a beat patrolman in Washington, D.C., in the early 1970s.

Dee had been Elvis's stepmother for eighteen years and

was ten years his senior. To McGriff she seemed to have the same problem as her late stepson in acting her age. Her makeup was thick enough for a quick game of tick-tack-toe. She had on enough hair spray to take on a wind tunnel. And she had stuffed herself like a sausage link into a one-piece, see-through jumpsuit without room to spare for underwear. As she effusively greeted McGriff, he could hardly avoid the spectacle of breasts jiggling in Dee's mostly unbuttoned jumpsuit top. "It wasn't any surprise to me that Vernon checked out if she would prance around like that with a total stranger," McGriff said years later.

After her divorce from Vernon, Dee married Lewis Tucker, who was five years her junior. She gladly accepted the subpoena from McGriff and said that she and her three boys certainly looked forward to detailing everything they witnessed during their many years at Graceland. Of course, Dee and her sons had just written their collective memoirs, *Elvis, We Love You Tender,* and there was no mistaking that any criminal proceedings against Dr. George Nichopoulos involving the Stanleys would be a windfall promotion for their book.

Meanwhile, Larry Hutchinson had drawn Ginger Alden's subpoena. During Hutchinson's visit to the Alden home, Ginger was as tethered to her mother as Charlie McCarthy was to Edgar Bergen. Any question that Hutchinson posed to Ginger seemed to overwhelm and dumbfound her. She continually turned to her mother for advice and answers. Hutchinson found Ginger's lack of intellect and self-assertiveness depressing. "She was an airhead," he said. "Everything she said, her mommy told her to say."

Also on the subpoena list was Al Strada, one of the few entourage members still employed at Graceland. For a time he managed to dodge his summons. But with some routine surveillance work, Hutchinson and McGriff collared Strada and explained both the consequences of failing to honor a subpoena and the criminal contempt powers of the Tennessee courts. The tough talk must have made an impression on Strada, because he meekly appeared before the grand jury, and among other things drew the jurors a sketch of Elvis's death scene.

Among other witnesses to appear before the Shelby County grand jury were Sam Thompson; Dee Stanley and her three sons; Ginger Alden; Pauline Nicholson and Lottie Tyson, the Graceland maids; Mary Jenkins and Nancy Rook, Graceland's cooks; Marian Cocke, Elvis's nurse; Sandra Miller, Vernon's last girlfriend and also a nurse; Tish Henley, Nichopoulos's employee, who lived in the trailer behind Graceland; Tommy Henley, her husband; Delta Mae Biggs, Elvis's aunt, who lived at Graceland and generally supervised housekeeping at the mansion; Billy Smith and Patsy Gambill, two of Elvis's cousins; George Klein, Elvis's longtime disc jockey friend; Alan Fortas, a sometime entourage member and patient of Nichopoulos's; Richard Davis, another minor entourage member; Marty Lacker and his wife, Patsy, coauthors of *Elvis: Portrait of a Friend,* which enumerated Nichopoulos's prescription habits; and Joseph Hanks, Elvis's accountant.

For the most part, those witnesses who were at Graceland at the time of Elvis's death confirmed what already had been published and broadcast. But there were some amplifications and nuances. There was a disagreement, for example, about whether an ambulance should be called before Nichopoulos arrived. Ultimately, the time needed for Nichopoulos to drive from Doctors Hospital to Graceland, once he was notified, prompted Joe Esposito to make a frantic phone call for a fire department ambulance. The grand jury also learned that Elvis obtained his final dose of drugs about 8:30 A.M. on August 16, 1977. The unlikely courier was his aunt, Delta Mae Biggs. This was two hours or less from the time Ricky Stanley delivered the Dilaudid prescription that Nichopoulos had called in for Elvis at approximately 4:00 A.M. Ricky, by his own admission, was zonked out on Demerol by 8:30 A.M. when Elvis was demanding more drugs. Elvis next attempted to call resident nurse Tish Henley in her trailer, but she had already left for work. Through Aunt Delta, Elvis contacted Tish at Nichopoulos's clinic in midtown Memphis. After determining what Elvis wanted, Tish telephoned her trailer and talked to her husband, Tommy, a deputy sheriff who also tended the grounds at Graceland. His instructions were to take a packet of pills—Tish told the medical board it contained Valmid and a Placidyl placebo—into the mansion and give it to Aunt Delta. Mrs. Biggs, who shared a room at Graceland with her mother, Minnie Mae Presley, took the packet to Elvis's second-floor bathroom, knocked on the door, and handed him the drugs. Apparently Aunt Delta was the last person to see Elvis alive.

———

At the end of March 1980 there was a lull in grand jury testimony, an opportunity for Hutchinson and McGriff to fly to the West Coast for witness interviews. Under Attorney General Hugh Stanton, Jr., though, the policy on travel was "See Memphis first." There wasn't any money in the budget for an extended investigation on the West Coast, Stanton pointed out. A special appropriation from the county commission funded this portion of the investigation, but as Hutchinson suspected, on the cheap. The cheapest rate he and McGriff could find was $85 a night at the Ramada Inn. Their per diem from the county was $40, covering room, board, and all other expenses. Traveling with them was Detective Bobby Armstead, who was on loan from the metro narcotics bureau, and that meant renting two rooms, minimum.

The Memphis threesome arrived at Los Angeles International Airport in late March, and in line with their budget they rented a subcompact auto. Hutchinson had signed off on their transportation when the suitcase problem arose. To fit themselves and their luggage into the car, they had to borrow rope from the car rental agency and tie two suitcases that wouldn't fit in the trunk to the car roof. Even so, Hutchinson and Armstead needed to stick the ends of other suitcases out of the car windows, while McGriff piloted the automobile through Los Angeles's clogged freeways. As Hutchinson recounted the spectacle, "We looked like well-armed 'Beverly Hillbillies.'"

The Memphis investigators soon discovered that higher prices weren't the only differences between the life-styles of their home town and Los Angeles in 1980. "Everybody we called had a damned answering machine and an agent, even the doctors, the hustlers, the con men, and the losers," complained Hutchinson. He telephoned Dr. Max Shapiro, better known as "Dr. Feelgood" or "Dr. Painless," and left a message on his answering machine. Returning the call at the Ramada was Shapiro's theatrical agent, then

Shapiro's attorney demanding to know why Hutchinson wanted to interrogate his client. Eventually an agreement was worked out through the attorney, who promised that Shapiro would arrive at the detectives' hotel room for an interview promptly at eight o'clock that night. Have a pot of coffee waiting for Dr. Max when he gets there, the attorney instructed. At the appointed hour Hutchinson, McGriff, Armstead, and fresh-brewed coffee were ready. While waiting they pulled out files of information and began discussing them. But no Dr. Max. As minutes became hours, they ordered more coffee. Still no Dr. Max. Hours passed. Around 3:00 A.M., they realized that they had consumed six pots of coffee at eight bucks a pop, and there was still no sign of Shapiro. Their nerves were shot from all the caffeine, a full per diem on coffee.

Their next interview attempt also went awry. Hutchinson phoned Priscilla Presley and again reached a ubiquitous answering machine. Priscilla's agent returned the call and brusquely informed the detective that Elvis's former wife was too busy studying her lines for a Colombian coffee commercial to talk with him. "She's so busy becoming the next Juan Valdez that she's got no time to talk about her former old man's drug habits? Terrific!" Hutchinson said, banging down the phone in frustration. He had been in Los Angeles less than twenty-four hours and was beginning to hate the place.

The Memphis team had been in L.A. for two days, their expenses were mounting, and they had accomplished absolutely nothing. Discouraged but undeterred, Hutchinson kept plugging away at answering machines and agents. Finally he managed to arrange an interview with Linda Thompson. The statuesque beauty had been Elvis's constant live-in companion for four and a half years; reportedly, Elvis had spent over a million dollars on jewelry for Linda during their romance from 1972 to 1976. When he was admitted to Baptist Hospital for drug detoxification during November 1973, she stayed with him in his hospital room. The hospital bent its rules and set up a cot for her.

Linda, then twenty-nine, arrived at the investigators' room at the Ramada wearing a simple, light-colored dress. It was 7:00 A.M. on Friday, March 28, 1980. She had scheduled her meeting with the detectives at this early hour so she and her current boyfriend, Bruce Jenner, could attend a boat race in Long Beach later that morning. During the interview, Linda had parked Jenner, an athlete who won the decathlon at the 1976 Olympic Games in Montreal, in the hotel lobby. (Linda married Jenner in 1981 and lived with him until 1987. After their split, Jenner became involved with Donna Rice, who came into disrepute with presidential candidate Gary Hart in 1987.) "Linda was kind of a breath of fresh air compared with the rest of the dirt bags we met who hung around Elvis. I liked her," McGriff said. She was an actress, a regular on the cornpone television series *Hee Haw.*

Hutchinson switched on his tape recorder as Linda began relating the first time she became aware that Elvis was heavily into drugs. It was on a trip to Las Vegas in September 1972, some four months after she began dating him. "I just noticed that he was very groggy that first night we were together. I had no experience at all with people taking sleeping medication, and he was just very groggy. I asked him what was wrong, and then I saw pills on, you know, the nightstand, and they were sleeping medication." Linda had never been around any addicts, and she asked Elvis why he took sleeping medication "every night of his life." At the time, he gave her a vague, equivocal answer.

Linda estimated that Elvis consumed about fifteen to twenty pills every night "and would sometimes knock himself out completely." Most of these drugs were sleeping pills, but some of them were potent narcotics, intended for patients suffering unbearable pain. Linda identified Drs. George Nichopoulos, Elias Ghanem, and Thomas R. "Flash" Newman as suppliers of Elvis's drugs. "Always" there was a ready supply of pills around him, and he also received regular injections from these same physicians. Elvis took so many drugs that frequently he passed out with food in his mouth and began choking. "He would fall asleep in the middle of eating, and I would have to clean food out of his mouth and out of his throat and turn him on his side and make sure that he was breathing," she said.

On occasion, her ministrations were not sufficient to keep him alive, and she was forced to seek professional medical assistance. "I had to call Dr. Newman, because Elvis had choked on food, and he was completely out of it. He came over and gave him an injection to help rouse him. Still, he didn't wake up for hours."

(Newman, who was practicing medicine in Las Vegas when contacted by the authors in 1989, denied ever treating Elvis for an overdose. Despite being identified by John O'Grady and Linda Thompson, he also denied ever being Elvis's doctor. "He was a real good guy and very religious," Newman said. "I used to read the Bible to him. He was more of a friend than a patient. Ghanem was his real doctor.")

Elvis was sensitive about his drug habits and hated to discuss them, but once Linda drew him out of his shell. "He at one point admitted that he had a self-destructive vein, felt that he was somewhat self-destructive. He just always suffered from insomnia even as a child, and I think from the age of nineteen on when he acquired world fame and all that goes along with it, you know, the pressures were so much and so intense that he really had a lot of difficulty sleeping."

Did she know of any other members of Elvis's tour group who ever overdosed on drugs? No, but she knew that Charlie Hodge drank a lot and frequently passed out stone drunk.

Perhaps Elvis's closest brush with death, Linda recalled, was during a flight from Las Vegas to Memphis on his private jet. As usual he had been taking drugs and suddenly fell to the floor, gasping for oxygen. His corporate pilot, appropriately named Milo High, dropped the Jet Commander's altitude in the hopes of making breathing easier for his stricken passenger. Elvis was moved near an air vent, located near the floor, and an oxygen mask was clamped over his face. These first-aid measures helped some, because his breathing and pulse began to steady. But when the plane landed in Memphis, Elvis still required hospitalization. He always carried narcotics everywhere he went, and he took his ready supply with him when he went to the hospital for detoxification.

Drugs often so blitzed Elvis out that he frequently "would never wake up throughout a performance," Linda told the investigators. "He would never quite become fully awake until the show was over, and he would say, 'Well, I'm just now waking up.' " On other occasions, he would be so wired from taking speed "or whatever he was taking affected him so that he was too high, strung out and giggling, you know, on stage—sometimes silly, and sometimes hostile."

Linda had been reared by strict parents who thought that even tasting alcohol was a sin. Her upbringing played a major role in her growing aversion to Elvis's excesses, which she discussed with Dr. Nick. "He told me I wasn't the kind of girl who should be around all that. He said, 'You are perfectly straight, you don't even smoke hash, and you don't do any of the stuff, and frankly my advice to you would be to leave, and I don't think you are ever going to change it,' because I had asked him how we could get him to stop doing all this." According to Linda, Dr. Nick's answer was, "I don't think that we ever can."

Hutchinson showed Linda a copy of the complaint filed against Nichopoulos by the Tennessee Board of Medical Examiners and asked her if she was familiar with the list of drugs contained in its bill of particulars. Nonplussed, Linda said she had witnessed Elvis take every type of drug listed. "From the years with Elvis, I saw those prescriptions prescribed at different times and would look them up in the PDR [*Physicians' Desk Reference*] that Elvis had." Elvis was "very well versed" on drugs and often thumbed through his PDR to check out the effects of various pills, when taken in combination.

Was he allergic to any of these drugs? Hutchinson asked. "Yeah, codeine," she replied. Sometimes Elvis would take Hycomine "or something that had codeine in it, and I think that sometimes he would get some sort of Tylenol—substances with codeine in them. I know that he had been prescribed codeine, and he would break out in a little rash."

McGriff's ears perked up. Was Elvis aware of his codeine allergy? he asked. "He was aware of the fact that he was somewhat allergic to codeine, and he would just break out in a little rash," she replied.

Did she believe that the doctors who prescribed the codeine were also aware of his allergy? They had to know, she said.

"Yet they continued to prescribe this medication?" McGriff asked. To the best of her knowledge, she said, the doctors including Nichopoulos continued to prescribe codeine to Elvis, even though they knew he was allergic to it.

The Death of Elvis

Linda said she had planned on marrying Elvis but left him "primarily" because of his drug problem but in a larger sense because she objected to "his entire life-style, and his entire person."

The interview had been going for about an hour when a loud knock interrupted the questioning. McGriff opened the door, and in stormed an angry Bruce Jenner. "Just when will you be finished?" he demanded.

Hutchinson, whose young son idolized Jenner, attempted to mollify the famous decathlon champion and asked for an autographed photo he could take back to Memphis. Rudely Jenner retorted that he would be in Memphis on a promotional tour later in the year. "See me about it when I'm there," he told Hutchinson.

At that point, Linda interceded and asked Jenner to return to the lobby. She promised to wrap up the interview as soon as possible.

With her boyfriend out of the way, at least for the moment, Linda resumed her account of life with Elvis. He required so much attention that she avoided drugs herself, "knowing that he might be lying there with food in his mouth. Someone had to be constantly there to take care of him." But occasionally she would take a Valium, as Dr. Nick had previously testified. With Elvis, though, you couldn't let your guard down. "I woke up at seven o'clock in the morning, and he was not breathing properly, because two or three days previous to that he had just been zonked out on sleeping medication—just walking around in a stupor when he walked around at all."

Would it be a fair statement to say that Elvis Presley "couldn't get up, couldn't go to bed, couldn't perform without medication?" Hutchinson asked.

"I think he thought he couldn't."

"Psychological dependence?"

"Yes, definitely."

Did drugs induce Elvis to be more generous in his gift giving? Linda thought that was a proper statement.

From 1972 to 1976 while Elvis was in Memphis, did she ever recall Elvis receiving any kind of drugs being shipped to him from Las Vegas?

"Yeah."

336

From whom?

"Dr. Ghanem."

What kinds of drugs?

"Amphetamines." She knew precisely, because she carefully monitored all of Elvis's drug sources. "All of the prescriptions that Elvis ever got were of great concern to me, because I viewed it as being like an alcoholic, someone who was a 'pilloholic'—it was like feeding a problem."

Did she ever see Elvis inject himself with a narcotic?

"Yes."

"Where did he inject himself?"

"His hip."

Did she ever inject Elvis?

"I have."

"Or assist him?"

"Yes, I have."

How did Elvis pay Dr. Nick when he was on tour?

"Elvis had to pay the entire Medical Group [Dr. Nick's medical partnership]. He had to pay all the other doctors, so that he could take Dr. Nichopoulos on the road with him. I think in the beginning Dr. Nick was just being paid himself, and then he came to Elvis and said all the doctors were upset, 'Because I am on the road, and they were having to take my patients, and they are not getting compensated.' So Elvis had to pay all the doctors in the corporation."

Was she ever present when Dr. Nick asked Elvis for a personal loan?

"I know that Elvis was going to loan Dr. Nick a large sum of money, and Dr. Nick was going to pay him back."

Linda said that since 1976 she spent much time reflecting on her times with Elvis. "I think, my God, how did I even tolerate that, you know, for as long as I did looking at that list of medications!" In the end, she finally walked out on Elvis, because there were fundamental differences "in every aspect of his life and mine."

Linda's turbulent years with Elvis became grist for a 1981 made-for-television movie, *Elvis and the Beauty Queen*. A clear consensus within the entourage was that Elvis would not have died on

August 16, 1977, if Linda Thompson had remained by his side to curb his drug intake and to revive him when he overdosed. These same insiders had been unsettled by Ginger Alden's flightiness and never believed that she could fill Linda Thompson's shoes, especially if Elvis overdosed while Ginger was alone with him. But Linda told the investigators that she had done as much as she could for the singer. His doom was preordained as long as he continued to abuse drugs.

As Linda left the interview room for Bruce Jenner and the boat races, Hutchinson, McGriff, and Armstead looked at each other. At last they had found a credible, forthright witness with firsthand information about Elvis's drug addiction and his relationship with Nichopoulos.

In mulling over the characters in this investigation, Hutchinson identified Linda and her brother Sam as the only two who had survived the Graceland cesspool of drugs, money, and deception with some wholesome values intact. That list wouldn't be growing much in the days ahead. Certainly nobody on the team was adding Sonny West's name to it.

The former bodyguard was then forty-one, still a strapping man who obviously had been down some hard, mean roads. When Sonny showed up at the Ramada for a late-night interview, he was dressed in rough work clothes, jeans, a faded plaid cowboy shirt, and Western boots. As a memento from the days of the Elvis gravy train, Sonny still had his 14-karat gold T.C.B. pendant hanging around his neck. Sonny admitted that he was experiencing some hard times and was shoveling out barns for his board and keep, but it was only temporary.

Sonny told Hutchinson that he had dropped by the movie lot where his cousin, Red West, was working and invited Red to tag along with him to the interview. "Red said he ain't going to talk to you. He'd just get mad and bust you in the mouth."

In fact, Red West did have a bad habit of busting people in the mouth, which was one reason why Vernon Presley fired him.

More powerfully built and two years older than Sonny, Red West had been friends with Elvis at Humes High School. Since his firing, Red had claims as an actor. Building on minor roles in some of Elvis's movies, he had appeared on television in *Baa, Baa, Black Sheep* and other productions of actor Robert Conrad. In 1979 Red made a Chevrolet truck commercial, but he also attracted some terrible publicity when a network news team taped him punching out a demonstrator in a clash between Iranian students and anti-Iran protesters in Beverly Hills.

While Red didn't plan to cooperate and give an interview to the Tennessee investigators, he wanted Sonny to relay a message that he was sticking to every word written in *Elvis: What Happened?* "That's all Red has got to say on the subject," Sonny reported.

Sonny said he knew of at least "four or five" instances in which Elvis developed serious breathing problems, like those earlier described by Linda Thompson, on his private airplanes after taking drugs. All of them were close calls and required major medical attention. Sonny swore that one of Elvis's Las Vegas physicians, Dr. Elias Ghanem, prescribed liquid cocaine "that Elvis used with cotton balls, which he put into his nostrils." He said Ghanem prescribed the cocaine to Elvis in combination with sleeping medication and amphetamines. Elvis also used nonprescription cocaine that Ricky Stanley obtained for him from a singer in one of Elvis's backup vocal groups. The backup singer apparently obtained the dope from a Nashville pusher. Red West found out about the deals, Sonny recalled, and threatened the vocalist "with harm if he got any more coke for Elvis."

Sonny said in the early 1970s he intercepted a bottle of liquid Demerol that Dr. Max Shapiro had ordered a pharmacy to deliver to Elvis, who was then living in a rented house in Beverly Hills. Because the prescription bore Sonny's name, he took it back to the pharmacy and ordered them never to put it on a prescription again. Sonny said he knew of other prescriptions for Elvis that had been written in the names of Sonny's wife, Judy, and his young son, Brian. Others, he said, were written in Charlie Hodge's and Joe Esposito's names.

When Elvis went to the hospital in Memphis for detoxification in 1973, he was extremely sick. "He looked so bloated, and they were trying to draw off fluid from him, and they couldn't get nothing, and yet his body was like a sponge. It just looked if you punctured it with a needle, you would be able to draw out all kinds of fluid. Also, his skin was such that you could press it, and an indenture would stay there for a little bit before it would go back out. It just looked like he was loaded with some kind of fluid or jelly or something underneath the skin."

Once at Graceland Elvis complained to Nichopoulos that he had attempted to get some drugs out of the doctor's black medical bag and discovered that it was locked. Henceforth, Elvis insisted, Dr. Nick would leave the bag unlocked when he visited the mansion. As Sonny recalled, Nichopoulos refused, and Elvis said, "Well, the next time you are up there I am going to blow that son of a bitch apart and get what I want."

Elvis's preoccupation with drugs was so abiding that he planned on buying his own pharmacy, Sonny said. Elvis's explanation was, "If I did that, I'd pretty much have what I wanted without the control that would have to be there on prescription stuff." Sonny argued with Elvis that there was the matter of obtaining a pharmacist's license and in time this outlandish notion faded.

Sonny said that Elvis had a particular fondness for Dilaudid. Hutchinson asked him if he knew what Dilaudid was normally used for. "Terminally ill cancer patients, right—and that pain is the ultimate in pain. A sprained ankle or an ingrown toenail or headache doesn't call for that. I mean, there is other medication you can take for that," Sonny replied.

By Sonny's calculation, the point when drugs began to affect Elvis's ability to perform on stage was 1972. "There were times he would go on a tremendous talking thing instead of singing. He would go off into stories about his life or something, or he would work out and do a big demonstration in karate instead of singing, which the people wanted to see him do. There were times, mainly in Vegas, when he would go out on the stage and would not be really ready to go on stage. And his voice would be 'tonguey,' very thick, and he would go out there and would make an excuse to the audience. 'Sorry, folks, I just got up, and I am not really awake yet.'

"He would have to walk—he looked kind of funny the

way he would have to walk. He would kind of keep his legs spread apart as he kind of walked, so he kind of swayed and everything in order to keep his balance. He couldn't, you know, just walk normally. Then, most of the time within about twenty or thirty minutes of the show, he got real good. But, there were a couple of instances where he would do the whole show, and he never got going."

And, of course, in most instances Nichopoulos was there to give Elvis his medication before and after each of these performances. "When he was performing, he would get medication," Sonny said. "He would get up to go to the performance, he would get medication after the performance. The next morning he would get up to leave town, and he would get medication to get up. He would get medication on the plane, if it was an hour or two ride. Then he would get up and come to the hotel, and if he had time for an hour or an hour-and-a-half nap, he would get more medication, lay back down, get up and do the show, and come back from the show and get more medication."

Also in 1972, Elvis's normal slim weight of 170 to 175 pounds ballooned on him. He had eaten too many hamburgers, French fries, pies, and other kinds of junk food, and taken too many downers to expect the weight to stay off as he aged. The pudginess came as a shock to him when he looked at himself in the mirror. Even Elvis couldn't just wish his fat jowls and bulging midriff away. The men around him were also putting on weight. The "Memphis Mafia" were beginning to look like the "Memphis Porkers."

Elvis tried standard diets, but they didn't work fast enough to suit his style. Hence he began a radical shock diet and ordered several of his aides, including Sonny West, to join him. According to Sonny, who weighed 235 pounds when he started the slimming program, the diet consisted of a daily injection of urine from a pregnant woman and no more than 500 calories a day of prepared food. Although this regimen disgusted Sonny, he was able to shave off about twenty-five to thirty pounds. Even though Elvis continued to take drugs, the diet helped him lose some weight, but not enough to satisfy him that he could perform on a live satellite television special to be broadcast in January 1973 from Hawaii to twenty-five countries around the world.

"He had me go on it again with him before I was supposed to," Sonny said. "You are supposed to stay off of it for three months or something like that before you take it again, and I did and I lost more weight. He lost the weight and he looked good, but the night after he had done the satellite show, he got totally out of it in Hawaii."

XXIII

PALLBEARERS AND PHANTOM FRIENDS

JOE ESPOSITO and Elvis both took basic tank training at Fort Hood, Texas, and became buddies when they were stationed together in West Germany. Elvis nicknamed him "Diamond Joe," a friend with a head for figures and a natural for keeping the Presley accounts straight when discharged from the army in 1960. Seventeen years later he was still working for Elvis and had become the top aide and highest paid employee. At Elvis's death he was earning $45,000 a year. In addition to Joe's base pay, Elvis showered him with custom-built cars, bonuses up to $60,000 a year, and expensive jewelry. Diamond Joe also served as Colonel Parker's official liaison and pipeline to Elvis's inner circle.

After Elvis's death, he opened the Sterling Coach Company, a Los Angeles limousine service, and later became the road manager for the Bee Gees. When he showed up for his interview with the Memphis officers, Esposito was dressed in designer jeans and a T-shirt. He was wearing gold-embossed, wraparound sunglasses and hardly seemed to be suffering from the hard times experienced by other members of the "Memphis Mafia." He was beginning to grow bald in back and was sporting a comfortable roll of fat around his midriff; like Sonny West, he had his gold and diamond-encrusted T.C.B. medallion around his neck and draped conspicuously outside his shirt.

"He was arrogant, and it was clear that he didn't want to talk with us," Hutchinson said. "But he wanted to see what we knew. When he learned that we knew what we were talking about, that we were not new babes, not new geese, he became more respectful."

For example, the investigators were aware that Esposito and Nichopoulos had been business partners in the abortive "Presley Courts" racquetball venture. When questioned about it, Esposito estimated losing $30,000 in this fiasco and said that Nichopoulos had lost another $50,000. Esposito blamed Mike McMahon, the real estate developer who had put the deal together, for his losses. "You see, I had to travel too much, and I had to trust people," Esposito said. "And you don't do that. I learned a lesson. Don't trust people."

Esposito, however, conveniently forgot that Elvis backed out of the deal without warning as bricks and mortar for the racquetball facility were in place. And twelve years later, the venture was continuing to haunt the Elvis Presley estate. With a $1 million loan from the estate in 1978, a limited partnership based in California but called Tennessee Racquetball Investors, Ltd., bought the facility, operated it as a racquetball club, and for several years made its payments of $9,100 a month. In 1981, the Presley estate lent an extra $41,848 to help keep the club in operation. The second loan was paid off in 1984. But somewhere between the bank and the lawyer's office there was a mixup. The estate issued and recorded a release that confused the two loans and apparently relieved Tennessee Racquetball Investors of responsibility for paying off the big loan. In late 1989 lawyers for the Presley estate were in court trying to void the flawed release, complaining that they don't have a current address for the general partner, and claiming a balance due of $882,783.48.

But at the risk of being reminded of sour episodes like the racquetball venture, Esposito was interested in talking to Hutchinson and McGriff to gauge what progress the detectives had made in their efforts to indict Dr. Nick. As the interview progressed,

Hutchinson allowed Esposito to gloss over Elvis's three stays at Baptist Hospital for drug treatment. But after a time, the detective wearied of hearing Esposito sidestep Elvis's real medical problems.

"For the record, Joe, when did it become apparent to you, if it did, that Elvis Aaron Presley was having problems with narcotics?"

Esposito looked as if the burly detective had slapped him across the face. "Hooked on narcotics you mean? No, I don't think Elvis Presley was never, ever hooked on narcotics."

This is the same Joe Esposito, Hutchinson mused, who sat through days of testimony before the Tennessee Board of Medical Examiners and heard Nichopoulos and Al Strada, to mention two, talk about Elvis's drug dependence. "You don't think he was?" the detective asked.

"Never, ever, ever! No way! And I will say that till I die! Because this man, I know, he would go times without ever taking a pill—thirty days. And anybody that's hooked on narcotics, they couldn't do that. . . . So, I mean, yes, he did take pills, and we all did."

What kind did Esposito take?

"Oh, I took uppers and sleeping pills. You've got some crazy hours. You wanna go to sleep, you go to sleep then. You wanna get up, you get up then."

Did he ever see Elvis overdose?

"I wouldn't say overdose."

How about pass out?

"Pass out and sleep. Yes, definitely."

How about explaining that?

"Well, we'd be sitting there talking, and he'd just fall asleep. Maybe that's happened."

Did he ever hear of Elvis falling out and hitting his head on a commode or something like that?

"I never saw him do that. I know he fell a coupla times. I know that, but I didn't see him actually do it. I know he fell."

Esposito traced Elvis's erratic behavior and emotional problems back to the divorce from Priscilla. And he was beginning to contradict his earlier statements.

Hutchinson doubled back to Elvis's hospital admissions.

345

"You never have seen him admitted to a hospital for detoxification from drugs?"

"Never in my life," Esposito declared. "He did not go in for drugs. Now, what they did in there is another story."

Hutchinson turned up the heat. "There have been no members of the entourage come to you, one Joe Esposito, and say, 'We're gonna have to do somethin' about Elvis Presley and his drug problems'? "

"Oh, definitely," Esposito replied. "Yes, they have. Sure they did. Sure. They told me many times. I said, 'What am I going to do about it? What can I do about it? I can't do nothin' about it.' "

Esposito added that he talked to Vernon Presley, who seemed incapable of any firm action, and Nichopoulos, who worried about the number of drugs coming in from Las Vegas. When confronting Elvis directly, though, Joe recalled being told, "You don't like it? Get the hell out!" He also recalled quitting a few times over "personal fights, a coupla arguments we had." Almost everyone around Elvis, including Nichopoulos, had fights with the singer from time to time and had either been fired or quit, he said. In Nichopoulos's case, Elvis wouldn't follow the doctor's orders about cutting down on drugs, and when Nichopoulos complained, Elvis fired him. To be reinstated, Nichopoulos had to "apologize and get back to work."

Of Elvis's collapse in Baton Rouge and the reason for his subsequent admission to Baptist Hospital in 1977, Esposito said, "Exhaustion, I was told."

Hutchinson scoffed. "I don't think anybody that has got [celebrity status], especially a notable person like Elvis Presley, is gonna say he was admitted to the hospital because of a drug situation."

"Oh, no. Of course not," Esposito agreed. "Well, once they said he was in there, and they said, 'Well, let's try and get him to quit taking some of these drugs he's taking.' I said, 'Hey. Great.' "

And Elvis wasn't addicted to drugs? Hutchinson persisted.

"I wouldn't say he was addicted. I would say he was taking a lot of medication," Esposito said.

346

"The coroner has even testified that he was addicted to drugs, Joe."

Esposito nodded. "I know what you're saying. I know what you're saying. Okay. I knew Elvis had a drug problem. He was taking drugs all the time. That's all there was to it. You know, I knew it the last year, you know, but there was nothing I could do about it."

Esposito added that he didn't like to talk about Elvis's drug problems. "I really don't because it's a personal thing. When Elvis died I kinda made myself a statement. I would never, ever say anything about Elvis. I wouldn't say anything bad about Elvis for any reason."

———

Compared to Joe Esposito's apparent prosperity, Charlie Hodge looked down at the heels in a sad sack sort of way. Hodge stood five feet three and sported black, slicked-back hair that was the same color he used to dye Elvis's every three to four weeks. Elvis once said that if he ever went bald, Charlie Hodge could find another job. A rhythm guitarist and gospel singer, Hodge first met Elvis in 1956 during a Red Foley country music show in Memphis. For years Hodge lived in a converted apartment, which he called "Charlie's room," behind the main house at Graceland and remained there months after the singer's death. He frequently claimed he had a voice like Elvis's and often bragged that he finished the fadeouts of Elvis's singing.

But Hodge was a bundle of nerves when he showed up for his interview and chain-smoked throughout. The gravy train was long gone. Hodge was forty-five and living on unemployment compensation. He listed his occupation as unemployed actor and said he didn't have a business address. "The guy was flat broke," Hutchinson said. "He was down and out. He was in love with Elvis and would tell any lie he could to protect Elvis's image."

Getting right down to cases, Hutchinson asked if Hodge had been aware of Elvis's drug problem.

"Not from what I understand a drug problem is," Hodge

said. "In other words, being someone who has to have drugs all the time, you know, or does it to stay high or something like that." However, Hodge went on to explain that there "was a lot of concern on the part of different employees who worked for Elvis, but to my knowledge I don't think I ever seen Elvis really abuse drugs or anything."

What about the incident in Palm Springs, California, when Elvis and his date were knocking down cough syrup and she nearly died? Was Elvis abusing drugs then?

"Uh, as far as I can remember, he looked normal to me and was acting normal. . . . They came and woke me up and brought her into my bedroom, and they called for an ambulance. They took her to the hospital, and she did OD. She didn't die, but she had an OD."

"Is it your statement then that Elvis wasn't aware that this girl was drinking his cough syrup?"

"I don't think so," Hodge said as he fumbled for another cigarette.

"Is it your statement that throughout all the years that you were with Elvis Presley that you never noticed him in a condition of intoxication as a result of taking too many drugs?"

"Well, again, I have seen him when he was, like, pretty tense and excitable and everything, but—and I'm not, you know, I could say that I was suspicious of him taking something, but since I didn't actually see him, you know, I can say I didn't see him."

Did Hodge remember Nichopoulos's telling Vernon Presley about three or four months after Elvis's death that his son was dying of incurable cancer?

Charlie acknowledged being present when Nichopoulos imparted that startling information to Vernon "in strictest confidence." As Hodge reconstructed the discussion, Nichopoulos told Vernon, "We discovered during the autopsy that Elvis had bone cancer, and it had spread all over his body. . . . Maybe the fashion that he died was better than to suffer the cancer."

In truth, Nichopoulos had been denied access to Elvis's autopsy until 1979. If he had seen it, he would have learned that Elvis's bone marrow had tested negatively for cancer. Hutchinson was as puzzled as the *20/20* team had been about the origin of this bone cancer story. He asked Hodge if he had kept his word to Nichopoulos about not repeating the story.

"Yes, I did," Hodge said. He added, however, that he had heard versions of the same story from hairdresser Larry Geller, singer Cathy Westmoreland, and maybe from Joe Esposito.

Was Hodge certain that he had not been the source of the cancer rumor to others in the Presley entourage, particularly his business partner, Dick Grob?

Again Hodge swore he had kept Nichopoulos's confidence.

Hutchinson produced a photostated copy of Grob's copyrighted synopsis, *The Elvis Conspiracy,* and read the portion relating to Elvis's bone cancer. "Where did Grob get this information, Charlie?"

"Well, I'm trying to remember if he had found it out himself or if—I don't think I told him anything. If I did, I don't remember it. I'm being very honest with you. But, Dick was investigating a lot of things after Elvis's death."

"Mr. Grob has given a deposition about this one statement. You know what his response to that is? 'It is a good way to end a book,' " Hutchinson snapped.

"Well, I suppose it is sensational. But I honestly don't remember whether I told Dick, or if he knew about it already. I know we did talk about it, but I don't remember if he knew it already."

"And you have not gone out and been the town crier and said anything about it—everybody else is coming to you? You don't know how Grob, your partner, got ahold of such information?"

"I'm not sure, again, whether I told him or he found it out himself." Then Hodge mumbled that he had discussed the cancer rumor with Billy Smith, Elvis's cousin.

"You blabbed to somebody, then?" Hutchinson pressed.

"No, I told Billy for a reason," Charlie pleaded. "Billy was living on the grounds and going through a lot of pain, you know. This was not too long after Elvis died. He was still living there, and I told Billy to kind of help relieve him from his pain a little bit. I told him that it was in confidence—that I was told in confidence. I felt in that case it was justified."

The Death of Elvis

———

Both Esposito and Hodge had been pallbearers at Elvis's funeral, and the Memphis investigators were about to meet a third one. Jerry Schilling had been one of Elvis's bodyguards from 1964 to 1975. A star football player at Memphis's Catholic High School for Boys, and he first met Elvis in 1954 during a touch football game. Schilling had attended Arkansas State University on an athletic scholarship. With just a few course requirements left for a college degree, Schilling allowed Elvis to twist his arm. He dropped out of school and joined Graceland's ever-swelling payroll.

Over the years Schilling would walk away from his Graceland job several times after bitter disputes with Elvis. But the two would patch up their disagreements. And it was Schilling who accompanied Elvis on the strange trip to Washington where he met President Richard Nixon and talked the President out of a federal narcotic agent's badge.

But Schilling was no flunkie. In his own right he had a knack for entertainment management, later working with singer Billy Joel and the Beach Boys. When the Memphis detectives interviewed him, Schilling had recently formed his own management firm and obviously was doing well. He was wearing a business suit, a crisp white shirt, and a conservative tie. He spoke softly and with precision, often pausing to think about his answers. He was almost too polite, but Hutchinson took an instant liking to him. Both had grown up in the same rough-and-tumble, blue-collar neighborhood in North Memphis. As Roman Catholics, they attended parochial schools but were graduates of arch-rival high schools.

After some light banter about the old days, Hutchinson and Schilling got down to cases. Elvis's health, Schilling was quick to note, took a vicious nose dive during the last three or four years of his life because of drugs. During Elvis's detoxification at Baptist Hospital in 1973, Schilling said he intercepted a narcotics shipment from Las Vegas and took it to Nichopoulos. "He [Nichopoulos] was trying to control the situation, and he wasn't getting any help from any of the other doctors involved, and he was very disappointed," Schilling said. As a test, Nichopoulos instructed Schilling to "take

350

the medication and give it to Elvis. I want to see if he lets me know that he has this." Two days later Nichopoulos reported that Elvis had never mentioned receiving the drug shipment. Nichopoulos covertly searched Elvis's medicine cabinet and located the pill bottle hidden in the back. The incident stood out in Schilling's mind. He believed Elvis was making a sincere effort to kick his drug habit, only to succumb to the temptations of out-of-town doctors. "Here the man had really tried. It was a very hard thing for Elvis to let his pride down. He never believed he had a problem to let people work with him. He let his pride go."

Schilling confirmed that within the entourage Charlie Hodge had medical problems and had been hospitalized more than once for nervous breakdowns. He also recalled carrying Alan Fortas, another entourage member, to UCLA Medical Center for treatment of a sleeping pill overdose in 1965. Fortas, a nephew of the late Supreme Court Justice Abe Fortas, became a bodyguard for Elvis in 1958. Fortas also was one of the patients the Tennessee health department accused Nichopoulos of overmedicating.

Schilling wasn't surprised that Elvis took more drugs as he grew older. "He ran himself for so many years that it was starting to catch up with him. He couldn't do at forty what he was doing at twenty. He took an amphetamine to get him up for the show, and he would build up a tolerance for that. To get him to go to sleep after the show and to counteract the amphetamines, he would have to take barbiturates. I think the more he worked on these touring situations, where it was night after night, turn on and turn off, he'd built up these immunities to them. And he would require more, and he would look for different things."

Schilling's interview contrasted sharply with the two previous ones. Under Tennessee law, the prosecution must vouch for the credibility of its witnesses. Hutchinson, McGriff, and Armstead agreed that in Schilling they had another Elvis insider worth putting on the stand. They couldn't say the same for Esposito or Hodge. Schilling later became a trusted member of the team that helped Priscilla Presley manage Elvis's estate.

The Death of Elvis

The final witness on Hutchinson's agenda for California was the legendary Colonel Tom Parker, Elvis's manager and mentor for twenty-two years. Parker was seventy when he met with the Memphis investigators. When he showed up at the Ramada Inn, the ex-barker, hustler, and huckster was wearing a sporty leisure suit and a porkpie golf hat. He looked as if he had just walked off a carnival midway. He smoked, chomped, and relit his ever-present cigar with vigor but otherwise was guarded and restrained, not the gregarious and voluble character the detectives had expected. The Colonel kept his natural gift of gab in partial check, and throughout the interview he conveyed to Hutchinson, McGriff, and Armstead that everything he told them was the unvarnished truth. They believed him.

The detectives didn't know that his real name wasn't Tom Parker, not that it would have affected the substance of the interview any. Parker was in fact a Dutchman who had lived illegally in the United States for nearly a half century; his military rank was honorific at best; and he had often given Elvis Presley poor advice, particularly when it came down to feathering Tom Parker's nest.

"He was a nice guy. He conducted himself like a gentleman. I don't care what people said about him later," Hutchinson said.

As was later revealed in a probate court battle over Elvis's estate, Parker's real name was Andreas Cornelis van Kujik. He was born in Breda, Holland, in 1909, and apparently stowed away on a ship bound for the United States in 1926. After living in America for about a year, he went home to Holland, but two years later, he stowed away on another ship, illegally reentering this country again, this time for good.

During the early 1930s, he enlisted in the U.S. Army, and for almost two years he served as a private in an anti-aircraft section of the coastal artillery at Fort Shafter, Hawaii, just outside Honolulu. Following his army discharge, he adopted the name Tom Parker (probably patterned after the name of an officer he met in Hawaii) and joined the carnival circuit that annually crisscrossed the southern tier of states.

In addition to working as a midway barker, Parker was an advance man drumming up publicity in small towns and drawing crowds to the carnival. During these years with the road shows, he normally spent his winters in Tampa, where he met and married the woman who would remain his wife for fifty-five years. In the late 1930s and early 1940s, he became less transient and ran the animal shelter for the Tampa Humane Society. He also became a master at concocting zany publicity stunts, often employing elephants and other exotic animals to attract customers to Tampa's larger department stores.

Despite his fondness for military rank and titles, Parker managed to avoid service during World War II. This deferment gave him a head start on other promoters and allowed him to obtain a toehold in the country music business. In 1942 he began managing the career of Eddy Arnold, then a twenty-six-year-old country music singer known as "the Tennessee Plowboy." During the mid-1940s, Parker obtained an honorary colonelcy from Jimmy Davis, another country music singer, who was elected governor of Louisiana. He later received a second colonel's commission in 1953 from Frank Clement, then governor of Tennessee. Eddy Arnold began recording his biggest hit songs in the late 1940s, and the singer's improving career made Parker feel confident enough of his own ability as a music promoter to shift his base of operations from Tampa to Nashville, which had then become the hub of the country music industry. The Colonel and his wife moved into Eddy Arnold's modest home lock, stock, and barrel. Their move caused a great deal of tension and consternation in the Arnold household, but somehow Arnold and Parker remained a team until 1953, when the singer's patience wore thin and he sent his manager a cable firing him.

As a result, Parker's career as a promoter went into a tailspin, and he had done some hard living by 1954, when he took over as general manager of Hank Snow Attractions. Snow, a Canadian-born country music singer and promoter, was still Parker's business partner in August 1955, when the Colonel signed a personal contract to manage the career of a fast-budding singer with the unlikely name of Elvis Presley. The two partners split over this deal, with Snow complaining bitterly that Parker cheated him out of potential millions of dollars that he should have earned in comanaging Elvis.

The Death of Elvis

Elvis already had a manager of sorts at the time Parker began persuading the young singer to let him manage his career. He was a Memphis disc jockey by the name of Bob Neal. Parker had little trouble running Neal off by paying him a pittance. But before he could place the underage singer under contract, he had to coax Elvis's suspicious mother into signing the agreement. Initially Gladys Presley smelled a king-size rat, but Parker finally gulled her into believing that he was a fine, Christian fellow who would make her boy a star and at the same time keep him on the straight and narrow path of clean and wholesome living. Once Parker had the contract signed and safely in his pocket, he sprung the news on his outraged partner.

The next year, when Elvis turned twenty-one, Parker signed another, even sweeter contract that called for Elvis to pay the Colonel 25 percent of all his earnings, plus reimbursement for all expenses. Some of the agreements that Elvis subsequently executed with Parker divided the earnings down the middle, fifty-fifty.

Not long after taking over as Elvis's manager, Parker moved his base of operations, this time to the West Coast, working out of posh offices in Hollywood, Palm Springs, and Las Vegas. A notorious tightwad who loved freebies, Parker made the movie companies, recording studios, and the hotels where Elvis entertained foot the bill for most of his expenses.

For sure, Parker wasn't risking Elvis's money-making abilities by departing from the gee-whiz, boy-meets-girl plot formula that kept on selling tickets.

In 1973 the need for ready cash to reach a divorce settlement with Priscilla prompted Parker to make a drastic financial decision. For $5.4 million, he signed an agreement with RCA Records, which controlled the rights to all of Elvis's recordings, to waive the singer's rights to all future royalties on an estimated 700 recordings that Elvis had already made. Since Parker's contract with the singer gave him a hefty 50 percent of the star's record income, that meant that the Colonel received $2.7 million from the sale. After taxes, Elvis was left with only $1.35 million for the rights to what may be some of the most valuable recordings ever made.

Although a 50 percent cut of earnings was out of line with entertainment management fees, the executors of the Presley estate in 1980 agreed to renew Parker's contract at that rate. But Probate Court Judge Joseph W. Evans questioned the agreement and appointed Memphis attorney Blanchard E. Tual to act as guardian at law to protect Lisa Marie Presley's rights and interests. Tual conducted an investigation of the Presley/Parker relationship and issued a report that blistered both the Colonel and RCA Records. His 1981 report stated in part: "There is evidence that both Colonel Parker and RCA are guilty of collusion, conspiracy, fraud, misrepresentation, bad faith, and overreaching. . . . These actions against the most popular American folk hero of the century are outrageous and call out for a full accounting."

In short, Tual charged that Parker's cut was too high, that during Elvis's lifetime he offered poor financial and tax-planning advice, and that he took advantage of Elvis's "naive, shy, and unassertive" character.

Parker's attorneys objected that Tual's report was immune to the normal rules of evidence and yet was subject to court protection against a defamation action. For his own part, Parker defended himself in *The Memphis Commercial Appeal* by saying, "Elvis and Vernon were well pleased with my services and desired to continue them over the years. Detailed explanations were regularly made of the transactions pertaining to Elvis and the companies with which we dealt."

Nevertheless, Judge Evans ordered the estate's lawyers to file a suit against Parker to recover money and against the record company to recapture royalties. The suit was settled in 1983. Parker agreed to sever all ties with the estate, and RCA agreed to pay the estate $1.1 million and to pay the estate royalties on recordings made after March 1973. Even though Hutchinson didn't know all the irregularities that would later be uncovered in Parker's financial dealings with Elvis, other people that he had interviewed told him that the Colonel was more interested in Elvis as a meal ticket than as a person.

"Was there a close relationship between you and Elvis Presley?" Hutchinson asked Parker.

"Uh, of a respectful nature, but not close socially," the Colonel replied.

Did he have any personal contact with Elvis while he was in the service?

"Oh, I think probably twice, three times when he called long distance, that's about all, and maybe a couple of letters or pictures. He wanted some pictures. But I kept promoting him. I worked with his father," Parker replied. "Elvis was not in the habit of writing letters. I think I got one letter the whole time—the twenty years—a short thank-you note."

In 1974, during the period that Elvis was performing in Las Vegas at the Hilton, he took time off to visit the Colonel at his home in Palm Springs.

"He didn't look well," Parker remembered. "I said, 'Do you want to take a rest? There's something wrong. I don't know what it is, but you don't look well. You don't feel good.' That's when Elvis told me, he told me, 'I do drugs. I don't tell you what to do with your life. I don't interfere with it. I don't want you to get involved in my personal life. I know what I'm doing, Colonel, no disrespect, but I know what I'm doing, and I'm fine.' "

Later, Parker became concerned with Elvis's radical weight gain. "I said, 'You've gained so much weight.' He said, 'I know what I'm doing, Colonel. Please don't interfere.' "

"You never did interfere into his personal life?" Hutchinson asked.

"I never had from the start," the Colonel replied.

As the interview neared an end, Parker invited the three detectives to drive back to Palm Springs with him and have dinner at the home of actor George Hamilton IV. The offer was tempting, but they declined. In Las Vegas they had located a little-known, never publicized girlfriend who had dated Elvis in Memphis during the same time that he dated Ginger Alden. Her name was Alicia Kerwin, and by reputation she was a lot smarter than Ginger was. Perhaps she could shed some light on Elvis's weird and destructive behavior during the last months of his life.

═════

At police headquarters in Las Vegas, Larry Hutchinson, David McGriff, and Bobby Armstead were referred to an officer named Rick, who looked more like a card sharp than a detective. Rick said he was assigned to the hotel and casino squad. Hutchinson briefed Rick on why they were in Las Vegas and why they were interested in gathering information—discreetly, mind you— about a certain doctor. "We don't want to spook him," McGriff added.

Quietly the detectives dropped the name, Dr. Elias Ghanem.

"No problem," Rick responded. Ghanem was a reserve Las Vegas policeman. "Besides," Rick said, "he's my doctor. What do you want to know?"

The Memphis detectives sighed. There wouldn't be a sly way to get at Ghanem, not now. Hutchinson simply asked for the phone number of Ghanem's attorney. Making connections later, the lawyer told Hutchinson that he already knew the Memphis cops were in town. His client had no desire to talk to them or to have any dealings with their grand jury. "We decided Ghanem was so well connected, had so much local juice, that there was no way we were going to subpoena him and make it stick. So we gave up," Hutchinson said.

The Las Vegas Police Department's detective bureau did agree to lend Hutchinson a third-floor interrogation room. By noon the investigators had it set up for Alicia Kerwin, twenty-three, a raven-haired beauty who had grown up in Memphis but now was working as a blackjack dealer in the California Casino in Vegas. She showed up on time in her Mustang convertible.

Alicia Kerwin was one of those witnesses that *20/20* had been aware of but was unable to contact. Jim Cole passed her name along to Hutchinson, who in turn had tracked her down by telephone. Alicia's reaction was that she didn't know too much about Elvis but would be willing to do an interview.

After graduating from high school in 1974, Alicia attended Memphis State University for about eighteen months before taking a bank teller's job. She was acquainted with George Klein, the Memphis deejay and longtime Elvis friend. In April of 1977, she accepted a spur-of-the-moment invitation from Klein to visit Elvis.

"I was shocked," Alicia said. "He [Klein] said that Elvis was upset. He and his girlfriend had had a fight."

That night she drove herself to Graceland, arriving at the mansion about 10:00 P.M. Billy Smith's wife, Jo, greeted her. "She was a very good friend of Elvis's. We talked for a long time, and then she took me upstairs to meet him in like this sitting room. There were a lot of people in the room." The only person she recognized other than Elvis was Charlie Hodge.

"They were fixin' to go on tour, so it was hectic, very hectic. And we just talked. I stayed maybe about two hours."

Did she have any conversation with Elvis by herself?

"Uhm hum. For about an hour, we just talked. He asked me what I did, how old I was, what I did for fun, you know, the normal things you would talk to someone about when you first meet them."

Did she notice anything odd about his behavior?

"No, not the first time. No, he was very . . . he was just very much of a gentleman."

What about his physical appearance?

"He was heavy, but other than that he looked very good. . . . His speech wasn't slurry. It was slow, but understandable. He seemed to be in very good spirits after the conversation." Elvis mentioned his troubles with Ginger Alden. "He said that they had an argument," Alicia said, "and he was upset about it. He felt like she was more or less after his money than anything else."

Alicia had a second meeting with the singer two days later. Elvis had personally called and invited her back to Graceland. It was quite late at night when she arrived, and Elvis made her wait another hour before greeting her. This meeting took place in his daughter's room upstairs near the master bedroom. With Elvis when Alicia looked in the doorway were Tish Henley, the resident nurse, and Arelia Dumont, a hair stylist who was cutting Elvis's hair. "His daughter had left that day, and he was a little despondent over [her] leaving. She had gone back to her mother."

One of Ginger Alden's sisters, Rosemary, came in the room, while Alicia was talking with Elvis. "She was just . . . she was real inquisitive and very rude, and she wanted to know who I was and what I was doing there. And, uh, she was bein' a female."

How much did Alicia know about Elvis before she met him?

"I was never a fan, and so I knew nothing about him whatsoever other than he had a daughter."

On this second visit, Elvis gave her a short tour of the mansion before she left. But the next day, he called her on the telephone and invited her back.

"I said no. I had a date. He thought I should break it. Of course, it was just regular old . . . it's the same thing that happens between a man and a woman when they want you to come over, and you say, 'No.' He hung up on me. And so I was getting ready [for her other date], and two seconds later he calls back, and he says, 'Well, what about tomorrow?' "

Elvis also asked Alicia if she could take a few days off from work and go with him to Las Vegas. She said she agreed and made the arrangements "because I'd never been there."

They flew to Las Vegas in one of Elvis's private planes, piloted by Milo High, and during the flight Alicia noticed a change in Elvis's demeanor. He seemed sluggish. After landing, they went directly to the Hilton.

"And, uh, did you stay with Elvis Presley that night in his room?" Hutchinson asked gently.

"Right," she answered.

She saw pill bottles and asked Elvis about them. "I remember talking about it. He either told me that they were muscle relaxers or sleeping pills."

During her three-day stay at the Hilton, Alicia remembered seeing Dr. Elias Ghanem, who visited Elvis in his room every day. She also remembered the obsequious behavior of Elvis's flunkies. When Elvis laughed, all the members of his entourage chimed in. "If something funny was on TV, whether anyone else thought it was funny or not, if he laughed, they laughed too. . . . You could tell the change in everyone when he walked into the room."

David Stanley, Elvis's stepbrother, was the worst of the bunch when it came to bowing and scraping and catering to Elvis's every whim.

"And you took offense to it?" Hutchinson asked.

"I just didn't appreciate it at all. . . . I just didn't give him that. I just didn't jump at his every beck and call, and he appreciated it very much."

From Las Vegas, Alicia and Elvis went to Palm Springs for two days. She recalled that Elvis was in good spirits. He bought her a car, which later was delivered to Memphis. Then unexpectedly Elvis got a telephone call from his father. "He got upset because he talked to his father, and he talked to the Colonel. And they were very upset with him, because we weren't supposed to be there. And he didn't tell them where he was going, so they had been looking for him for three days and couldn't find him. So everybody was upset, and in turn, then he got them upset. He was being scolded."

After their return to Memphis, Elvis left on a concert tour and from time to time would call her from the road. Alicia next saw him in mid-June. Already she had relayed a message to Elvis through his cousin Billy Smith—that she had decided to break off the relationship. "It was just too much for a young kid," she said, "just the idea of Elvis Presley."

"Too much?" Hutchinson asked.

"Too much, too fast," she said.

"Just too much to handle?"

"Way too much. So, uh, he called me back a few hours later and wanted to know if I'd come to see him, so I said, 'Yes.'"

After a family dinner party celebrating her sister's birthday, Alicia drove to Graceland to meet Elvis. He was in a somber mood. "He wished he could go out on Saturday night like everyone else, and he couldn't. He was just depressed about it. He liked you to tell him about places that you'd been, uh, a club you go to. He liked you to, you know, describe in detail what it's like to walk in there and have nobody really know you. So we just talked, and then I went home about three o'clock in the morning."

Did she notice a great difference in him then? Hutchinson asked.

"He just seemed more depressed than I'd ever seen him, . . . and he didn't want me to leave when I left. He liked me to just stay right there, you know. When he was ready to go to sleep,

360

he wanted to make sure that there was somebody in the same room with him, just someone close by."

Alicia remembered making one more late night trip to Graceland later that summer, arriving at 4:00 A.M. and leaving four hours later. "I just took my stuff to go to work and would only stay a few hours. I stayed a few hours, and I had to get ready to go to work, and he was asleep by the time I left for work."

Was she ever curious about why Elvis always seemed to have a physician around him?

"Of course, I was curious, but like I said, I never asked questions."

What was Elvis's attitude, his mental state, the last time she saw him?

"He seemed just depressed. He looked sad. I didn't notice his changing, his voice, or anything. I only know that he was very sad. . . . I read to him for a long time till he went to sleep."

Having grown up in the early 1970s, Alicia told Hutchinson that she couldn't help being familiar with drugs. "I had seen Quaaludes there [at Graceland] before, but not very many. . . . There were also little orange tablets at one time there. They were some kind of speed, some kind of amphetamine."

"Were you of the impression that Elvis Presley was addicted to drugs?"

"Uh, I felt like he took more pills than he should, but as far as being addicted to drugs?" She paused. "I think he was."

"And you knew what the medications are, and the abuses that people had with them. Didn't it seem strange to you that Elvis had a doctor in Memphis, and a doctor in Las Vegas, and also a doctor in Palm Springs?"

"Yes, it did seem strange."

"You stated that you really didn't want to get involved with Elvis, and you really wanted to discontinue the alliance. Was this because you had heard something about Elvis? Were you actually too young for the man, or what?" Hutchinson asked.

"I was a twenty-year-old girl, and it was just too fast. I had never been used to this. I mean, you stay up all night with people around constantly, and it just wasn't what I wanted at this time."

The Death of Elvis

Was Ginger Alden ever present at Graceland while Alicia was there?

"Uhm, she came over once, and he wouldn't see her, so she left. Uh, she called a lot when I was there, and she'd know I was there. She would ring the phone off the hook."

Did she ever have any personal contact with Ginger?

"Uhm, I would meet her on the street. I would see her in clubs quite often. We tried to avoid each other as much as possible, and I saw her quite a bit. I would see her at least once a week. For some reason, she and I would always cross paths, if not at a stoplight or the dress shop, but somewhere we would see each other quite a bit."

As he wound down the interview, Hutchinson had a few short questions for Alicia.

Did Elvis ever mention to her that he had cancer?

"No, he didn't."

Did he mention any other medical problems?

Only a strained muscle.

After Hutchinson turned off the tape recorder, Alicia began to sob. She wanted to answer the question that the Memphis investigators were too polite to ask. Despite spending several nights with Elvis, she said, they never had sexual relations.

"And you know what?" Hutchinson said later, "We believed that little girl. We believed everything she told us was sincere and honest."

But apart from Alicia's own credibility, Hutchinson and his colleagues had another reason for believing that Elvis wasn't the womanizer of his younger days. Recently the investigators had acquired some valuable evidence—photocopies of documents that were in a medical bag stolen from a Mercedes owned by Dr. George Nichopoulos. The theft occurred just months before Elvis's death and coincided with the time that Alicia was seeing Elvis. Metro narcotics officers recovered Nichopoulos's bag. But before returning it, Detective Mary Ann Case had the presence of mind to run off copies of the documents inside the bag. One of these documents, which Detective Case subsequently turned over to Hutchinson, showed that Nichopoulos was administering daily doses of testosterone to Elvis. Testosterone is a male hormone, often used to treat men suffering from impotence.

The documents were known as "Protocols" and were in Nichopoulos's handwriting. They broke down what drugs Elvis was to receive in six stages during the course of a day on tour. Stage 1 was administered about 3:00 P.M., when Elvis normally woke up, and consisted of a "voice shot" (which Nichopoulos noted had been devised by Ghanem), vitamins and herbs, medication for dizziness, a laxative, three appetite suppressants, and testosterone. Stage 2, an hour before Elvis's performance, consisted of a second "voice shot," medication for vertigo, a decongestant laced with codeine, an amphetamine, and sometimes Dilaudid. Stage 3, just moments before his performance, consisted of a dose of caffeine, dexedrine, and Dilaudid. Stage 4, administered immediately after his performance, consisted of a pill to lower his blood pressure, an antihistamine, a tranquilizer or a sedative, and a diluted form of Demerol. Stage 5, just before Elvis went to bed, consisted of a Quaalude, Placidyl along with an amphetamine, a laxative, a blood pressure pill and three other sedatives. Stage 6, used only if Elvis were restless and unable to sleep, consisted of more Quaaludes and Amytal.

Hutchinson, McGriff, and Armstead left the Las Vegas Police Department's headquarters the same time that Alicia did.

During April 1980 the Shelby County grand jury heard more witnesses and tied up more loose ends, as it edged ever closer to indicting George Nichopoulos. Hutchinson still hoped to answer one nagging question before the grand jury returned its indictment and adjourned: Who ordered the maids to clean up the bathroom between the time Elvis's body was taken away from Graceland and the time Dan Warlick and the homicide detectives arrived? Three people—Vernon Presley, Joe Esposito, and Aunt Delta Mae Biggs—had authority to issue those orders. Vernon was in such bad health on August 16, 1977, that Hutchinson seriously doubted that he had either the strength or foresight to do it. He eliminated Joe Esposito, who had accompanied the ambulance to the hospital and would not have been present to supervise the job. The maids were very evasive in their answers to questions about Mrs. Biggs and seemed to be afraid of her. In effect she was Graceland's housekeeper and customarily supervised the maids. Aunt Delta was Hutchinson's top choice, but he was never able to prove it. However, he was confident that his investigation had established two more important points: One, that Elvis was a hopeless drug addict; two, that drugs had certainly killed him.

"Had this been the death of a routine, ordinary person," Hutchinson said in retrospect, "it would not have taken almost three years to get to this point [to a grand jury]. Everybody knew what really happened to Elvis. This shows you what occurs when fame and money enter into the picture. In my mind Elvis had a very bad, a tremendous drug problem, and it resulted in his death. And that problem overshadowed all the good things that he did for the city of Memphis and overshadowed his great talent and entertaining ability." To Larry Hutchinson, who had been a great fan of Elvis Presley, the long investigation was saddening.

On May 16, 1980, the Shelby County grand jury indicted Dr. George Nichopoulos.

XXIV

THE TRIAL

THE CRIMINAL PROCEEDINGS against Dr. George C. Nichopoulos got off to a false start when Judge Bernie Weinman set the case for trial on September 29, 1981. Soon after inking the date in on his calendar, though, Weinman's gentile colleagues on the criminal court bench were razzing him in the judges' break room as a Jewish backslider. September 29 was Rosh Hashanah, the Jewish New Year. Sheepishly, Weinman reset the case for the following day.

To casual observers, the postponement was a humorous aside in the Nichopoulos case. But to those who spent much time around criminal court, here was yet another example of Bernie Weinman fumbling his way through our system of justice. While intelligent, fair minded and up to date on criminal case law, Weinman scarcely projected the image of a forceful, take-charge judge. In response to a hotly argued motion, Weinman was almost certain to leave opposing attorneys confused by his broken sentences, incomplete thoughts and recapitulations qualifying what he had said earlier. He would ramble on in a quaking voice that sounded like he had just finished a package of Saltines. Put a fishing hat on him, and he bore a striking resemblance to Bob Denver, Gilligan on the

TV series, *Gilligan's Island.* While he spoke, Weinman's eyes would be focusing on books, pads, and pencils in front of him, avoiding eye contact as maybe an interference with the voice of Solomon, which suddenly might rescue him from a close call.

In dealing with pretrial motions in the solitude of his office earlier on, Weinman had ruled against the double-jeopardy argument brought by the defense. According to this stratagem, Nichopoulos could not be tried criminally because he already had been penalized by the board of medical examiners. Siding with the prosecution, Weinman noted that a medical license was a state privilege regulated administratively. By removing that privilege, the state hadn't deprived itself of the necessity, indeed the duty, of prosecuting crimes arising from the same actions and circumstances—in this case, the immense number of prescriptions that Nichopoulos was writing.

When a case attracted publicity, Weinman was quick to call conferences at the bench with the lawyers during trial. It was his way of airing disputes and short-circuiting press coverage while claiming that the discussions were being recorded and one day would be part of the public record. But in the Nichopoulos trial, only the testimony of one witness was transcribed later, and at least at this writing these bench conferences never have seen daylight.

All put together, there wasn't much decisiveness in the way Weinman ran his courtroom, not many declarative statements from the bench that made for concise reading in the newspapers. What was hyped as a showdown-type case to be filled with heaps of excitement, scintillating oratory, heated confrontations, and new revelations about Elvis turned out otherwise. Over the long haul of many weeks it would be dull, uneventful, and maddening, particularly when it was Bernie Weinman's turn to talk.

Stepping in to fill the leadership vacuum in the trial was attorney James Neal of Nashville, the famed Watergate prosecutor. Neal was in the middle of a poker game when a Memphis lawyer called about the Nichopoulos case. Neal was none too happy to be dragged away from his cards but after hearing the fee would be substantial, he agreed to meet Nichopoulos. Square-jawed, clean-cut, and confident, Neal appeared to embody the fundamental virtues of a straight-arrow, Hollywood hero. His reputation was as a dazzler, but lawyers who had observed him closely knew otherwise. Jim Neal didn't win cases; he just prepared himself so well that he didn't lose them.

Nichopoulos had discharged John Thomason and Frank Crawford, the defense attorneys who had failed to wiggle him off the hook before the board of medical examiners. With the help of the Greek community in Memphis—primarily Charles Vergos, owner of the Rendezvous rib emporium, and Father Nicholas Vieron, pastor of Annunciation Greek Orthodox Church—Nichopoulos came up with an estimated $150,000 to hire Jim Neal to fight this indictment. (In an interview with *American Medical News* after the trial, Nichopoulos calculated his legal bills at $300,000.)

One Sunday afternoon before the trial began, a police dispatcher called Larry Hutchinson at home. There had been an anonymous call from a woman on the Crime Stoppers tipster line. It had been taped. The caller claimed to be a nurse whose husband had just attended a fund-raising meeting at a Memphis church along with a judge, some attorneys, and other prominent citizens. The purpose of the meeting, the caller said, was to raise $50,000 to hire a hit man from Houston to kill Larry Hutchinson for his role in directing the Nichopoulos investigation. Hutchinson, who was no stranger to threats, took this one seriously after listening to the Crime Stoppers tape. He was more mindful to strap on his service revolver in the morning. Each night he placed a coin on the hood of his car and checked to see if it was there before starting the engine. Even so, he ordered his twelve-year-old son to remain in the house until the motor was running. Then Hutchinson would drive him to school. During the trial, Hutchinson asked Father Vieron, Nichopoulos's pastor, if he knew anything about the fund-raiser. Vieron expressed shock and adamantly denied any knowledge of it.

Hutchinson's best friend headed up the prosecution side of the trial. Jewett Miller, a career prosecutor, was second in command of the attorney general's office and "hard-nosed" and "unmerciful" were adjectives invented for him. Whenever a defendant appeared in court, Miller scowled and by instinct asked himself, "Why isn't this lowlife doing time in the state pen? And why can't

I be doing more to put him there?" Miller was hard on his staff, but most of all hard on himself.

Hutchinson had attracted Miller's interest in the Nichopoulos case. All the drugs involved triggered his emotions about how society was losing out to drug abuse and the violent crimes so often related to it. But Miller's bombastic, vengeful style wasn't well suited to this prosecution. And as executive assistant with management responsibilities, he had lost touch with the courtroom.

Behind the scenes, Weinman had met with both sides to decide just how Elvis's autopsy would fit into the proof. Documents under court seal, then and now, thrashed out the relevancy of the autopsy record. However, the upshot was Weinman's ruling that the toxicology report was admissible for the limited purpose of showing what drugs were in Elvis's body at death. The cause of death, the judge ruled, was irrelevant.

Jury selection dragged on for the better part of two weeks. When the process was over, the panel's character was decidedly blue collar—a grocery cashier, two nurse's aides, a retired hospital worker, an auto parts handyman, a waitress, and a secretary. Other jurors were a hardware store manager, an advertising agency musician, and a housewife. During the course of the trial, one of the nurse's aides would be excused because she couldn't find anyone to take care of her young children. Another juror, an alternate, would be dismissed after court bailiffs caught wind that he not only knew Elvis Presley personally but also knew about his drug problem. Ultimately, the Nichopoulos case would be decided by six women and six men—one among them a bed-wetter.

After the jury was sworn in, the prosecutors read the indictment. Nichopoulos was accused of overprescribing drugs to ten patients plus himself. Two of those patients were Elvis Presley and Jerry Lee Lewis, both identified as drug addicts. Hence Nichopoulos faced a related complaint under a Tennessee law that makes it a crime to prescribe drugs to known addicts. Two other patients were former members of Elvis's entourage—Marty Lacker and Alan Fortas. Five more patients made up what the prosecution called "the group," a network of close friends in the habit of dropping by Nichopoulos's office unexpectedly and walking out with

Schedule II refills. The medical board had found Nichopoulos guilty of overprescribing to all five although by pretrial order from Weinman the prosecutors weren't allowed to mention those verdicts. "The group" was made up of Ivan and Drew Cook (the twin brothers), Barbara Kaplan, Gail Clifton, and Barry Underberg. Underberg was now dead, another fact Weinman didn't want slipped into the trial. Underberg, owner of an interior decorating firm, was found shot to death in his downtown studio on October 1, 1980. Police never solved the case.

The last patient named in the indictments was Robert Deason, who received a large quantity of drugs but was being treated for cancer. Expert testimony would be divided over Nichopoulos's handling of Deason's case.

In his opening statement, Miller talked about "accepted standards of medical practice" that licensed physicians were obligated to observe. There was a line between what was acceptable and what wasn't. Doctors in Tennessee understood their duty was to stay above the line. Then he rattled off numbers in Elvis's case showing how the flow of pills intensified as the addiction worsened. "He [Nichopoulos] wasn't even close to that line," Miller said. "He was well below that line."

Of course, that wasn't how Jim Neal saw the case at all. The issue—and he would repeat it countless times—was whether George C. Nichopoulos was trying to help. "I suppose that we all think that Elvis Presley was a fine young man, a fine entertainer. But the proof in this case will show that he had many, many, many problems," Neal said. If Nichopoulos's intentions were good, then he wasn't guilty of a crime. He was more like the Good Samaritan than a criminal defendant.

Already the Elvis dynamic was repeating itself. His case would overshadow the rest and would meld them into one extraordinary issue—just how do you handle a celebrity with a powerful personality, unlimited resources, and an insatiable appetite for prescription drugs? By comparison, the professionalism of a doctor prescribing uppers and downers to skinny patients with manipulative claims of obesity and insomnia—as the proof showed with "the group"—would become lost in the glitter of Elvis Presley.

The state's first witness was Robert Muehlberger, a hand-

The Death of Elvis

writing expert with the U.S. Postal Service. With the exception of thirteen prescriptions written for Jerry Lee Lewis and containing alterations increasing dosages, all were written and signed by Nichopoulos, Muehlberger testified. Miller, who was handling the direct examination, flipped through some pages and directed Muehlberger's attention to the handwriting sample that Nichopoulos had given. What did the sample say? *"20/20* sucks," the handwriting expert replied.

During a recess moments later, James Neal was muttering about how Miller had blindsided him with Nichopoulos's ill-advised vulgarity. "It was a cheap shot," Neal said to no one in particular.

The prosecution then called Jack Kirsch, the pharmacist who had filled most of the prescriptions. In April 1980 Kirsch had surrendered his pharmacist's license for a year and pleaded "No Contest" to a complaint from the state pharmacy board accusing him of unprofessional conduct in supplying Presley with "a medicine chest" of drugs. There were approximately fifty prescriptions without signatures, and Kirsch confirmed that Nichopoulos had called these in by telephone. On cross-examination, Neal sparked a squabble when he began asking Kirsch how Nichopoulos tried to curb Elvis's drug problem. Miller objected. Judge Weinman went into a dither but finally agreed that Kirsch was qualified to answer questions about Nichopoulos's professional state of mind.

"Isn't it a fact," Neal asked Kirsch, "that on various occasions he had to intercept drugs from people who apparently were giving drugs to Elvis Presley?"

"Yes, sir."

"Did he bring some to you and say, 'Jack, tell me what they are giving Elvis behind my back'?"

"Yes, he did."

"What kinds of drugs were they?"

Kirsch rattled off a pharmacopoeia of uppers and downers and added, "Some of them, I had no idea what they were."

Many prosecution witnesses were reluctant ones, such as Marty Lacker, who regretted that the nitty-gritty of his dependence on Nichopoulos and Placidyl was ever printed in his book, *Elvis: Portrait of a Friend.* The book had encouraged Larry Hutchinson

370

and his investigators to keep their eyes peeled for prescriptions to Lacker. The prescriptions they turned up showed that Nichopoulos had prescribed 1,745 Placidyls to Lacker between December 6, 1975 and October 28, 1976. That comes to more than five doses a day. Despite that sort of unrestrained medical treatment, Lacker declared, "I really don't appreciate being depicted as a drug addict. All I did was take pills to go to sleep."

But Lacker's wife Patsy wasn't quite so inclined to gloss over the severity of her husband's drug problem, or Nichopoulos's nonchalant attitude toward it. "At one time at Graceland, I asked him to please stop prescribing sleeping pills for Marty. He didn't respond. He just turned and walked away without saying anything."

Patsy Gambill, Elvis's cousin and longtime bookkeeper at Graceland, identified a series of canceled checks showing that Nichopoulos was being paid at a rate of $800 a day while on tour with Elvis. The checks also established that Elvis's drug bills increased dramatically throughout the 1970s while at the same time that the quality of Elvis's handwriting degenerated to that of a child. "He became, well, not a recluse totally, but he didn't spend as much time out as he had before—you know, going to the movies, riding his motorcycle, and things like that," she said.

Adding to its stack of documents—the prescriptions, the canceled checks—the prosecution then came forward with the toxicology report from Bio-Science Laboratories and its chief toxicologist, Dr. Norman Weissman. Given the same frustrations of enforced silence as the Baptist Hospital pathology team, Weissman was prepared to disclose and discuss the full autopsy in the Presley case. Reporters from across the globe hunched forward with their notepads on their knees as Weissman took the stand. And while the jury no doubt was unaware of the central role that Weissman heretofore had played in the Presley case, the panel wasn't immune to the now suspenseful atmosphere of the courtroom. At last, close followers of the Presley case told themselves, what really happened was about to become public knowledge.

Ever so slowly the questions and answers established Weissman's education and position as a biochemist, described Bio-Science's role in the autopsy, and listed the drug concentrations found in Elvis's blood samples. There were fourteen of them, including three metabolites, Weissman testified. "I've never seen the number of drugs we found in this case in any other specimen," he added. Two drugs, codeine and methaqualone, were above therapeutic ranges, and codeine was ten times a therapeutic level.

But Bernie Weinman cut the direct examination short. What Weissman's testimony about these drugs had to do with Elvis's death was immaterial to the case on trial. The conclusion to the autopsy was irrelevant. Even the effects of the drugs which Bio-Science identified on the human body, not specifically Elvis's, were inadmissible, Weinman ruled. Picking up on Jim Neal's argument, the judge noted that Norm Weissman was a biochemist, not a medical doctor.

Well, how about Eric Muirhead? Medical doctor. Chief pathologist at Baptist Hospital. Internationally recognized authority on hypertensive heart disease. First signator on the suppressed Elvis Presley autopsy. Again Weinman cut the testimony short. The prosecution called Muirhead as an expert witness, but he was permitted to provide little more than links in the chain of evidence —that blood, urine, and tissue samples from Elvis's body were in fact shipped to Bio-Science Laboratories, that no stomach contents were shipped because of the snafu in the emergency room, and that results from tests on those samples came back from Bio-Science. What were those results? What was the cause of Elvis's death? Muirhead wasn't allowed to say.

At that juncture when Muirhead left the witness stand, the Nichopoulos prosecution became an overprescribing case, not a death case as reporters eager for the big revelation had hoped it would be. In addition, the trial became tedious. Prosecutors began calling drug treatment specialists and internists like Nichopoulos to look at the prescriptions and explain how they represented substandard medical practice. And this form of laborious proof opened a hole for Jim Neal. It allowed him to take potshots at experts who might disagree on minor points of good medicine. And by default it permitted him to become the lawyer who wanted to move the trial along.

Probably the best expert witness on the prosecution side was a doctor who didn't want to testify at all. Dr. David Knott, a drug treatment specialist who had treated both Elvis and Jerry Lee Lewis, resisted his summons but was forced to testify under court order. While Knott said he believed that Nichopoulos was trying to get the two entertainers off drugs, both repeatedly were in need of detoxification from what he described as "recreational polypharmacy."

Nonetheless, Knott, a cool, often haughty individual, seemed genuinely astonished when shown the immense number of drugs that Nichopoulos had prescribed to Elvis. The year-by-year breakdown showed:

Year	Amphetamines	Sedatives	Narcotics
1975	1,296	1,891	910
1976	2,372	2,680	1,059
1977*	1,790	4,996	2,019

*Through August 16, 1977.

In Jerry Lee Lewis's case, Knott testified that he recommended withdrawing Lewis from high-powered amphetamines and sedatives. This ran counter to Nichopoulos's frequent method of supplying patients with the type of drug to which they were addicted.

"Did you ever advise Dr. Nichopoulos when he called about Lewis that he could control his addiction to amphetamines by prescribing amphetamines?" Miller asked. Knott conceded that he hadn't.

On cross-examination, Neal used Knott to plug away at his central defense. "Did you conclude that Dr. Nichopoulos was trying to help his patients?"

"Yes, I did."

"You saw Dr. Nichopoulos with Jerry Lee Lewis on more than one occasion. Did you conclude he was trying to help his patient?"

"Yes, I did."

Dr. William Lerner, a drug rehabilitation expert from the Medical College of Virginia, outlined a three-step approach to treating drug addicts—reducing their intake while substituting weaker drugs; controlling outside sources; and continuing lengthy therapy. But whatever the merits of Lerner's traditionalist methods in drug treatment, his testimony became lost in a sideshow of credentials. Obviously Lerner wasn't a frequent contributor to learned medical journals. He recalled contributing an article years earlier but couldn't remember to which publication. Ever prepared, Neal began naming medical journals, and after each asked Lerner, "Was that it?" But Lerner couldn't remember. And as the number of journals Neal named reached ten and headed toward twenty, the smirks in the courtroom turned to snickers and then guffaws.

Lerner's testimony marked a turning point in the trial and undermined the prosecution's confidence in its expert proof. Miller and his assistant, James Wilson, had assembled five Memphis physicians to testify about the poor quality of Nichopoulos's methods in treating the patients named in the indictment. They were Drs. Alvin Cummins, Hall S. Tacket, and Hamel Eason, all internists; Dr. Stewart Nunn, a cardiologist; and Dr. Jason L. Starr, an oncologist.

Cummins, perhaps the strongest in this lineup of Marcus Welbys, described the amounts and combinations of drugs Nichopoulos prescribed as "outrageous and dangerous." But to extract these descriptions the prosecution needed to go through each case at some length. Cummins was on the stand for two days. Eleven counts multiplied by five physicians totaled forty-five recitations. And sometimes the five experts would disagree.

Meanwhile, Neal let his impatience show at every opportunity. And with each yawn and wiggle in the jury box, his message appeared to be getting through. So that in the middle of Stewart Nunn's testimony, when Neal offered to stipulate that the other physicians would substantially support Alvin Cummins's testimony, Jewett Miller rose to the bait.

"At the time I agreed with the decision," said Jim Wilson, Miller's partner in the prosecution and now a Memphis attorney in private practice. "We were getting bad vibrations from the jury and thought we ought to abbreviate our proof. Cummins and Nunn were our strongest witnesses, and we didn't think the testimony would get any better.

"Looking back, though, it was probably the worst tactical move we could have made. It would have been better to have

374

differing expert opinions arrive at the same conclusion—that Nichopoulos was practicing medicine below accepted medical standards. As it was, we left the jury cold.

"There's an old saying around the courts that if you can't prove it, then you don't need it," Wilson added. "We should have let the jury have a look at all five of those doctors."

When the prosecution rested its case, Neal asked that the jury be excused and then went into a tizzy. The state hadn't called Linda Thompson to the stand, he noted. Originally the Nichopoulos trial had been scheduled for the previous May but had been postponed because Linda Thompson was pregnant. Neal ranted that the state should be cited for prosecutorial misconduct or compensate Nichopoulos for the time and expense of delaying the trial. Judge Weinman denied the requests but ordered that Linda Thompson, who was in Nashville, remain in Tennessee and be available as a possible witness later.

Again, as Jim Wilson explained later, the prosecution eliminated several marginal witnesses to shorten the trial. "Linda would have helped the defense as much as she would have helped us. Even though she would have testified that Elvis was an addict, she didn't really blame Dr. Nick for it." Falling into the same marginal category were Alicia Kerwin, Colonel Tom Parker, Jerry Schilling, and, for sure, Joe Esposito.

At the end of the state's proof, Judge Weinman dismissed the indictment involving Robert Deason, the cancer patient. He also dismissed the one about Nichopoulos himself. Prosecution witnesses admitted that doctors frequently prescribed medicine to themselves to keep on hand as needed.

The first portion of the Nichopoulos defense was largely a rerun of what had been presented to the Tennessee Board of Medical Examiners in 1980, but with an important substitution. Again, Dr. Walter Hoffman, a partner in the Medical Group, testified about how compassionate Nichopoulos was in treating problem patients. Again, Al Strada testified that he and Nichopoulos slipped placebos past Elvis as often as possible.

Then Neal called the defense's star witness. Dr. Forest Tennant, Jr., a boyishly vibrant physician from Los Angeles, took the stand to tell the jury about the latest in drug rehabilitation. Frequently the traditional strategy of withdrawing patients slowly to drug freedom just didn't work and was unrealistic, Tennant testified. And this was quite true, he added, in the cases of Elvis Presley and Jerry Lee Lewis. "Drug maintenance," the strategy of supplying drugs to keep a patient functional, was a sensible medical treatment and fell within contemporary standards of good medical practice, Tennant testified.

Tennant was a more confident, forceful witness on drug maintenance theory than those presented by Nichopoulos's attorneys in the medical board hearing. His testimony allowed Neal to argue that Nichopoulos not only was trying to help his patients but also was practicing medicine on the cutting edge of drug rehabilitation research.

The defense's last witness was Nichopoulos. The questions and answers between Neal and Nichopoulos were calm, smooth, and direct. Repeatedly Nichopoulos declared that his constant goal was to help his patients kick their drug habits. In treating Elvis, he said, "I'm satisfied I did the best I could."

The stack of prescriptions, the canceled checks, and the state's ace in the hole—the drug protocol in Nichopoulos's own handwriting, which hadn't been introduced—became lost in Miller's bullying of Nichopoulos on cross-examination. A low-key prosecutor with an even-handed sense of the ridiculous, such as prescribing uppers to the string-beaned members of "the group," would have made Nichopoulos into a fool, which in many instances he was. But against Miller's bombast, Nichopoulos came across as the beleaguered physician, falsely accused and now being vilified.

Deft detective work from Larry Hutchinson had retrieved a copy of the handwritten protocol from old metro narcotics bureau files. Unmistakably it showed that the number of drugs Nichopoulos fed Elvis was without limit. But it was lost on the jury as Miller ranted on. Even those court observers pulling for the prosecution were embarrassed.

Hence, it came as no surprise to those who followed the trial that Jim Neal's portrayal of George C. Nichopoulos as "the Good Samaritan, the physician who stopped to help" carried the day in the jury room. He was acquitted on all counts.

Afterward an uncontrite George C. Nichopoulos was wearing his gold T.C.B. tie pin once again when he agreed to an interview about his legal battles with the sympathetic *American Medical News.* "I felt that I did a very poor job during my 1980 trial before the medical board," he said. "Had the criminal trial been held first and I had been acquitted, I'm sure the medical board thing would have been forgotten. As it worked out, it was double jeopardy."

XXV

THE STORY THAT WON'T GO AWAY

IN THE FINAL ANALYSIS Elvis Presley was fighting to control the uncontrollable—age, drug addiction, public image, and press. Like most celebrities, Elvis as well as his spokesmen had no qualms about lying to protect his privacy and preserve an image. But over a period of time Elvis began to confuse self-image and reality. Elvis wasn't a deep thinker. Headstrong and heedless of good advice, he lacked a reflective personality, the sort of psychological gearshift that would have allowed him to pull out of the fast track, step back, and look at himself honestly. Instead, when realities didn't suit him, he popped pills to change them.

Yet the realities remained. Each year Elvis was adding one more candle to his birthday cake like everybody else. His music, that dynamic talent that had set the world to a new rhythm, declined because he quit working at it, fine-tuning it. His wealth was up and down because business and financial decisions left him with a sense of inadequacy. His waistline spread because he refused to shed the undisciplined eating habits of a teen-ager. And his health, as demonstrated by severe intestinal problems and impotence, was on a steep downhill slide—all because of drugs. Ultimately Elvis's means of control turned on him.

In early 1977 even sympathetic entertainment writers were encouraging Elvis to take a break, to quit recycling hits by other artists, and to try something different. If you were a fan toward the end, to watch Elvis perform was like seeing Babe Ruth gracelessly strike out. Then afterward you tried to persuade yourself that the Babe really had hit the ball out of the park. If you were a member of Elvis's entourage, you didn't ask too many questions about why the boss was painting his life into a corner. You just banked another paycheck.

———

After Elvis's unexplained death, the man in control became Jerry T. Francisco, who also was headstrong and heedless of good advice. Francisco belittled the healing arts board suspension of Nichopoulos's medical license. Dr. Nick was just "a sloppy record keeper," a failing that a network news outfit blew all out of proportion for its entertainment value while at the same time reviving a death investigation that should have been closed permanently in 1977.

The prescriptions? The cause of death in the Presley case? There was no relationship, Francisco assured his colleagues at the 1980 meeting of the National Association of Medical Examiners (NAME) in New Orleans.

Francisco projected a series of newspaper headlines on a screen to illustrate his message that the press was no place to settle forensic disagreements. Reporters embellish things, jump to the wrong conclusions, and fail to recognize coincidences for what they are, the medical examiner said as he punched the slide button on his projector. Click. Nichopoulos's friend, for example, Dr. Langford, sitting a row back from Dr. Nick at the football stadium soon after Elvis's death. Click. Struck by a bullet, thought somehow to be associated with the death. Click. Tightened security. Click. But ultimately dismissed as a stray shot. Click. Just as coincidental as Elvis's death was to those prescriptions that Nichopoulos wrote. Click.

"This is not an indictment of the press," Francisco disclaimed, as he convened his one-man grand jury. Tarring respectable news organizations with the same brush as the scandal sheets, he talked about unruly reporters, one-sided news presentations, and single-source stories. In retrospect, the medical examiner's bill of particulars against the press was unremarkable. However, tucked away in Francisco's running commentary as the slides came and went was a broad hint about why he had covered up the Presley case.

"The medical examiner is frequently privy to many details surrounding the death investigation that are immaterial to our job in classifying a death," Francisco said. "We often are deceived by a reporter who is hungry for a story. Many of the details we possess would make great stories. The press is very good and very attuned to protecting the privacy of a source. However, privacy of the memories of the relative from public exposure varies with the sensitivity of the reporter. . . ."

As a refrain in his presentation, Francisco raised the question, "How much should a medical examiner reveal?"

If in fact Francisco hid the evidence in Elvis's death investigation in order to protect the privacy of the Presley family, as his comments in New Orleans suggested, then at the same time he deprived the district attorney, the grand jury, and state administrative authorities of evidence of reckless and, arguably, criminal acts in the dispensing of dangerous drugs.

In the process Francisco managed to muzzle his critics while portraying himself—sometimes the private consultant and sometimes the public official—as the only authority qualified to speak on the subject of what caused death.

"Truth will take a buffing," Francisco warned his colleagues, when disputes in forensic pathology are fought in the press. What he neglected to say was that truth was buffed up big time when the Shelby County medical examiner announced his official ruling without warning to the Baptist Hospital pathologists, and when the Shelby County medical examiner turned Dr. Robert

Blanke's consulting opinion upside down and failed to explain why.

If Francisco had acted responsibly, the full Presley autopsy would have gone into the medical examiner's file as a public record. The proper authorities would have been alerted to the overwhelming evidence of drug abuse and done their duty. The press would have reported these facts and moved on. Most everybody would have felt sorry about the trade-offs Elvis made in his life the same as they did with hard-drinking, pill-popping Hank Williams a generation earlier. And the world would have gotten on with the memories of another celebrity who paid a price for wealth and fame.

Instead, the Presley case had a medical examiner searching for a cause of death that would close the case and gloss over the bad news. Instead of laying the case to rest, it festered. And it waited for a news organization besides the listless *Commercial Appeal* to open it up and find what was there.

How much should a medical examiner reveal? The answer then and now is clear—everything that's in the file and that otherwise belongs in the file. That is how truth would have emerged in the Presley case—quickly, forthrightly, and openly. Given a fair reading, that is the intent of Tennessee's postmortem statute.

However, Francisco took advantage of a loophole in that statute to suppress the Presley autopsy. State law reads that the local prosecutor orders an autopsy on the medical examiner's recommendation. In practice, though, the medical examiner reviews hospital records and autopsies and may adopt them as his own before going through formalities with the prosecutor in a suspicious case. In the Presley case, a gap in the law permitted Francisco to make use of the hospital autopsy, admitting that an autopsy was necessary in an inexplicable case like this, while arguing it was a private record, protected by state confidentiality statutes, because the prosecutor hadn't ordered him to have it performed.

This was Shelby County's primary argument in defending Francisco in the suit filed by *20/20*. A tacit defendant in the case, however, was the Elvis Presley estate, which at a key moment in the Nichopoulos hearings let it be known to Chancellor D. J.

381

"Tene" Alissandratos that nobody had waived confidentiality of the autopsy as a medical record.

Abruptly ruling on *20/20*'s lawsuit on February 6, 1981, Alissandratos spared ink and clerical time. He adopted *20/20*'s designation of record as his findings of fact and the county attorney's opinion, the same one written eighteen months earlier without benefit of those facts, as the court's opinion on the law. In other words, the autopsy wasn't a public record.

At that point Geraldo Rivera and news executives at ABC put pressure on Charlie Thompson to drop the suit. Thompson passed the word to Jim Cole, who balked at the idea. "We'll be kicking ourselves for the rest of our lives if we don't appeal it," Cole argued. And it didn't take a bit of heat off Thompson when Cole promised to appeal the case at his own expense if ABC no longer would back it. Ultimately, Thompson persuaded ABC to go along with an appeal if Mike Pleasants would agree to reduced fees. Pleasants agreed.

Thompson and Cole spotted a bad omen when their case was argued on appeal before the Tennessee Supreme Court. Also on the docket was Jo LaVern Alden's case, the one claiming that Elvis promised to pay off the mortgage on her house.

The men in black bought Jerry Francisco's argument that he was acting as a private consultant. To do so, the justices ignored Francisco's toxicology tests in the case—the ones run at Francisco's state-funded laboratory, commissioned by Francisco not as a private consultant but as Shelby County medical examiner, the tests that officially never have seen the light of day.

At ABC, the money changers chided Thompson for wasting money on the appeal. Cole, meanwhile, was consulting with Pleasants about filing a motion to rehear based on the justices' misreading of the facts. Given the unanimity of the decision, Pleasants regarded the chances as practically nil that the court would overturn its own decision. For obtaining the autopsy through the courts, it was the end of the line. But for Thompson and Cole, it wasn't the end of the story.

The Story That Won't Go Away

Ever since the *20/20* broadcasts in 1979, authors, television promoters, and crackpots frequently would call Thompson for information about Elvis Presley. Among the first was Albert Goldman, who called Thompson in late 1980 and asked him point-blank for a copy of the Presley autopsy. "I've been told you have it," Goldman said.

"Part of it," Thompson said.

"How about giving it to me? It would make my job a lot easier," Goldman persisted.

"Not on your life," Thompson replied.

"Did he die of drugs?" Goldman asked.

"That's a pretty safe assumption," Thompson answered.

Later, Thompson told his brother-in-law about his conversation with Goldman. They concluded that without any autopsy records Goldman would rely on conjecture in portraying the postmortem phase of the forthcoming biography. "He also asked me a lot of questions about Elvis's interest in little girls who wore white panties," Thompson added.

Goldman's book, entitled *Elvis,* appeared in 1981. Given its preoccupation with sleaze and its condescending tone, Goldman's episodic telling of Elvis's life hardly pleased the fans. It relied considerably on the anecdotes of Lamar Fike, a onetime Graceland insider whose main claim to fame was his stomach bypass surgery, which was financed by Elvis. In concluding that Elvis died of a drug overdose, Goldman echoed *20/20*'s broadcasts and relied on a portion of the toxicology report he managed to acquire from ABC's files. His closing chapters contained a number of factual mistakes. For instance, Goldman had Ricky Stanley picking up Dr. Nick's last prescription the day *before* Elvis died, and never grasped why this last drugstore request might be important. Goldman had Elvis sitting in a leather chair instead of on the toilet. And he had Elvis absorbed in the Shroud of Turin instead of the stunning picture book on astrology and sexual positioning.

To compensate for a dearth of source material on Elvis's autopsy, Goldman relied on typical autopsy procedure and assumed that the pathologists acted accordingly. One erroneous result was that Goldman had the pathologists in Memphis replacing Elvis's vital organs, which wasn't done. Another was the fanciful and false description of Elvis's liver as "so diseased that it looked exactly like pâté de foie gras," which showed that a New Yorker's familiarity with goose liver was no prerequisite to discovering what really killed Elvis Presley.

In 1990 Albert Goldman would declare in *Life* magazine that after years of research, "I was wrong." Collaborating with David Stanley, who was taking his third crack at explaining what really happened, Goldman wrote a cover story in the June 1990 issue of *Life* and concluded that Elvis killed himself. It's a cleverly written hypothesis but collapses under close examination. For example:

- The Goldman/Stanley article argues that the discovery of Elavil (amiltriptyline) and Aventyl (nortriptyline) in Elvis's body signaled a suicidal state of mind. In fact, traces of these antidepressants were found in the liver, but the concentrations were too scanty to be quantified. As the complete toxicology reports show, Elavil and Aventyl had little if any bearing on the cause and manner of Elvis's death.

- To prevent anyone from interfering with the suicide, the article claims, Elvis gave emphatic instructions to Ricky Stanley, David's brother, that he wasn't to be disturbed. In fact, Ricky told *20/20* in 1979 that Elvis merely said, "Rick, I'm going to bed. I'll call you if I need you." Later that morning Elvis tried to find David, to Ricky's relief, for a third pack of pills. David couldn't be found, and Elvis's aunt, Delta Biggs, delivered the third pack.

- The Goldman/Stanley article still has Elvis reading about the Shroud of Turin. In fact, isn't it more plausible that Elvis asked for privacy because he wanted to be alone with *Sex and Psychic Energy*?

- Goldman and Stanley contend that Elvis had "a purloined manuscript" of the bodyguards' book and on the day of his death was depressed about how the fans would react to its publication. In fact, *Elvis: What Happened?* hardly would have stunned Elvis on August 16, 1977. It had been in the bookstores for more than two weeks. Furthermore, the belated Goldman/Stanley assertion that on the morning of the death with manuscript in hand, "Elvis insisted that Rick get down on his knees and pray with him" is quite simply unworthy of belief.

- Does it make sense that Elvis Presley, the king of glitz and largess, would have planned a suicide that would have resulted in such an embarrassing scene in the bathroom? "If Elvis Presley had committed suicide," scoffed Joe Esposito before a live television audience in 1990, "he would have done it in fashion. He would have dressed up in a tuxedo, a jumpsuit or something. He would not have committed suicide and ended up dying in a bathroom. I'm sorry."

- As part of his secret scheme to do away with himself, is it likely that Elvis Presley would have visited his dentist for work on a couple of fillings? Or is this a chore he would have chosen to postpone?

- For the suicide theory to work, Goldman's narrative must put David Stanley at center stage—for example, in the hospital emergency room catching "a glimpse of Elvis laid out naked on a steel table with an incision running from his neck to his abdomen." In fact, even giving David the benefit of the doubt about arriving at the emergency room before the Harvey team gave up, the only incision made up to that point was a small circular one in Elvis's side, a thoracotomy, made in an attempt to restore a heartbeat.

- On the secrecy of the autopsy, the Goldman/Stanley article declares, "Ask for a copy of the autopsy report and all you get are three pages on which all the revealing passages have been blacked out." In fact, the official ruling is contained in a four-page file with nothing blacked out. It just doesn't say much. The medical examiner's two-page report states that Elvis died of heart trouble, and a two-page press release adds that the full autopsy report is private. The full record, counting consultants' reports and pertinent scientific studies, is more than forty pages long.

The Death of Elvis

To its credit, however, the Goldman/Stanley article admits that "exactly what the doctors discovered is still a mystery."

———

Echoing this mystery theme within a month of the Goldman/Stanley article's appearance, Dr. George Nichopoulos played one-upmanship and claimed that he and only he had the answers. Working with free-lance writer Murray Silver, Dr. Nick declared that Elvis was probably murdered. And how was he murdered and who was the most likely suspect? A book proposal prepared by Nichopoulos suggested that the most likely cause was a karate chop to the neck or to the head. He said a broken neck would not be readily discoverable in an autopsy and was quick to note that David Stanley was a karate buff who often practiced that sport with Elvis.

There are four problems with Dr. Nick's murder theory, particularly if David Stanley is his primary suspect:

One: David Stanley last saw Elvis alive on August 14—two days before the death. Independent sources corroborate the fact that David was not at Graceland until noon on August 16, and the medical evidence shows that Elvis was dead by that time.

Two: During the autopsy the pathologists dissected Elvis's neck column, removed his brain, and found absolutely no evidence of blunt trauma or foul play. Dr. Jerry Francisco was chagrined to hear about Nichopoulos's murder theory and made a rare appearance on Memphis television to denounce it.

Three: Beginning two days after Elvis's death, Dr. Nick always maintained that Elvis had died of natural causes. In fact, on August 18, 1977, he attempted to file a death certificate that ascribed death to heart problems. And he never raised murder as a defense before a panel of doctors and a criminal jury. One long-time friend of Dr. Nick said, "He's never mentioned murder in thirteen years. He's really baying at the moon on this one."

Four: Why, thirteen years after the death, did Nichopoulos raise such a bizarre theory? As his book proposal says, Dr. Nick is sick and tired of being blamed for Elvis's death.

386

The Story That Won't Go Away

Each year in Memphis, particularly when the calendar approaches August 16, swarms of fans engulf the city to pay their last respects to Elvis for yet another time. Parallel to that phenomenon at the beginning of summer, Jim Cole begins fielding telephone calls about Elvis.

In 1985 Geraldo Rivera left *20/20*. He embroiled himself in a fight with ABC's Roone Arledge—and lost—over the airing of another correspondent's program about Marilyn Monroe and the Kennedys. From there Rivera did several syndicated news specials, the most memorable being his live peek into "Al Capone's vault," which yielded a couple of empty gin bottles. As part of a proposal to establish his own talk show, Rivera agreed with the Chicago Tribune Entertainment Company to do regular "investigative features" on *Entertainment Tonight*. And that put him back in touch with Jim Cole in Memphis.

Rivera's story idea was straightforward enough. There was a new book coming out entitled *Are You Lonesome Tonight?* by Lucy De Barbin, who claimed to be Elvis's secret girlfriend and mother of Desiree, Elvis's love child. The coauthor was Dary Matera, a Florida writer. The sheer absence of place names, dates, and other factual material that could be checked independently was a dead giveaway to Rivera and the production team he assembled that this book was preposterous. But it was grist for a full-blown series on *Entertainment Tonight*.

Pulling out his old notes and telephone numbers from the *20/20* investigation, Cole rounded up people like George Klein for interviews and set up shoots with Elvis's probate court records and on the grounds and in the trophy room at Graceland. Jack Soden, executive director of Graceland Enterprises, was delighted to have Rivera's help in launching torpedoes at books on Elvis like *Are You Lonesome Tonight?* While in Memphis, Rivera also interviewed the coauthor, Dary Matera.

In 1989 Charlie Thompson left *20/20* to go to work for *60 Minutes*. He was in the Miami area conducting an investigation and was talking with media attorney Ellis Rubin. Somehow their conversation drifted to Elvis, and Rubin brought up Dary Matera. The confrontation with Rivera had so enraged Matera that he hired Rubin to review transcripts of the interview and sue to recover damages for lost sales. Matera didn't have a case, Rubin told Thompson.

Rivera has delved back into the subject of Elvis on his daily talk show. Late in 1989, for example, Billy Stanley appeared on *Geraldo* to promote yet another stepbrother book, this one entitled, *Elvis, My Brother.* On the broadcast Billy rehashed the story in the first Stanley book, *Elvis, We Love You Tender,* claiming that his first wife, Anne, had an affair with Elvis. At the same time Billy told Rivera his book is different from the others because it puts Elvis "in a positive light."

In September 1988 *Memphis* magazine published a cover story entitled "Dead Reckoning." It took a long look at the Shelby County Medical Examiner's Office, without Dr. Jerry T. Francisco's cooperation. The story focused on a police case with some familiar ingredients—black suspect, witness reports of nightstick beating, official ruling of cocaine overdose, case closed. As Francisco must have expected, *Memphis* magazine led its readers to the underlying question of whether there should be a change at the medical examiner's office. Judging from the political consequences of "Dead Reckoning," the answer is No.

In looking over Francisco's years in office, the magazine naturally included a summary of the Elvis Presley case. That portion of the story drew a response from one of Francisco's colleagues, Dr. Ronald K. Wright, chief medical examiner of Broward County, Florida. He's also known among forensic pathologists as "Ron 'Never Wrong' Wright."

Sending in a letter to the *Memphis* magazine editor, Wright said: "Dr. Francisco has a tremendous deserved reputation for honesty, integrity, and quality of death investigation amongst medical examiners. I had the opportunity to review his work in the death of Elvis Presley and, Geraldo Rivera's opinion notwithstanding, I concur wholeheartedly in Dr. Francisco's conclusion of sudden death from hypertensive heart disease."

Of course, all that's contained in File 77-1944 at the Shelby County Medical Examiner's Office is a scanty two-page form and Jerry Francisco's press release on the death of Elvis Presley. Presumably, to "concur wholeheartedly in Dr. Francisco's conclusion," Ron Wright must have looked at far more information than that.

———

Dr. Harold Sexton would have thought so. Sexton, the point man of the Presley autopsy team, left Baptist Hospital in the mid-1980s. Despite long-standing heart problems that led him to the relative tranquility of the pathology lab, Sexton returned to his original specialty, internal medicine. He opened a clinical practice in Water Valley, Mississippi, but kept in close touch with his friends in Memphis. On July 17, 1988, Harold Sexton died. His coronary problems caught up with him. His obligations to maintain confidentiality were over.

A few months later, Cole received an unexpected telephone call. It was from an intermediary he had begun to know ten years earlier. And the call was about the autopsy. "Harold wanted you to have this material," the caller said. Cole didn't forget to say thanks.

———

The Elvis story wouldn't go away for Dan Warlick. Since the last time that Thompson and Cole had been in touch with him, Warlick had gone into private law practice and in a few short years had made quite a reputation for himself, both in Memphis and in Nashville, as a medical malpractice attorney. Through the law firm that had represented *20/20,* Warlick tracked down Cole in late 1986. "I've been thinking that the Elvis case was an important episode in my life, and that I would like something to remember it by," he told Cole. What he had in mind was a copy or possibly even the original drawing used in the *20/20* broadcast, which showed Warlick looking at the handwritten message, "EP OD? DOA BMH."

Yes, Cole replied. Charlie Thompson still might have access to some of those drawings. Perhaps they all could get together the next time Thompson came through Memphis. "Good," Warlick said. "Then we can sit down and I can tell you how Elvis Presley died."

Two years of conflicting schedules would pass before Thompson, Cole, and Warlick would have that sit-down conversation. Warlick had a copy of his deposition from the *20/20* lawsuit lying on his desk. Motioning to it, he said, "Obviously I would have remembered little details better then than now, but there were things I couldn't talk about in 1979 even though I considered that everything I did was in my official capacity as investigator for the Shelby County Medical Examiner's Office."

Thompson interjected that he and Cole had recently acquired key information about the autopsy that had been unavailable.

Warlick nodded. "Then what I saw and heard at Graceland and in the autopsy room on August 16, 1977, is even more important to you." Warlick launched into a monologue about his role in the Presley death investigation that went on for most of that rainy winter morning. Thompson and Cole listened in rapt silence, rarely interrupting, even when Warlick threw in an obscure medical term. From time to time, Warlick referred to a picture-laden book on how autopsies are performed to illustrate a point.

Warlick traced his movements and observations from the medical examiner's office to Baptist Hospital, to Graceland, and back to the hospital, and inside the autopsy suite. He recalled how Jerry Francisco had rewritten his investigative report the next day and what his last contribution had been to the Elvis investigation. The day after the death, Warlick said, he called Dr. Lester Hofman, Elvis's dentist, and confirmed that Elvis had received codeine to help kill pain from the dental work.

Warlick also focused on the essential points that led him to his conclusion about how Elvis died. More than ten years later, Warlick was still chagrined that the bathroom had been cleaned up by the time he got to Graceland. "However, I was still able to locate the place that his head had lain when he died, because I found a mixture of vomitus and saliva on the carpet," he said. Warlick estimated that he was about the same height as Elvis was. He lay down on the carpeting, positioning his head on the wet spot and stretching his frame out as far as he could. His feet came several feet short of touching the toilet bowl. "This led me to the conclusion that Elvis had not just fallen off the pot, but had crawled several feet before dying."

Warlick remembered one of the bodyguards told him (he was uncertain who) that during the cleanup of the bathroom he had flushed the toilet even though there was nothing in it. He remembered the raunchy book graphically blending astrology with sexual positioning, how it lay open and facedown amid cologne bottles knocked akimbo on the long mirrored counter as if it had been tossed aside. This scene led him to two conclusions. "One, you don't read rank pornography to lull yourself to sleep. Considering what Elvis was reading, I was now even more certain that he didn't doze off on the throne and quietly die there. Two, the book appeared as if it had been hurled and had hit the counter, knocking over the cologne bottles. Thus, I concluded that Elvis probably threw it, as he felt death grabbing him."

Warlick believed that Elvis's death had been neither quick nor painless. "Elvis knew he was going to die. He felt it, and he struggled on the floor for some time before he finally died." Warlick's discovery of the two syringes and the empty medical bag in Elvis's living quarters made him especially suspicious that drugs had somehow played an important role in his death. But when Warlick interrogated Dr. George Nichopoulos and Ginger Alden about drugs, at best he obtained only vague and misleading answers.

As Warlick began discussing particulars of the gross autopsy, Thompson suggested that they break for lunch, not an ideal combination. Warlick continued to talk about the autopsy during a rainy walk to a nearby cafe. After placing their orders, Warlick looked pointedly at Thompson and Cole. "I know you're going to disagree with me on this, but this is how Elvis died." He described Dr. Noel Florendo's shock at discovering that Elvis's lower intestinal system was clogged and distended with chalky-white, hardened fecal material. "The man was in agony. Elvis obviously hadn't moved his bowels for some time," Warlick said. The distended colon left Warlick convinced that at the bottom of Elvis's death was a phenomenon called a "Valsalva maneuver."

"He's straining so hard to take a dump that he presses all his guts together, all his bowels together, all this fecal material together so hard that he increases the pressure in his belly," he explained. "The pressure is higher than his blood pressure, which means he can't pump blood. And that means he has smashed or mashed the abdominal aorta, and it shuts down his heart. And then, BAM! He'd feel his heart stop, and it would start to hurt, just like a heart attack. He'd lose all his breath, and it would be just like somebody kicking him in the chest. And he'd jump up, and if he were reading a book, then he'd just throw the book away. Maybe he would take a step and fall. That's the picture we would have. It's not as glamorous as anything else might be, but it appears to me to be the best explanation of what happened to him."

When Warlick finished, Thompson silently toyed with his salad. Cole went back over the Valsalva theory point by point and asked Warlick what relationship drugs had to Elvis's death.

"Well, he had obviously been abusing drugs for some time. The downers had virtually paralyzed his lower intestinal system, causing his chronic constipation," Warlick answered.

"So you are saying that even with your theory, drugs were important, that they were a contributing factor in the death?" Cole asked.

"I believe they played a role, but I don't think the Baptist Hospital theory of polypharmacy is the viable answer," Warlick replied. "Polypharmacy is a zebra. You've heard the story. If you hear hoofbeats in Arizona, don't start looking for zebras."

Cole raised the question of anaphylactic shock, a phenomenon that forensic pathologists often see among street junkies. If a heroin addict, for example, were to buy a relatively undiluted supply of the drug and not know it, then in injecting the drug his reaction might be systemwide. In fatal overdose cases like this, syringes flipped from forearms have been found imbedded in plaster walls like so many Bowie knives. In other instances, when a person takes a strong dose of a substance to which he is allergic, then the acute and often explosive reaction would be diagnosed as anaphylactic shock.

Warlick said he doubted that anaphylactic shock was the cause of death, because Elvis had a previous history of taking the drugs that turned up on the toxicology tests.

"I don't know, Dan, your theory is a little far out. I buy Baptist Hospital's theory," Cole argued. "It was backed up by every consultant that they used."

"I told you that you wouldn't be happy with my theory," Warlick said. "It's not the most glamorous way to go, but that's what I believe happened."

Walking back to Warlick's office after lunch, Cole asked what Francisco's assistants thought of the Valsalva theory. "Jim Bell liked it, thought it might work, but when Jerry decided that heart disease killed Elvis, why then Dr. Bell thought that was the right theory," Warlick said. "Jerry never explained where he got the heart disease. He had convinced himself that Elvis was being treated for that at Baptist Hospital during the times he was really in the hospital being treated for drug abuse. I guess Jerry bought the cover story."

Warlick emphasized again that Francisco seemed uninterested in both his findings at Graceland and his observations during the autopsy. "Jerry kept getting these calls from Vernon Presley, and he made up his mind that Baptist Hospital was wrong. He never said why they were wrong or was really very interested in what I had seen or heard."

Warlick put forward two more arguments against the Baptist Hospital theory that an interaction of drugs had killed Elvis. "A drug death doesn't involve somebody thrashing around. And besides, how many rulings of death due to polypharmacy do you think there have been in Shelby County? None."

Cole countered that he had run across several multiple-drug deaths. They might not be called "polypharmacy" in Shelby County, but the term was commonly used among pathologists. Further, other forensic experts vigorously disputed the notion that the scene of a drug death was always nodding-off-to-sleep peaceful.

As the get-together wound down, Thompson, Cole, and Warlick agreed to work together and to pool information. They might disagree on the exact mechanism of Elvis's death, but they all believed that Francisco was off base in ruling that drugs played no significant role in Elvis's death.

During that same visit to Memphis, Thompson and Cole looked up Larry Hutchinson and David McGriff to compare notes. McGriff was still investigating cases for the attorney general's office. Hutchinson, however, had retired as chief investigator but was holding down a part-time job running the property room for the criminal court clerk.

A year earlier Hutchinson had urged Cole to review the tapes and transcripts from the criminal investigation of George Nichopoulos. He agreed to go with Cole and meet with Attorney General Hugh Stanton, Jr., and argue that the tapes were public records.

"Well, they're not grand jury [records], not medical records," Stanton said. "I think you're entitled to them."

Once over that hurdle, Cole went through dozens of boxes of material with Hutchinson and McGriff. Even after weeding out confidential records, they found plenty of useful material and duplicated it. Certain tapes never had been transcribed. Thompson and Cole commissioned that themselves later, but spent many fascinating hours listening to the tapes and putting it together with files already in hand.

Meeting with Thompson and Cole, Hutchinson heard about Warlick's theory about Elvis's death. "Dan is a good man. All the cops like and respect him," the detective said. He was mindful of Warlick's description of the death scene and knew about the dirty book, but as a career detective, Hutchinson looked for and believed in patterns. This perspective led him to a different conclusion about how Elvis died.

"We had knowledge the man had seizures or blackouts," he said. "Remember, when he was on the airplane and had an overdose and couldn't get his breath, they always put him down on the floor near an air vent. His body was found in the plush carpeting and he had been there some time before he was discovered. I think he was struggling to get air and ended up strangling on the thick pile carpet pile."

Thompson and Cole began shaking their heads in disagreement. "Just think about it," Hutchinson said. "I may be wrong, but that's my best theory."

―――――

For ten years Thompson and Cole had kept tabs on Dr. John Feegel, who frequently helped on stories unrelated to Elvis. Feegel had resigned his post as associate medical examiner in Atlanta and had converted an old fire station into a law office in Tampa, where he was practicing full time. Like Warlick, Feegel was specializing in medical malpractice cases.

Once new material began to flow in on the Presley case, Thompson and Cole were calling Feegel's firehouse with greater regularity. Having reviewed all the evidence that Thompson and Cole had passed along, Feegel's reaction to both Warlick's and Hutchinson's theories was negative. "They're both pretty far out and equally shaky," he said.

What about anaphylactic shock?

"I know you guys have always liked that theory, but it's another exotic. Go for polypharmacy. It's a good, solid diagnosis," Feegel said. "As far as Jerry Francisco not recognizing it, that doesn't mean anything. It's in the textbooks, it's in the literature. The other argument about all drug deaths falling asleep is another old wives' tale. It just ain't true."

Several months later, during a trip to southern California, Thompson went over the same four theories—Valsalva maneuver, carpet strangulation, anaphylactic shock, and polypharmacy—with Bob Cravey at his laboratory in Orange County. "Only one works, Charlie, and it's polypharmacy," the veteran forensic toxicologist said. "That's what Bio-Science said, and that's the bottom line."

Cravey and other forensic specialists quarrel with Francisco's notion that clinical pathologists, such as Eric Muirhead, are unqualified to determine causes of death. Muirhead's colleagues, as well as some of Francisco's, point out that he helped establish the medical examiner system in Dallas. Further, when Elvis died, Muirhead had been in pathology, particularly the study of cardiovascular disease and hypertension, for forty years. Muirhead's reaction to the official ruling was memorable to those around the

Baptist Hospital pathology lab. "Jerry claimed you had to be a forensic pathologist to determine the cause of death," he told his associates. "I said, 'But, Jerry, you're invading my territory. I'm the authority on hypertension.' I disagree with Francisco 100 percent."

The key element of the autopsy report, which Harold Sexton wanted in the open, is the summary of Bio-Science's findings. It reads:

> The levels in the body fluids and tissues exceed some other known identifiable multiple-drug overdose cases where codeine has been implicated. Of particular note is the combination of codeine and ethchlorvynol (Placidyl) and barbiturates. Codeine was present at levels approximately 10 times those concentrations found therapeutically. This case must be looked at in terms of the cumulative pharmacological effect of drugs identified by this report.
>
> Altogether, 14 drugs were identified with codeine being found at 10 times the therapeutic level and methaqualone (Quaalude) on the borderline of toxicity.
>
> Drugs are likely to have enhanced and prolonged effects on patients with liver abnormalities (which were also found). On the basis of the toxicology results, we classify this as a polypharmacy case.

Elsewhere in the final report, forensic experts outside of Francisco's office noted ample evidence for concluding that when stricken, Elvis didn't die instantly. The suppressed autopsy report stresses four points: (1) Minor edema, or accumulation of fluid, was found in the lungs; (2) there were petechiae, or small hemorrhages, from a line of demarcation at the abdomen up to the neck; (3) there were signs of conjunctivitis or an edema-type condition around the eyes; and (4) there was a cyanotic or bluish condition around the abdomen from lack of oxygen in the blood. All four indicated that Elvis had lived for a short time, allowing the vessels to hemorrhage.

Baptist Hospital's summary noted Elvis's oversized heart,

the moderate narrowing of his coronary arteries, and a genetic abnormality in the blood called "Alpha One Antitrypsin Deficiency." This deficiency can be serious if the genes causing it are inherited from both parents. Elvis's blood was typed "MS," signifying that he inherited the deficiency from one parent. This "MS" blood classification shouldn't be confused with multiple sclerosis, commonly known by the same initials. Perhaps this finding accounts for the phony bone cancer theory of Elvis's death. The Baptist Hospital team attached no importance to Elvis's antitrypsin deficiency and included it under the heading, "Additional Comment."

The clincher paragraph in the autopsy falls under "Toxicologic Studies." It reads:

> In accordance with interpretations made by our consultants versed in therapeutic and toxic drug levels in body fluids and tissues, and in accordance with our interpretation of results on drug levels and their clinical significance as recorded in the literature, it is our view that death in the case of Baptist Memorial Hospital A77-160 resulted from multiple drug ingestion (commonly known as "polypharmacy"). Of particular note is the combination of codeine, ethchlorvynol and barbiturates detected in body fluids and tissues. The levels in the body fluids and tissues exceed some other known identifiable multiple drug overdose cases where codeine has been implicated.

Even with the autopsy results finally in hand, Thompson and Cole still weren't satisfied that they knew what really happened to cause Elvis's death. For years Elvis had been experimenting with drugs and not without some close calls. Why was it that Elvis crossed over the line on August 16, 1977?

The first clue came from an unlikely source. The *20/20* team looked right over it. Elvis's nurse, Marian Cocke, noted in her memoir that Elvis was allergic to codeine. Linda Thompson, Elvis's longtime girlfriend, told the Shelby County investigators how Elvis reacted to codeine. He broke out in a rash. He became short of breath. He panicked.

Discovering that he had picked up codeine at the dentist's

office, no wonder Elvis called Dr. Nick at 4:00 A.M. and asked for Dilaudid instead. We know that the Dilaudid prescription was filled, that Ricky Stanley picked it up and presumably delivered it to Elvis in the bedroom suite. If we can believe what Nichopoulos volunteered in his *20/20* interview, Elvis never took the Dilaudid —all tablets were accounted for in the bathroom. As the complete Bio-Science report shows, toxicologists specifically searched for Dilaudid but found no trace of it. On this issue, the dumped stomach contents were a crucial loss.

Assuming that Elvis didn't take any Dilaudid, then why did he take the equivalent of ten therapeutic doses of codeine, a drug he couldn't tolerate?

Dilaudid is manufactured in tablet form and comes in four strengths ranging from 1 to 4 milligrams. The tablets are round, pale yellow in color, and labeled with the numbers 1, 2, 3, or 4, depending on the dosage. Nichopoulos prescribed the strongest dosage—4 milligrams with the number "4."

Codeine comes in several forms, but a typical one for dentists, as investigators for the Tennessee Board of Medical Examiners discovered, is Empirin with codeine in tablet form. These tablets are round, white in color, and labeled with the numbers 1, 2, 3, or 4, depending on the dosage. The strongest dosage is a full grain, labeled with the number "4."

Given the number of similarities between these two drugs, Thompson and Cole became convinced that Elvis mistook codeine for the Dilaudid he especially requested. He must have taken close to ten codeine tablets. And he took them long enough before being stricken for the codeine to have metabolized into his urine.

While sitting on the toilet, Elvis's allergic reaction kicked in. He began to feel itchy. He grew short of breath. He was struggling. He had trouble calling for help. No one was on duty in the valet's bedroom. Ginger Alden was in a deep sleep. Suddenly his book was heavy, an encumbrance. He threw it aside. With much effort he stood but stumbled as he tried to pull up his pajama bottoms. He fell forward on his chest with his head to one side, pressure on his neck and his knees flexed. Moments later the king of rock 'n' roll was dead. Despite the official ruling, Elvis died from polypharmacy, an accidental overdose of multiple drugs.

BIBLIOGRAPHY

Court Records

Lane v. Integon, U.S. District Court, Western District of Tennessee, 1971.

State of Tennessee v. Louis Montesi, Criminal Court, 16th Judicial Circuit, 1965.

Tennessee Board of Medical Examiners v. George C. Nichopoulos, M.D., complaint, deposition, proceedings, 1979–80.

State of Tennessee ex. rel. James P. Cole and Charles C. Thompson v. Jerry T. Francisco, Shelby County Medical Examiner, and Hugh W. Stanton, Jr., District Attorney General for 16th Judicial Circuit; Chancery Court, pleadings and depositions; Tennessee Supreme Court, ruling, Tenn, 643 S.W. 2d., 105.

State of Tennessee v. George C. Nichopoulos, M.D., Criminal Court, 16th Judicial Circuit, indictment, proceedings and investigative interviews.

Government Documents

U.S. House of Representatives, Select Committee on Assassinations. "Investigation of the Assassination of Martin Luther King, Jr." Washington: Government Printing Office, 1979.

Copyright Office of the United States of America, Library of Congress, Number TXu 18-490: Grob, Richard, as told to Dan Mingori. *The Elvis Conspiracy,* book synopsis, 1979.

Bibliography

Medical Sources

Butterworth, Bernard B. *Laboratory Anatomy of the Human Body.* Dubuque, Iowa: William C. Brown Publishers, 1975.

Gresham, G. Austin. *Color Atlas of Forensic Pathology.* Chicago: Yearbook Publishers, Inc., 1975.

Hansten, Philip D. *Drug Interactions.* Philadelphia: Lea & Febiger, 1979.

Houts, Marshall, Randall C. Baselt, and Robert H. Cravey. *Courtroom Toxicology,* Vols. 1–6. New York: Matthew Bender, 1989.

Martin, Eric W. *Hazards of Medication.* Philadelphia: J.B. Lippincott Co., 1978.

Merck Manual of Diagnosis and Therapy. Rahway, N.J.: Merck & Co., Inc., 1977.

Nursing 88 Drug Handbook. Springhouse, Pa.: Springhouse Corp., 1988.

Physicians' Desk Reference. Oradell, N.J.: Medical Economics Co., 1976 ed.

Smyth, Frank. *Cause of Death: The Story of Forensic Science,* foreword by Colin Wilson. New York: Van Nostrand Reinhold Co., 1980.

Wecht, Cyril H. "Post Mortem on Elvis Presley Won't Die." *Legal Aspects of Medical Practice.* December 1979.

News Sources

ABC News, *20/20 News Magazine,* "The Elvis Cover-Up," transcripts, September 13, 1979, and December 27, 1979.

American Medical News, "Examiner Is Firm: Heart Disease Fatal to Presley," October 12, 1979; "Presley MD Hearing Put Medicine on Trial," February 8, 1980; "Presley's MD Struggles for a New Life," December 11, 1981.

Los Angeles Times Magazine, "Eternal Revenue Why Elvis Is Worth

More Now Than the Day He Died," by Robert Hillburn, June 11, 1989.

Memphis magazine, "Stalking the Grim Reaper," by Tom Martin, March 1980; "Dead Reckoning," by David Lyons, September 1988.

The Memphis Commercial Appeal, assorted articles.

The Memphis Press-Scimitar, assorted articles.

Memoirs, Biographies

Baden, Michael M., M.D., with Judith Adler Hennessee. *Unnatural Death: Confessions of a Medical Examiner.* New York: Random House, 1989.

Brewer-Giorgio, Gail. *Is Elvis Alive?* New York: Tudor Publishing Co., 1988.

Burk, Bill E. *Elvis Through My Eyes.* Memphis: Burk Enterprises, 1987.

Cocke, Marian J. *I Called Him Babe: Elvis Presley's Nurse Remembers.* Memphis: Memphis State University Press, 1979.

De Barbin, Lucy, and Dary Matera. New York: *Are You Lonesome Tonight?* Villard Books, 1987.

Geller, Larry, Joel Spector, and Patricia Romanowski. *"If I Can Dream": Elvis' Own Story.* New York: Simon & Schuster, 1989.

Goldman, Albert. *Elvis.* New York: McGraw-Hill, 1981.

Gregory, Neal, and Janice Gregory. *When Elvis Died.* Washington, D.C.: Communications Press, Inc., 1980.

Haining, Peter, ed. *Elvis in Private.* New York: St. Martin's Press, 1987.

Helpern, Milton, with Bernard Knight. *Autopsy.* New York: St. Martin's Press, 1977.

Hodge, Charlie, with Charles Goodman. *Me'n Elvis.* Memphis: Castle Books, 1984.

Hopkins, Jerry. *Elvis: A Biography.* New York: Warner Books, 1971.

Bibliography

Hopkins, Jerry. *Elvis: The Final Years.* New York: Berkley Books, 1983.

Lacker, Marty, Patsy Lacker, and Les Smith. *Elvis: Portrait of a Friend.* Memphis: Wimmer Brothers Press, 1979.

Noguchi, Thomas T., with Joseph DiMona. *Coroner at Large.* New York: Simon & Schuster, 1985.

Presley, Priscilla Beaulieu, with Sandra Harmon. *Elvis and Me.* New York: G. P. Putnam's Sons, 1985.

Rooks, Nancy, and Mae Gutter. *The Maid, the Man, and the Fans.* New York: Vantage Press, 1984.

Stanley, Billy, with George Erikson. *Elvis, My Brother.* New York: St. Martin's Press, 1989.

Stanley, David, with David Wimbish. *Life with Elvis.* Tappan, N. J.: Fleming H. Revell Company, 1986.

Stanley, Dee, et al, as told to Martin Torgoff. *Elvis, We Love You Tender.* New York: Delacorte Press, 1979.

West, Delbert "Red," Sonny West, and Dave Hebler, as told to Steve Dunleavy. *Elvis: What Happened?* New York: Ballantine Books, 1977.

Worth, Fred L., and Steve Tamerius. *Elvis: His Life from A to Z.* Chicago: Contemporary Books, 1988.

INDEX

Alden, Ginger, 10, 13–14, 24, 25–26, 31, 53, 57, 63, 74, 126–27, 142–43, 145, 160–72, 182, 211, 212–14, 238, 256, 257, 258, 303, 313, 315, 329, 330, 338, 358, 362, 391, 398
Alissandratos, D. J. "Tene," 254, 259, 304, 308, 381–382
Allen, Glen, 88–89, 95
American Medical News, 247–49, 265, 367, 377

Bailey, Lewis, 147, 153, 154, 156
Bale, Dr. George, 34, 40–41, 48
Baselt, Dr. Randall C., 289–90
Bell, Dr. James S., 5–6, 82, 242, 243, 244, 262–63, 393
Bilsky, Steve, 203, 215–16, 218–19, 235, 239, 278
Bio-Science Laboratory, 72, 77–80, 85, 96, 100–102, 105–106, 107, 110, 155, 182, 183, 230, 245, 248, 251, 287, 288, 306, 307, 371–72, 395, 396, 398
Blackburn, E. B., 82, 83, 96, 99–100
Blanke, Dr. Robert, 188, 244, 250–52, 265, 273–74, 380–81
Brandon, Bob, 175, 219–220, 225, 227, 229–231
Breo, Dennis L., 248–49, 265
Brinkley, David, 56
Burch, Peggy, 75–76, 86
Burk, Bill, 68

Caughley, James K., Jr., 320–27
Chesney, Dr. Thomas, 34, 40–42, 45–46, 48, 49, 51, 52, 254
Cocke, Marian, 117–18, 283, 330, 397
Cohen, Steve, 215
Cole, James P. (author), 92–94, 98–100, 105–311 *passim,* 357, 382, 389–98

Cooney, Hayes, 293, 294, 298, 302–303, 304–305, 308
Cravey, Robert H., 78–80, 287–90, 395
Crawford, Frank, 253–55, 276–86, 293, 299, 309, 367
Crosby, Charlie, 15–19
Crump, E. H. "Boss," 65

Davis, Richard, 182–83, 330
Death of Elvis:
ABC lawsuit to obtain autopsy report, 108, 114–15, 142, 149, 184, 238, 247, 248, 253–72, 293, 304, 313, 381–82
autopsy, 20, 28, 30–42, 45–54, 64, 70, 71, 72, 75, 80–83, 113, 145, 238, 255, 383–84, 389, 391–92
autopsy report, 76, 80–84, 106–108, 141, 143, 176, 183, 190, 244, 246, 256, 272, 293–94, 306, 307, 308, 311, 381–83, 385, 396–97
bone cancer question, 143–45, 171, 179, 260, 261, 348–49, 362, 397
day of, 1–11, 15–29, 158–59, 165–68, 207–208, 212–13, 233, 238, 330–31
drugs and, *see* Drugs, Elvis and; *names of doctors prescribing drugs to Elvis*
medical examiner's conclusion about cause of, 81–86, 113–14, 147–48, 169, 210, 238, 242, 247, 250–52, 263, 266, 288, 289, 291, 305–306, 379, 385, 388–89, 390, 393, 394
murder theory, 386
stomach contents, 3, 156, 158–60, 184, 189, 231, 238, 245, 270, 398
suicide theory, 384–86
Valsalva theory, 391–93

Index

Droege, Joan, 246, 272
Drugs, Elvis and, 22, 23, 27–28, 49,
  50, 52, 63, 70, 177–78, 179, 190–94,
  204–40, 263–398
  detoxification for, 51, 52, 151, 168,
    234, 283–84, 300, 302, 332, 339–
    40, 350
  known drug habit, 13, 18–20, 26,
    35–36, 52–53, 67, 68, 117, 119,
    120–26, 133, 135–38, 150, 167,
    169, 204–12, 233–35, 284–85, 303,
    314–18, 323–26, 333–38, 339,
    350–51, 356, 361
  overdose, suspicion of, 5, 6, 16–17,
    18, 27–28, 41, 64, 182, 186, 262,
    269
  overdose as cause of death, 80–81,
    84, 85, 97, 109, 110–12, 144, 148,
    184, 238, 251–52, 265–66, 274,
    288–89, 290–91, 364, 383, 393,
    395, 396–98
  sources of drugs, *see names of*
    individual doctors
  start of problem, 137
  toxicology results, 71–72, 77, 78–80,
    85, 96, 99, 100–102, 105–106, 107,
    108–11, 144–45, 152, 155–56, 169,
    182, 214, 231, 233, 238, 244, 245,
    251, 307, 368, 371–72, 383, 396–
    98
Dughman, Joe, 203, 215–19, 235, 239,
  278, 292–95, 297, 302–303, 305, 306,
  309
Dunleavy, Steve, 56

Ellenhorn, Dr. Matthew, 108–10, 238,
  248
Elliott, Maurice, 8–9, 54, 80, 81, 107,
  157–60, 183, 199
Elvis and Me (Presley), 179
"Elvis Cover-Up, The," 237–48, 296
Elvis: Portrait of a Friend (Lacker), 133–
  38, 164, 182–83, 330, 370
Elvis: What Happened? (West et al.), 67,
  68, 73, 74, 124, 211, 321, 339, 384–
  85
Esposito, Joe, 9, 10, 11, 17, 21, 23, 24,
  31, 61, 62, 67–68, 94, 122, 134, 143,
  150, 166, 167, 178, 181, 206, 269,

  282, 283, 302, 313, 314, 323, 330,
  339, 343–47, 363–64, 375, 385

Feegel, Dr. John, 253–55, 262, 263,
  273, 291, 292, 294, 296, 307–308,
  309, 395
Fink, Dr. Robert D., 284, 285, 300
Finkle, Dr. Brian, 188, 244, 250–52,
  265, 273, 291, 292, 294, 306–308
Florendo, Dr. Noel, 34, 41, 46, 48, 50,
  51–52, 146–48, 149, 183–84, 238,
  240, 243, 391–92
Fortas, Alan, 134, 298, 330, 351, 368
Fosbinder, Jack, 201–202, 215–16, 278
Francisco, Dr. Jerry, 4, 5–6, 55, 59, 61–
  62, 63, 64, 71, 93, 106–108, 112–14,
  183, 184–85, 214–15, 231, 247–50,
  267, 272–73, 286, 291–92, 379–81,
  386, 395–96
  autopsy and, 20, 28, 31–34, 40–41,
    48–53, 76, 78, 80–83, 113
  career of, 103–105
  depositions of, 185–90, 264–66
  determination of cause of Elvis's
    death, 81–86, 113–14, 147–48,
    169, 210, 238, 242, 247, 250–52,
    263, 266, 288, 289, 291, 305–306,
    379, 388–89, 390, 393, 394
  at Nichopoulos hearings, 305–306
  rebuttal of, 242–47, 307

Geller, Larry, 37, 126, 261, 349
Ghanem, Dr. Elias Farad, 132–33, 151,
  234, 239, 283, 313, 324, 333, 334,
  337, 339, 357, 359, 363
Goldfarb, Danny, 116–19, 126, 127–33
Goldman, Albert, 383–86
Grehl, Mike, 87, 93, 95
Grob, Dick, 17, 19–20, 34, 56–57, 138–
  43, 144, 145, 163, 164, 168, 171,
  175–77, 178, 181, 213, 214, 256–62,
  299, 314–15, 317, 326, 349

Haggit, Dr. Roger, 34, 48
Harbison, Dr. Raymond, 298
Harlan, Dr. Charles, 242, 243, 244,
  262, 263–64
Harrell, Chuck, 142, 183, 184, 185,
  253, 259–62

Hebler, Dave, 13, 56, 67, 68, 124, 135, 211, 321
Henderson, Isaac, 35, 39–40, 47, 48
Henley, Tish, 19, 26, 27–28, 151, 169, 212, 266, 283, 301, 303–304, 330, 358
Hodge, Charlie, 10, 17, 21, 139, 143, 167, 176, 177–79, 180, 261, 282, 316, 326, 334, 339, 347–49, 351, 358
Hoffman, Dr. Walter K., 195, 304, 375
Hofman, Dr. Lester, 14, 27, 140, 154, 155, 235, 317, 389
Holbert, Dr. James, 34, 41, 48, 145
Hookstratten, E. Gregory, 120, 121, 123
Hughes, Howard, 19, 92
Hutchinson, Larry, 271–72, 298–99, 312–64, 367–68, 370–71, 376, 394–95

Jones, Ulysses S., Jr., 15–19, 269–70

Kelly, Jack, 17–18, 121, 124–26, 239
Kelly, Dr. Raymond, 105–106, 238
Kennedy, John F., 8, 110
Kerwin, Alicia, 356, 357–63, 375
King, Dr. Martin Luther, Jr., 103, 214
Kingsley, Jim, 64, 66–67
Kirk, James, 142–43, 172, 213–14, 257–58
Kirsch, Jack, 190–201, 219, 226–29, 235, 240, 279, 370
Klein, George, 134, 161, 162, 182, 330, 357–58, 387
Knott, Dr. David H., 284, 285, 300, 372–73

Lacker, Marty, 133–38, 179, 182, 202, 238, 313, 330, 368, 370–71
Lamin, Dr. Raul, 34, 48, 51–52
Lauter, Phil, 175, 219–220, 229–230
Leech, William, 293
Lerner, Dr. William, 373–74
Lundberg, George David, 290–91

McCachren, Sam, 6–7, 8, 10, 20, 21, 22–29, 38–39, 55, 82, 186, 266
McEachran, Angus, 73, 82
McGriff, David, 318

McMahon, Michael, 94, 150–52, 160, 195, 196, 198, 267–68, 344
Masterson, Ken, 236, 253
Matera, Dary, 387–88
Me 'n Elvis (Hodge and Goodman), 179, 261
Memphis Commercial Appeal, The, 61–68, 69–70, 72–75, 82–87, 88–89, 93, 95, 99, 106, 189, 258, 270–71, 305, 355
Memphis Press-Scrimitar, The, 65, 68, 75–76, 81, 86
Miller, Jewett, 319, 367–68, 369–76
Miller, Sandy, 80, 330
Millican, Roy, 21, 22
Mingori, Dan, 141, 142
Monroe, Marilyn, 79
Montesi, Louis, 103–104
Muirhead, Dr. E. Eric, 32–33, 40, 41, 48, 49–50, 71, 72, 73, 80–81, 83, 84, 105, 107, 146, 148, 149, 160, 183, 184, 238, 243, 270, 288, 296–97, 304–305, 308, 372, 395–96

Nash, W. S., 152–56, 239
National Enquirer, 54–55, 142–43, 164, 172, 213–14, 257–58
Neal, James, 366–67, 369–76
Newman, Dr. Thomas, 324, 333–34
Nichopoulos, Dean, 182, 276
Nichopoulos, Dr. George C., 7, 11, 15, 17–18, 58–60, 73–76, 146, 149–52, 161, 167, 182, 188–200 *passim,* 215, 242, 253–56, 261, 272–73, 335, 386, 391
autopsy and, 31, 34–35, 48
charges against, 219, 221–22, 229, 232, 236, 237, 247, 254, 272, 274, 279
civil hearings, 291–310
criminal indictment and trial of, 364–77
criminal investigation of, 312–64, 394
deposition of, 274–86
drugs prescribed by, 27, 50, 119, 133, 135, 136–37, 152–56, 160, 169–70, 194, 202, 206, 216–19, 222–25, 228–29, 232–33, 239–40, 266, 268, 271, 280–85, 292, 293,

Index

Nichopoulos, Dr. George C. *(cont.)*
296–310, 317, 333, 335, 362–63,
366, 369, 371, 373–76, 398
Elvis's business dealings with, 58,
94–95, 150–51, 169–70, 200, 221,
294, 301, 337, 344
financial problems, 195–200
Rivera interview with, 220–25, 229,
235, 239–40, 277–80
Noguchi, Dr. Thomas, 78, 79

O'Grady, John, 18–19, 119–24, 125,
239, 313, 334
Orynich, Dr. Ronald, 72

Parker, Pat, 120
Parker, Colonel Tom, 10, 23, 122, 123,
134, 150, 178, 210, 280, 313, 317–
18, 326, 343, 352–56, 375
Peel, John C., 9, 10, 21, 22, 28, 39,
266–67
Pitcock, Dr. J. A., 34, 48
Pleasants, Mike, 108, 114–16, 117,
142, 143, 149, 183, 185–90, 240,
253–56, 258, 259, 262–65, 267, 296,
304–305, 382
Presley, Elvis, *see* Death of Elvis;
Drugs, Elvis and
Presley, Gladys, 12, 174, 175, 263, 354
Presley, Lisa Marie, 14, 20, 21, 22,
170, 211, 315, 355, 358
Presley, Priscilla, 13, 14, 20, 123, 161,
179, 315, 332, 345, 341, 354
Presley, Vernon, 8, 12, 16, 18–19, 21,
22, 23, 28, 34, 66, 80, 83, 126, 140–
41, 164, 167, 169, 170, 204–205,
245, 338, 346, 363, 393
background of, 174–75
death of, 88
Elvis's drug use and, 17–18, 120–21,
123, 137, 206, 323–24
Nichopoulos and, 57–58, 59–60, 74,
80, 121, 256, 261, 348
Presley, Vester, 320

Reed, Dwight, 79
Rivera, Geraldo, 56, 88, 90–92, 100,
105–106, 108–10, 121–26, 129–32,
147–49, 157–72, 175–83, 203–41,

247, 267, 270, 272–74, 277–80, 288,
296, 299, 309, 382, 387, 388
Rose, Dr. Earl, 7–8
Rothman, David, 141
Rout, Jim, 107, 114, 198
Ruhl, Gayle, 190, 299

Scanlon, Frank, 276–86, 293, 294, 296,
302–303, 309
Schilling, Jerry, 350–51, 375
Sexton, Dr. Harold, 33–34, 41, 48, 70–
72, 77, 80, 96, 107, 108, 159–60,
183, 184, 287–91, 296, 311, 389
Shapiro, Dr. Max, 124, 125, 126–32,
133–34, 234, 239, 317, 324, 331–32,
339
Smith, Billy, 14, 26, 165, 180–81, 208,
303, 330, 349, 360
Smith, Gene, 181
Smith, Leslie S., 135–36
Smith, Dr. Vasco, 214–15
Sorrels, William, 67
Stanley, Billy, 204, 205, 329–30, 388
Stanley, David, 15, 56, 145, 164, 204,
205–11, 239, 256–57, 282–83, 313,
316–17, 329–30, 359, 384–86
Stanley, Davida (Dee) Elliott, 204–
205, 232, 328–29
Stanley, Rick, 56, 145, 152, 153, 164–
69, 204, 205, 207–208, 211–12, 229,
232–35, 238, 239, 242, 256, 282–83,
313, 316–17, 329–30, 339, 383–85,
398
Stanton, Hugh, Jr., 114, 237, 271, 272,
293, 312, 319, 331, 394
Stauffer, Jerry, 8, 20–24, 267
Stivers, Dr. Robert, 296–97
Strada, Al, 10–11, 16–17, 18, 24, 26,
31, 64, 143, 166, 182, 209, 269, 303,
329, 345, 375
Sunshine, Dr. Irving, 288

Tamke, Beth J., 69–70, 72–75, 81–87,
93–94, 97, 189, 251, 305
Tennant, Dr. Forest, 375–376
Thomas, Billy Joe (B. J.), 318–19
Thomason, John J. "Buddy," 293, 295,
297, 298, 305, 307, 309, 310, 367
Thompson, Charles C. II (author), 88–

100, 105–311 *passim*, 382–83, 387–88, 390–98

Thompson, Linda, 13, 68, 138, 161, 162, 283, 314, 315, 327, 332–38, 375, 397

Thompson, Sam, 12–15, 18, 19–20, 22–23, 57, 208, 209, 313–18, 329, 338

Wade, Allen, 196

Warlick, Dan, 3–11, 20–28, 55, 63, 64, 184–85, 190, 231, 238, 262, 263, 267, 314, 389–92

    autopsy and, 31–42, 45, 46, 50–53, 54, 76, 83, 184, 186, 389, 391–92

Wecht, Dr. Cyril, 110–14, 238–39, 248–49

Weinman, Bernie, 365–366, 372

Weissman, Norman, 72, 77–80, 251, 288, 371–72

West, Red, 13, 67, 68, 124, 134, 135, 152, 179, 205, 210, 211, 282, 321, 322, 327, 338–39

West, Sonny, 13, 56, 67, 68, 124, 134, 135, 136, 152, 179, 205, 210, 211, 282, 321, 326, 327, 338, 339–42

Westin, Av, 230, 235–236, 237, 241, 267

White, Jim, 272

Wilson, Jim, 374–375

Wright, Dr. Ronald K., 388–389

Wruble, Dr. Lawrence D., 52–53, 117, 304